MENTAL HANDICAP AND THE HUMAN CONDITION

What is the sense in 'stupidity'? This book is not only about the people officially designated mentally handicapped, but also about the ways in which all of us suffer from the limitations and self-limitations which can be discerned from clinical work on the inner world of these individuals.

More particularly, why should severely and profoundly handicapped people be deprived of psychoanalytic psychotherapy? Mental or multiple disabilities have handicapping effects and entail emotional suffering. This is the first book to focus, from the perspective of psychoanalytic psychotherapy, on both processes in the individual.

Ranging over questions of loss, bereavement, sexual abuse and the process and meaning of thinking, it is based on more than ten years' practice in the field. It is stimulating, innovative and very moving.

Valerie Sinason is Principal Psychotherapist in the Child and Family Department, Day Unit and Adult Department, Tavistock Clinic, London, and Psychotherapist Convenor of the Mental handicap Workshop there. She is a highly regarded poet and writes regularly on mental health issues in *The Guardian*.

'Valerie Sinason's book challenges us to know what we know, and can plainly see before us, in the lives of people with learning disabilities. Our avoidance and denial of knowledge may be because we accept what we are told uncritically, or because the truth about people with learning disabilities may be too painful for us to confront. She invites us not to be rendered "stupid" ourselves by the trauma of their pain.'

– Professor Sheila Hollins, Head of Division of Psychiatry and Disability, St George's Hospital Medical School, London

MENTAL HANDICAP AND THE HUMAN CONDITION

New Approaches from the Tavistock

VALERIE SINASON

Free Association Books / London

Published in Great Britain in 1992 by
Free Association Books Ltd
57 Warren Street, London W1P 5PA

The publication of this book was made possible by
generous grants from Kirsty Hall and
The Human Nature Trust

A CIP record for this book is available from
the British Library

ISBN 1 85343 176 1 pbk

Impression: 99 98 97 96   7 6 5 4

Printed in the EC by J.W. Arrowsmith Ltd, Bristol, England

CONTENTS

Acknowledgements

In learning to work with people whose thinking, speech and communication have been damaged by internal or external forces, I have had time to appreciate anew the life force of language – verbal, written, emotional, physical.

I would like to thank my parents Stanley and Tamar Segal for their valuing of speech and creative writing as well as for their lifelong work with mentally handicapped children and adults. As I read English Literature at London University, followed by a teaching diploma, my own teacher, Margot Heinemann, was a source of inspiration. The combined power of literature and fine teaching as an aid to understanding meaning has percolated through the writing of this book as well as in my work as a child psychotherapist and poet. Mattie Harris, an English literature graduate and one of the founders of the Child Psychotherapy Training at the Tavistock Clinic, encouraged this cross-fertilization.

To the Tavistock Clinic I owe thanks for both my training in child psychotherapy and support for the work in mental handicap. If psychoanalyst Neville Symington had not started the Tavistock Clinic Workshop on Mental Handicap, my knowledge and interest, stimulated by my family's involvement, might never have found a home. I am grateful to Jon Stokes, with whom I convened the Workshop for several years. Our work together laid the groundwork for further theoretical and clinical development.

Special thanks go to Sheila Bichard, with whom I now convene the Workshop and whose research clinical skills are enhancing the current development of the work. We are working together on a major research project both to understand the link between emotional and cognitive functioning and to evaluate the impact of therapy.

As this is the first book to be devoted to psychoanalytical psychotherapy with this client group there are many people to thank. As well as benefiting from the thoughts of Workshop members past and present, including Harriet Meek, Jenny Sprince, Isabel Hernández Halton, Andrew Arthur, Janet Bungener, Stella Acquarone, Brendan McCormack, Janice Uphill and Anne Wells, I am grateful to the Tavistock Clinic itself. As a major National Health Service training and treatment centre and an international centre of excellence it has managed to welcome and support this new development. Without that supportive external framework the internal work would not be able to develop. Anton Obholzer, Maurice Caplan, Judith Trowell, Jon Stokes, the Tavistock Foundation and the Special Committee have been especially important here. My own discipline of child psychotherapy, chaired by Margaret Rustin, has encouraged the development of this work. Thanks to Jill Walker for her fundraising efforts for mental handicap, to librarian Margaret Walker, and to Judith Usiskin and Davina Carrol.

Outside of the Clinic, there are several people and organizations who have helped the spread of psychoanalytic thinking to the area of handicap. I would like to thank Nick Temple, past chairman of the APP (Association for Psychoanalytic Psychotherapy in the National Health Service) for offering support for a Mental Handicap Section and the colleagues, in England and elsewhere who have joined the Section Committee, including Pat Frankish, Margaret Heal, Michele Pundick, Susanna Isaacs-Elmhirst, Frances Tustin, Tony Taylor, Wai Yung Lee (Canada), Yvonne Gilljam (Sweden), Arnold Wellman (Canada), Annie Stammler (France), Mariá Eugenia Cid Rodríguez (Spain) and Richard Ruth (USA). Joan Bicknell and Sheila Hollins from St George's Hospital have enriched the APP Section as well as international practice through their inspiring work. David Morris, sadly now dead, encouraged a space for psychodynamic thinking at the Royal Society of Medicine's Forum on Mental Retardation as well as supporting the APP Section.

Thanks are due to Dilys Daws and the Child Psychotherapy Trust for their economic support of training ventures in handicap across the country; to the Association of Child Psychology and Psychiatry for including the topic of handicap in the Abuse Study Group; and to Margaret Kennedy and the British Association for the Study and Prevention of Child Abuse and Neglect (BASPCAN) for their major work in protecting handicapped children and adults from abuse. In the growing area of awareness of abuse of people with handicaps I am also indebted to Ann Craft, Helen Armstrong, Hilary Brown, Margaret Kennedy, Eileen Vizard, Arnon Bentovim, Beverley Loughlin, Judith Trowell, Marcus Johns, Moira Dennison, Jane Walby and Nadia Poscotis.

For help in working with patients who were both mentally ill and mentally handicapped I am grateful to John Corbett (who is also a mine of historical understanding on the subject), Nick Bouras, David Wilson, Frank Menolascino, Sabah Sadik, and Joan Bicknell, and for supervision, to Susanna Isaacs-Elmhirst and Anne Alvarez.

I am indebted to the commitment and variety of experiences of members of work discussion groups and trainers past and present, who include music, art and drama therapists, psychologists, psychiatrists and social workers including Vicky Turk, Sandra Baum, Alison Cantle, Anne Sloboda, Simon Cregeen, Nigel Beail, Joyce Howarth and Clare Woodcock. Thanks also for help and encouragement to Isca Wittenberg, Juliet Hopkins, Eileen Orford, Sandy Bourne, Frank Orford, Eileen Francis, Jenny Allen, Eleanour Morgan, Issy Kolvin, Peter Hobson, Derek Moore, Tony Lee, Rob Hale, Mannie Lewis, Liam Hudson, Joyce Piper and Linda Kaufman from the Tavistock Clinic and Doris Wills from the Anna Freud Centre.

Thanks to writers David Cook and James Berry for inspiration from their work as well as permission to quote them. Thanks to my son, Marek, and my daughter, Marsha, for their interest and support.

Thanks to Bob Young of Free Association Books for his enthusiasm and his willingness to commission this book; to Selina O'Grady for her painstaking and creative editing; and to Ann Scott for her imagination and expertise in initiating and completing the task. Thanks to Mandy MacDonald for her detailed copy-editing; and to Anita Kermode and Linda English for their accurate and astute proofreading and indexing, respectively.

My own psychoanalysis was crucial in understanding my own areas of handicap as well as those of my client group and I am grateful to my former psychoanalyst, Jane Temperley.

My thanks to the parents, foster-parents, social workers and escorts who have been willing to travel long distances to ensure that their children or clients have access to the treatment they need, and my thanks to all my patients, past and present, who have been willing to show me what they knew and patiently wait for me to lose my handicaps.

Finally, my thanks to my husband, Michael Sinason, whose work on psychosis has provided many thought-provoking links with my work and whose help towards my computer literacy eased the labour pains of this book.

The following papers of mine are reproduced or expanded here by kind permission of Robert M. Young, Editor of *Free Associations*: 'Face values: a preliminary look at one aspect of adolescent subculture' (1985) 2:75–94 (now in Chapter 2). By kind permission of Robin Anderson, Editor of *Psychoanalytic Psychotherapy*: 'Secondary mental handicap and its relationship to trauma', *Psychoanalytic Psychotherapy* 1986 2(2):131–154, and 'Smiling, swallowing, sickening and stupefying', *Psychoanalytic Psychotherapy* (1987) 3(2):97–111 (now Chapters 5 and 6). By kind permission of Sue Kegeiris, Editor of *Journal of Child Psychotherapy*: extracts from 'Richard III, Hephaestus and Echo: sexuality and mental/multiple handicap' (1988) 14(2):93–105, and 'Interpretations that feel horrible to make and a theoretical unicorn' (1991) 17(1):11–23 (now in Chapter 10). By kind permission of Bob Hinshelwood, Editor of *British Journal of Psychotherapy*: extracts from 'Dolls and bears: from symbolic equation to symbol. The use of different play material for sexually abused children' (1988) 4(4): 350–363, and the poem 'Headbanger' (now in Chapter 10). By kind permission of Hilary Brown and Ann Craft: extracts from *Thinking the Unthinkable*, Family Planning Association, 1989 (now Chapter 11). By kind permission of Free Association Books: extracts from 'The psycholinguistics of discrimination', in Barry Richards, ed. *Crises of the Self: Further Essays on Psychoanalysis and Politics*, 1989. By kind permission of Anton Dosen, Logon Publications: extracts from

'Individual psychoanalytic psychotherapy with severely and profoundly mentally handicapped patients', in *Treatment of Mental Illness and Behavioural Disorders in the Mentally Retarded: Proceedings of the International Congress, May 3–4 1990, Amsterdam* (now in Chapter 12). By kind permission of *The Tavistock Gazette:* the poem 'In Memoriam'. By kind permission of Gladys Mary Coles, Headland Press: poems from *Inkstains and Stilettos*.

In addition, I am grateful to Penguin Books for permission to reproduce extracts from Cicero, *On The Good Life*, trans. Michael Grant, 1982; and Confucius, *The Analects*, trans. D. C. Lau, 1986. Every effort has been made to trace the holders of copyright material. My apologies if I have inadvertently omitted to approach a copyright holder.

Introduction

Shall I tell you what it is to know? To say you know when you know, and to say you do not when you do not, that is knowledge.
Confucius, *The Analects*

Distress removes from the Soul all Relation, Affection, Sense of Justice, and all the Obligations, either Moral or Religious, that secure one Man against another. Not that I say or suggest the Distress makes the Violence Lawful; but I say it is a Tryal beyond the Ordinary Power of Humane Nature to withstand.
Daniel Defoe, *A Review* (entry for 15 September 1711)

The struggle of man against power is the struggle of memory against forgetting.
Milan Kundera, *The Book of Laughter and Forgetting*

All of us, as babies, children and adults, are faced with the predicament of not knowing; we are faced with actual gaps in our knowledge; gaps in our capacity to acquire or retain kinds of knowledge; gaps in our emotional motivation that make us unable to learn certain things, quite apart from not knowing what is genuinely out of our own control. What is it, internally, externally or both simultaneously, that can make these issues so painful? And if it is painful for everyone at times to have to acknowledge their own limitations, what is it like for those whose limitations are more concretely defined by brain damage or chromosomal abnormality?

This book, with the aid of psychoanalytical theory and clinical practice, explores the way we all use and abuse our unique constitutional resources when faced with the pain of not knowing. It seeks to throw light on the emotional factors that can inhibit our potential intelligence as well as on the ways in which we deal with our actual intellectual limits. This book needed to be written, as to date no other book exists that is solely concerned with psychoanalytically informed psychotherapy, as practised by a formally-trained practitioner, of those individuals who are emotionally suffering at the same time as dealing with the handicapping effects of mental or multiple disabilities.

Sometimes the handicapping factors are external and this points to the need for social change. A wheelchair user, for example, is made handicapped by an architect not thinking about ramps. Someone with no verbal speech is handicapped by the lack of electronic communication devices. A blind individual is handicapped by cars parked on the pavement and a deaf person is handicapped by the lack of knowledge about sign language in the hearing community.

However, this book is more concerned with how the primary handicap (or disability) is made worse by defensive exaggerations (secondary handicap). For some of us, an area of disability is particularly vulnerable to the most damaging secondary handicapping processes. I call this 'opportunist handicap' (Sinason, 1986) and it is where every destructive aspect of the self finds a home in the disability. In Chapter 10 I show how this process works. The concepts of primary, secondary and secondary opportunist handicap are seen as universally applicable.

Central to this book is the factor of trauma as a handicapping agent – the damage done to the emotions and intellect when we are crippled by intolerable knowledge. Some people have memories of incidents that are so traumatic that they become numbed with grief, stupefied. In order to protect themselves from painful memories, they throw away part of their brain, their memory. In Chapter 1, I look at the way 'stupidity' affects and handicaps all of us. As I show throughout the book, 'stupid' means numbed with grief and the process of 'going stupid' handicaps all of us at different times.

The existence of disability, handicap and handicapping processes is so painful that each culture and historical period has tried to evade the issue by a frequent change of terms. No other subject has been prey to this amount of change. Within my own working life there have been the terms 'retardation', 'subnormality', 'handicap', 'special needs', 'learning difficulty' and 'disability'. In

Chapter 2 I explore the psycholinguistics of euphemism and definitions in this field. There is a history in these changes that needs to be understood from a psychoanalytical perspective. Otherwise, we handicap ourselves further.

The importance of history cannot be overestimated. Milan Kundera (1980, p. 3) has pointed out that 'the first step in liquidating a people is to erase its history' and that 'the struggle of man against power is the struggle of memory against forgetting'. Writing this book is a way of ensuring that these issues, the links between trauma, disability and handicapping processes, are recorded. It does not matter whether it is disease, brain damage (see Chapters 4, 5, 8 and 9), sexual abuse (Chapters 6, 10, 11 and 12), environmental deprivation (Chapter 5) or psychosis (Chapter 12) that has ravaged someone's mind or memory, or indeed closeness to colleagues, clients, friends or relatives who are suffering from any of these. When there are people who cannot think, remember (see Chapter 4), speak or write (Chapters 7, 8 and 9), it matters that others take up the scribe function. This applies as much to political prisoners as to individuals with a mental handicap.

When I travelled, for teaching purposes, to a country where I had no understanding of the language, I was doomed, without the interpreter, to illiteracy and lack of any communication beyond pointing. Even with her, conversation was a tiring process needing all sentences to pass through her before I could understand and be understood by the professionals I had come to see. Because my words were considered valuable, my colleagues had bothered to provide an interpreter. Handicapped adults and children are still too rarely seen to have words and thoughts of value inside them and only too rarely provided with a means of interpreting them or having them interpreted. It is not surprising that they can give up the exhausting and unequal struggle for communication and keep their thoughts locked up in their heads forever (Chapters 8 and 9). However, unlike diaries or poems or books that are hidden away, thoughts unformed and unspoken become a storehouse of pain. This is even more damaging for the handicapped individual and a major aim of this book is to address that issue.

In its aims of valuing and exploring the experience of mental handicap this book is very much a child of its time. Following the cultural changes of the last decade, our new decade has already seen the first publication of a book solely on the treatment of depression in handicapped people (Dosen and Menolascino, 1990) and the first four books on handicap that include any details of psychoanalytically orientated work (Brandon, 1989; Conboy-Hill and Waitman, 1992; Brown and Craft, 1989; Craft, in press).

My knowledge comes largely from twelve years of treating clients whose mental handicap coexists with severe emotional disturbance. (There are, of course, people with disabilities who are not in need of any psychological treatment and are in far better emotional shape than some people without mental disabilities who are emotionally handicapped.) This book could not have been written earlier, for previous psychoanalytical psychotherapists did not stay in this field long enough or only took on one or two patients with a mild handicap. This was a historical and cultural tragedy as psychoanalytic psychotherapy can aid the process of recovery, the retaining of thoughts, the uttering of speech and the sharing of history, and can treat the ravages of opportunist handicap as well as coexisting psychosis. However, there is still very little chance that enough people will gain the necessary treatment. What happens, then, when the child or adult with a mental disability is also deeply emotionally disturbed? What is the history of psychoanalytical treatment for this group? Unfortunately, it is painfully short (as I describe in Chapter 3).

Each time a psychoanalyst or psychotherapist has 'rediscovered' the emotional and treatment needs of this group and underlined the fact that verbal abilities and performance intelligence are *not* needed for psychotherapy to take place, she suddenly leaves the field and takes on no further patients with handicaps. Ten years later another psychotherapist is reinventing the wheel. In England I am one of only a handful of child or adult psychoanalytical psychotherapists or psychoanalysts specializing in working with this client group. There are a few others who have taken on one such patient. This is not any longer because of lack of interest (see Chapter 3) but because altogether there are not enough such practitioners in this country. There are only 230 child psychotherapists in England at the moment. A child psychotherapist is a graduate, usually in his or her late twenties or early thirties, who undertakes a six-year postgraduate training in Child Psychotherapy. In addition to treating intensively (three to four times weekly) a child under five, a junior-aged child, an adolescent, and less intensively a family, perhaps a group, and a range of other cases, plus taking theoretical classes and work discussion groups, a trainee has to fund her own psychoanalysis. Although child psychotherapists work almost entirely within the National Health Service they have to subsidize their own lengthy training. The theoretical and clinical foundations of the training are psychoanalytical. There are similar child psychotherapy trainings in Europe but not in the USA.

A psychoanalyst is a graduate who has undergone a training at the Institute of Psycho-Analysis, seeing two patients for psycho-analysis (five times a week), having their own psychoanalysis and a range of theoretical seminars and work discussion and supervision. Although some psychoanalysts work in the health service the training is a private one. The detailed and intensive work of psychoanalysts informs psychoanalytical psychotherapy and thereby enriches public sector treatment. Psychoanalysts also support health service psychoanalytical psychotherapy by taking on trainee therapists as their patients. There are about 400 psychoanalysts in the UK and 2,560 in the USA. These numbers are swelled by psychoanalytically orientated art, music and drama therapists, psychologists, social workers, nurses and psychiatrists, amongst others. However, the numbers are small, the service is patchy and there is little supervision or support. All too often, a hard-pressed residential worker is expected to manage a Unit and counsel residents and other workers who labour under even less support, no adequate training and a complex blurring of boundaries. Facilitative work can make enormous changes to people who have been deprived of communication and whose lives have been given no meaning. However, when it comes to treating deep-rooted emotional disturbance there is an abyss in provision. You cannot love someone out of mental illness.

Twelve years ago in the UK there was no formal psychoanalytical psychotherapy treatment offered to mentally handicapped patients, although there were a few pioneering psychiatrists (for example, Joan Bicknell, Sheila Hollins and Sophie Thompson at St George's Hospital in London), psychologists (like Pat Frankish and Nigel Beail in Yorkshire) and art and music therapists who were working within a psychoanalytically orientated framework. Neville Symington, a psychoanalyst and clinical psychologist, worked in the Adult Department of the Tavistock Clinic, the largest National Health Service training and treatment centre in the UK. In 1978 he was referred an adult male patient who was mildly handicapped. He grew so involved in the implications of this man's treatment that in 1979 he started a workshop on Psychotherapy for Subnormal Patients. (As I stated earlier, names and terms have changed dramatically within the last twelve years: see Chapter 2.) He pointed out some basic facts that had been lost for over twenty years. For example, since handicapped patients had conscious and unconscious processes at work that could be enriching or debilitating, they might need access to psychoanalytical treatment just like the rest of the population and indeed might merit extra access by virtue of the burden of their handicap.

Why psycho- analytical treatm. [handwritten margin note]

Symington drew together a group of interested colleagues, mainly psychologists and psychiatrists, but after he emigrated to Australia only two remained from the original group: Jon Stokes, an adult psychotherapist and clinical psychologist, and myself, a child psychotherapist. Over a four-year period we increased our clinical commitment. I took on severely and profoundly handicapped patients too. A period of writing began as we wanted to make clear that it was 'stupid' to deprive severely and profoundly handicapped patients of psychoanalytical psychotherapy. We started ten-week psychodynamic introductory courses for workers in the field of mental handicap, introduced open monthly meetings and met weekly to offer each other peer supervision.

The theoretical conclusions were obvious once we came to them! Firstly, we concluded that no handicap in itself meant that a patient could not make use of therapy. There could be emotional intelligence left intact and rich regardless of how crippled performance intelligence was. This finding had been voiced every ten years since Freud first created psychoanalysis but somehow it kept getting lost again and needed to be refound. We felt we could say it with added conviction and power as we were treating far more severely handicapped individuals than the analytic literature had ever mentioned before (see Chapter 3, for a psychoanalytical history, and the Glossary of Psychoanalytic Terms at the end of the book).

Secondly, however fixed some aspects of organic impairment were, we saw handicap as a fluid state that people moved in and out of throughout the day. Hence, the patient who could open the door easily at one moment might not be able to lift his hand a few moments later. We therefore saw the need for expectancy to be at the highest level but for there to be provision for the lowest. Thirdly, we saw that the secondary handicap, the way clients defensively exaggerated their difficulties, could be more debilitating and handicapping than the primary handicap. As far as theoretical foundations for the workshop went, we needed access to the important main body of psychoanalytical literature. The only difference we found in working with this group was the extra impact of abuse and post-traumatic stress disorder.

From one of my first patients with a severe mental handicap (Chapter 6) I learned about the coexistence of sexual abuse and handicap and the way abuse itself could be a primary cause of handicap when there was no brain damage. When a paper of mine was published on that subject several years later, in 1986, it is hard to believe now the surprise and shock it created. Letters started pouring in to the workshop (meaning to just two of us) at a rate of over sixty a week as well as urgent referrals and lecture requests. When any one person opens her eyes and sees something more clearly it allows others to do the same. In the workshop we were aware of how Alice Miller, a former psychoanalyst, aptly illustrates this point in her book *Thou Shalt Not Be Aware: Society's Betrayal of the Child*. Looking at the impact of the French obstetrician Leboyer on techniques of childbirth, she comments, ' . . . only one obstetrician had to gain access to his feelings in order for the cruelty of present day childbirth methods to be exposed' (Miller, 1985, p. 213).

Perhaps the biggest shock was that we had all managed *not* to see something; we had gone 'stupid', knocked silly by the grief we were witnessing. From this I learned how stupidity could be a defence against the trauma of knowing too much of a painful kind. I was helped in facing these issues by the general cultural awakening to the existence and impact of sexual abuse, trauma and severe deprivation.

It seemed an important piece of historical synchronicity that all these pieces of work came together in the late 1970s and early 1980s, the same time as the People First self-advocacy movement came to England. This movement began in America and consisted of people with handicaps helping themselves and others to speak up. Some English individuals with learning difficulties were inspired by an international conference organized by the People First movement in America and brought the idea back. Some of these groups are initially facilitated by advocates who are not handicapped.

This was also the period in which the concept of normalization was developed in Denmark and Sweden (by Bank-Mikkelson and Bengt Nirje) and taken up in the USA by the President's Committee on Mental Retardation in 1976. Normalization is a process in which those deprived of ordinary living experiences and attitudes because of the nature of their institution or handicap are given support to have these ordinary experiences and values. This philosophy aided the move towards returning people to the community from long-stay institutions.

In 1987, Jon Stokes became chairman of the Adult Department of the Tavistock Clinic and had to give up belonging to the Mental Handicap Workshop. I convened the Workshop by myself for a year until Dr Sheila Bichard, an educational psychologist who had trained at New York University, joined because of her interest in exploring the connections between emotional and cognitive development. Her previous research had been on specific reading disability. Her psychodynamically orientated clinical work as a senior staff member of the Tavistock Clinic had made her aware of the complex interrelationship between internal and external factors in assessing handicaps.

The idea of joint research on these crucial areas soon gained ground and it was agreed that she would provide psychological tests for most of the handicapped children and adults I took on for long-term therapy. This would enable us to provide a fuller service for the patients who came to us and the wider referring network. Repeated yearly, it would also provide some understanding of the nature and meaning of change for some twenty-four individual and group patients.

As our plans grew firmer, it was clear that the Workshop needed a new name to reflect its new tasks and in Autumn 1989 it duly became the Tavistock Clinic Mental Handicap Psychotherapy and Psychology Research Workshop with Sheila Bichard as co-convener. The preliminary results of our research will take time to monitor and will be a book in its own right.

SOME DEFINITIONS

What is handicap? What is the difference between handicap, disability and learning difficulty? In Chapter 2 I discuss in length the reasons for all the different words and terms in this field. At this point, it needs stating that the term 'mental handicap' came into prominence in the 1970s, replacing the terms 'mental retardation' and 'mental subnormality'. As a general term it deals with the emotional and social consequences of an individual's mental impairment.

The World Health Organization (WHO) has defined impairment (1980) as any loss or abnormality of structure or function. A disability is defined as a restriction resulting from an impairment and a handicap is the disadvantage to an individual resulting from an impairment or disability.

Some people prefer the definition contained in the US Developmental Disabilities Act (1984 PL 98–527, Section 102), which links mental and physical handicaps by defining mental or physical impairment (or a combination of the two) as something that is liable to continue indefinitely and results in substantial functional limitations in three or more of the following: self-care, receptive and expressive language, learning, mobility, self-direction, capacity for independent living and economic self-sufficiency. This definition also reflects a person's need for interdisciplinary or generic care, treatment or other services which are of lifelong or extended duration and are individually planned and co-ordinated.

Ian McDonald, Director of Brunel University's Mental Handicap

Services Unit, has created his own definition of disability, which is painfully emotionally accurate: 'the irreconcilable difference between imagination and realisation' (1988).

In this book, whilst supporting the WHO definition of impairment, disability and handicap, I do not use the same terms. I often use the term 'primary handicap' as a synonym for disability and 'secondary handicap' as a synonym for handicap. The words we are brought up with, like our surnames, become deep-rooted and it is very hard to change them. For a single marriage it is possible but in this field, where linguistic divorce is so frequent, I am still biding my time! (See Chapter 2 for a full exploration of these linguistic issues.)

Since the 1920s a division has been made between those who are mildly and moderately handicapped (IQs in the 50–70 range) and those who are severely handicapped (IQs below 50). Profound handicap registers in the 0–24 range. These scores are just one useful indicator of cognitive functioning. So long as they are seen that way they cannot be abused.

INCIDENCE AND SOCIAL FACTORS

The social figures concerning handicap that is not caused by brain damage or chromosomal abnormality (organic causes) are shocking. Eighty per cent of the total number of mentally handicapped children and adults in the UK are only mildly handicapped (Ricks, 1990, p. 518). Most of these are from social class V and have experienced a socially disadvantaged environment. In many cases, the handicap is environmentally caused. Although mental handicap caused by brain damage or chromosomal abnormality is spread across all social classes (Office of Health Economics, 1973) the majority of handicap worldwide is environmental and linked to poverty.

Michael Rutter and colleagues (1970) found maternal absence, paternal unemployment, large number of siblings and foster-care significantly linked with this group. Richard Rieser and Micheline Mason (1990) estimate that at the start of the 1980s 100 million children in the world were disabled by malnutrition. If we add those handicapped by war, torture, accident, pollution we can see that the number handicapped by birth trauma or organically is very small. If we include all physical and mental disabilities, the number, for adults, in the UK would reach 6,202,000 or 14.2 per cent of the adult population (Office of Census and Population Surveys, 1988) Even when looking at physical disability alone we find that incomes are substantially lower than average.

In the UK over one million adults and children are in the mildly handicapped range. In the USA there are between five and six million handicapped children and adults, an estimated 3 per cent of the population. As in the UK, poverty was found to have a close connection to mild handicap. Draft rejections caused by mental handicap during World War II were fourteen times heavier in states with low incomes, whilst in some slum areas 10–30 per cent of school children were handicapped (Kennedy, 1963). The interim findings of the National Commission on Children, published in Washington on 28 April 1990, estimated that malnutrition affects 500,000 children in the USA, directly creating an illiterate underclass. An estimated 100,000 children are homeless. Eleven million children have no direct access to a family doctor. One child in five lives below the poverty line and it is considered that the figures for black children are even higher. In 1987 the poverty rate among black children was 45 per cent, among Hispanic children 39 per cent and among whites 15 per cent. In the US *Guardian* newspaper on 30 April 1990, Democratic Senator John Rockefeller of West Virginia said, 'These are personal tragedies and they are also a staggering national tragedy.'

Insurance companies are skilled in assessing the stress levels caused by divorce, unemployment, bereavement, illness and moving home. With each additional burden they can financially estimate the extra emotional cost. Many of our mildly mentally handicapped citizens have experienced a complete set of life's worst experiences. The Office of Census and Population Surveys study of disabled children (1989) found that boarding or alternative provision was needed for 48 per cent of children who were at physical or emotional risk in their home environment.

When we come to organic mental handicap, 300,000 severely mentally handicapped children and adults live in the UK on average

(Ricks, 1990, p. 518). Most have coexisting physical disabilities and, not surprisingly given the burden they carry, there is an increase in emotional disturbance in proportion to the severity of the handicap.

A child who is born with something wrong is often experienced as a disturbing challenge to our sense of biological autonomy and control. Where something is seriously wrong that cannot be repaired we often seem to be reminded of our mental and physical frailty and mortality. This leads to some of the most inspired preventative or reparative work on the one hand or to blaming, scapegoating, disowning on the other. At the most extreme end of this process is what Wolfensberger (1987) has aptly called 'death-making'. The damaged child is written off as pre-born or pre-human and therefore the value of his or her life is under threat.

Devalued children and adults have, with a few shining historical exceptions, received the worst services, the worst schools, the worst teachers, the worst medicine, the worst hospitals and homes and little pioneering treatment except of an experimental kind (for example contraceptive injections). Over twenty years ago, before the concept of normalization was articulated, my father, educational pioneer Stanley Segal, encapsulated his philosophy in his book title *No Child Is Ineducable* and impressed on me the importance of proper training and valuing of teachers working with handicapped children. 'Otherwise you get the "C"-stream teachers teaching the "C"-stream children.' At one time he taught the 'F' stream in a comprehensive school and later pointed out that had the comprehensive been larger it could have been an 'L' stream. To combat the feelings of worthlessness in his pupils he wrote special textbooks on space with sophisticated knowledge expressed in the right primary-level vocabulary, and soon his class had access to high-status knowledge on Sputniks and offered something to the rest of the school. A series of books and articles followed, because as well as high-quality teaching, training and planning he emphasized the importance of writing.

This book, like the Tavistock Workshop, is a way of providing a space to hold a history of this work as well as becoming a focal point for other people's hitherto lost information. As the person who has spanned the different stages in the life of the Workshop, I have been able to offer long-term treatment, an average of six years of once-weekly psychotherapy. This means patients have had the time to unravel their own histories, the history of what they knew but could not own previously. This book is therefore also a history of the unravelling of their intelligence.

The actions I take and the words I use are in the context of psychoanalytical psychotherapy treatment. They are not the same as those I would have taken in my previous role as a teacher. In other words, readers are asked to take ideas that might be relevant for their own work and apply them in their own words and their own fashion. For example, if a child is behaving aggressively in the therapy room with the aim of being rejected because his father has just left home, I might interpret that. I might say he is seeing if his angry words and actions are powerful enough to get rid of me. In the classroom, as a teacher, I would see those same angry actions disrupt the class. As the class teacher I would understand that the child's aim was to see if he could re-enact the driving out of a parent. However, it would not be appropriate in the classroom to say 'You are angry because your father has left home'. It would be necessary to stop the disruptive behaviour first and then quietly have a word later.

This book is specifically about psychoanalytical psychotherapy as a treatment for secondary handicapping processes. This necessary focus in no way denies the value of the increasing good treatment practices that have developed in other disciplines over the last decade.

Writing this book has been both a painful and inspiring task. Human limitations, whether caused by internal or external factors, bring out both the worst and best in individuals and society.

I have tried to throw light on the inner experience of mental handicap as well as to show the ways handicapping processes operate in all of us. I hope that in exploring the universality of these processes I have not diminished in any way the extra difficulties experienced by individuals with disabilities.

To protect the confidentiality of treatment, the names, physical description and background information of clients have been changed.

PART I:
THE BACKGROUND

1   THE SENSE IN 'STUPIDITY'

Listen to others, even the dull and ignorant; they too have their story.

Anon., 'Desiderata'

It was a splendid mind. For if thought is like the keyboard of a piano divided into so many notes, or like the alphabet is ranged in 26 letters all in order, then his splendid mind had no sort of difficulty in running over those letters one by one firmly and accurately, until it had reached, say, the letter Q. But after Q? What comes next? He knows only a few people reach Q and Z is only reached once by one man in a generation but it hurts him not to be able to get to R. A shutter, like the leathern eyelid of a lizard, flickered over the intensity of his gaze and obscured the letter R. In that flash of darkness he heard people saying – he was a failure – that R was beyond him. He would never reach R.

Virginia Woolf, *To the Lighthouse*

The Master said, 'There are, are there not, young plants that fail to produce blossoms and blossoms that fail to produce fruit?'

Confucius, *The Analects*

Twelve years ago, when I was waiting to assess for psychotherapy my first severely mentally handicapped patient, I realized I was frightened. The fear of not understanding what my patient might say was predominant as I knew that brain damage had seriously affected his speech. Two memories came to mind that helped me, one of my grandmother and one of an uncle.

I had a grandmother who refused to wear her false teeth. She had also refused or been unable to learn much English despite fifty years in this country. When she spoke to me I didn't understand what she said. As a small child I felt angry with her. I knew she was handicapping her communication with me by not wearing teeth or learning English. I also had an uncle with Parkinson's disease who struggled bravely to communicate with me despite the permanent physical discomfort he was experiencing. As a child, I smiled stupidly, clutching onto the couple of words I did understand. I always felt guilty when I saw him. My uncle was trying to make himself understood whilst I became the stupid smiling idiot. In both those cases there was a primary deficit – loss of teeth, loss of a native country due to persecution, loss of physical control and clarity due to an organic disease. However, far more disturbing than the primary handicap or disability can be the defensive secondary handicap used to cope with it, or rather not to cope with it. My grandmother, in not bearing the loss of her Russian past and the loss of her teeth, made her communication problems even worse while my uncle suffered the consequences of having a relative unable to bear his primary handicap.

I can now say to patients with severe speech defects, or, indeed, to colleagues with unintelligible accents, 'I'm sorry but I did not understand what you said. Please say it again.' However, the child I was could not bear admitting she did not understand. To pretend to more knowledge than you have rather than face openly what you do not know is indeed handicapping. How many calls to service engineers for washing machines, televisions or household implements that have gone wrong are due to this issue? Many of us omnipotently fiddle with different buttons in the mad hope of fixing something rather than ask for help and admit lack of knowledge. One highly intelligent adolescent, coming for a first assessment meeting, raced ahead of me in the corridor, turning in the wrong direction. He preferred to be called back and told the right direction rather than wait and face the fact that he was in a new building and did not know where we were going.

A while back, with a colleague from the Tavistock Clinic, child psychotherapist Eileen Orford, I was at Rome airport looking for the right terminal for a domestic flight. We were on our way to provide a teaching day for a centre for mentally and physically handicapped children and adults in Bari with Dr Marco Urago, the director. Having learned just a few sentences in Italian, approximating to a two-year-old's vocabulary, I wanted to try one out. To my initial pride and relief my sentence was understood. In fact it was too well understood. The Italian airport official responded with several sentences of fast Italian. I understood nothing. I felt extremely stupid and realized that in my grandiose wish to deny my linguistic paucity I had only added to my difficulties. Humbled, I returned to speaking English, which the official, of course, spoke fluently!

Thomas is a teenager with a severe mental handicap. He was very proud that he knew the sign and the word for 'Gentlemen' when he needed to use a public toilet near his leisure centre. He ignored his key worker's comments about the different coins needed in different places. One day, in a new area, he found himself faced with a toilet that required 10p placed in its slot. That was a sign and instruction he had not encountered before. For a long while he waited, refusing to believe his knowledge was not adequate. Finally, he walked back up to the main street and managed to say to a passer-by that he could not read and needed help.

Both Thomas and I were in the same predicament of finding it intolerable that the precious small resource of specific knowledge we had was not adequate for the particular task needed. In the circumstances mentioned we both managed to deal with that hurt and admit we needed help. We were able to demonstrate what Confucius considers true knowledge, an understanding of what we did and did not know.

Here is a more familiar example. A professional adult needed to ring his doctor's surgery to change an appointment time. All the receptionist needed to hear was the time and date being changed and the time and date wanted. However, disintegrating dramatically, the adult struggled with a long-winded apology that was completely unnecessary for the receptionist to hear. There was the problem of this co-existing other self who was going to be so furious at having anything changed that they required total submission.

Dealing with that internal person is made much harder when there is a real external one to match. Admitting you do not know something and asking for help only to be met with a shocked or contemptuous 'What? You don't know that? Where have you been all your life?' makes it harder. If you face someone who cannot or will not ever tell you something you need to know, it can be easier to stay stupid and give up on learning. For example, Tom (aged 8) had never been told why his father had left home when he was a baby. He picked up very powerfully the signs that his mother could not bear even to consider that question and managed to stifle it in his own mind. However, stifling that question always meant stifling many others that she *could* answer. He ended up unable to read or write, his emotions clearly affecting his ability to learn. There, trauma in both the mother and the child had led to handicapping. As well as the hurt self saying, 'Please don't talk about that as it hurts me too much', we have the arrogant, omnipotent self saying, 'Don't you dare mention anything I don't want you to think about.' Trauma and deprivation excite false internal friends. Tom and his mother turned out to have an internal comforter who initially helped them over their loss of husband and father. However, that comforting voice soon became an abusive one, only offering help if it was implicitly obeyed. That particular constellation is as present in individuals with an organic handicap as it is in ordinary individuals who are handicapped by particular problems.

We all share the struggle not to spoil or handicap the basic inheritance we have. Needless to say, some are a lot luckier than others with the outcome of the genetic or constitutional lottery. Two three-year-olds are sharing biscuits. One of them, with great difficulty, breaks off a small piece for the other. It looks as if he is very greedy and indeed he is. However, what is not seen is that for that particularly greedy child to manage to give even a tiny piece to someone else could have represented a greater act of personal generosity than for the other child to give half. Our genetic inheritance is very unequal and so is the use or abuse we make of it. Thus, though we might agree with the concept that we are all handicapped and that it is only a matter of degree, the extent of the degree is of great significance.

Opening your eyes after adolescence to the realization that you will not be an Austen, Einstein, Madonna or Picasso can be painful enough to the ordinary adolescent. Opening your eyes to admitting you look, sound, walk, talk, move or think differently from the ordinary, average person, let alone a cult hero or heroine, takes greater reserves of courage, honesty and toleration of one's own envy. It can be easier to behave like the village idiot and make everyone laugh than to expose the unbearable tiny discrepancy between normal and not normal on the human continuum. This is what is involved in the 'handicapped smile' (Chapter 6). Although it resides most prominently on the faces of the handicapped, an understanding of its process is helpful both in understanding the impact of sexual abuse and in understanding ordinary embarrassment.

Every way an individual struggles with the predicament she is in provides an understanding of that process in other people. Looking at handicap means looking at difference and at a difference that is painful. This sheds light on the way all people deal with differences of education, accent, appearance, class, family structure. If the actual difference, when it is not favourable, is seen as primary, how it is *not* dealt with represents the secondary handicap.

There seem to me to be three main areas where secondary handicap plays a part in the difficulties of the individual even though there is regular overlap between the three groups. (I will be looking at these in more detail in Chapters 5 and 6.) The first is mild secondary handicap. Here, individuals compliantly exacerbate their original handicap to keep the outer world happy with them. For instance, some handicapped people behave like smiling pets for fear of offending those they are dependent on. This can involve cutting their real language and intellectual abilities. This type of secondary handicap also has wider political application. When people depend for their lives on cruel regimes they need to cut their intelligence and awareness. Black slaves and their descendants in the USA learned to show their intelligence in private and adopt a 'stupid' appeasing way of talking in front of whites. In *I Know Why the Caged Bird Sings*, Maya Angelou reveals her 'crying shame' when her uncle is subservient even to 'poor white trash children' (Angelou, 1969, p. 27). Alex Haley's *Roots* vividly showed the two tiers of understanding. As his character Fiddler puts it, 'If dey [white folks] eatin' an' talkin' nigger gal servin' 'em actin' dumber'n she is, 'memberin' eve'y word she hear. Even when white folks git so scared dey starts spellin' out words, if any niggers roun', well, plenty house niggers ain't long repeatin' it letter for letter to de nearest nigger what can spell an' piece together what was said' (Haley, 1978, p. 258). With the advent of *glasnost* and *perestroika* we saw that Soviet citizens were aware of the massacre at Katyn as well as other devastating acts of Stalinism. Similarly, the unification of Berlin led to further discussion and understanding of Nazism. Only in a period of safety is it possible for people to reclaim the understanding they did have but were unable to acknowledge consciously.

Second, there is opportunist handicap, by which I mean that added to the original handicap there is severe personality maldevelopment linked to the handicap in which all internal disturbance amalgamates. Howard (see Chapter 10) was physically and mentally handicapped. He was referred because of violence to his residential workers amidst angry outbursts that the staff had not provided him with a woman. He treated handicapped women with contempt and disgust. He had the pain of severe handicap to process, a major primary handicap. However, he could not deal with it. His hatred and envy found a home in opportunist handicap.

I do not consider it surprising that opportunist handicap should exist as a more serious version of secondary handicap, nor that secondary handicap should exist. We are all aware of how children or adults can use minor or major ailments to 'carry' other emotional states, but if we are lucky these are of short duration. Even with a short, non-life-threatening illness, such as a cold, it is hard to retain one's normal balance. When environment, constitution and original handicap are themselves severely debilitating it takes greater courage than normal to avoid secondary mild or opportunist handicap.

The Office of Health Economics paper on mental handicap (1973) describes mental ability as the product of three factors: 'inherited constitution, modification or injuries caused by pre- or postnatal injury or disease and conditioning and training of the intellect'. Friedrich and Boriskin (1976) have pointed out that 'within the population of maltreated children the handicapped are over-represented'. In addition, the majority of those with mild handicaps are from the most deprived social backgrounds (Rutter *et al*, 1970). Similar conclusions have been reached in the United States. At the 1977 multicultural seminar on mental retardation among minority disadvantaged populations, held in Norfolk, Virginia, it was estimated that 85–90 per cent of the mildly handicapped were disadvantaged by 'poverty, racial and ethnic discrimination and family distress. Correspondingly, the retardation rates for blacks, Puerto Ricans, Cubans and disadvantaged whites living in urban and rural poverty are especially high' (Pollard, 1982, p. 19). We are therefore looking in some cases of mental and multiple handicap at severely deprived individuals who have received poor parenting or even abuse.

Along with mild or opportunist secondary handicap, the third type of secondary handicap is handicap as a defence against trauma, which will be looked at more fully in Chapter 6. This is where the handicap is used in the service of the self to protect it from unbearable memory of trauma, of a breakdown in the protective shield (Freud, 1920, p. 29). We find trauma to be a regular constituent in the experience of handicap. When we look at the emotional experience of mental handicap we are looking automat-ically at loss and trauma. Almost every patient who is referred, almost every case brought to supervision groups, reflects the painful centrality of trauma. Trauma can cause handicap (by sexual, physical, environmental, political and emotional abuse); it can exacerbate the experience of the handicap, and the handicap can itself be experienced by the individual and those around as traumatic.

When Shirley Hoxter (1986, p. 89) considered the plight just of the physically disabled child she commented, 'The physically disabled child is often himself experienced as a source of trauma. Perhaps for the parents this occurs almost invariably, but to a large extent this may also be the situation for the care-givers and for society as a whole, and the defences mobilised can often be recognised as typical of the responses to trauma'. If we add mental handicap to that already burdened situation some embryonic concept of the multiply handicapped individual's plight is possible.

When we properly take into account the impact of severe or profound handicap we can understand why psychiatric disturbance increases in proportion to the severity of the multiple handicap. It is not that the handicap creates emotional disturbance as part of its process, but rather, that the burden of a handicap depletes what resources an individual has, leaving him or her prey to what is internally unresolved and disturbed.

Daniel Defoe (1711, p. 130) was sharply aware of the internal

impact of difficult external circumstances and wanted to differentiate between virtue that was a product of good fortune and lack of
stress and internal strength that was tried and tested: 'The man is
not rich because he is honest, but he is honest because he is rich.'
Defoe was extremely understanding of the predicament of those
who lost economic resources and his words apply equally
powerfully to the effect of all internal or external depleting
processes. 'I tell you gentlemen, in your poverty, the best of you
will rob your neighbour; nay, go further, as I said once on the like
occasion, you will not only rob your neighbour, but if in distress,
you will EAT your neighbour, ay, and say grace to your meat too –
distress removes from the soul, all relation, affection, sense of
justice, and all the obligations, either moral or religious, that secure
one man against another. Not that I say or suggest the distress makes
violence lawful; but I say it is a trial beyond the ordinary powers of
human nature to withstand' (Defoe, 1711).

Although mild handicap is predominantly linked to deprivation,
organic handicap is spread across all social classes, as are, of course,
the momentary states of stupidity and handicap all people pass in
and out of. For we all try to deal with differences that are
unfavourable. As a teacher I was well aware of the phenomenon of
the 'C-stream stare, the one each backrow inherits' (Sinason, 1987,
p. 48). It was shared by highly intelligent grammar school children
who came last in their own culture's hierarchy and those who came
last in classes for handicapped children. Being seen to be different
in an unfavourable way has its own emotional impact.

Different cultures and different periods in history have their own
rules for defining acceptable levels of knowledge, appearance,
manners, but the internal processes of dealing with the situation
have remained the same. At one period in the 1960s when there
was a fashion for boys to grow their hair long I remember a joke
about a son complaining, 'Beethoven had long hair,' and the father
replying, 'Yes. But if he lived now he would have short hair.' With
handicapped people the discrepancy between current and past
standards is not humorous. I am reminded of a patient's comment:
'A long time ago only the King could read.' For it is no help to
consider that the mildly handicapped child or adult today would
have been seen as far more intelligent a few hundred years ago when

only the privileged were taught to read. We cannot minimize the plight of those considered handicapped now by saying they would not have been perceived that way three hundred years ago.

Nevertheless, if we go back a thousand years to when Alfred the Great wrote 'On the state of learning in England', it is salutary to note that 'So utterly had learning declined in England that there were very few on this side of the Humber who could understand their prayer-book in English . . . and I think there were not many beyond the Humber. So few of them, there were, that I cannot think of even one single one to the South of the Thames when I became King. God Almighty be thanked we now have a supply of teachers' (Onions, 1966, pp. 4–6). King Alfred brought in Irish monks as teachers. I have often wondered if the way the Irish are used as idiots in English jokes stems from an unconscious historical memory that once they taught the backward English! Now, the low esteem in which education is held in England currently has meant that to ensure a supply of teachers recruitment is again being made overseas!

Each time there is progress and new educational goals are set, a new group is created just outside of the curve of normality. What is defined as handicapped, retarded or slow is therefore a relative term dependent on what is perceived as average in any culture. Yet, there *has* been progress and it is as a result of our social progress and the fact that we offer education to all that we can now feel more free to consider the emotional plight of the handicapped. Countries in the midst of disasters, poverty, hunger or war cannot concern themselves with learning difficulty, let alone the emotional aspects of learning difficulty. Richard Rieser and Micheline Mason (1990) aptly point out that worldwide, most handicap 'is not caused by an Act of God or nature; it is allowed by political neglect'. First must come the provision of basic survival needs, then education. When literacy comes, it becomes easier to see the mildly handicapped. Before literacy, those who were only mildly handicapped might not have been noticed so clearly. However, those who are profoundly handicapped stand out even when the educational level of the community is basic.

Major difference from the norm, even in ways that seem advantageous, can carry its own difficulties. Someone considered beautiful in any culture has to cope with being looked at admiringly or enviously. Although a beautiful voice, face or body are positive attributes, they pose problems. There was a time when film star Paul Newman took to wearing dark glasses because people staring at his famed blue eyes proved such an intrusion. Famous opera singers sometimes refer to their voice as 'the voice', not 'my voice'. The object of difference, however beautiful, is split off from integrated ownership.

Wealth and title can prove a similar problem. Fairy-tales are full of beautiful princesses or handsome princes who pretend to be poor in order to make sure that they are loved for 'themselves' rather than for their trappings. Again, it is hard for the trappings of wealth, fame or beauty to be successfully integrated and accepted. Hence, some upper-class British boarding schools excel in providing monastic conditions of poverty.

Sometimes, individuals who are gifted in some ways deal with internal and external envy by offering a handicap as a sacrifice.

The image of the 'dumb blonde' provides a degraded way in which someone can apologize for their sexual beauty, seductiveness or knowledge by massacring their intellect. Marilyn Monroe was a victim and perpetuator of this process, a familiar one in sexually abused children. Margaret Mahler (1942), delineating this process in children and adults, used the term 'pseudo-imbecility' to convey the way stupidity could function as a cover to conceal illicit sexual life or knowledge. The public willingness to join in with this stupidity is not surprising. In admiring the dumb blonde's sexual knowledge whilst denigrating her intellectual ignorance or innocence the child in all of us is simultaneously coveting, attacking and gaining access to forbidden parental knowledge. In the field of mental handicap, there is a further twist. Some parents and workers talk as if their handicapped charges were bereft of any sexuality. They are seen as wondrous permanent children who inhabit a Never-Never Land where sexuality will never intrude. Or, if they do show signs of anything sexual, like masturbating, it is seen as an infantile regressive act. Reciprocally, there are adults and children with handicaps who split off all sexual knowledge.

A child who is noticeably handicapped receives the same amount of attention as a child who is abnormally beautiful. Strangers stare unashamedly, some people giggle, some become sentimental. The child and the parent have to deal with instant celebrity without any of the positive rewards that can bring. Sometimes the curiosity is excited and voyeuristic, like the curiosity that can accompany a disaster. The sight of damage, of something gone wrong, induces an excited disturbance in such onlookers. Sometimes, there is a turning away, a fear and a hostility, a sometimes spoken wish that such sights should be hidden from public view; there is a fear of catching the damage or having to recognize that such an event is possible.

The handicapped child and its parents and workers therefore carry a double burden. Not only do they have to face public scrutiny of varying kinds, making a simple walk to a local shop the equivalent of running the gauntlet, they also are burdened by the projections that come their way of other people's responses to damage and handicap. Salman Rushdie (1984, p. 123) understands this very well in the persona of his handicapped heroine Sufiya Zinobia. In looking at the projections that came to her and to other handicapped people he saw such people as given the task of being 'janitors of the unseen, their souls the buckets into which squeegees drip what-was-spilled. We keep such buckets in special cupboards. Nor do we think much of them although they clean up our dirty waters.' In 'Metamorphosis', his terrifying tale of transformation, Kafka (1916) has provided a similarly powerful parable of how someone different is dealt with. A man wakes up to find himself transformed into a giant insect. His family feel horror, disgust, shock, kindness, hatred and, finally, lethal negligence.

Being made the recipient of hostile, patronizing or demeaning projections is an experience all minorities experience. Perhaps it is not a coincidence that most members of the Tavistock Clinic Mental Handicap Psychotherapy and Psychology Workshop are from other countries or second- or third-generation British. The American writer Maya Angelou (1969, p. 12) understood the projections she and her family received as blacks as well as the extra projections received by her crippled Uncle Willie. 'The tragedy of lameness seems so unfair to children that they are embarrassed in its presence. And they, most recently off nature's mould, sense that they have only narrowly missed being another of her jokes. In relief at the narrow escape, they vent their emotions in impatience and criticism of the unlucky cripple . . . In our society, where two-legged, two-armed strong Black men were able at best to eke out only the necessities of life . . . Uncle Willie was the whipping boy and butt of jokes of the unemployed and underpaid.'

Different groups are also recognized by accent. How accent is perceived as a sign of intelligence provides a useful example of aural prejudice. 'Received pronunciation', the voice of higher education, is the most popular accent in Great Britain (Honey, 1989), whilst the four least favoured accents are London Cockney, Liverpool (Scouse), West Midlands (especially Birmingham) and Glaswegian. A standard accent can aid in job opportunity and enhance credibility in court. Honey was shocked to find (p. 60) that readiness to stigmatize these accents was shared by great numbers of the speakers of those stigmatized varieties themselves. Honey quotes Janet Street-Porter, a television star with a Cockney accent, as commenting 'The British think I must be working class, they think I must be thick.' Interestingly, she added that people expect her to be cheerful and funny because of her accent. Again, the pressure to link unfavourable difference with 'fun' is made.

Where can fun be made of difference? British comedian Jasper Carrott has a running joke about the stupidity of *Sun* readers (the *Sun* is an English tabloid newspaper). If there were no Page 3 pinups of teenage girls and a more serious level of news reporting, albeit with a primary-school vocabulary, we would be pleased that the paper had succeeded in interesting those with limited reading ages. We would also feel sad that such a large percentage of the population was unable to read anything more complex. However, the joke is permissible because we can see that there is a perversion of intelligence in the pretence that it is providing news instead of titillation and that this is being exploited by the publishers. Otherwise, humour about disability, as about all widespread minority experiences, needs to come from the specific groups themselves.

Humour aside, the strength of the desire to make the immigrant, the handicapped, the fat or the ugly smiling and cheerful unerringly covers over our precise knowledge of the opposite. It takes a lot of knowledge and intelligence to get something completely wrong!

We show our understanding of that process by the words we use. Take this scene, for example. In the park on a tarmac playing area two children are playing ball. One of them throws the ball too hard and it goes into the sandpit. 'You stupid idiot!' cries the other angrily. That scene is repeated in varying ways all over the country. The choice of language is extremely important. It shows that an idiot is not seen as someone without any sense. If an idiot really was understood to be someone without rudimentary intelligence then the adjective 'stupid' would not be enlisted to qualify it. If you really thought someone was an idiot you would not be calling them one and you would not need to add an extra adjective. Otherwise you would be behaving like the angry adult who says to a child, 'Don't be so childish.' In other words, it is understood that the perpetrator of a stupid action is not stupid but is in the grip of a process that can be experienced as an attack by those around.

A thirsty adult takes a carton of orange juice from the fridge and with unerring accuracy opens it the wrong way, ignoring the 'open this end' signs. 'You idiot,' says a watching friend. Again, the word 'idiot' is used to convey an awareness of misused intelligence. It takes a perversion of real intelligence to manage to spoil a task so assiduously. We are all aware of individuals who are highly skilled in their stupidity. To manage always to find the worst person to fill a job vacancy, the worst partner, the worst way of dealing with written instructions, takes knowledge. Something has to be known well in order to be transformed into accurate error.

Because moments of being stupid are so universal there is often an attempt to see such episodes as accidents, unfortunate occurrences that have no unconscious meaning. Anthea Able, for example, arrives at work and then realizes she has left her keys at home. 'I'm so stupid,' she says. Her work colleagues generously say that everyone has an accident like that sometimes and chime in with examples of their own acts of forgetting. In therapy, it emerges that she is shortly about to move. For her, at that moment, denying herself access to her old and about-to-be-lost home was a way of unconsciously responding to the meaning of change and loss. The universality of occasional states of stupidity meant that the meaning of her state was ignored.

Only where such episodes occur with unremitting frequency are they given any extra attention. Anthony Arkwright, for example, forgets his appointments regularly. His colleagues cannot keep up the pretence of an 'accident'. Their use of the word 'stupid' then has to decline. Anthony is perceived as having a 'problem'. There is therefore a curious quantitative borderline between what is perceived as stupid and what is understood as a 'problem' although we can see that underneath the two issues form part of a continuum. Beryl Bank jokes that she is 'stupid about machines'. Hoovers, toasters, videos and computers are totally avoided by her. She is not perceived as having a problem, however, because enough people share her behaviour to normalize the meaning of it.

What happens then when a mentally handicapped person does something stupid? In our experience in the Tavistock Clinic Mental Handicap Workshop it is exactly the same. Doris Dot is a severely mentally handicapped woman. She had expressed the wish for a 10 a.m. appointment. Unfortunately, I had no such time available and could only offer her a 3 p.m. one. She turned up for her session at 10 a.m., apologizing profusely but cheerfully for her 'silly mistake'. In her afternoon session she used both her handicap and the concept of a mistake to avoid looking at the meaning of her action. It took time for her to realize she was angry that her own choice of time was not possible. By coming early, she was demonstrating the power of her omnipotent self that refused to accept being thwarted. Long-term psychoanalytical psychotherapy with the mildly, severely and profoundly multiply handicapped shows how we all misuse our emotional and cognitive inheritance.

Let us look again at the thirsty adult who has opened the carton of orange juice the wrong way. 'Open this end' are three simple words. They are easy to understand. There can be no excuse that technical jargon is making the consumer's task harder. There can be no excuse that the language was at a higher level than the average consumer's reading ability. What we have, when we look at a minute example like this, is an individual disregarding an instruction because, at that moment, it is unbearable that there is a right way to do something. In an omnipotent state of mind individuals want to create their own laws, their own language.

A profoundly handicapped man pours a packet of breakfast cereal over the table, missing, with exquisite accuracy, his cereal bowl. A residential worker comments, 'Poor fellow, fancy being so handicapped he cannot even pour his cereal. We need some more physiotherapy to help him control his hand movements.' I draw the worker's attention to the fact that everything on the table – knives, forks, spoons, salt and pepper, sugar bowl – is covered with cereal except the cereal bowl. I comment on the carefulness of the aim that has managed to leave untouched the very receptacle that should have contained the cereal. The worker thinks for a moment and then embarrassedly says, 'You know, I always feel angry when he does that but then I feel guilty and prefer to think it is an accident.' Of course there are people with all sorts of disabilities that powerfully reduce or change their ability to manage certain tasks. However, when a task is mismanaged with perfect accuracy we can see that there is intelligence, albeit misused. We often show we recognize this process by feeling irritated. 'Come on now, I showed you that just half an hour ago and you knew how to do it then.' To feel that an action is 'stupid' means we have the knowledge to know that the person committing the act is not always in the state that produces such actions.

What then is stupidity? We have seen that the word 'stupid' actually means 'numbed with grief'. We are all aware of that meaning in the word 'stupefy' but somehow lost our understanding of it in the concept of 'stupidity'. To be stupid is to be numbed with grief and those who bear the burden of a mental handicap carry an enormous amount of grief.

Let us look first at how this process operates in everyday life. Charles Charlesworth is an energetic man in his late seventies. He has some part-time freelance work and enjoys a range of hobbies. One afternoon, his wife complains bitterly that he is being 'stupid'. He has walked across the traffic lights before they were red and risked being knocked down. 'Leave him alone,' says their son, 'it must be his eyes. Perhaps they need checking.' Perhaps they do, but what his wife has picked up is that he is angrily committing an unsafe act.

Further exploration reveals that Mr Charlesworth feels such a loss of vigour as he grows older that he tries omnipotently to deny his physical state. In this state he feels he is more powerful than any car and any young man driving it and he is more important and powerful than any traffic light. Charles Charlesworth takes an afternoon rest when he is tired from his part-time job. He can at times be aware of and cater for his increased physical vulnerability. But facing the busy street and its fast traffic he moves into a state where awareness of his fragility is so unbearable it has to be thrown away. However, when he throws this awareness away he has also thrown his intelligence away.

Unfortunately, we cannot choose to remove from our brain tiny specific pieces of knowledge. David Davidson, for example, has a forthcoming appointment with his local hospital. He is terrified he may have cancer. In trying to deny the pain of that possibility he has wiped out knowledge of all his current appointments. As professionals we become stupid at times for similar reasons. Many training events I provide on mental handicap or sexual abuse include the following processes. Workers start by apologizing for their lack of knowledge and lack of training (regardless of their level of seniority or professional background). Then they show they know a lot about the difficulties of their clients. Then they start revealing extracts from some of the many horror stories they carry on their grossly overloaded 'caseloads'. Finally, they are aware that they said they knew nothing because they knew a lot and could not bear what they knew when they felt unable to change much in the lives of their 'caseload'.

Starting a new job, joining a new course, beginning a new training: all these starts can re-evoke feelings of helplessness, memories of first day at infant school. Sometimes people feel bereft of their adult selves for a considerable amount of time before they are able to settle. Before working in handicap I saw such experiences in myself, in colleagues and in patients only in terms of reminders of being little and helpless. Now I view the situation differently and see two alternative or additional factors.

Firstly, it only matters feeling little and helpless if there is also another self who is furious at not being all-knowing. It is that arrogant self who wakes up in a rage at learning that its healthy twin has admitted it needs to know more! Stupidity in some cases can therefore be linked to arrogance, as Bion (1957) shows us most clearly. This has enormous implications for the meaning of teaching. If we were to become stupid about Mr Charlesworth, for example, we might suggest he needed a social education programme. A worker would go with him to teach him to cross the road. Unfortunately, this kind of stupidity is widespread and many scarce education resources are wasted in such unnecessary and inappropriate tasks.

For example, Frances Farlow, a profoundly handicapped woman, was always stripping her clothes off in the middle of Sainsbury's. She had recently been moved to a community home after her long-stay hospital had closed and staff were eager for her to enjoy the benefits of local shopping. Their first move when faced with the difficult behaviour of Frances was to suggest an education programme to explain body parts and privacy. This failed. The next step was an enormous *volte-face* with staff deciding that it was the shoppers in Sainsbury's who were all wrong. Their client had the freedom to express herself how and where she liked and it was the silly shoppers who had the problem. At the root of this problem there is something painful. A young woman is drawing attention to her body in a public area. There is something troubling her. As well as her handicap, she is burdened by emotional disturbance. In a hospital ward her behaviour might not have been treated adequately, but it would not have caused the same disruption as it did in a community setting. Moving to a community home does not make her suddenly able to deal with herself let alone with the community.

I suggested to the staff that stripping off was not appropriate behaviour in a large shop, that Frances's behaviour and their own attempts to accommodate it were causing strain and stress to all concerned. Slowly in therapy we uncovered Frances's hurt and shame about her deformed body and how exposing it was one way of smearing others with a sight she could not bear. However, for staff to not become stupid and for the client to see, support is necessary. A child whose mother has died and who has muddled up past, present and future tenses in his news book does not require a grammar lesson. Education and psychoanalysis and psychoanalytical psychotherapy need to form a partnership to try to disentangle these issues.

One organization that struggles with that task is DUET (Development of University English Teaching). It is the brainchild of the School of English and American Studies at the University of East Anglia. Founded by Professor John Broadbent, it aims to link the academic with the experiential. Broadbent (1982) saw the design of DUET as being similar to the experiential working conferences of the Tavistock Institute. He therefore wanted a focus on the process of DUET workshops and conferences as well as on the actual academic texts that were going to be studied. He hoped that participants would rediscover the potential of their chosen subject by this process. Integration of many splits was also a prime aim. Specifically, he saw a need to heal the split between reading and writing, betweeen the choice of syllabus set texts and the mode of teaching them, between teacher and learner, between sacred text and profane reader.

I joined the staff of DUET for a one-week summer course, using my combined qualifications as an English literature graduate, teacher and psychotherapist. The week provided me with an impetus to rethink my ways of teaching psychoanalytic theory. How could one combine analytic understanding of the learning process with the need to have a set text? An invitation to teach a one-year introduction to Freud's work offered me the chance of exploring this and using some of the ideas offered by DUET.

I felt there was a particular problem for highly educated postgraduate professionals who were beginning to read psychoanalytical theory and history, sometimes for the first time. They could either be disconcerted by reading a 'sacred' text, the origin of the profession they were hoping to train to enter, or, alternatively, irritated at having to read someone 'old' instead of contemporary. There are similar problems for students undertaking a literature degree as well as GCSE or 'A' level. The very concept of a 'set text' challenges the individual's omnipotent wishes. Accordingly, I prepared some notes on the way we were going to approach the subject. The core concept was crystallized by a DUET sentence that meanings were neither in the text nor in the reader but in the meeting-space between them. I added that there were many different ways of studying Freud, or indeed any major thinker/ writer. We could focus on the individual man and see his work as an expression of his life. We could look at the historical, political, religious and cultural background. We could ask individuals in turn to give a short talk on the relevant extracts to be studied. The tutor/lecturer could give prepared lectures. However, whatever the method, there is often an unspoken assumption that the method chosen is 'objective'; that there is a reality 'out there' (author, text, society), of which everyone shares knowledge.

The fact is, though, that readers respond differently to texts, perceive them differently, notice some things, miss others. The texts are not shared Esperanto objects. Each of us makes the text exist for ourselves and what exists for each of us depends on our associations to the text: our fears, memories, hopes, gender, class, age. We all know this, and yet the pressure to wear the Emperor's new clothes, the pressure to pretend to the knowledge that is not personally true for us, can be enormous. We need therefore to stress these aims in trying to gain the most we can in sharing the experience of becoming familiar with a new text.

The aims of my introduction to Freud were to understand that learning is not a linear incremental process; that insight can come suddenly and unexpectedly; that it matters to be honest when the text is temporarily dead for us. I wanted to achieve as real a familiarity as was possible with the text being studied at an individual level but within the context of a group that could help people see more than they would have done individually. Students were asked to write out two sentences they most liked or disliked from the text we were discussing, giving their reasons. These were shared with the group at the start of each seminar so that everyone had a way of reaching the text via the group's experiential responses. I also raised the issue of 'skipping'. I suggested that skipping through text should be legitimized. For the set reading people were asked to do the best they could with the text but not to stay with lines they did not understand unless they wanted to. They could note particularly incomprehensible sentences and words.

To my fascination, one major piece of learning was that if students trusted their responses and were honest about not understanding, we could often see that the paragraphs that were not understood were very badly written! Freud is a most elegant and lucid writer. However, where he feels defensive his language is transformed. A student feeling handicapped by awe and aggression would not dare to ascribe responsibility for misunderstanding to the maestro! No teaching method can be foolproof because fools are so un-foolish. However, it is important to think of how to maximize the potential of students, whatever their age and however difficult the text.

In teaching the basic concepts of the psychoanalyst Melanie Klein to a group of graduates I found it useful to provide a verbatim clinical extract for everyone to read. However, I deleted Klein's interpretations of the child's behaviour. Without the 'answer' in front of them to become a vehicle for prejudices about Kleinian practice, the students were asked to fill in what they would say. To their surprise they largely gave more sexually explicit interpretations than Melanie Klein did and were shocked to see how prejudice affected their learning abilities at a postgraduate level.

More and more teachers are coming to the Counselling Aspects of Education courses for teachers at the Tavistock Clinic, organized by Margot Waddell, because the emotional aspects of learning difficulty, at whatever educational level, are so powerful. However, when it comes to children and adults who are severely handicapped, professionals can sometimes shut their eyes and go stupid not just because it is painful, but because it is unbearable to see damage and not be able to repair it, not be able to put it right. Here is a frequent example social workers provide. A family is desperate for respite care for their multiply handicapped child, having managed valiantly all year with little support. They are near breaking point. The social worker has only one local resource available and knows that it is appallingly run, that there is abusive behaviour between residents and that the child or adult will witness awful events. Rather than facing the fact that beggars can't be choosers and admitting the place is poor but there is nowhere else, or, alternatively, blowing the whistle on an unprofessionally run place, the worker smiles to the parents about the break they will have; the parents smile back. The child smiles at going. Everyone is behaving stupidly and everybody knows the truth.

Beryl Bank, in avoiding machines, is trying to avoid knowing that her parents used machinery in a murderous way. Her father committed suicide by smashing his car against a wall and she herself was the product of a failed abortion. To avoid continuing with that lethal identification she has gone in the opposite direction, therefore losing the benefits that non-abusive use of machinery would give her.

In *What Maisie Knew* Henry James (1897, p. 24) provides a powerful example through the character of Maisie, a child whose separated parents use her as a receptacle for their aggressive thoughts about each other. Maisie's soul is treated as 'a boundless receptacle'. In realizing the terrible function she held for them she takes the only avoiding action she could manage. 'Her parted lips locked themselves with the determination to be employed no longer. She would forget everything, she would repeat nothing, and when, as a tribute to the successful application of her system, she began to be called little idiot, she tasted a pleasure new and keen' (p. 25).

This type of process and its results are powerful enough in the ordinary population who have more resources, but what happens when someone is already brain-damaged to begin with? Geraldine, a child of ten, was born multiply handicapped. Her parents never recovered from the shock of her birth. By the time they were able to feel for her she had disappeared into a universe of her own. Being deaf, blind and dumb to their approaches was a way of protecting herself from the memory of that first awful shock. However, it meant that she was depriving herself of the love they could now offer. Since she had less to begin with than Maisie, cutting off her intelligence in the same way for the same reasons meant she ended up more handicapped.

There are two further features of Geraldine's life which highlight the essential place of trauma in the emotional experience of handicap. It is thanks to the understanding of my daughter that the first feature became apparent. In writing a song about a baby with Down's syndrome she included the line 'I don't look like my family, why don't you cross me off the family tree?' I had not consciously appreciated until that moment what the impact was of looking more like another handicapped person than your own family. This can be especially true for people with Down's syndrome. After I relayed the line from my daughter's song to the Mental Handicap Workshop several of us then remembered moments when patients spoke of seeing 'someone like me'.

This led to an even more painful finding: that handicapped

people not only belonged to a handicapped tribe, they belonged to a tribe that was becoming extinct. All over the world medical and nutritional progress means that some handicaps are being eliminated. Where the handicap is not eliminated early enough, apart from those whose religious beliefs rule it out, abortion is seen as a sensible act.

In the *Daily Mail* on 11 September 1989 a famous female pop star discussed her hope of having a baby at the age of fifty. Like all women over the age of thirty-five she was concerned by the prospect of a handicapped child: 'as an older woman, I might produce a deformed baby. And if that seemed a likelihood I would have to have an abortion, no matter how much I want her. You see, I'd never be able to put her in a home.' Only a small number of people would find any reason for disagreeing with that statement. It is repeated all over the world by women and men. However, what does it sound like to handicapped children and adults? It took me a long time to bear to realize how devastating this was for my patients. Although the wish to eradicate future handicap is shared by most of my handicapped patients, sometimes it is hard for them to draw an emotional line between the external death-wish – 'I wish you had never been born' – and a murder threat – 'You should not be alive now' – especially when both may be true.

Biological advances mean that certain handicaps can be eliminated *in utero*, not that there is a 'final solution' for those with handicaps who are alive. However, facing threat of abandonment, staff changes, physical and emotional abuse, makes this distinction hard to stay with. It is not surprising, then, that faced with an internal and external death-wish the handicapped child or adult can cut off his or her intelligence further so as not to see, hear or understand what is going on in a hostile world. Only when we take that on board can we understand better the stupid smiling and behaviour. However, as well as the tragedy of that experience, which was hidden in Geraldine's behaviour, there is also great anger involved in the decimation of internal resources. Geraldine had found a way of continuing to bear and display the first scars, just as Miss Bank continues to attack her childhood parents with each act of machine-avoidance. Tragically, the fight continues with an internal enemy when the outside enemy is no longer there.

2   EUPHEMISMS AND ABUSE

To fail to speak to a man who is capable of benefitting is to let a man go to waste. To speak to a man who is incapable of benefitting is to let one's words go to waste. A wise man lets neither men nor words go to waste.
Confucius, *The Analects*

Words are truly people, magic people, having birth, growth and destiny.
John Steinbeck, *Of Mice and Men*

Sticks and stones may break my bones but names will never hurt me.
Children's skipping song

I've got four handicaps. I've got Down's syndrome, special needs, learning disability and a mental handicap.
Young woman with Down's syndrome

When Neville Symington founded what we now call the Tavistock Clinic Mental Handicap Psychotherapy and Psychology Research Workshop, he called it 'The Subnormality Workshop', using a term that was then in use. Had he founded it a few years earlier it could have been called the Mental Deficiency Workshop, the Mental Retardation Workshop or the Backwardness Workshop. Going back even further it could have been called, with no offence at the time, a Workshop on Feeblemindedness, Imbecility, Dullards, Dotards, or Idiots.

No human group has been forced to change its name so frequently. The sick and the poor are always with us, in physical presence and in verbal terms, but not the handicapped. What we are looking at is a process of euphemism. Euphemisms, linguistically, are words brought in to replace the verbal bedlinen when a particular word feels too raw, too near a disturbing experience (Sinason, 1984, 1986, 1989c).

Hence, although Jon Stokes and I changed the name of the Workshop to 'Mental Handicap Workshop' when we took it over in 1985 and the title expanded into 'Mental Handicap Psychotherapy and Psychology Research Workshop' when Sheila Bichard became my co-convener in 1988, we decided it was important to try to hold onto the term 'handicap' even though the process of euphemism soon meant it was no longer a completely approved term. The *Journal of Social Work Practice* grappled with this in a pioneering special issue (in 1989) entitled 'Mental Handicap or Learning Difficulty?' In the USA the current favoured term is 'people with developmental disabilities', which is replacing 'mentally retarded'. This does not mean that any name in itself, whether 'handicap', 'disability', 'learning problem', or 'special needs', is necessarily better than any other. But it is important for workers to be aware that abuse lies in the relationships between people, not in the name used. As Orwell (1946) stated, 'The great enemy of language is insincerity. When there is a gap between one's real and one's declared aims, one turns as it were instinctively to long words and exhausted idioms, like a cuttlefish squirting out ink.' One young woman, highly irritated by her key worker's descriptions of her, announced to me with a tired grin: 'I've got Down's syndrome, special needs, learning disability and a mental handicap.' A young man with cerebral palsy wistfully said, 'I wish I did have a learning difficulty; not being able to learn is the least of my problems.'

Each worker introducing a new term hopes that the new word brings new hope and a new period of healthy historical change. Each time the new word is coined, it is coined honourably. It is not deliberately created as a euphemism but becomes one because of the painfulness of the subject. Nearly every book on mental handicap written in the last hundred years begins with a chapter on definitions and words chosen. Each such chapter praises itself for its hopeful new term. It is therefore doing a grave disservice to past pioneers to point contemptuously to their chosen terms. Within another five years the process of euphemism will already be affecting the brave new words. On an individual level I use the terms my clients choose for themselves just as I always check how a name is pronounced and whether someone likes to be called by their formal title or their Christian name. However, individual choice is a different matter from succumbing to different pressure-group choice. It will indeed be a major step forward when internationally we all use the same term and the WHO definition is binding.

As I mentioned in the Introduction, the WHO (1980) defined impairment as any loss or abnormality of structure or function. A disability is defined as a restriction resulting from an impairment and a handicap is the disadvantage to an individual resulting from an impairment or a disability. However, a name change is not casual and each person changing his or her name (as for women entering marriage) needs to think long and hard about the meaning. The term 'disability' has, in the English language, been specifically linked with physical handicap for several hundred years. This means that the extension of its use for mental handicap is experienced by many as a euphemism.

The word 'euphemism' is a euphemism in itself. It derives from the Greek and literally means 'fair-speaking'. It originated in religious ceremonies where it was forbidden to speak in case the spirit would be offended by ill-omened words. Thus its practical meaning is not to speak fairly but to be absolutely silent. The fear that saying something could make it happen; the fear that words or thoughts could concretely cause events to happen, especially bad events, is something we are all now especially aware of in young children's thinking. Freud (1912) used the term 'omnipotence' to describe this state. Melanie Klein (1952a) underlined the way the young child enters such a powerful state as a defence against anxiety. Embedded in euphemisms, therefore, are psycholinguistic signs as to what evokes anxiety, guilty wishes and terror in any society.

It is the small child who most resorts to omnipotent thought. For children, being small and relatively powerless compared to adults, omnipotent thinking is one way of defending the self against painful realizations of difference. When I was an infant teacher it always struck me how children enjoyed the fable of the little mouse who sits on an elephant's back and says, 'Boy, didn't we shake that bridge!' They knew the mouse could not really shake the bridge but they sympathized with its predicament and its 'stupid' and omnipotent arrogance and the gentle humour of the story allowed them to recognize the process. Euphemisms deal with differences that are painful.

In fact, gender, sexuality, mortality, religion, mental illness, handicap and race are the areas around which euphemisms have always clustered. These are the areas where wishes cannot change or put right differences; they are differences that thwart omnipotent wishes to be able to change and control. They are also about differences that are perceived to be unfavourable. Sometimes a caringly coined term is transformed *so that it is experienced as if it were an abusive term*; sometimes the word used is abusive. It is extremely important to be able to differentiate between these two options.

What happens if your ability to choose is more refined than someone else's? What happens if you have a 'discriminating' taste? The history of that word provides a fascinating study in psycholinguistics. From the 1660s onwards the word 'discriminate' meant to be able to differentiate, to perceive the difference between things. In the seventeenth and eighteenth centuries, and still a little today, the ability to tell the difference between things was and is seen as a good quality, and a person of discrimination was someone who could distinguish between things and therefore was distinguished! However, in 1885, the term 'discriminate *against*' was first used. Interestingly, this use of the term was coined to discriminate against certain imports from the United States. Since then, the term 'discriminate' has largely lost its important original meaning of differentiation. The use of the term 'positive discrimination' has hastened the breakdown of the original meaning. To feel the need to add the adjective 'positive' means that differentiation is seen only in a negative, rejecting way. Freud (1909, p. 225) has aptly commented that 'the thing which is warded off invariably finds its way into the very means which is being used for warding it off'.

When a word deals with an area of difficulty, for example the Anglo-Saxon word 'mad', it is allowed to have a historical life until the painful feelings connected with the word are no longer held by it, but leak out. Then a new word is brought in, often from the Greek or Latin. In the fourteenth century the Latin word 'insane' was imported to ease the pain of 'mad' but when that too became burdensome the Anglo-Saxon 'mad' returned. There is a hope that the foreign word will be a blank which will be free of unpleasant associations – 'chemise' for 'shift', 'intoxication' for 'drunkenness', 'perspiration' for 'sweat'. Word changes are symptomatic, they do not solve problems. Some organizations now use the term 'special needs' or 'print-impaired'. The school for maladjusted children where I used to work is now an EBD (emotional and behavioural difficulty) school; ESN (educationally subnormal) is now MLD (moderate learning difficulty). There is often, as I have said, true hope that a new word could usher in a new climate. Clinically, however, we must take it as a diagnostic feature of difficulty when a word keeps changing.

With regard to handicap, mental illness and actual damage, we are often scared of facing differences because of guilt (Sinason,1986). The guilt of the worker at not being handicapped turns into a collusive identification with the omnipotent self of the handicapped client. A true understanding that we are all equal souls and all handicapped in different ways gets transmuted into a manic desire to erase difference. My handicapped patients often choose the word 'stupid' for themselves. The original meaning of 'stupid' is 'numbed with grief' and I feel the original meaning of the word does shine through because a lot of the pain and secondary effects of handicap is to do with the grief of internal and external trauma.

A Historical Vocabulary

With the aid of Ted Onions' *Shorter Oxford English Dictionary on Historical Principles* (1980), I present below a brief linguistic history of some of the commonest words used in describing mental illness and handicap. The dates in brackets after each word indicate the first recorded usage of the word.

backward (Middle English) in the direction of one's back, of retreat; shy and bashful (1599); to put back or retard (1660). The word was first used in terms of learning by Hume.

blockhead (1549) a wooden head or a wooden block for a hat or wig. The block is therefore a facsimile head. The word was used abusively, meaning somebody stupid, from the same period.

changeling (1642) an exchanged child; half-witted.

cretin (1779) one affected with cretinism, a combination of lack of growth and backwardness due to congenital thyroid deficiency. The name was first linked to handicapped people in certain Alpine valleys, and originally meant Christian.

daft (Old English) mild, gentle, meek. In Middle English it meant 'silly' or 'stupid'. By 1536 it meant 'crazy' and in 1575 it also meant 'crazily over-excited'.

defective (Middle English) having a defect, incomplete (1472). One who is defective (1592). In America from 1881 it referred to deficiency in physical powers.

deficient (1581) from the Latin expressing failure, lack, wanting something necessary for completeness.

dense (1599) from the Latin, meaning crowded. The word was used about ignorance in 1877.

dim (Old English) not clear, dull; not bright. In 1729 it meant 'dull of apprehension'.

disable (1485) to render unable or incapable; to cripple (1491).

disability (1492) want of ability, impotence leading to legal disqualification. This term has now been rehabilitated and is used in the WHO definitions of handicap. It denotes a restriction resulting from an organic impairment.

dolt (1543) a dull stupid fellow, numskull.

dope (1880) as a verb, to mix, adulterate. In 1889 it was used to refer to opium for horses, thence any drug.

dotard (Middle English) an imbecile. In 1787 it was used as a description of a decayed tree without branches.

dull and **dullard** (Middle English) stupid, inert; slow; depressed.

dumb (Old English) stupid; destitute of the capacity to speak; that which does not or will not speak. In 1606 the word meant 'mute', and later in the seventeenth century came to mean 'silent' or 'unable to speak'.

dummy (1598) a dumb person or an imaginary player at whist or bridge. In 1796 it denoted a dolt or blockhead; in 1845 a counterfeit or sham, thence a baby's dummy.

dunce (1527) from John Duns Scotus, a scholastic theologian who died in 1308. His disciples, the Dunses, were discredited in the sixteenth century and the term changed to apply to a pedant or a sophist, and then in 1577 to a dullard or a blockhead.

feeble (Middle English) weak, lacking moral or intellectual strength.

fool (Old and Middle English) from French *fou*: mad. It applied to a silly person; one who counterfeits folly for the entertainment of others; one who has little or no reason or intellect.

handicap (1653) from the phrase 'hand i'cap' – hand in the cap. This was a game described in *Piers Plowman*, where forfeit money was put in a cap. Players drew out empty hands or full hands. Later, the term was used in horse-racing, where the superior horse was penalised; thence, for penalization of any superior competitor in a race.

idiot (Middle English) an ignorant person; simple; deficient.

imbecile (1549) without support, weak, feeble; idiotic.

impair (Middle English) make worse, less valuable; damage, injure. To be impaired was to suffer loss. **Impaired** meant unequal, unsuitable (1606); odd, made worse (1839). Since 1980 the term **impairment** has been rehabilitated by the WHO definitions of handicap. It now refers to any loss or abnormality of structure or function.

jobbernowl (1592) stupid.

mad (Old English, Middle English) insane, foolish, wildly foolish.

maladjusted (1611) from the French: unable to compose and harmonise discrepancies or differences.

mental (late Middle English) from the Latin: pertaining to the mind. This has been used abusively to mean 'mad' only in the twentieth century.

mongol (1738) one of an Asiatic tribe inhabiting Mongolia. In 1828 the word was used of 'a type of idiot resembling the Mongols in physiognomy'. Since the 1970s the term 'Down's Syndrome' has been used, naming the chromosomal abnormality after the doctor who first described it.

moron (1912) from the Greek word meaning 'foolish'. The term is used to refer to a person whose intellectual development is arrested.

ninny (1593) a pet form of 'innocent', meaning 'simpleton', 'fool'.

numskull (1717) blockhead, thickhead.

oaf (1625) elf's child, referring to a misbegotten, deformed or idiot child.

retard (late Middle English) from the Latin: to hold back, delay (1489). Bacon spoke of a 'retardation of reading'. In 1891 it was being used educationally.

shallow-brain (1592) having no depth of intellect.

silly (Middle English) deserving of pity, poor. Later meanings were helpless, defenceless (1500); feeble-minded, imbecile (1550); stupefied as by a blow (1886).

simple (Middle English) innocent, honest; poor; humble. By 1604 it meant 'deficient in learning', 'stupid'.

slow (Old English) not quick or clever; taking a long time. This word has kept both its meanings.

spastic (1753) relating to a spasm or sudden contraction. From 1822 it meant 'performing involuntary physical movements'. The term has been used abusively only in twentieth century.

special (Middle English) excelling in an unusual way, held in particular esteem. It has been applied to handicapped children and adults only in the late twentieth century.

stupid (1541) stunned, with one's faculties deadened; stunned with surprise, grief; slow-witted, dull. In 1778 it meant 'boring', 'dull'.

subnormal (1710) from the Latin. The word began as a geometric term describing the part of the axis of abscissae which is intercepted between the ordinate and the normal at any point on the curve. In 1890 it meant 'less than normal', 'below normal'.

thick (Old English) dense. By 1597 it meant 'slow' (referring to mental faculties), 'stupid'.

A painful history emerges from these terms that is only too alive today. If we take 'blockhead', for example, it is worth noting that from 1541 the block meant the executioner's block, on which the condemned man laid his head. Whilst the execution block represented the end of the head, the wooden block on which wigs could be rested also implied a substitute for a real flesh-and-blood head. I believe the link between trauma and handicap was understood in the term. A terrible attack to the head, to thinking has caused damage. However, that knowledge cannot be borne and the term deteriorates into abuse.

Similarly, words that originally dealt with a specific quality like 'silly', 'simple', 'feeble' cannot be tolerated. They are turned into abuse. Words that straightforwardly note a deficit are unable to survive, neither are directional terms like 'retarded', 'slow'. The new term 'learning difficulty', I predict, will also not last, as it shows there is a problem, even if the real problem is emotional, psychiatric or organic rather than to do with learning. The currently respected term 'disability', in showing a deviation from 'ability', is only a rerun of a term that became contaminated in the sixteenth century. Similarly, 'impairment' is a rerun of a contaminated term. There is nothing in its form or history that makes it objectively any more useful a term than 'retarded', 'slow', 'subnormal' or 'defective'.

Interestingly, all the terms reveal what a struggle it is to understand the meaning of handicap. What has happened to make people different in this particular kind of way? Have they lost colour and brightness (dim, dull), have they received a terrible blow (stupid); are they slow (retarded, backward) or are they missing something they will never regain (deficient)? Is their simplicity honourable (simple, silly) or is there something aggressive that makes them refuse to understand and become dense (thick, dotard), or are they weaker than others (feebleminded)? The terms also struggle with whether something is organic or perverse, tragic or sadistic. Whether they are coined honourably must be distinguished from whether they are intended as abuse. A similar intelligence must be used in understanding when a word is experienced wrongly as if it were an abusive term.

Aggressive terms for handicap are coined when it is recognized that intelligence is being perverted, hence 'dolt' and 'numskull' or, again, the current application of 'idiot' to people who are not really seen as idiots, an example I gave in Chapter 1. It is part of the human condition that we all move in and out of different states of being and the same person who wins sympathy for being an organically handicapped person can, in a different state, evoke anger for the perversion of their intelligence.

Malcolm, aged sixteen, is deaf and mildly mentally handicapped. His mother has long found that if she is talking quietly about a family outing, or a present, Malcolm has no problem in hearing. If, however, she is discussing something he does not like, for example the need to tidy his room, he will 'go deaf'. The only times she has angrily shouted at him using 'deaf' as an insult have been when he has perverted his real capacity to hear.

I am not referring here, of course, to the painful situations where individuals are the recipients of abuse regardless of their own actions. Miss M was physically and mentally handicapped and walked with a pronounced limp. In a therapy session she said, 'Whenever I walk down my street there is the gang of children who run after me calling me a spastic. I tell them they are lucky they are not spastics and then they go away. But sometimes I don't feel like leaving my flat.' Being persecuted for being different, becoming a scapegoat or a dustbin for the primitive fears of others, is another major (though linked) issue. I am trying to differentiate here between the way a caringly coined term is transformed *so that it is used or experienced as if it were an abusive term* and words that are used as an insult from the start. As Miss M reveals, the same word can be used in several ways. She is content to define herself by a medical term, 'spastic'. However, when she is called that aggressively it becomes a term of abuse.

In 1935, Professor Cyril Burt wrote a book called *The Subnormal Mind*. He took great care to explain how any differentiation between normal and not normal was in danger of being used abusively. He pointed out that the vast majority of abnormal mental states were exaggerations of impulses which exist in everybody but that defining, nevertheless, helped to ensure provision and services. He tried to differentiate between children whose minds were 'dull' but who had some capacity for learning and those whose minds were inherently 'defective'. In our Workshop at the Tavistock we also differentiate between children and adults whose emotional disturbance has affected their learning adversely and those who are more severely handicapped and whose intellectual functions are thus limited regardless of emotional disturbance.

The subsequent discovery that Burt's research findings were fabricated has tended to discredit some of his good work. He did, for example, clarify issues on labelling in a thoughtful way. Reading his words of 1935 provides a graphic example of how our language has changed. 'Children such as these are not inherently defective; they are merely dull and educationally retarded. Their minds, though slow, are nevertheless sound; but their progress in the classroom lags two or three years behind the progress of their fellows. To group them with genuine defectives, who may be but little above the rank of imbeciles, . . . seems unfair . . . It has therefore become increasingly urgent to know what is to be done with this huge intermediate group; and the attention of both psychologists and administrators has of late been largely diverted from the problem of the mentally deficient and focused upon the problem of the backward and dull . . . Our definition is bound to be somewhat arbitrary; as we have already seen, the defective merge into the dull, as the dull merge into the normal and bright, by insensible transitions and gradations.'

We now have schools for children with mild learning disabilities (MLD) and severe learning disabilities (SLD). These schools used to be called ESN (educationally subnormal) and SSN (severely subnormal). The same problem of obtaining the best provision and the most suitably trained teachers exists. So does the attempt to differentiate between kinds and levels of handicap. However, the words have changed.

In 1982 in America there was a National Symposium on the black mentally retarded offender. In a paper on the effects of labelling, Douglas G. Glasgow (1982) points out some linguistic dangers. For example, he saw the use of the term 'drop-out' as an active term implying that it is totally the responsibility of the adolescent if he drops out. Glasgow has used the term 'underclass' to explain the link between background, handicap and crime. The concept of an underclass was not used in a pejorative manner. It did not subscribe to the notion that those in a static, immobile state were there primarily because of their own disability. In England the concept of an underclass is also being re-examined, but both here and in America there have been angry attacks on the term. 'Under' is, after all, only the English for the Latin 'sub', which became seen as abusive in the term 'subnormality'. It seems that, regardless of how committed any worker is to egalitarian principles and how careful we are in our choice of language, there is no safe way.

For the moment 'over' and 'under' would seem the least contaminated terms. However, a report presented to the Equal Opportunities Subcommittee of the Inner London Education Authority (ILEA) on 7 December 1984 showed two new terms already in difficulties. 'Over-represented' and 'under-represented' try to do justice to complex statistical, social and emotional issues. The now-abolished ILEA carried out a major survey of the characteristics of pupils in its 133 special schools and units. It was found that the majority of the 8,000 pupils involved suffered from at least two 'disabilities' and came from homes affected by low income and unemployment. Boys outnumbered girls by almost two to one. After this, the facts became more painful. The first report compared the social and ethnic backgrounds of pupils and found that children from Afro-Caribbean backgrounds were 'over-represented' in special schools but 'under-represented' in schools for delicate pupils and for those with motor impairment.

In several reports the term 'over-represented' implies 'there are too many and this is wrong'. Now nobody would be implying that there is something wrong in the relatively small number of children of Afro-Caribbean background having physical handicaps. In other words, it is all right to point out difference if it is favourable, but if it is not it is felt to be abusive unless there is no possibility of blame. Curiously, there was little concern that boys 'outnumbered' girls two to one in special schools. Perhaps that was held to be biological or genetic. However, were that word to be used over racial as opposed to gender issues, the response would be very different.

The coining of new terms in policy documents, government Acts and new theories is fascinating to watch. In the 1960s Karl Grünewald put forward an important theory of 'normalization' for handicapped people. He argued that 'only when the normal resources are not sufficient must special ones be used'. A colleague working in a residential hostel for handicapped adults put this into practice by trying to use taxis or minicabs for outings instead of a social service minibus. Michele Pundick (1989), pioneering a leisure project in Barnet for handicapped adults, similarly encourages access to normal social venues and activities. However, the concept and term normalization have also been abused.

For example, a young man was moved from a long-stay psychiatric hospital to a community home. The hospital was being closed down as part of a much-heralded 'return to the community' campaign (itself a term that is sometimes open to euphemism, sometimes meaning a return to ageing parents and sometimes meaning a move to a place with less provision). He was encopretic (smeared his faeces), incontinent and self-mutilating. He was clearly mentally ill as well as mentally handicapped. In America, the new term 'dual diagnosis' has been coined for such a person.

In the community home his violence and disturbance were unmanageable. He pulled the wires off electric toasters, knocked over saucepans containing boiling liquids and destroyed the extra freedom some of the other residents could have enjoyed without his presence. The staff, highly committed to community care, added many safety features to the kitchen as well as instituting different programmes to enrich his life. It made little difference. When I commented that perhaps he could not live in a community home and might feel far safer on a ward there was both shock and relief. The staff protested that their aim was normalization. I reminded them that normalizing means providing proper access to normal services and life except 'when the normal resources are not sufficient' (Grünewald, 1978). However, even culturally enriching new concepts and terms are open to contamination.

In 1969 the UNESCO General Conference had reaffirmed the needs and rights of handicapped children to education. Parents' organizations and specialist teaching organizations flourished. In 1978 the English Warnock Report found that 20 per cent of all children had special needs, let alone the most severely handicapped 2 per cent. The 1981 English Education Act, which implemented some of the recommendations of the Warnock Committee, underlined the new terminology. Now children were seen as having 'special educational needs'. The positive thinking behind the 1981 Education Act and the international concept and practice of normalization and community care have sought to point the way to linguistic and social integration. There was concern that some handicapped or disturbed children were being deprived of the wider and richer curriculum available in the mainstream.

However, going to a 'normal' school does not bring internal normality with it and providing such children with extra classes or a support teacher can only work if the child herself is integrated enough and the host school has adequate practical and emotional resources and provision. Mrs Anne Chatfield, former head teacher of a school for emotionally and behaviourally disturbed children (EBD) underlined that point at a 1986 conference for EBD teachers. 'It is no good talking about the wider curriculum of an ordinary school when the children are excluded from everything because of their disruptive behaviour. When they come to us they have lessons, go to the theatre, school journeys, all the things they missed out on before.'

The 1981 Act hoped to help the rejected child by seeing his problems as a mismatch between the child and his environment. In other words, if a child did badly at school it was because the environment was not right for him. Certainly, teachers and schools with low morale damage the emotional and educational prospects of their pupils. However, the disturbed child carries his own lack of integration wherever he goes. Having his disturbance named can be a relief from fear and guilt about difference. Nevertheless, the lower referral figures for EBD schools since the 1981 Act can reflect the way 'fear of labelling' is a displaced way of dealing with 'fear of stating difference'. After all, going to special classes or units within an ordinary school carries as large a message to other children as going to a different school altogether.

In England, the 1986 Fish Report took the idea of integration even more seriously. Teachers in MLD and SLD schools as well as those working in off-site units and schools for emotionally disturbed children were all concerned that thought was not being given to those children who were unable to be integrated. As a psychotherapist in an EBD school at that time I was vehemently opposed to the idea of integration on the cheap. I was also aware of the irony of my position. For hundreds of years children and adults had been locked away and ill-treated. By the time there was a sufficiently angry response to those injustices and a move did begin to promote integration, the moment, and some of the children chosen, were already wrong. In order to rescue the child from one wave of historical rejection exemplified by some kinds of segregation society moves to another extreme which can be equally simplistic. This is a painful psychohistorical process whereby the answer to a past problem is unerringly consolidated when it is no longer helpful or necessary.

The creation of special schools for profoundly handicapped children represents a triumph for the notion of educability (Segal 1967) that was hard won. Yet in some cases the very term 'school' is not an appropriate one. One teacher who works with seven profoundly handicapped children commented that she had never ever taught them. 'They need holding, toileting, mothering, and that is fine but I don't think by any stretch of the imagination that could be called teaching'.

If we cannot bear to see when someone needs *different* provision verbally and practically we all end up being stupid.

One linguistic trend that I do not welcome is censorship of a descriptive term coming before a noun. Hence 'a disabled woman' is seen as an abusive term whereas 'a woman with a disability' is seen as correct. I consider this to be an unnecessary lengthening of language. I am a middle-aged woman, not a woman of middle age. When I become an old woman I do not want to be described as a woman who is old. I am also content to be named a short-sighted woman rather than a woman with impaired vision. Of course we need to subscribe to the concept of putting the person before their handicap or disability. However, to think that a person is not being thought about unless any adjective describing her comes after a noun is not true. Nor do I consider that I should give up expressions such as 'I see' when in the company of blind colleagues, friends or patients. Words have been hard earned and are precious. Where the term is not itself an abusive one, abuse is in the intention, conscious or otherwise, of the speaker. When one school I worked in was struggling with its policy on racial issues it became clear that there were complex divisions between some colleagues. Some Asian teachers, for example, liked the term 'black' to describe themselves; one felt that was completely wrong as it linked her with Africans or West Indians and she considered her Asian origins different; others preferred the term 'non-white' to highlight politically the racism that they felt was hidden in all the terms. However, regardless of how abusive some terms were considered, they could clearly be differentiated from terms that were specifically geared to abuse, like 'nigger' and 'Paki'.

Differences in gender, race, size, shape, ability, appearance, culture, voice are intrinsic to a rich experience. Otherwise we would all live in a world of autistic sameness. However, difference evokes envy (when we perceive ourselves to be lacking) or guilt (when we perceive someone else to be lacking). In Sonnet 29 Shakespeare understands the 'outcast state' where the poet enviously wishes he was someone else and loses all contentment with his own lot. Then the thought of his love retrieves him from that state. As I showed in the Introduction and Chapter 1, some differences are not fair and need to be socially tackled. Some are not fair but cannot be changed, and some are fair. Then how we each deal with our own unique inheritance determines whether we become outcasts, prey to secondary and opportunist handicap, or whether we manage the true and sane path.

3 A SHORT HISTORY: MYTHICAL AND PSYCHOANALYTICAL

The further back in history one goes, the lower the level of child-care, and the more likely children are to be killed, abandoned, beaten, terrorised, and sexually abused.

Lloyd de Mause, *The History of Childhood*

There is no man in the world so hapless, nor so needy, so weak in thought, nor so dull-minded that the beneficent Giver strips him of all skill of mind or mighty deeds, wisdom in thought or in speech, lest he should despair of all things he did in life, of every benefit. God never decrees that anyone shall become so wretched.

Anon. Anglo-Saxon poet, 'The Arts of Men'

For the serpent, where the tree of knowledge stands is always Paradise.

Nietzsche, *Beyond Good and Evil*

There is one history of mental handicap but it is made up of two shifting states of mind. The first is full of understanding and wisdom. It contains all that is finest and sanest in ancient and modern civilization. It contains some of the noblest aspects of religions and philosophies. Its insights were relevant at the dawn of history and remain valid today. Writing in about 45 BC, the Roman orator and philosopher Cicero understood, in his essay 'On the State', that if a law was true its validity would have to be universal. 'It is unchangeable and eternal. Its commands and prohibitions apply effectively to good men and have no effect on bad men . . . There will not be one law at Rome, one at Athens, or one now and one later, but all nations will be subject all the time to this one changeless and everlasting law' (Cicero, trans. M. Grant, 1982, p. 11).

The second state is similarly timeless. It is one of madness, cruelty and pain. It is also there from the start, the dark twin, the serpent, the fallen angel. At its most dangerous it tries to sound like an angel. Hence, the Catholic Inquisition or the Protestant Luther could 'reasonably' declare that a handicapped child was created by the devil and should be killed. Against these shifting attitudes to mental handicap there is the possibility of a gradual historical trend of improvement. The psychohistorian Lloyd de Mause (1974) argues that there has been a general psychogenic evolution in parent–child relationships, despite appalling fluctuations. There is certainly more likelihood in the West now of handicapped people having an improved quality of life. However, this is still extremely patchy and we have to say that the Ten Commandments, one for each finger, are still too much of a handful for any culture or period of history to keep to!

Psychoanalytical theories of personal history provide a similar double perspective. There can be a developmental pattern against which different states, integrated and disintegrated, flicker and fluctuate. Anna Freud offers us the concept of developmental hurdles and progress while Melanie Klein defines the shifting states of disturbance and integration. It was in 1946, in 'Notes on some schizoid mechanisms', that Klein described the fragmented persecuted state she named the paranoid–schizoid position. The integrated state was called (Klein, 1935) the depressive position.

In the 1930s Kleinians saw the tiny infant as especially prone to paranoid–schizoid fears. However, Melanie Klein noted from observing babies that some very tiny ones were capable of longer moments of integration (1948, p. 34). Child development research, such as that by Daniel Stern (1985) and others, agrees with this. There are times when, observing a tiny baby feeding, we see the baby gaze into its mother's eyes. At that moment, although the baby's mouth is attached to the nipple, the baby is taking in the whole of its mother, not just one part of her. An adult male staring at a topless pinup is only taking in part of the person, on the other hand. Writers and philosophers have long struggled with this issue.

Nietzsche (1886, p. 76), for example, commented, 'Mature manhood: that means to have rediscovered the seriousness one had as a child at play.' However, if all goes well, the hope is that the adult will be able to maintain a whole-person orientation more than a baby or a small child can.

As well as the fluctuations in mental states, history also provides us with an important sense of developmental progression as a backdrop. Knowledge and learning, for example, were linked first to religion and the cultural elite. Prior to technology, the invention of printing and the possibility of ordinary people having access to the written word, a chained holy book (within Western Christianity) was the only source. Where there was no access to books the great religions still initially promoted knowledge of reading and writing and, paradoxically, have therefore played a part in the defining of handicap. For if no-one can read or write then only those with the most severe handicaps will be noticed. The majority of the handicapped, who are only mildly handicapped, would not have been noticeable. Hence the developmental act of noticing and acquiring knowledge creates new definitions of those who fall short, just as each new law can create more criminals. However, Sir Brian Rix (1990 p. 14) warns us against having any illusions about a golden age for handicapped people in the past or in poor areas. 'I want us to be aware of the enormous problems in third world countries where people with a mental handicap are rejected and marginalised today in their own rural communities.'

IN THE BEGINNING

In the beginning, in creation myths, there is Chaos or an Abyss. Nothing is clear at all. There is no differentiation between day and night, land and sea. Then a process of differentiation begins. For the Greeks, the Earth gave birth to the Sky. From Chaos, Erebus and Night produced Day. For the Egyptians, Num, the primordial ocean, comes first, then the Sun and the Sky. In Indian mythology, in the Brahmanas, the world is unknowable darkness and then the Brahma seeds himself and makes heaven and earth, air and water. In the Old Testament Genesis, 'God said, let there be light, and there was light.'

Whether the sea comes first or the earth there is an understanding of the difference between light and dark (sun and eclipse, day and night), up and down (heaven and earth), hot and cold (fire and water, and in Icelandic myths, ice), wet and dry (earth and water). Differentiation between male and female usually comes later, although in some myths (Assyro-Babylonian, for example) a male and female dividing principle is understood from the start. It is usually after these first differentiations are understood that ignorance and knowledge, love and hate, good and bad, are dealt with, either between people or deities or within the same person or deity.

Often, the primitive chaos of Genesis is seen as necessary at first but dangerous if it continues. Tiamat, the Sea and Feminine principle (in Assyro-Babylonian myth), gives birth to the world but then is seen as a primitive threat by her intelligent children and Marduk the Wise is asked to kill her so that order and progress can be achieved. Often, the mother Goddess produces giant or deformed children who are then killed off by the next generation.

These creation myths seem to mirror the growth of the human infant. Only when she is held secure after the chaos of birth, and when love and order prevail, can sense be made of the surroundings. A sense of temperature, of dark and light, of mother and father follows. Then, a capacity to think can come into being. After weaning and moving from bodily fusion with the mother to a sense of separateness aided by speech, the growing child struggles for further differentiation, seeking to 'take arms against a sea of troubles' and not to regress back into the symbiotic sea of pre-birth and infancy. Moving away from a symbiotic relationship is especially hard for handicapped children (Frankish, 1989). In order to have a mind, the child must give up its animal or monstrous primordial self. Language is an essential part of this.

Brahma's wife, Sarasvati, invented Sanskrit. The ancient Egyptians believed the God Thoth invented writing and all the languages of the world, and a scribe was highly venerated. In the Old Testament the act of creation is linked to language. God 'said' there should be Light and what Adam 'called' each animal was the name it was given. The Ten Commandments were *written* for Moses by God, showing the value of writing, and within Judaism the scribe was always honoured. 'The tablets were the handiwork of God, and the writing was God's writing, engraved on the tablets' (Exodus 32:15). Such was the power of language that when Noah's children sought to build a tower to the heavens they were scattered to all parts of the earth so that humans could not share a common language. 'Therefore is the name of it called Babel; because the Lord did there confound the language of all the earth; and from thence did the Lord scatter them abroad upon the face of all the earth' (Genesis 11:5-9).

Religious myths honour language and writing and show that the deities themselves seek it but, as Bion points out (1963, p. 67), the gods can also be hostile to humankind because of this. A fall from grace can follow the link of knowledge with procreation. Bion points out that with the Sphinx in the Oedipus myth, and with the Tower of Babel and the serpent, there is the concept of a deity who is hostile to mankind's search for knowledge and will threaten death or exile.

Language in the form of words comes first in order both to help produce and communicate thoughts (Kristeva, 1981 p. 7) and writing has to come later. Writing involves understanding the presence of an other or others who wish to be receptive to the communication. It involves understanding that even in personal absence, a written communication can have power over time and space. Written language even defies mortality by continuing to communicate even after the writer's death.

I have emphasized the early religious significance of the *written* word because on the whole it has been the growth of mass literacy that has highlighted the incidence and prevalence of mild handicap, although severe and profound mental and multiple handicap would have always been noticeable. The interweaving history of physical handicap is a somewhat different one in that compassion for those with physical handicaps who were otherwise sane and intelligent has always been easier. As Cicero commented in his 'Discussions at Tusculum' (trans. M. Grant, 1982, p. 112), 'When Democritus lost his sight, it is true that he could no longer distinguish black from white, yet he could still distinguish good from bad, just from unjust, right from wrong . . . whereas if it had been the comprehension of ideas that he lacked, a happy life would have been out of the question.' Unlike those who try and convince themselves and others that 'ignorance is bliss' (see section on smiling in Chapter 6), Cicero understood that the inability to understand could not be a true source of happiness.

The different ways in which religions and child development theories describe beginnings are mirrored in the way handicapped children and adults account for their genesis. A young profoundly handicapped girl lifted up a male and female doll. She made them kiss on the lips and examined them intensely from each angle as if she wanted to be able to see inside that kiss. There was a painful silence. I asked if she was wondering how she was made, what happened for her to be born as she was. She lifted up the hair on the female doll and pointed to where the hair came from. 'Gone wrong,' she said simply. 'Right from the root.' She knew, as every handicapped child and adult I have ever seen knew, that she was different. She also knew that she felt that difference was not a good difference but was a sign of something having gone biologically wrong. The act of procreation that brought her into being was somehow flawed. 'God farted' was one angry adolescent's explanation for his handicap. A first impression of a school for the profoundly handicapped made one therapist (Hoxter, 1986) 'want to protest as at some wicked trick of creation'. A multiply handicapped woman who could not speak cried when she turned the key of a musical box and sound came out (Chapter 9). Even an inanimate object created the sound that she could not. There is the struggle of feeling part of a flawed creation, 'children of a lesser god'.

The inner feeling of being flawed is made worse by external validation. In Exodus 24:13 we learn that no man with a defect can offer a sacrifice, whilst the Ayatollah Khomeini (1979, p. 79) commented it was not advisable to allow a feeble-minded person into a mosque. The first mention of handicap in psychoanalytic history is similarly painful. It is also an exclusion. Assessing which kinds of patients were suitable for treatment, Freud (1904, p. 254) considered that 'a certain measure of natural intelligence and ethical development are to be required'. There was nothing unique about this exclusion. Freud also had doubts about the mental elasticity of patients over the age of 50 and psychotic patients. Given that eighty-six years later only small inroads have been made into the treatment of these other groups we should not be so severe towards Freud over this. At least he had the humbleness and wisdom to add, 'I do not regard it as by any means impossible that by suitable changes in the method we may succeed in overcoming this contra-indication – and so be able to initiate a psychotherapy of the psychoses' (p. 264).

Although he was not then intending to address the issue of mental handicap, all his major theories are relevant and some have a particular resonance for handicap. For example, in 1901 Freud formulated the theory of secondary gain, which could be derived from an illness and which is the central factor in what is now referred to as secondary handicap. He gave the clear example of a crippled bricklayer who was making a successful living as a beggar. He commented that this man would not be pleased to be cured as he had obtained a secondary gain from the primary injury. Whatever the grief the injury caused him in the first place he now lives by it and is terrified of being helpless if it were to be taken away. A patient of mine, Betty, aged 16, was profoundly handicapped and could not speak or walk. She had an extremely intuitive and sensitive mother who was able to understand her moods and wishes without any signs. Betty could have learned Makaton sign language but for her it would have spoiled the reward she received for her awful handicaps – the infantile satisfaction of being understood without words.

Freud also described 'somatic compliance', the way bodily ills with their organic base are the result of a mental and physical interplay and can become fixed with a 'psychical coating', a particular emotional investment (1905 p. 83). For an example, he describes how his patient Dora had a real throat irritation; however, this real organic base 'acted like the grain of sand around which an oyster forms its pearl'. Dora had a continuous cough which expressed both its real organic base and her sexual and guilt feelings about her father.

In my practice, for example, 23-year-old Carole has an organic handicap which makes her head jerk uncontrollably. However, in addition to that organic lack of control there is a noticeable way that her face jerks upwards when she is upset. After a year of once-weekly therapy she was able to recall a traumatic incident in which her mother slapped her face before having her moved to a hospital.

In his paper 'The unwelcome child and his death instinct' (1929, p. 105) Sándor Ferenczi describes how unwanted children are 'unwelcome guests of the family' who could get colds easily, are prone to psychosomatic disorders and epilepsy, and want to die. His understanding of the projections of hatred poured into such children is very helpful in understanding the depression and self-destructiveness of disturbed patients with a mental handicap. He also delineated how as a result of trauma some individuals remain at an infantile level with only a tiny fragment of their personality adapting to reality. That too is relevant for this work. Ferenczi retained a profound belief that such individuals required an experience of parenting and normal nursery life as well as analysis.

I am indebted to Martin Stanton's excellent new book on Ferenczi (Stanton, 1991) for the information that in 1903 Ferenczi wrote a paper on cretinism. However, although Martin Stanton is in the process of having it translated it will be too late to include in this book. With Ferenczi's unrivalled awareness of the emotional implications and experience of abuse, epilepsy, organic illness and other trauma I would expect this paper to be an important one. Ferenczi has been disturbingly undervalued as a pioneering psychoanalytic practitioner and theorist and Martin Stanton's book is a major step in gaining access to his ideas.

1930–60

Thirty years after Freud (1901) formulated the gains that could come from illness there was a sudden interest in the predicament of patients with mental handicaps, promoted by Leona Chidester and Karl Menninger, two American psychiatrists and psychoanalysts. The previous lack of advance in this field was due to psychoanalytic indifference rather than anything else. Parents had had the intelligence to refer their children, but in vain (Jelliffe, 1914).

Chidester and Menninger pointed out (1936, p. 616) that 'mental handicap has long been looked upon as an organic condition, therapeutically hopeless, and probably for this reason few psychoanalysts have attempted to apply their methods to the study of retarded children'. Henry, a boy of twelve, was given psychological tests every few months throughout his analysis to evaluate the emotional aspects of his learning difficulty. In September 1931 his IQ was 62. Four years later, in November 1935, his IQ was 90. He was a child who had experienced some traumatic events, especially the desertion of his mother. From our current stance, Henry would be seen as a child with a learning difficulty caused by emotional disturbance, and child psychotherapists and child analysts currently treat large numbers of such children. The first treatment of a severely or profoundly organically handicapped child or adult was yet to come.

Melanie Klein was extremely interested in the emotional aspects of learning difficulty and in the meaning of intellectual maldevelopment. However, like Leona Chidester and Karl Menninger, her work was largely with children handicapped by their emotional difficulties rather than with organically handicapped children. She threw major light on learning difficulties and her development of analytic techniques for treating children as well as her pioneering contributions to psychoanalytic theory have been seminal for all client groups. In *The Psychoanalysis of Children*, she discusses her treatment of a six-year-old girl, Erna, who rocked and masturbated excessively and had 'a very severe inhibition in learning' (Klein, 1924, p. 57) and was seen as 'ineducable'. Erna was not organically handicapped and was capable of speech and play; however, arithmetic and writing were shown to symbolize violent sadistic attacks for her and until this was interpreted she could not develop. In 1931 Klein's ideas on these issues were to be further developed in 'A contribution to the theory of intellectual inhibition'.

Although Melanie Klein did not treat an organically mentally handicapped child herself she extended the analytic boundaries to include children suffering psychosis and schizophrenia. She also pointed out most forcefully that early psychological processes in a baby's development could, if disturbed or not processed satisfactorily, lead 'to inhibition of intellectual development which may contribute to mental backwardness and – in extreme cases – to mental deficiency' (1952b, p. 304).

In 1933 Pierce Clark became the first analyst specifically to consider applying analytic insight to the organically or environmentally mentally handicapped. In *The Nature and Treatment of Amentia* he suggests that the foetal postures adopted by many severely handicapped patients were a specific regression. He also pointed to the way some individuals could deal with trauma by avoiding reality. Ernest Jones specifically investigated hemiplegic patients – patients who had paralysis of one side of their bodies either from a stroke or a tumour. He also studied the articulatory function in normal and defective patients. He tested two thousand patients and found, amongst other things, that girls used lip-reading as a way of learning to talk. However, he did not think of applying analytic insights to this group (Jones, 1959, pp. 120, 145).

In the 1930s and '40s leading psychiatrists interested in handicap were part of the psychoanalytical movement. Emmanuel Miller and Lionel Penrose in England, for example, were both analysed and that informed their thinking on learning difficulty and handicap. Emmanuel Miller looked at emotional aspects of learning difficulty in a 1933 paper, although his cases, with their relatively high IQs of 80, were not really examples of handicap. However, after this period a division begins in England with psychiatrists involved in mental handicap and psychoanalysts failing properly to inform each other of developments. The advent of non-medical psychoanalysts also meant a dramatic diminishing of the number of analysts who worked in long-stay psychiatric or mental handicap hospitals.

Harold Bourne (1955, p. 11) commented that some analytic work was also lost to mental handicap professionals because although some of the patients they worked with 'are plainly very defective to judge from the description, both as a topic and a diagnosis mental defect goes conspicuously unmentioned'. Either mental handicap went unmentioned or it was hidden under a different name.

Margaret Mahler, for example, coined the term 'pseudo-imbecility' (1942). By this term she meant a process in which some individuals could appear stupid in order to cover up their sexual knowledge. Harold Bourne, in a talk given to the Tavistock Mental Handicap Workshop (1989), pointed out that Beate Rank (1949) used the term 'atypical children'. She saw these as being young children whose development was arrested at a primitive level due to gross emotional deprivation. An important link between trauma and arrested development was made but because of the new term chosen and the lack of a two-way process between mental handicap workers and psychoanalysts it got temporarily lost.

Similarly, the pioneers who have transformed our understanding of institutional damage and the effects of separation, R. Spitz (1953), John Bowlby (1951) and James and Joyce Robertson (1951), do not specifically name the handicapped. They make it clear that trauma in the form of separation affects all development and that lack of personal attention is catastrophic. Spitz (1953, p. 329) described how children faced with long periods of deprivation 'offer pictures reminiscent of brain-damaged individuals, of severely retarded or downright imbecile children'. In showing how babies and small children can experience clinical depression Spitz underlines how deterioration includes bizarre hand movements and 'imbecile' expressions before the succumbing to infection. Thanks to their pioneering work nobody could pretend not to have the knowledge that separation and trauma affect development. From the major work of these psychoanalysts and therapists we can now transfer that knowledge not only to those who are organically handicapped even before trauma takes its toll, but to those whom trauma *makes* handicapped. In other words, trauma does indeed create not just pictures *reminiscent* of handicap but *real handicap*.

However, moments of curiosity did not add up to any substantial continuous history. In 1955, in England, Harold Bourne made a pioneering study at the Fountain Hospital, a hospital for 600 mentally and multiply handicapped children. He had noted that mental deficiency had little contact with psychoanalysis or other professions and felt that psychogenic defect was a uniting theme, or should be. Accordingly he set out to investigate whether severe mental defect could result from social and psychological adversity in infancy. The new term he created for such psychogenic handicap was 'protophrenia'. He wrote a paper about this for *The Lancet* (Bourne, 1955) and it caused an initial stir but little follow-up work.

Within the Fountain Hospital itself, however, Bourne's work had created a lot of interest. Lydia Mundy, a psychologist, commented in the *British Journal of Clinical Psychology* that 'it is sometimes assumed that psychotherapy with the mentally retarded is inadvisable because of their limited insight and poor verbal development' (Mundy, 1957, p. 3), a familiar refrain and one that ends up having to be repeated because its truth has not been adequately accepted! She drew on American research by Saranson (1952), Cotzin (1948), Thorne (1948) and Fisher and Wolfson (1953) to show that therapy for this group was effective, both individual therapy and group therapy.

It is important to note the pioneering role of the *American Journal of Mental Deficiency* in publishing all these papers and indeed the leading role America had at that moment in applying psychodynamic ideas. One researcher not mentioned by Lydia Mundy was Sara Neham (1951), whose paper 'Psychotherapy in relation to mental deficiency' also appeared in the *American Journal of Mental Deficiency*. Nevertheless, most of the authors were psychologists working psychotherapeutically, but not psychoanalysts or psychoanalytical psychotherapists. This meant that the work did not percolate properly through analytic circles. In addition, those who were interested in working in client-centred ways in America were held back by Carl Rogers's opinion (1957) that client-centred therapy was not suitable for handicapped people. His comment was half a century after Freud's and people are still repeating it now. Many of the patients I treat come from clinics where they were met with the response 'Handicapped people cannot make use of psychotherapy.' It does not seem fair to continue blaming Freud! Somehow pioneers receive the blame for what they didn't do as well as for what they did!

Physical disability, however, was another matter. The Hampstead Clinic, started by Anna Freud in 1951, was concerned with the predicament of blind children. Dorothy Burlingham had always had an interest in this disability and she was able to follow it further when in 1954 the Royal National Institute for the Blind asked the Clinic for help in treating blind children under the age of five, with whom they had had no success. Doris Wills and Dorothy Burlingham, in particular, carried out this work. Dorothy Burlingham (1963), drawing attention to regressive physical movements in blind children, commented that they too looked like mentally retarded movements and often caused blind children to be wrongly classified. Because of Anna Freud's deep interest in the meaning and importance of developmental stages the Clinic had a commitment to understanding in what ways a physical disability impeded integration.

Although Anna Freud was extremely aware of the way emotions affected learning, this never became a predominant issue in thinking about handicap. In 'Four lectures on psychoanalysis for teachers and parents' (1930, p. 129), Anna Freud describes an ill-treated eight-year-old who 'pretended to be stupid, and so cleverly, that in several places she was diagnosed as mentally defective'.

In England, major psychoanalytic advances were being pioneered by Wilfred Bion throughout the fifties and sixties (and by him in California in the seventies). A tank commander in the First World War, Bion worked with schizophrenic patients, aided by Melanie Klein's breakthrough in working with this group. He did not work with mentally handicapped patients but his theories on the meaning and act of thinking are essential. Bion (1959) developed Klein's concepts and showed how the analyst could become a container for the intolerable experiences of the patient, just as a mother could receive the cries of her baby and transform them, by the way she processed them, into something manageable. The concept of shifting states of handicap, which I mentioned in Chapter 1, Jon Stokes likened to Bion's differentiation (1957) between psychotic and non-psychotic personalities.

It was in 1957 that Bion identified two radically different personalities that exist in the same person. As psychoanalyst and psychiatrist Michael Sinason (1990) has emphasized, 'The implications of having two personalities which are functionally and organizationally distinct and with very little awareness of the existence or significance of the other personality is so horrific that there is a very strong pull within patient and therapist alike to re-simplify matters and revert to a patient with one ego using mechanisms of defence.' This crucial central concept of ego-splitting is one to which I keep returning throughout this book and I am indebted to Michael Sinason for his work on this subject (1989, 1990). He points out that if patients are seen as unitary entities then they are unfairly held responsible for all their actions.

For example, if I cannot find my keys and am distressed at their loss it is no help to me to be blamed for my negligence. The 'I' who is looking for the keys is the victim of the 'I' who hid them. We share the same name and body but have completely diffeent structures and mechanisms. Similarly, the patient who hurts his head is not the same person as the one who is hurt. Without this recognition no real progress in treatment or understanding is possible.

1960–1990

In the 1960s there was a renewal of interest in handicap in France, Canada and the United States. In France, the torch for psychodynamic thinking in mental handicap was carried by psychoanalyst Maud Mannoni. She studied psychiatry and criminology at the University of Brussels, went to Paris in 1948 and became interested in the work of the psychoanalyst Jacques Lacan. She was appointed Chef de Service at the Centre of Child Psychology in Paris but subsequently withdrew from routine duties to devote more time to research and writing. In 1965 she wrote 'A challenge to mental retardation', which appeared in a special edition of the journal *Esprit* devoted to the subject of handicap. She commented, as others have done before and since, that 'Many psychoanalysts turn away from the problem of mental retardation and evade the exchange of ideas taking place on the subject. It took some time to admit psychosis into the analytic kingdom; even Freud believed it was inaccessible to analysis.' She added that now schizophrenia and psychosis were seen as treatable there should be a similar extension to certain cases of mental handicap.

Mannoni makes clear that the psychoanalytic approach does not deny the existence of organic damage but 'does not regard this as a basic explanation' (1969, p. 212). For the first time, in such books as *The Child, his 'Illness' and the Others* (1968) and *The Retarded Child and the Mother* (1973), we have, fully documented, the emotional experience of handicap in child, family and institutions. Psychoanalysts continuing in this field at the moment in France are also largely Lacanian. However, as elsewhere in the world, the numbers are still small. Annie Stammler and Genevieve Haag are amongst this group. Annie Stammler works with severely multiply handicapped children in the hospital ward where necessary. She is the French representative for the Mental Handicap Section of the Association for Psychoanalytic Psychotherapy in the British NHS.

The psychoanalytic interest in mental handicap in Canada in the 1960s was largely due to the influence of one man, Clifford Scott, and his dual role as a psychiatrist and psychoanalyst. (That task is now continued by psychologist and psychotherapist Dr Arnold Wellman of the Midwestern Hospital.) Clifford Scott was secretary of the Canadian Psychoanalytic Institute and was also very active in psychiatric circles. This meant that on 15 June 1963 the Canadian Psychiatric Association could hold a Symposium on Psychotherapy in Mental Retardation. Clifford Scott, like Melanie Klein, did not actually treat a severely mentally handicapped patient himself. His own patient had an IQ of 80. However, work with this patient did prove to him how treatment could aid her. He then reported on the work of a colleague, Dr S. F. Lindsay from Dundee, Scotland, who treated analytically a woman with an IQ of approximately 53. After one year her IQ was 70 and after two years, 77. Dr Lindsay then also treated a mildly handicapped boy whose IQ rose from 72 to 86. He offered brief treatments to a 16-year-old girl with an IQ of 63 and two young men. Unfortunately, Dr Lindsay has not written anything himself and it is not known whether he continued to treat other handicapped patients.

In the same Symposium, G. Sarwer-Foner, Assistant Professor of Psychiatry at McGill University, gave a report on seven years of intensive psychoanalytic psychotherapy with an adolescent who had mild cerebral palsy and was 'pseudo-mental defective' (1963, p. 296). Sarwer-Foner clearly understood the nature of secondary handicap and produced a dramatic change in his patient in the first meeting when he commented, 'You know, when you wave your arms about, shout and drool . . . you make people believe that you are much worse than in fact I believe you to be.' Again, this patient was only mildly handicapped. At a pre-treatment test his IQ was 76 and after one year, 85. After seven years his IQ was 90, to all intents and purposes normal.

The third and final paper from the Symposium was by William Ogle, a clinical instructor at the University of Washington, Seattle.

A psychiatrist working with a mildly handicapped girl whose IQ was in the high fifties or low sixties, he was very keen that psychiatrists should deal with the 'group embarrassment . . . concerning the application of psychodynamic understanding to the treatment of people with limited intelligence. This group embarrassment has, up to this stage, worked against sustained advance in the whole field of treatment of the mental deficiencies. It is suggested that if psychoanalytical understanding is not significantly brought into the treatment of the mental deficiencies, then the advances through the other disciplines, no matter how valuable, will be insufficient to make a really serious impact upon this large, individual and social problem' (Ogle, 1963, p. 307). The particular case he described involves a girl who had been chronically sexually abused by her father. The theme of sexual abuse is one I return to again and again in Chapters 6, 8, 10, 11 and 12.

The lack of psychodynamic resources for handicapped patients was noted most sharply in America in the 1960s. The American psychoanalyst and psychiatrist Irving Phillips in his book on prevention and treatment of mental retardation (1966) pointed out that the unavailability of psychotherapeutic services was still due to the misconception that behavioural or emotional problems were a function of mental retardation. Still, even this idea was an important step forward. Previously, the rationalization for not providing or pressing for such services was laid on the lack of intellectual ability. To consider that there might be an error in not differentiating disturbance from the coexisting handicap is clearly significant. (I am indebted to Professor John Corbett in the UK for the information that Irving Phillips is currently Director of the Langley Porter Clinic in San Francisco and that psychoanalytic treatment is offered to handicapped patients there.)

In 1968, Anna Freud suggested that psychoanalyst Arthur Couch should visit Harperbury Hospital (a long-stay hospital for individuals with a mental handicap, in Radlett, Hertfordshire) in order to explore how handicap affected ego and psychosexual development. After discussion with John Bolan of the Child Guidance Training Centre a meeting was arranged with Dr Shapiro of Harperbury Hospital and once weekly for a month Arthur Couch observed life on the wards. Watching disturbed individuals for six hours per visit he found a traumatic experience. The lack of history in the case notes of patients meant that evaluating changes in development was extremely difficult. However, there had not been any intention in Anna Freud's mind that such patients could or should be offered psychoanalytic treatment.

Indeed, it was not until 1974 that an American child analyst who studied at the Hampstead Clinic worked with a blind boy with 'limited intelligence' (Lopez, 1974, p. 277). Thomas Lopez begins his paper with the familiar and painfully true statement, 'therapeutic efforts in which a prolonged and intimate relationship between child and therapist is central are, to judge from the literature, extremely rare with children as limited as Ronny' (p. 278). Even here the term 'therapeutic effort' is provided rather than 'psychoanalytical treatment'.

The work of psychoanalyst and child psychotherapist Frances Tustin (1972, 1981) provided further inspiration and understanding of learning difficulties for those working in autism and mental handicap. She specified how cognitive defects could be acquired and how the autistic state could be a reaction to traumatic awareness of separateness. Theoretically, some kinds of autism and handicap can spring from similar relationships to trauma and although the two groups are largely separate I am now treating handicapped patients who also are autistic.

Frances Tustin did not work with an organically mentally handicapped child herself but an understanding of her work is extremely important. She kindly became an advisor to the Mental Handicap Section which I convene at the APP (Association for Psychoanalytic Psychotherapy in the National Health Service) even when she was not well enough to travel. Her book *Autistic Barriers in Neurotic Patients* (1986) applies her understanding of autism to those autistic aspects in all of us. Thanks to her efforts and the work of child psychotherapists Anne Alvarez and Susan Reid, as well as the interest of psychiatrists, there has been a longer and more substantial history of psychodynamic work with autistic patients than with mentally handicapped ones. An English psychiatrist, Heaton-Ward (1977), examining the 1,300 papers that had been presented at five International Congresses for the Scientific Study of Mental Deficiency (ICSSMD) held in the previous fifteen years, found that only 40 were concerned with mental illness or its treatment. Half of those 40 reports involved autism and only two were concerned with psychosis.

In the last twelve years there has been a wider interest both in psychoanalysis itself and in its application. The growth of the Tavistock Clinic Workshop in London since it was first founded in 1979 has been considerable. In 1981 Neville Symington's first paper on work with a handicapped patient was published in the *British Journal of Medical Psychology*. A mildly handicapped man, Harry, 'felt there was something wrong with him and he was extremely anxious lest people did laugh at him for that and so he exaggerated the process and was thus able, within himself, to say that he was really perfectly all right. But what caused him pain and anxiety was a sense that there was something wrong.' Like my patient Evelyn (Chapter 10), Harry was able to show that he had more intelligence available to himself than other people expected. Although no-one thought he was capable of travelling on his own he managed to do so. Harry was able to show the depth of his distress about his handicap and the way he could not maintain his highest levels of functioning for long. 'I am capable of more than anyone thinks but there is tomorrow and Sunday and Monday.'

Neville Symington and his wife, psychoanalyst Joan Symington, developed Pierce Clark's concepts of regression to a foetal memory. They felt that a retreat to a foetal position was a way of getting back to the womb at a point before there was prenatal or birth injury. They gathered other interested psychoanalysts, psychologists and psychiatrists to the Workshop, including Dr Bernard Barnett, Dr Chris Holland, Adrian Pantlin and Paul Upson. However, few of the Workshop members, other than Alan Pantlin, saw more than two patients and those given treatment were largely in the mild handicap range. The Symingtons made the first links, which have proved lasting, with Joan Bicknell, Professor of the Psychiatry of Disability at St George's Hospital, London, and Neville Symington also excited interest within and outside the Tavistock Clinic. The psychodynamic work of St George's, started by Joan Bicknell and continued by Sheila Hollins, has paralleled the work of the Tavistock. A special area of interest at St George's has been the impact of bereavement.

In 1985 the Symingtons moved to Australia and, although they retain an interest in the subject of handicap and have given several lectures there, further clinical work in this area is yet to come. Joan Symington merits a special place in psychoanalytic history for succeeding in taking on a handicapped patient as her training case for her psychoanalytical training.

An adult and child psychoanalyst and child psychiatrist, Dr Judith Trowell, former chair of the Tavistock Clinic Child and Family Department, combined work with both mentally handicapped and abused children and adults. Her ability to stay with both those difficult subjects allowed wider social recognition of the problems. Similarly, psychoanalyst and child psychiatrist Dr Arnon Bentovim included moderately handicapped children in his structured groups for abused children at both Great Ormond Street Hospital, London and the Tavistock Clinic from the late 1970s. The link between workers in the area of child abuse and mental handicap has remained constant. Psychoanalyst Mervyn Glasser at the Portman Clinic in London has worked with mildly handicapped sexual offenders.

From 1985 to 1988 the Tavistock Clinic Workshop was co-convened by Jon Stokes, an Adult Department psychologist and psychotherapist, and myself. We started to hold monthly open meetings. Anyone working in the field of mental handicap was welcome to attend. This created the start of a successful networking process. Colleagues visiting from other countries would come to the Open Meeting and then write or make extra time to tell us of the work in their areas. As a result of the Open Meetings I made contact with Yvonne Gilljam, a psychologist from Stockholm. She informed me that in Sweden there was an organization, ARKTIS, made up of psychodynamic psychologists specializing in the treatment of psychosis and handicap. Over the years more and more members from ARKTIS and other linked Swedish organizations have visited and Yvonne Gilljam has become the Swedish representative for the APP Mental Handicap Section.

We were also inspired by the ideas of others. Dr Vicky Turk (now researching abuse and disability at the University of Kent at Canterbury) asked me to run a ten-week course on psychodynamic thinking for workers in the mental handicap field. It worked so well that I continued, and ten-week introductory courses on mental handicap and psychodynamic thinking continue to run. In them ten workers from different professions think together about the meaning of their work. Both of these ventures, the open meetings and the ten-week courses, proved highly successful. With my new co-convenor educational psychologist Sheila Bichard, a one-year intermediate course in psychodynamic understanding and mental handicap was planned and piloted in Autumn 1990 to provide a follow-on to the ten-week course. After a successful trial year, it has now become part of the regular trainings on offer.

THE CURRENT SITUATION

What, then, can we offer colleagues? Most basically, an underlining of the fact that all human beings have an inner world as well as an outer one, an unconscious as well as a conscious, and therefore those with a handicap need just as much attention to these aspects of life as others. We therefore disagree with A. Reid (1982) when he comments, 'the scope for individual therapy is limited. Such patients do not have the intellectual resources to benefit from in-depth psychotherapy.' As Jon Stokes (1987) has aptly expressed it, 'we find it useful to distinguish between cognitive intelligence and emotional intelligence'. In other words, however crippled someone's external functional intelligence might be, there still can be intact a complex emotional structure and capacity. To reach and explore this emotional intelligence a great deal of guilt must be dealt with, guilt of the patient for his handicap and guilt of the worker for being normal.

One of the tasks of the Tavistock Clinic Workshop, since its inception, has been to rebuild the bridge that existed in the '30s between psychoanalysis and other professions. This has several hopeful implications. Firstly, we can try to transmit to workers in mental handicap the crucial concepts of, for example, Freud, Klein, Bion, Bowlby, Tustin, and Rosenfeld. Secondly, we can also encourage psychoanalytic colleagues to include the mentally handicapped in their frame of theoretical reference. Although psychoanalytic workers in this area are small in number they can play a considerable part in helping other professions to increase their understanding. The number of formally trained psychoanalysts and psychoanalytical psychotherapists engaged in this work (with more than one patient in this category) does not amount to more than four, with two or three trainees. This number is augmented by several hundred music, art, drama, physio-, and occupational therapists who work from a psychoanalytic framework, and a similar number of psychologists and psychiatrists.

In 1988 the APP (Association for Psychoanalytical Psychotherapy in the National Health Service) welcomed my suggestion for a Mental Handicap Section. The idea of this Section is to encourage other colleagues to open their services to the mentally handicapped as well as to provide extra training and support for workers already in the field of mental handicap. However, at this moment, the number of psychoanalysts and qualified psychoanalytical psychotherapists is very small. This committee includes only one English psychoanalyst, Dr Isaacs-Elmhirst (who was supervised by Bion and worked with Winnicott), one honorary psychoanalyst, Mrs Frances Tustin, and one Indian-trained psychoanalyst, Dr David Bassa. Nevertheless, each additional paper or conference adds to the chain of national and international contact and the APP Mental Handicap Section now has representatives from several countries: Annie Stammler (doctor and psychoanalyst, France) Wai-Yung Lee and Arnold Wellman (social worker and psychologist, Canada), Richard Ruth (psychoanalyst and psychologist, USA), Rudi Vermote and Johan De Groef (psychoanalytical psychotherapist and psychoanalyst and director of the Institute Home Zomnelied, Belgium), Maria Eugenia Cid Rodríguez (Spain), Christian Gaedt (Germany) and Anthi Agrotou (Cyprus).

International links piece together the gaps in psychoanalytical history as well as providing for a shared future. On 2 May 1990, PAOS, the Netherlands Organization for Postacademic Education in the Social Sciences, together with the World Psychiatric Association Mental Retardation Section, held a historic International Congress on Treatment of Mental Illness and Behavioural Disorder in the Mentally Retarded. As well as having the pleasure of meeting colleagues from all over the world I also found answers to some gaps in the history. I met Dr Richard Ruth, a psychoanalyst and psychologist at the Community Psychiatric Clinic, Gaithersburg,

USA. Since the early 1980s his clinic has had a contract with the county government to provide free/low-cost psychoanalytic psychotherapy for mentally handicapped people. There are eight workers in the clinic. The leader and pioneer was social worker Mary Ann Blotzner. She and the other five clinical social workers have all had personal therapy and a postgraduate two-year course of training followed by two years of psychoanalytic supervision and then a further four-year training. Supervision and clinical work is undertaken by the two psychoanalysts – Richard Ruth, who is also a psychologist, and Dr Rachel Ritvo, who is also a physician.

Within the UK I am pleased to say that although child psychotherapists are so few in number (only 230) and overwhelmed with rising referrals for sexual abuse, effects of deprivation, and all the ordinary ills that beset childhood, we are now very concerned with this client group. Robin Balbernie, Marta Smith, Lesley Ironside, Shirley Truckle, Jenny Sprince, Janet Bungener, Sheila Spenseley, Trevor Hartnup, Wendy Feldman and Anne Wells are just a few of those who have taken that interest further.

Psychoanalyst Sandy Bourne co-convened an Adult Psychotherapy group with me; other psychoanalysts or psychoanalytic psychotherapists have offered research help (Peter Fonagy, Peter Hobson, David Taylor, Rob Hale), clinical supervision (Susannah Isaacs-Elmhirst, Nick Temple, Caroline Garland), have referred patients (Mike Brearley, Eglé Laufer), supervised primary workers (Patrick Casement, Don Meltzer), or provided forensic liaison (Chris Cordess, Estela Welldon, Mervyn Glasser, Richard Davies).

Psychoanalysts like Shapiro who mainly worked as psychiatrists have had an incalculable effect and there must be others in that dual position. Perhaps even more importantly for the future, some colleagues already working in mental handicap who came to the Tavistock for the ten-week or one-year course have since decided to add on a child psychotherapy training. Out of ten professionals in the first two supervision groups, eight are now taking the Observation Course, a two-year course in its own right which is also an essential prerequisite for clinical training at the Tavistock. It builds up observational skills by requiring the once-weekly observation of a baby, attendance at a baby observation seminar, a work discussion group and a theoretical seminar. Indeed, in the long term, the biggest psychoanalytic impact on mental handicap will come from professionals in the field, adding on psychoanalytic or psychoanalytically informed training and taking it back to mental handicap.

By the time that the twelfth ten-week course came to an end a curious change had taken place. In the beginning, the workers on those courses were pioneers, not believed in their own institutions, who dared to believe that handicapped patients had feelings and intelligence. As we have become more successful in spreading our views and as, historically, we have coincided with the self-advocacy movement, the courses have taken on a more established atmosphere. Workers are still relatively unsupported in their institutions but they are not disbelieved to the shocking extent they were.

The part psychoanalytic ideas and practice have played in the field of mental handicap is a small but crucial one. Although the work of Freud and ideas on emotion and education continued by Klein, Anna Freud and Bion have slowly percolated, because they were not primarily addressed to the mentally handicapped population they have been slow to be taken up.

In the last few years the term 'psychotherapy' appears more frequently on computer searches of this subject; however, the nature of the therapy offered or the rigour of the therapeutic training is very diverse. What most share is a belief that there is meaning in the actions and feelings of people with severe disabilities and that if the therapist is able to lend himself adequately to the task, change will happen. Hence psychiatrist Kenneth Day's special unit for handicapped male offenders at Northgate Hospital, Morpeth, England, includes counselling and supportive therapy; and social worker Robert Fletcher's Ulster County Mental Health Service (UCMHS) in New York State, USA includes individual and group psychotherapy.

What most share, whether acknowledged or unacknowledged, is the same ancestor, Freud! Interactional analysis (and Berne was interested in mental handicap), Rogerian client-centred therapy, relationship-therapy, pre-therapy all share the benefit of a base-line of psychoanalytic understanding – even where their pioneers disowned this shared inheritance.

The developmental psychotherapies in the Netherlands, for

example, as written about by Anton Dosen (in Dosen and Menolascino, 1990), and Prouty's work on pre-therapy in the USA (1990) derive from John Bowlby's work on attachment and bonding. John Bowlby's psychoanalytic training and insight enrich his internationally acclaimed work on attachment. Unfortunately, the historical inability of his analytic colleagues in the 1950s to accept the central importance of his work meant that students following his work perceived it as something totally separate and unanalytical. All breakups and tensions in the psychoanalytic family lead to inter-generational conflict.

At one conference in America and another in Amsterdam I was told by surprised-sounding professionals that I sounded like a Rogerian. It seemed they regarded 'unconditional valuing of the client' as a concept that only fitted with Carl Rogers's counselling or John McGee's Gentle Teaching. (John McGee founded his concept of non-aversive teaching and wholehearted valuing of handicapped clients in response to punitive behavioural pro-grammes.) They did not see it as a psychoanalytic concept. Some of the blame for this must lie with some psychoanalytic practitioners who fail to make constructive use of the theories available to them. One American proponent of Gentle Teaching commented that the American psychoanalytic attitude to self-injury, insofar as there was one, was that 'the patient should have known better', thus blaming the patient for his or her own illness. When faced with lack of interest in the analytic community or attitudes like that, it is not surprising that America proliferates with alternative therapies that have a kindlier attitude to the handicapped patient and are sometimes in danger of representing the flip-side philosophy; that there is nothing destructive or ill anywhere in the handicapped individual, only in the outer response to them. If the implications of Bion's work on ego-splitting were fully taken on board this polarization would not exist. Without it, no real progress in treatment or understanding is possible. As Michael Sinason puts it (1990), if you ascribe the wrong action to the wrong self of the patient there are serious implications. If you attribute sane motives to psychotic actions 'the patient thinks you are sanifying what you cannot stomach about their psychotic personality. If you misattribute psychotic ambitions to the sane personality there is a deep despair which leads to the rapid emergence of a confusional state.'

PSYCHOANALYSIS AND MENTAL HANDICAP

I am hoping, therefore, that this book will be a further step in righting some of those attitudes. In 1990 I presented some preliminary findings to the Applied Section of the Institute of Psycho-Analysis in London. Amongst those present was Frank Orford, an English psychologist and psychoanalyst who had worked at the Fountain Hospital, taking part in Harold Bourne's research. Together with my colleague Sheila Bichard, we presented our research also to the Institute of Psycho-Analysis Research Forum. The subject is no longer out in the cold.

As no history has been written of psychoanalysis, psychoanalytical psychotherapy and mental handicap I am aware that there will have to be major gaps in this account. Where psychotherapists have not written up their work it does not appear on computer printouts! I would be grateful for missing pieces of the history to be sent to me.

In my work I rely on the body of psychoanalytical theory, having available for myself the concepts that particularly help me at different moments. For the understanding of trauma and the internalizing of painful external events I am particularly indebted to the Independent and Freudian Schools and for the understanding of internal shifting states I would not be able to work without the concepts of Klein, Bion and Rosenfeld. This chapter has looked at the small number of psychoanalysts or psychoanalytical psychotherapists involved intensively in mental handicap work, but, of course, that small group of us relies on the vast amount of psychoanalytic literature that cannot be more than briefly mentioned here. That literature is also available nationally and internationally for hard-pressed workers trying to make sense of the anguish of their clients, residents, patients, family and friends.

A small glossary of key terms is included at the back of this book; where those terms are important in particular chapters I provide further explanations. Whilst this book is intended to help all interested professionals in applying the concepts raised here rather than to be a technical exploration of psychoanalytical theory and technique, there are a few issues that do require extra attention.

The lack of involvement of more psychoanalysts or psychoanalytical psychotherapists is also due to the fact that such clients are not referred to them. Workers who tried to refer patients unsuccessfully ten years ago have all too often given up trying again. In addition, they have been slow to avail themselves of supervision opportunities. A *cordon sanitaire* can be two-way.

First comes the issue of assessing for psychotherapy. As this work is still in its relatively early stages we are still accumulating clinical evidence about suitability. However, I have found it increasingly helpful to think of an assessment as my way of exploring whether I think I have anything to offer a particular person. Where an individual has few communication abilities and many emotional difficulties, grounds for taking somebody or rejecting them can be related to personal resources and foibles. Someone who can work with violent patients well might not tolerate someone who sits and spits or urinates.

Secondly, working with severely and profoundly handicapped children and adults who are also emotionally disturbed is a very specific application of psychoanalytical psychotherapy. It lends itself particularly well to a child psychotherapy training and perhaps it is no coincidence that the Tavistock Clinic Workshop has attracted more therapists trained to work with children than adults. Children, especially young children, communicate their unconscious wishes and fears through their play, often without words. The child psychotherapist is trained to pay particular attention to the non-verbal communication whilst the adult psychotherapist or psychoanalyst may rarely be involved in face-to-face contact. The child psychotherapist and child analyst is also more likely, when working with the very young, to place particular importance on the countertransference.

Bion (1959) explored the concept of the analyst as a container for the patient's intolerable experiences, just as a good-enough parent is the container of her baby's nameless fears. The younger the child or the more severely handicapped the child or adult, the greater the need to work more by understanding the countertrans-

ference or the nature of the communication the patient has sent to
the therapist to be held.

Where a baby sends out distress signals and his parent can
tolerate receiving them, the painful, messy signals are clarified and
made manageable and the baby receives back something manageable. Where the parent cannot bear the communication a
handicapping process is begun. Hanna Segal comments that the
containment of anxiety is the beginning of mental stability and also
the basic model for the therapeutic endeavour of the analyst.
Containment is an essential prerequisite for any therapeutic change
and especially crucial for this group. Irma Brenman Pick (1985,
p. 158) points out that some patients listen to the mood rather than
the words in an interpretation. An inability to bear the grief and
anger and extent of handicap would make null and void any
interpretation as an agent of psychic change.

In addition, where there is substantial external and internal
trauma and an organic condition, technique has to adapt. Where
abuse is a fact on a file, distanced as something in the past, the
Marlovian defence can rear its head, crying 'But that was in another
country, and besides, the wench is dead.' Where death, damage,
torture, decay, chromosomal abnormality and organic malfunction-
ing are alive in the session the therapist has the task of facing the
real hurt, the fantasy about it and a double countertransference.

In one setting where I worked there was a family with an
epileptic child. The child was unable to separate from the parents,
fearing death. The parents were unable to separate from the child,
fearing death. They slept together, worked together and, apart from
school, functioned as a single unit. Skilled psychologists worked
with the family over practical and emotional issues such as baby
alarms and other equipment so that the child could sleep by itself.
The child died on the first night of separation. In other words, for
some children the equation of separation with death is not just a
fantasy. In the same way, Second World War orphanage children
could die of a broken heart when they were not loved.

In many homes where there is a handicapped child, the child
is only tolerated if she stays 'unborn', a fetishistic object for the
parent, usually the mother. There has been such hurt that the
child will not grow up normally that the only way of managing

is to demand that the child stays a baby. It matters that the child's fear that growing up will lead to rejection or death is not only a fantasy.

Shirley, aged fifteen had Down's syndrome and came to therapy in short white socks and a smocked dress as if she were eight. She wore no bra despite her well-developed breasts. She was referred for split-off acts of violence that jarred with her 'loving disposition'. Her mother was over-protective. Shirley's happy smile and her regular looks at her mother for approval or corroboration were very noticeable. 'Smart shoes,' she said to me. 'You like my shoes and dress.' I was aware she was exploring me as a replica of her mother. Someone, in the transference, who wanted her as a smart baby. The force of her statements was also an invitation to agree. A few years ago I might have made a transference comment on her wish to please me and be smart for me – but without detailing what that involved. The next stage might have been to say she wanted her clothes to be smart as she was worried her mind and body may not be because of her handicap. Currently, my comment was that she wanted me to notice how smartly she was dressed but that she was not dressed like a young woman, she was dressed like a little girl. Perhaps she was scared that if she showed me she had breasts and was growing up I would get rid of her; I would only want a handicapped little girl, not a young woman; and perhaps she was worried her mother felt like that too. She burst into tears, tore up the paper on which she had drawn a tidy picture and shouted, 'I am fifteen. I am nearly sixteen. What about when I am seventeen? White socks at seventeen?' Then we could think about her predicament.

Hanna Segal (1973) clearly shows that a full transference interpretation should make links between the inner and outer world, the relationship with the therapist and the relationship to parents. Nevertheless, there is a strongly felt myth that Kleinians do not make outer-reality interpretations. Harold Blum (1983, p. 615) comments, 'A "transference-only" position is theoretically untenable and could lead to an artificial reduction of all associations.'

Some of the attack on 'reality' interpretations seems to have come about because such comments were linked with analysts who felt they had to present themselves, as Rosenfeld puts it, as 'real objects to the patient in order to bring about a mutative change'. Rosenfeld notes (1972, p. 456) that 'patients get very disturbed when the analyst points out or discusses a reality situation during analysis or makes non-analytical comments during a session . . . It certainly does not help the patient to face reality.' Now forcing external reality onto a patient because of fear or inability to deal with the internal world is clearly abusive at worst or inadequate at best. Freud clearly shows where he has not helped a patient by bringing in outer reality. He wrote (1911, 1913, p. 141), 'Every time I repeated her mother's story to the girl she reacted with a hysterical attack and after this she forgot the story once more. There is no doubt that the patient was expressing a violent resistance against the knowledge that was being forced upon her. Finally, she simulated feeble-mindedness and a complete loss of memory in order to protect herself against what I had told her. After this, there was no choice but to cease attributing to the fact of knowing, in itself, the importance.'

As well as showing vividly here how we do go stupid and handicapped when faced with unbearable facts, Freud was showing the progression in his clinical technique, his sensitivity to timing as well. However, I am wondering if, because some people have brought in outer reality in a non-analytical way, the concern has been generalized to other uses of outer reality, leading to a movement too far in the other direction. With some traumatized children and adults I suggest we are dealing with a different reality, where the outside has to be linked in rigorously.

On Saturday 20 July 1991 a historic conference was held at the Tavistock Clinic. A joint meeting between the APP Mental Handicap Section and the Tavistock Clinic Mental Handicap Workshop, the day focused on boundaries in psychoanalytical psychotherapy with abused handicapped children and adults. Psychoanalyst and child psychiatrist Dr Judith Trowell began by emphasizing the primacy of child protection issues within psychoanalytical psychotherapy. She made clear that in any assessment for therapy she holds in her mind the possibility of abuse and it affects the nature of her clinical work. Dr Sheila Bichard, Professor Joan Bicknell and I equally stressed the fact that abuse meant a boundary had been broken. There was less room for inner fantasy at a time of trauma. The external event took up all the space and needed addressing and containing before the inner world could be strengthened.

Similarly, as I saw on a visit to the mental handicap asylum in Leros, Greece in April 1992, pioneering psychoanalytical psycho-therapist and psychiatrist John Tsiantis and his inspiring team needed to plan a major primary rehabilitation programme before offering therapy. However, the psychodynamic knowledge of the team, which included Fani Bithazi, Angelos Voutsas, Penny Papanikolopoulou and Makis Kolaitis, meant the importance of both outer and inner needs could be held in mind. It is a matter of international pride for psychoanalytical psychotherapists in this field that such physically and emotionally life-saving work is being carried out by colleagues.

PART II:
CASE STUDIES

4 THE MAN WHO WAS LOSING HIS BRAIN

Patient: Doctor, I'm really worried. I don't know what to do. I keep forgetting things.
Doctor: Don't worry. Just forget about it.

A tree on earth shall suffer in its leaves, lament its branches.
Anon. Anglo-Saxon Poet

Life is full of losses. From the moment of birth we are dispossessed of our first country, the womb. Weaning and displacement by the birth of siblings follows. Each new stage in normal development involves loss. Starting junior school means saying goodbye to infant school. As well as basic losses we can add the loss of loved ones, country, job, health. Underlying all of these is awareness of our mortality, the eventual loss of our life itself. Whilst some workers in mental handicap (Hollins and Grimer, 1988; Bicknell, 1983) have long understood the crucial connection between handicap and loss others have subscribed to the hopeful myth that 'ignorance is bliss'. Ignorance is not bliss and neither is knowledge.

In facing the tragedy of incapacity there is no easy stance. Where a condition is incurable and the progression is one of unremitting mental deterioration it is not surprising that the wish for ignorance should be strong. However, in the end repression of reality does not work. As Freud (1909) commented, 'the thing which is warded off invariably finds its way into the very means which are being used for warding it off'. Unbearable feelings are often displaced in this way.

Our own personal life circumstances determine which kinds of incapacity or damage we find most difficult. If we mourn more the loss of what was once fine and whole, then we might be vulnerable to displacing onto those who have never experienced true wholeness all the feelings we find most painful. 'At least my child did once walk,' said a mother of a paralysed seven-year-old, transferring her emotions to the plight of a neighbour's child who was limbless from birth. On the other hand, a patient who was blind from birth was full of compassion for a friend 'who wasn't brought up blind and doesn't know how to manage it. How will she manage just hearing and smelling?'

As biological organisms we seem to carry within us a sense of the whole. Two babies, for example, are struggling to sit up. One will manage it in another month or so. The other will never be able to. At this exact moment of time neither of them consciously knows its future. Each is striving towards the next developmental stage. There can be no concept of a deficit yet. As the child grows the sense of what is whole does pinpoint discrepancies. For example, a child born with one hand is still born with a concept of two hands just as a child without a father still has an image of a father and two parents. Brendan MacCarthy (personal communication, 1987) pointed out, for example, that the term 'one-parent family' was a misnomer. There was really a two-family child. A child or adult without a fully functioning brain lives with the shadow of the missing part.

The emotional experience of the individual with a late-onset physical illness or handicap is very similar to that of the mentally handicapped individual. My purpose in providing the following clinical description of a man suffering from Alzheimer's disease is to share the tragic though inspiring process of one person's journey from the heights of intellectual achievement into severe mental handicap. I hope this will highlight the emotional experience of both mental handicap and any impairment .

A baby experiences its arms and legs as separate beings. When a baby finally discovers that the shape she is waving belongs to her and can be brought under her personal control, it is a delight to watch. From a kaleidoscope of different moving parts and fragments there emerges an understanding of unification. When a lucky-enough individual enters adulthood there is an emotional expectancy, based on family history and experience, of particular kinds of losses that will come with ageing. Going bald or going grey, being more prone to backache, becoming arthritic, developing cancer, heart problems . . . Some people, in more affluent countries with better diets, can age gracefully with very few adverse effects. However, any change that goes beyond what is realistically expected and emotionally prepared for attacks our central belief in ourselves as autonomous beings. With the advent of a sudden pain, illness, injury that was not self-inflicted, we face yet again our own mortality.

With Alzheimer's disease, there is not only a physical impact, there is a measurable mental deterioration too. From knowing, possessing knowledge, words, thoughts, there is a downward path to not knowing. It means returning back to the first chaos of infancy when not an infant and having possessed knowledge at its fullest and finest. The difference between someone at the start of Alzheimer's disease and someone near the end is as large as the difference between someone who is normal and someone who is profoundly handicapped. The total continuum is experienced in the mind and heart of a single being.

A note on Alzheimer's Disease

Freud's professor at the Vienna Medical School, Theodor Meynert (1833–1892), wanted to understand mental illness from a purely anatomical basis. He perceived delusions and hallucinations as being due to subcortical irritations (Zilboorg and Henry, 1941, p. 442). Alois Alzheimer was influenced by Meynert's research and in 1906 (p. 146) he reported on a disease in which he found that changes in the brain were similar to those found in senile psychoses. Alzheimer's disease is now seen as the most frequent of the pre-senile dementias, partly because of the increase in longevity. Dr Gerry Bennett (1989) points out that a hundred years ago only 4 per cent of the population were over 65; now the figure is 15 per cent, with more people over the age of 85 than ever before. This means the numbers who suffer from some form of confusion are also growing. Population projections suggest the number of over-85s will double between 1981 and 2001, with as many as one in five suffering from dementia.

Alzheimer's disease tends to start in the mid-fifties and brings memory disturbance, gait disorders and eventually dementia in its wake. Like non-organic mental handicap its cause is largely unknown; heredity plays only a small part. Treatment is largely supportive rather than transformational and 'the end point, like all dementias, is appalling' (Willis, 1976, p. 144). Although, as with organic handicap, there is clear brain damage and deterioration, emotions play their part in how the disease is experienced, and possibly, too, there is in some cases an interplay between body and mind in the timing of the onset.

Lily Pincus, a founder of the Institute for Marital Studies at the Tavistock Institute for Human Relations (1981, p. 107) states most clearly that despite organic authenticity there is still a question as to why dementia should happen, and asks us not to see all emotional disturbance in dementia as being caused by it. She provides the example of a woman for whom grief at a flood in her basement flat 'led to the onset of steadily growing confusion'.

EDWARD JOHNSON

Edward Johnson was at the height of his profession. A university academic with a post of responsibility, he was respected by staff and students when at the age of 56 the onset of Alzheimer's disease led to his enforced retirement. He was referred to me by his GP, who was concerned by the devastating emotional and cognitive impact of the condition.

Edward Johnson's memory loss was already so great that he could not manage to visit his GP any more. Home visits were essential. Even leaving his home to visit his next-door neighbour could involve his forgetting where he was going. 'He prided himself on the breadth and depth of his academic scholarship and travelled the globe to share that knowledge. Now even a few steps and he is lost,' wrote the GP. He added that Edward Johnson was a widower with two grown-up sons who lived nearby but that he did not want to move in with either of them. The home help who had been with the family for over twenty years now lived in and, against the wishes of his family, Edward Johnson was determined to stay independent as long as he could. The GP had referred him to me as he thought it might be possible that help with the emotional issues would assist with the practical problems.

Following past experience with two other patients with Alzheimer's disease I decided to hold open the possibility of treating him in his own home should therapy prove useful. Unless he was able to provide an escort he would clearly not manage to come to me or even remember his appointments. This involved considering boundary issues very carefully. A usual prerequisite for therapy is a specially designated consulting room in a clinic, hospital or elsewhere. The room needs to have its privacy respected with no-one coming in or knocking on the door. However, important work with children in hospital wards and in day units and schools has managed to go on without these essentials. As I had worked in school and hospital settings and now also work in the Tavistock Clinic's Day Unit I felt used to dealing with these issues. In a school, all the children know which pupils go to therapy and the pupils see their therapist in the corridor, in the staffroom and elsewhere. When I take nine-year-old Mary to the therapy room, we might be jealously approached by ten-year-old Steven saying 'Isn't it my turn yet ?' In a Child Guidance Clinic where children do not know who else comes, there is room for fantasies about rival siblings who share the attention of their therapist. In a school or hospital it is known concretely who shares the therapist and also at what time. In a hospital, therapy sometimes has to take place on a hospital bed if the child is too ill to move. This is not easy. If the bed is the doctor's territory one moment, then the nurse's five minutes later, then the therapist's, the physiotherapist's, then the family lounge, the teenage den, the back row of the cinema, all the staff need to share the problems involved. Once these issues have been thought about and shared there is the reward of taking essential treatment to a client group who would otherwise been deprived. (See Judd [1989] for details of ward-work.)

First visit

My first visit was arranged to take place with both sons present. At 11 a.m. on a Monday morning I rang the garden flat bell. Edward Johnson came to the door, a tired-looking, elegant man in corduroy trousers and polo-neck sweater. He smiled at me welcomingly, looking very much like the university don he had been. But then his face went blank, then exhausted and then questioning. 'You must be – must be – ' he began. He repeated his words so that I did not have the chance to say my name and rescue him from his memory loss. However, holding onto the fabric of his past memory, the imperative words 'must be', which denoted a confident certainty, were clearly easier than admitting he needed to be helped. His sons, whom I will call John and Peter Johnson, professional men in their middle and late twenties, helpfully appeared and made the introductions, ushering me into a room that looked out onto the garden.

When I was seated they made it clear that they lived nearby with their young families and were each able and willing to have their father live with them. John, the eldest, emphasized that while it was all right for his father to live alone now there were nevertheless worries for his safety. Suppose he left the cooker on and forgot to turn it off; suppose he locked himself out; suppose he got lost? Edward Johnson froze and then looked completely blank while they spoke. I felt the burden of worries his family carried as well as Edward Johnson's distress and anger. I said it was frightening and upsetting for all of them to consider what it was like now, let alone in the future, and that was one of the reasons why Dr X had suggested my coming. It must also make them feel angry.

Edward Johnson turned his head towards me and said haltingly that he was lonely. 'Honestly,' exclaimed John angrily, 'You've just refused coming to move in with Helen and me and now you say you are lonely.' Peter then quietly told me that their father received lots of invitations from old friends but was embarrassed to see many of them. 'Or they're embarrassed to see me,' added Edward Johnson sharply. John quickly added that his father got tired easily and when he stayed the weekend with either of them the grandchildren tired him out and he longed to get home again. Edward Johnson smiled awkwardly. I said maybe the loneliness then was not to do with physically being alone, it was an inner feeling of isolation and loss that he carried about inside himself even if he was in company. He vigorously agreed, saying he was not short of 'physical bodies' in terms of visitors. His eldest son relaxed.

I explained that if Edward Johnson would like me to come, I could see him in his flat so that if he forgot he would not have the experience of getting lost on his way to me. He looked relieved but then said angrily, 'I do still go and get my evening paper across the road.' John then reminded him of how he had got lost just the day before. 'But I got back,' he proudly replied. 'Lots of people get lost. Everyone made such a fuss. I never fussed about you two like this. A right old woman you'd have thought me.' There was a painful pause. I said how hard it must be for Mr Johnson. As a father he had gone through the stage of worrying if his children were back safely and now because of Alzheimer's his children had to worry about his safety and his life.

'I do not like it. But there you are. That's what happens.' There was a long pause. 'And I did get back.' I said yes, he had, but his sons were also worrying about when things would get worse. I added that while he was being so brave and saying 'these things happen' he was not allowing himself or his children to worry. Edward Johnson laughed. 'That's right. I do worry and I don't like to let myself.' I said it helped him that he was so brave but perhaps he also needed to recognize the Edward Johnson who was upset at losing his job and his memory. Peter then quietly said they felt their father was missing his wife too. She had died three years ago. I said something about the way a loss stirs up the memory of other losses and maybe losing even a word or a thought stirred up these other losses for him. Edward Johnson nodded. There was a long silence.

Peter said they had not directly spoken about how badly their father must be feeling about losing his memory; they just focussed on incidents like his getting lost. 'It's not that bad,' said father. John commented on how fluent his father was this morning, usually he kept losing words.

I then brought in what I had understood from the GP about the process of Alzheimer's; how it could take several years in which memory would get worse. John said he and his brother and their respective partners shared visiting so that someone popped in each day and they kept a shared diary so that they knew where their father should be. Peter added that Edward Johnson did not like other people controlling his diary and life. I said he might also feel that way about the prospect of therapy. They all laughed.

I arranged to make an exploratory visit to see Edward Johnson on my own. I discussed confidentiality, explaining that what was said in our time together was private but that I would let both sons know if anything serious happened, such as accelerated deterioration or not finding Edward Johnson in. We also discussed whether they would like to meet as a family to discuss the impact on them all, but they clearly felt that they most needed their father to have something for himself. When I stood up John whispered to me that his father had been ill for a couple of years now. He was letting me know that his father was only expected to survive a few more years.

As I left, Edward Johnson pointed to his back garden. 'This is why we moved here. We needed somewhere smaller after the boys flew the nest. We both loved gardening and would only live in a garden flat. Look at the – those – long ones – you know – near the – ' The words had left him but the shape of the plants still carried their own iconic meaning. I said I was sorry, I did not know the names of those plants or the tree near them; sometimes I would know the word he was looking for but not always. He looked relieved. It is essential for therapists to be able to bear not knowing what they do not know and being honest about it. Otherwise, what hope is there for their clients?

That very first meeting resonated with me in many ways. I thought about the friends who were embarrassed to visit and the way Mr Johnson himself declined contact. One friend who was widowed told me that the hardest part was seeing acquaintances cross the road to avoid talking to her. 'They thought they were being kindly and were avoiding upsetting me but what they were really being was scared of being contaminated by my misfortune.' I thought too about the difficulties of holding onto past knowledge, like names and the hard balance between going out – to the point of taking a dangerous risk – versus staying in – being safe but losing all hope.

I went home and looked out at my own garden, at trees that could last longer on the earth than I could and felt sharply the comfort Edward Johnson received from his garden. I was to end up seeing him once weekly for a year. For a man who loved nature so much it seemed that going through all the seasons once with him carried its own symmetry.

First session

I arrived for my first exploration. Edward Johnson was looking out at me from his study window, clearly expecting me. He smiled warmly when he saw me and ushered me into his drawing room. We had arranged for the phone to be taken off the hook so we would not be disturbed for the fifty minutes. I commented that he was pleased to see me and also pleased he had remembered I was coming. There was a pause. 'These friends, so kind, old friends, they came today, earlier, just in case, because I am . . . ' He could not find his words. I added that I too was here like his old friends because he wasn't well. He laughed at the connection. 'They told me about a party. As if I wouldn't know. They felt they had to tell me. They – their name – old friends.' I said I did not know if he had really forgotten the name of his friends or if he had lost it just for the moment because he was cross because they assumed he had lost his memory for something that he had not forgotten. He agreed. I said how hard it was for him and his friends when his illness meant that he would have to be reminded already of some things, and gradually more and more things. Friends ran the risk of hurting him if they assumed he had forgotten something and yet they needed to check. There was a long silence. 'Please tell me something,' he said, turning his head away.

I said it was very painful that he was losing his memory. 'Yes. It makes me feel so lonely. I am in this large flat, rattling about, when all I need is a little room. Perhaps I should move.' I said he wished a smaller room could prune down and minimize his loneliness and his loss of memory but it was not the physical space that caused it. There was a long silence. 'My oldest friend, in Sussex, he is meeting me at the station this weekend and I will stay for the weekend. But only the weekend. I wish it was longer. My children keep asking me, but it is hard work being with the grandchildren when I am like this. But my children and friends – they are so kind.'

I said there were all these people he liked, perhaps including me, who offered him nice things when what he would like best would be to live with his oldest friend. 'Dead right.' I commented on his choice of the word 'dead' and wondered if he also wished his wife was still alive. He wiped away a tear. 'Do you know, sometimes I forget my wife's name.' He cried. 'Sometimes I forget what she did, what her job was. And we were married for thirty years. I don't try and go back and remember – what's the point – sometimes I can't.' I said managing now was so hard he felt he had to see each day through at a time rather than look back. There was a long silence. He turned his head away from me. 'Tell me something.'

I said maybe being in the flat he had shared with his wife, even though he felt lonely, helped him, as the rooms held the history for him; so that although he could not manage to look back now it meant that when and if he did it would be around him despite what he had lost. His eyes filled with tears and he said, 'That is one of the nicest things I have heard.' Then he spoke of the old home help who managed the whole flat beautifully but who spoke English poorly and was sometimes difficult to understand. I said I had just said something that he felt put his house in order just as his help did even if I also felt hard to understand or slow. He laughed. 'I'm sorry. That's not very polite of me.' I said politeness mattered a lot to him but understanding was not to do with politeness.

He put his hands on his head and struggled with a memory. 'My son – er – he will be seeing – us – I mean me. He lives – near here. Road with lamp-posts.' He looked at me pale and exhausted. I commented that he had said 'us' instead of 'me' and this had hurt him. He said it often happened. I then wondered if he had lost his son's name and address because he was so upset at the loss of his wife.

'John,' he said proudly and then sighed and relaxed. I said there were some words his brain was losing all by itself and he could do nothing about that but some words he was losing all by himself. He grinned. Then there was a very long peaceful silence. 'Why didn't I mind that silence?' he asked. I said perhaps the tears had comforted him, had made him part of a couple, a him who cried for himself and a him who grieved. His face brightened for a moment and he said, 'In my room, there is a book I am trying to read on the birth of the labour movement. It is hard but I want to finish it.' I said there was some labour movement going on here despite the attacks on it and he knew that inside him there were the tools for marching on despite the end that would come. He wiped his eyes. When I told him it was time for me to go in a minute he commented it had been cold when I came, then the sun had come out and now it was miserable again.

He decided he would like me to come for an extended exploration because he did not know how long he would have the strength to stay thinking. We decided on once a week to begin with. He said he would tell his sons and I too could let them know. I carried his last sentence back with me, admiring the dignified way he acknowledged his wish to be in charge as well as awareness that he might not be.

That first meeting also raised many of the issues that handicap does. Some things are organic and nothing can be done about them. Yet in order to accept what cannot be changed it matters being able to explore the extent of knowing. Only then will it become possible to know what is a secondary handicap and can be changed. Within that first meeting it became clear that real organic loss shared a parallel existence with temporary emotionally caused impairment. This relates to a theme that is echoed throughout this book. Until you open your eyes to your own predicament you cannot see the extent of it. However, if opening your eyes means seeing sexual abuse (Chapter 6 and 8) or devastating limitations, is it bearable?

Therapy is a reciprocal treatment that cannot occur without consent. There is therefore some kind of self-selection.

An ability to bear the painful reality of the experience is needed by the therapist or no treatment is possible.

This session also raised the question of dignity in the face of impairment. A handicapped adult who cannot manage on his own and requires the help of others is in a difficult position. Mr Johnson was able, at this stage, to wash himself and perform his own toilet. However, a small number of severely physically and mentally handicapped children and adults are not able to do this. How can those around allow the greatest dignity and privacy? When his sons and I clearly and honestly spelled out certain dangers or realities, Mr Johnson was able to deal with these dangers. However, in many hospitals, schools and hostels I have seen people in wheelchairs being suddenly pushed and moved with nobody speaking first, asking where someone wanted to go or explaining why somebody had to move.

Second session

On our second meeting Edward Johnson excitedly led me to the drawing-room to point to a blossoming tree in the back garden. 'Isn't it beautiful? It has been so dark and dismal, the weather, and then that happens and the blossom is just perfect at the moment. It is not falling yet. It just stays there. It is held.' I thought about his illness and how grateful he was for thoughts that stayed intact; his appreciation of the beauty of life. I did not say anything. I felt his words carried their own answer. He then sat down and held his head in his hands. This was his usual position. His head, with its dying braincells, was the injured baby that needed holding and mourning with and for.

There was a long silence. He sighed and began a long complicated story of friends calling for him to take him to a party. He had lost lots of words. He had lost the names of his friends, the purpose of the party and the words 'food' and 'dinner'. 'These people – nice people – I know them – on the doorstep. Why? They said they'd take me. Lots of people there. I was very tired. They gave me – you know – on a plate – ' His frown grew as he searched for the word. 'Tuck. They gave me tuck. I was so tired.' I said it seemed a lot had happened. As he had lost control of remembering his own calendar other people had that function but when they came for him it felt sudden and unexpected and maybe when I came it felt like that too and then he felt tired out. He smiled both at the aggression implicit in what he had said and at his recognition of it. Then he shouted 'School!' He banged his fist on the table. 'Staff party. End of term. University.' As in my work with mentally handicapped patients it seemed that anger unlocked the door of remembering so that then he was able to recall the meaning of the party. It was a staff party at his university. Going to the party had meant showing former colleagues and junior staff the level of his deterioration. One way of dealing with that trauma was to lose his memory and intelligence about the party so that it should remain only 'tuck' and being tired. 'Tuck' in itself seemed a childhood word for him from his boarding school days. More adult words for eating had gone. I found myself thinking of Hal, the computer, in the film *2001*. As it was dismantled its language returned to first nursery rhymes.

Edward Johnson had managed, with great difficulty, to integrate his memory and knowledge. However, as with other organically handicapped people, the moment of integration could not last long. In his next sentence he was losing things again. 'My oldest friend – Sus? Suspect? Coast – right hand of map.' 'Sussex?' I asked. 'Yes,' he replied with enormous relief. 'You remembered from what I had told you before.' It felt to me that one of the functions of working with a deteriorating patient was to hold their memory, their knowledge, their choice of words. Edward Johnson could lose words but he still knew if I had remembered them correctly; hearing them said by another voice could still be understood when his own internal syntax had lost the word. 'I'd like to live there. Beautiful trees, all the year round.' I said how nature helped him, the way trees did stay in the same place even though their leaves and blossoms might get buffeted. I then added that perhaps he had lost the word 'Sussex' and replaced it with something 'suspect' because he was angry his friend was not offering him a permanent place and perhaps too he wished I could offer a permanent forest of remembering.

Another integrated few sentences followed. His son Peter had one daughter – 'only the one. Only one.' He sounded very sad. I commented that he was one of a previous grandparent couple, and a 'one' felt sad, like the end of a line. He looked surprised and pleased. 'Just the one and nanny,' he added uncertainly. I said he did not sound so sure about the nanny. 'Why a nanny when there is only one?' he asked faintly. I wondered aloud whether his experience of being ill and dependent made him feel like a child, but one with a nanny, not a mother. Perhaps I was experienced as a paid nanny. 'You know, I had a nanny when I was a child and I hated it. I was at boarding school too. But then when my wife went to work we got a nanny for my children. And now they do the same. I wish I could do more for my grandchildren. Only two, one each. They never saw my – my wife. I feel I should play with them but I get tired so quickly. It is hard for my children too. I am not really of much use to them. Or them for me. I need people my own age. But isn't it wonderful that the season is changing and I love my garden. I cannot remember the names of all my favourite plants and maybe one day I won't be able to say 'tree' but I will still see it. To think I was a – I used to know – tell children the names.' It was time for me to go and as I left he spoke again of the beauty of the blossom.

Some weeks later he was not in when I rang the bell for our seventh session. He rang me exactly when his session time would have finished. That immediately made clear to me it was not due to his illness that he had forgotten his session. It was too accurate for that. 'I'm ready now,' he said in a faded voice. I said he had missed his time today and I would see him next week.

Again, that is a familiar finding with children and adults with severe and profound handicaps who are thought to have no concept of time. Steve (see Chapter 5) had little verbal speech and was severely multiply handicapped. But he made it clear he knew when a session ended. Similarly, Maureen (Chapter 9), a profoundly handicapped young woman, showed her workers she knew when her therapy day and time was. To make an unerringly accurate mistake requires intelligence.

Eighth session

When I arrived he greeted me coldly and angrily. 'I have had a good day, what about you?' I said he was angry that I was not here for a social chat. I linked that with his behaviour of last week when he phoned just when his time was over to say he was ready, as if I were a friend waiting at home for an invitation. He nodded and agreed and then said, 'A – friend – woman – came with a car and took me to – up a hill – to see – other friends. There is a man. He can't speak. It is not cancer.' He went very white. There was a long painful silence. I asked if the man was dementing. I knew from the painful feelings stirred up inside me during the silence as well as from the way I was needed as a receiver and transmitter for Mr Johnson's innermost fears. 'Yes. He can't speak or move without being helped.' I said he had caused me to lose my tongue and speech last week when those facilities in me might have helped him. Maybe he feared that I would be this motionless inarticulate person who was supposed to help. 'I have done a little thinking,' he said quietly. 'Not much. It tires me. He – the man – said my name. I think he remembers me. It must be hard for his wife.' I said he had missed his time to explore how hard to bear he might be when his illness got worse. Perhaps he feared I would not bear him.

He suddenly cried and briskly wiped his eyes. 'I am frightened. But then I also like being on my own – with my live-in help. My children don't think I can manage. But the garden helps. So beautiful – and it will get sunny soon. How green. The trees.' I said the garden and trees were beautiful and stayed there, they did not go away. He could be sure of them. 'Yes. Like the cherry blossom. Look at it. The other blossoms have gone but it still hasn't dropped its blossoms. It will of course. It will all drop and fade. But not yet.' I said he did appreciate the nature and greenery around him and maybe at this moment he also appreciated his thoughts as they too were like the blossoms, very beautiful and precious, especially as they would fall. 'Yes. I agree. And that is hard and that is when I get busy doing things and tiring myself.'

It was at this point that I felt in need of the support of a colleague and had two meetings with child psychotherapist Anne Alvarez.

Session 10

Two weeks later the first blossoms were falling from the tree. Edward Johnson was whiter and there were deep lines on his face. For the first time, his trousers looked creased and his shirt crumpled. 'Saw – you know – people. Car. Wheels. Feet. We walked.' I said he looked very tired and it sounded as if he had lost more words. 'Yes.' He held his head in his hands and then banged his fist on the coffee table. A flashcard that said 'Table' fell on the carpet. I looked at it. So did he. He nodded sadly and then angrily. A full sentence then appeared. 'I have been thinking about killing myself. Before I lose all my brain.' He pointed to the cherry tree. 'Look,' he whispered. I said the blossom was falling but the tree was still holding some of them, some of them were still intact and when the blossom fell the tree would still stand there. 'And if it doesn't know?' he asked. I asked if he meant if life had any meaning if the tree or person didn't know they were alive. 'Yes.' I said that would indeed be a death, to be stripped of meaning. It would be the death of the mind. 'Good,' he said. 'Good.' He kept on nodding, relieved I was not minimizing his forthcoming tragedy.

As I have pointed out (Sinason, 1991, p. 16), in the first interpretation I commented on the fact that the tree was still there, some blossom was still intact. I was commenting that my patient had managed to stay alive and had some thoughts, and there was some human value in that. That interpretation was not a defence against the unpleasure of the terrible predicament he was in. Thinking of Anne Alvarez's paper 'Beyond the unpleasure principle' (1988), I was aware that there is indeed, as Anne states, 'another kind of reality'. That Edward Johnson had not killed himself merited a mention just as for some patients just turning up is all we can expect of them. It is enough. When he then took the image through to the next stage – the stage he would shortly be in – the stage of having no intelligent life left, that needed acknowledging as a fact. To have made a dyadic in-the-room transference interpretation at that time, on the grounds of, say, 'You wonder if I would care for you when you have no brain left', would have been easy to say and, I think, useless against the nature of the reality I was dealing with.

He picked up a letter and 'read' it to me in order to show me he could no longer recognize all the words. 'So that's that. That's that,' he said. I said he did not know all the words in the letter and they were words he used to know and that meant reading hurt him now although it used to relax him. 'I'm stupid now. I can't read. I'm dumb. Me. I can't read. Once, I told – boy – what do you say – student – he was an idiot. He did not understand – Derrida – if he knew. I am nothing.' I told him that 'stupid' meant numbed with grief and he was numbed with grief and he was realizing what it was like to be mentally handicapped, to pick up a book and only know a few words and to have your brain hurt when you tried to think more.

I travelled home struggling with unshed tears. For a while I was unable to write my notes on the session. Then I wrote a poem. Then I was able to bear to remember the session and to be able to write it.

ALZHEIMER'S
(To Anne Alvarez)

He sits with his head in his hands
on the stiff armchair

In the spare bedroom
the home help sleeps
Together they have watched the flat
empty itself

The children left like a flock of birds
The leaves left the trees
Even the cars left the street
Leaving the houses like thin stalks
And his brain is leaving him

Day by day it erases itself
Each sentence ends in a silver trail
A daily funeral

Yesterday all place names left him forever
Today it was numbers
Today the old help forgot
to make him lunch
Today he forgot he had not eaten

Looking at the family photographs
repeating the names in a fading braille
He sits holding his head
on the stiff armchair

The actual act of writing carried extra meaning when thinking of the devastation it caused to Edward Johnson to lose that ability. I remembered a hostel for adolescents with severe handicaps. The staff found they were keeping no notes. At first they felt this was due to an ideology that equated writing notes with 'labelling' but then they realized they found it unbearable to admit they were the possessors of the skill to write when their charges were unable to. My poem was also a way of preparing for the future, when his senses would be even more restricted.

Session 20

Now he was even whiter. He was huddled on his armchair in a crumpled cardigan and trousers that were unbuttoned. 'Tuck,' he stammered. There was a quiche and salad on a plate on the floor. There were crumbs round his mouth. He was trying to tell me he was still eating. It was 3.30 p.m. It was the first time he was clearly not ready to see me. As I was entering his home rather than him coming to see me I had decided there were certain important ethical issues regarding his consent. I asked him if he would like me to come back later or see him next week. 'Next week,' he said with a sigh of relief.

Session 21

The next week it was a cold rainy day and before I rang the bell I was already feeling a sense of loss that was displaced onto the cherry blossom. I knew all the blossom would have fallen. It was somehow easier to think of that than the pain of the brain cells that were dying. The home help opened the door, the first time I had seen her. 'Mr Johnson says to come in – he is resting on the couch. He is very tired, poor gentleman.' In the drawing room Edward Johnson lay on his chaise longue looking out at the fallen blossom. 'Gone,' he said, pointing to the bare tree. I nodded. He held his head in his hands. I said it was hard work for him holding onto what was precious inside his head, just like the tree holding onto its blossom. 'That's it. It is so tiring.'

His room, his elegant spacious room, was filled with flashcards. Clock, heater, newspaper, book, pen.

He said with great difficulty that the wife of the dementing man had phoned him and wanted him to come over but he could not bear it any more. He said more names had gone and he found it tiring seeing friends and not having words. Sometimes he had sentences, sometimes only disjointed words that I could link together, the holder of his memory. 'My oldest friend – from – Suspect – where – ' I reminded him of Sussex. 'Ah yes. You remembered. It has gone and do you know I could not remember my street name this morning.' I said it might be that those names had gone forever. 'Yes. Isn't it stupid.' He giggled. 'Do you know I can draw his home for you.' He took a pencil and struggled to remember where a piece of paper would be. Laboriously he opened a drawer and took a piece of paper out and drew a creditable map of England. He placed a dot in the Sussex region. 'He lives there.' I said that was right. 'So what can I do? What can I do?' I said what he was doing; that if he found a part of his brain had gone he had to find other ways of expressing the same word. 'Do you know, I know my speech is worse. Anyone who meets me now knows my brain is affected.' I agreed and said how painful it was that he knew what was happening and could do nothing to stop it. 'That's right. I can do nothing about it. And I have to think about how it will be.'

I thought of the aptly named *One Hundred Years of Solitude* by Gabriel García Márquez where the villagers suffer an insomnia plague that brings on memory loss. José Arcadio Buendía labels items with their names but then he realizes a day might come when he remembered the name but not what it meant. Then he added on extra labels. 'This is the cow. She must be milked every morning so that she will produce milk, and the milk must be boiled in order to be mixed with coffee to make coffee and milk.' However, even with that labelling 'they went on living in a reality that was slipping away, momentarily captured by words, but which would escape irremediably when they forgot the values of the written letters' (García Márquez, 1967, p. 46).

There was a long pause. 'My – son – my son. The first one. I've forgotten his name.' He cried loudly. I said John. 'Yes. Yes. My son John. John, the computer programmer. John, black hair, 28 years. Blue eyes. Son. Boy. Man. You see it is no good writing it on paper any more.' He pointed tearfully to large flashcards that said 'heater', 'diary', 'clock'. 'You see, they are no use if I can't read. If I am just plain stupid.' He started giggling and rocking in his chair. 'Flashcards for dopes. They're mad. Give me words to help me and I can't read the damned things.'

At this stage I spoke to both sons about arranging for extra help from a local psycho-geriatrician. A sharp deterioration began.

Session 30

Edward Johnson looked confused when he first saw me. His face was unshaved and his hair uncombed. I was shocked by the increased pallor of his face. 'Hello? Am I expecting you?' He stood by the door looking uncertainly at me. I asked if he knew who I was. 'Valerie,' he said and then smiled triumphantly. There was an aggression in his removing my formal title of 'Mrs Sinason'. 'Want tuck?' he asked me as he led me into the kitchen. I felt disorientated at being in the kitchen instead of the drawing-room and realized how often Edward Johnson would have to bear that feeling, being incomprehensibly in the wrong room at the wrong time. I said no thank you, I did not want food but perhaps he was feeling hungry and that was why he had led me into the kitchen instead of where we normally had our session. I looked around the kitchen, realizing that it too had been transformed like the drawing-room by the large flashcards. Cooker, oven, saucepan, plate, knife, fork.

'I don't know' he said. 'I don't know any more if I have eaten. Do you know – she – my help had the flu and stayed in bed the other day and I completely forget she hadn't brought me or her any – tuck – food – so I did not eat anything.' I said I felt I should let his sons know that. He put his head in his hands and massaged his head. I said he wished he could make his head feel better. 'There's something wrong in the kitchen.' 'Something wrong?' I asked. 'Yes. Yes,' he snapped angrily – 'What do you call it? The box. You know, the box in the kitchen.' 'Fridge?' I asked; 'breadbin? What sort of box?' 'Box,' he shouted at me. 'Don't you know what a box in the kitchen is, you idiot?' He burst out crying and smashed his fist on the table. I said how awful it was for him to feel an idiot, not to know the word. What was in the box? Could he use other words. Could he point? Perhaps that was why he wanted me to be in the kitchen. He shouted loudly and then with his old dignity apologized for shouting. He stood up and led the way back to the drawing room. He looked out at the garden, stroked his head and sat down.

'It's a box this high' – he pointed to his waist – 'and you put things on it that you heat up.' 'A cooker?' I asked. 'Oh, a cooker,' he exclaimed, thrilled. 'A cooker. A cooker.' It was as if he hugged the word to himself now he had recovered it. 'A cooker. I need a new cooker. A cooker. How wonderful. A cooker.' I said how wonderful it was to get a word back. 'Yes. Yes. It is. It makes up for things. It is hard. I am trying to get my affairs in order. What do you say? It is a metal thing – this high – ' he pointed to his forehead – 'it has drawers in it for papers.' 'Filing cabinet?' I asked. 'Yes. Yes. Filing cabinet. Cooker and filing cabinet.' I said once he had managed to bear his stupidity at not getting the word 'cooker' he had been able to more calmly get help for finding 'filing cabinet'. 'Yes,' he agreed. 'And now there is something else. I want to look for something else. There is a play I want to see and I saw the name in the paper and I don't want to lose it. I am sure I have it somewhere.' I suggested he go through the paper then. I sat there silently for twenty minutes while he slowly went through a pile of newspapers. First I thought of the complete long sentence he had just managed.

Then I sat thinking of the tree in the back garden. I felt if I stayed silent whilst he searched that would be the most useful thing I could do. When he found it, as somehow we both knew he would, he held the paper up slowly and pointed: *Under Milk Wood*. We both sat very quietly for a while. I said perhaps the title of the play was saying something to him all by itself. He smiled quietly and nodded. 'Knock twice and ask for Rosie,' he said with a Welsh accent, a shadow of his former academic self.

The week after, the home help again showed me in. 'My poor gentleman very tired but peaceful.' Edward Johnson had a beautiful multicoloured scarf round his neck which he kept stroking with his fingers. On the scarf were trees and birds. I commented on it. 'My mother made this when she was pregnant with me. She never did anything like it again. Isn't it beautiful. It's funny. I had a nanny, I told you. My mother didn't spend that much time with me. She didn't even make me a baby shawl. She made this instead and of course no baby or child could use it. But it really comforts me. I found it last week. After I went to the theatre. I did go. I went. I phoned for a cab. I said the time of the play and I remembered my address although – er – my – son – the computer – he wrote it down for me. The acting I did not like. I liked the written version better.'

I was astounded at his fluency. I said he had managed to go to see the play after managing to remember and find the title and maybe being in touch with something his mother had made when he was a little baby inside his mother had made him feel looked after. I commented too on Captain Cat in the play, whose friends and loved ones have all died like his parents and his wife.

He smiled and stroked the scarf. Then he picked up a leather-bound book from the coffee table. 'This was my father's hobby – bookbinding.' I said he had something from his mother and father inside him and outside of him to help with his journey. 'Do not go gently – ' he began a Dylan Thomas poem. I said he was struggling between going gently and raging. He nodded, then his language fell away from him. 'The new – box – kitchen –' 'Cooker?' I asked. 'Yes. It is in the kitchen but it is useless without being fixed.' He giggled. I said parts of his brain also felt useless but there were things to see that worked even though one important piece of equipment didn't. He grinned and said he had slept better.

Session 36

He was white and anguished again when he opened the door. He looked at me carefully and then gave a warm smile. He had clearly not recognized me and did not know what to do about it. In *One Hundred Years of Solitude*, García Márquez understood that process painfully (1967, p. 47): 'He greeted him with a broad show of affection, afraid that he had known him at another time and that he did not remember him now, but the visitor was aware of his falseness. He felt himself forgotten, not with the irremediable forgetfulness of the heart, but with a different kind of forgetfulness, which was more cruel and irrevocable and which he knew very well because it was the forgetfulness of death.'

I stood on the doorstep feeling equally lost. 'I am Mrs Sinason,' I finally managed; 'Have you forgotten my face?' It was somehow easier to say that than to ask 'Have you forgotten me?' In feeling the experience of being lost to memory, wiped out, even momentarily,

I was experiencing just a tiny moment of what Edward Johnson had to live with. His face relaxed back into exhaustion and he walked back to the drawing room, leaving me to close the door. Perhaps having closed the door on me closing the door felt too painful a task. He sat down and held his head for a moment. Then he reached for a gilt-edged invitation to an official party of an organization in which he had been prominent.

'What – what – can – I went to – when – when I was elevant? Elevant? Important. When I was important. I sat opposite – you know – man in – big hat. You know. The most important man.' 'Royalty?' I asked, 'a crown?' 'No. Bigger than that. Big face.' I tried uselessly. We could not between us retrieve the missing information. He shouted. 'Please, please, say names.' I said it frightened him when I too was stupid and ignorant and did not have the words he wanted. He picked up the scarf. 'What seas did you sail, Captain Cat?' he said. Then he smiled calmly at me. I said when he felt furious with me and full of despair with me and himself he could remember his triumph that day in finding the name of the play and remembering something of it and in holding and finding what his mother had given him.

He smiled and spoke of an outing he had had the previous night. 'Old friend. Tuck. Beautiful – castle? House? – very beautiful. Everything perfection. Wood. China. We had – tuck – beautiful.' I said it seemed that beauty and friendship could help him even when other things had left him. 'Yes. I can't go out – driving. Things – round things – money. I don't know it.'

Session 38

He answered the door in his gardening gloves and shouted 'No' when he saw me. Then he looked at my face carefully. I said fine, I would go away and see him next week. The next week he also answered the door in his gardening gloves. 'Gard– gardening,' he said. His face looked more relaxed. I said it looked as if he found gardening more help than seeing me at the moment. 'I am so sorry,' he said with his old politeness. 'I do not want to be rude but I don't want to think any more.' I said he had done a lot of thinking and now he wanted to do the gardening as that helped him now. He smiled. I said I would ring his sons and we would have a last meeting together.

And so, one year after our initial meeting, we all sat again in that drawing-room. Edward Johnson sat holding his father's book. He had no more sentences left. Words came out, sometimes correctly, sometimes not. He looked at the book mainly. I said we were all here together to say goodbye and think about the future. I said Mr Johnson was now clear he would like to stop seeing me and that he found thinking harder and preferred gardening. Edward Johnson nodded. We discussed again what might happen in the future, when the time came that the home help would not be adequate to the task. We also discussed other local services. I said I would be happy to come again at any time in the future if Mr Johnson would like to see me or if his family would. Edward Johnson picked up a biscuit and crumbled it over his trousers. 'Father,' said Peter with embarrassment. Edward Johnson smiled inanely and touched the biscuit crumbs happily. We said goodbye.

As I left I found myself thinking of a lecture Jonathan Miller gave at the Tavistock Clinic in 1987. He spoke of the way some smiling could be the body apologizing for its stupidity, its dementia. I also thought of the infantile pleasure Edward Johnson could allow himself under the umbrella of dementia and paradoxically, that thought made the ending more bearable. I never heard from him again. Peter Johnson informed me of his father's death one year later. Edward Johnson had died in his own flat, attended by a private nurse. He was holding his father's academic book in one hand and his mother's scarf in the other. He was watching his tree in the garden. 'I don't want to think any more' had been the last complete grammatical sentence I heard from him.

He had held onto thinking, as represented by my presence, as long as he could. According to his sons, therapy allowed him to come to terms with his degeneration, with the unpicking of the fine embroidery that had been his brain. However, once it got to the point of the last unravelling, when he knew mindlessness and death lay ahead, he felt better equipped to go with nature (the tree) and his mother (the scarf) and his father (the book).

5 PRIMARY AND SECONDARY HANDICAP: STEVEN

HEADBANGER

The man kicked the telly right
so he smashed smashed
with his great fists
at the stubborn interference
in his brain
His knuckles grew lumps
his forehead grew bumps
but the picture did not change.
'Birdbrain,' cried his mother
feeding him plaster and flannels
helmets and hugs
She could see
it was an injured eagle
that flickered
in the half light of his eyes
that never would be right
and when he let his eyes
open wide
he kicked the television
to pieces

                              Valerie Sinason

In children or adults with an organic handicap there is genetic, chromosomal or brain injury. This is real, measurable and incurable. However, the defensive use or abuse the individual makes of the primary damage can sometimes be more powerful than the original handicap itself. This distinction between primary and secondary handicap dispenses with an earlier view held in both the USA and UK. An American exponent of this earlier view was E. Doll. In his pioneering paper, 'Counselling parents of severely retarded children' (1953), Doll distinguished between 'true' subnormality and the 'pseudo-mentally-deficient' whose intelligence is blocked by background and emotions. At first this theory represented an important recognition of psychogenic factors but it became prey to simplistic abuse.

If, because of better staffing or institutional life, a handicapped patient progressed, the meaning of the change was denied by the statement that he or she was not really handicapped to begin with. Similarly, the emotional plight of the organically handicapped individual was disregarded with the blanket excuse that the emotional disturbance was part of the handicap. In England, the psychoanalyst and child psychotherapist Frances Tustin became so used to having changes in her autistic patients ascribed to the fact that they could not have been really autistic in the first place that she took the decision to have each patient she took on assessed by a leading psychiatrist first (personal communication, 1989).

A mark of contemporary progress is that we have dispensed with the notion that the 'true' handicapped patient has a condition caused only by brain damage. Researchers (Segal, 1971; Shaffer, 1977) have found that incorrect. Psychiatrist D. Shaffer, for example, found that 'brain-injured non-readers do not appear to differ from non-readers without brain injury . . . most of the effects of brain injury on behaviour appear to be indirect' (p. 202). Although nearly all children with an IQ below 50 have organic brain damage (Crome, 1960) and are more susceptible to psychiatric disorder (Rutter *et al.*, 1970), researchers such as Professor John Corbett (1975) are very aware that the brain damage cannot be the sole causative factor and that the reason for the extra vulnerability is therefore open to question. Roger D. Freeman (1970) points out that emotional disorders in the adolescent with cerebral palsy are frequent but not directly related to brain damage. K. Goldstein (1948), discussing the 'catastrophic rages', the temper outbursts in children with epilepsy often attributed to brain damage, considers they may be due to a number of factors such as over-protection from the usual consequences of bad behaviour, the imposition of painful, unwelcome procedures or excessive and unreasonable environmental pressures.

The difficulties in defining handicap due to organic damage as distinct from secondary handicap are substantial. The WHO, in trying to promote an international consensus on the classification of psychiatric disorders, has devised a system in which disorder on several axes can be recorded. This is known as the Multi-Axial Classification of Child Psychiatric Disorders. Rutter, Shaffer and Shepherd (1975) originally devised five axes, the clinical syndrome, specific developmental delays, intellectual level, medical or organic condition and psychosocial familial situation. Even with this tool, they make it clear that there is no consensus as to the degree of behavioural disturbance that can be expected as part of mental retardation.

In our Workshop at the Tavistock Clinic we have found the IQ to be a useful gauge of the state someone can be in at the time of taking a test. Jon Stokes's (1985) useful definition of handicap as a state in and out of which people move needs to be held in mind for this. Clearly, where someone is profoundly handicapped, the amount of time 'in' a handicapped state is longer, but even so, a quantitative signpost of the extent of the state has its uses. It is worth noting that the only handicapped patient who did not like having an IQ test with my colleague Dr Sheila Bichard was Tomás (Chapter 7), the one patient who could not manage long-term therapy. All the others found it satisfying to be with someone who was undertaking to highlight differences for them.

Among children and adults who are severely or profoundly physically and mentally handicapped, there has been a particularly high level of referrals of males for violence directed against themselves or others. Attacks on the head were the commonest form of violence against the self, posing a question of whether the organic damage left a feeling of physical discomfort within the brain, as well as raising psychodynamic questions as to the nature of the attack. Therapy, in all cases, has unfortunately only been once weekly. This has been partly due to a situation of national handicap. As psychoanalytical psychotherapy with this group is so new there has not been the financial provision for it. When I started this work it was with just two permanent sessions a week (seven hours). Because of the urgency and nature of the referrals I soon found myself adding on another eighteen hours or so of my own time which my Clinic managed occasionally to subsidize partially with research grants. A year ago, the Tavistock Foundation appointed a voluntary appeals co-ordinator, Mrs Jill Walker, who has managed to secure extra funding for mental handicap work. This covers my clinical work for two years. In addition to my own limited time, many of the most handicapped and disturbed patients live at least two hours away from the clinic. Their disturbance is so great that staff consider it worth the time to spare an escort and driver for what ends up being over half a day a week.

With a fifty-minute session, after discussion with the medical consultant concerned, I can think carefully about the meaning of the self-attack and not use restraint. However, staff who are with such clients for eight-hour periods cannot take that attitude or their patients would die. Some can inflict such terrible wounds upon themselves that without restraint death would occur. Obviously, I would not allow actions that could cause severe bodily harm. Nevertheless, for fifty-minute periods it is possible to reflect on the meaning and nature of each blow. I will know from my own countertransference feelings whether the blow was aggressive, hopeful; whether it was to knock something bad out or something good in.

Here is a boy of ten who had organic brain damage in the form of cerebral palsy, one of the most common causes of handicap in the boys who were referred to us. For him, his secondary handicap protected him from the memory of both primary organic damage and environmental difficulty. I was to see him for six years of once-weekly therapy until he was sixteen and moved to an adult hostel too far away for us to continue direct contact.

STEVEN

This boy, whom I shall call Steven, was the second of three children. At the time of his birth, his parents' marriage was already in difficulties owing to the strain caused by the deteriorating physical condition of the oldest daughter, Mary, who was born with a physical handicap. (She has since died.) Depression over the serious illness of the daughter meant that there was little time for Steven and he adapted to this, being seen as a 'perfect quiet' baby. Only a routine clinic visit picked up his cerebral palsy.

When Steven was two, Carole, a healthy daughter, was born. Although there was relief she was normal, the pregnancy had not been consciously planned and the new arrival added to marital strain. Father's unemployment was an extra difficulty. Placed in a daycare nursery so his mother could manage the new baby and the older sibling, Steven displayed aggressive behaviour. By the time his father left home, when he was three, Steven's attacks on himself were so dangerous he was admitted to hospital.

Father had behaved violently to mother prior to their breakup and there was some worry that Steven might have been hurt as well as having witnessed violence. Each time Steven left hospital his attacks on himself recurred. Behaviour therapy helped temporarily but in the end only changed the part of his body he attacked. At six he was admitted to a residential home for severely multiply handicapped children but his violence continued and was so great both to himself through headbanging and to staff through biting that there was fear of what would happen when he was older and stronger.

Further help was sought from a behavioural assessment unit. This was to provide invaluable management help for the residential staff. For example, it was found that being woken up in the morning precipitated a violent state. The behavioural approach was to speak gently so that he would wake up in a slow gradual way. The worker was to keep at a physical distance when waking him. However, although pointers like this lowered the number of violent outbursts, his self-injury was still a cause of great concern.

Steven was finally referred to me when he was ten. The referral letter pointed out that no nearby child guidance clinic wanted to take on such a patient but they could provide an escort and a driver if we could offer him a place. This has been a curiously common situation in the referrals we have received. Whereas parents and workers of other children are usually highly ambivalent about the prospect of therapy, there has been great support for it with this group.

It was agreed that I would make an initial visit to the children's home. The referral letter had mentioned difficult staff shift systems in the short-staffed home and we wondered whether some of Steven's fury was linked to that. However, a visit to the home emphasized the fact that although the shift system was disturbing, it was a caring home that gave the children ample warning of all changes. Steven, it was emphasized, found all changes unbearable, even down to moving into a standing position from a sitting one and vice versa. We agreed that I would meet with Steven for some exploratory sessions.

First meeting

In the waiting room, a slumped, twisted, ferocious-looking boy was jammed between his mother and a key worker. I could not see his face. When I introduced myself his legs went into an amazing forceful action as if they had a life of their own. Realizing I would not be safe on my own with him I asked his mother and worker to bring him to my room and to stay with us. I tried to sound casual, as if that had been my plan all along, but I felt most fearful. I was not only frightened by the violence of this child whose face I had yet to see, my fear had also eroded my professional confidence. I also felt apologetic to the home staff. When the referral letter had mentioned that his violence meant two staff were needed to be with him at all times I had responded disbelievingly. Now I understood.

Steven grunted and screamed all the way to the room but once inside he moved into a foetal position and then said clearly and distinctly the word 'shy'. His voice was low and guttural and there was a slur from his brain damage but there was no mistaking the word. The social worker looked sad and I felt immensely moved. His mother said he had never said the word 'shy' before, she did not even know he knew it. Steven started ferociously banging his head. The sound really hurt but I restrained his mother from moving to hold his hands.

I started talking, saying how he had said he was 'shy' and that wasn't surprising as I was a stranger to him. He didn't know me. His fist stopped in mid-air. I carried on speaking, saying he was telling all of us that he knew his mum and key worker and all the people at the children's home. He was used to seeing lots of people. But he didn't know me. His hand flopped onto his lap and I was then at peace, knowing that meaning was there and I was at work.

I then explained why he was coming, how people were worrying about him hurting his head and how they felt he was sad. I explained he would come to this room a few times and that there were toys on the table. The moment I mentioned toys he ferociously banged his head. When I said he was worried at being in this new room with toys he stopped banging. Other features of this first session were that he banged his head whenever there was a sound from outside the room. Alternatively, he would curl up and close his eyes like a baby. When I said there were five minutes left he moved the vestigial fingers of his deformed hand and hid them under his head. I wondered aloud whether he was showing me his struggling handicapped hand now it was time to go and maybe there was a struggle with the Steven who had powerful legs and could run and a handicapped Steven. When it was time to stop he kicked the table at me with great force.

Second meeting

At the second meeting, again with his mother and worker present, he screamed and banged all the way to the room but was quiet on sitting down. He did not utter a word, but fell asleep, only to stir to bang his head whenever the wind blew or there were footsteps. At one time when there was a loud noise he fell into a newborn falling reflex. This is the involuntary survival response a tiny baby instinctively demonstrates when startled. I wondered here whether the tiredness was because of all the energy that went into maintaining an unborn state where no other life existed.

Third and fourth sessions

It took me until the third session to tell Steven I did not feel ready to see him on my own until I felt I could protect him and me from his violence. I thought we must be connecting more for him to allow me to have that thought and utter it and for him not to bang his head when I said it. Fifteen minutes before the end of the session he fell asleep. I was taken by surprise by my own difficulty in saying aloud that I did not feel safe. I learned a lot from this experience. When I have seen any violent patient since I have always commented on why we are not going to meet on our own. As professionals who pride ourselves on understanding the meaning of violence we can rather stupidly at times consider that means we do not need to fear it. At a meeting in Leeds, with Yorkshire psychologists in mental handicap who work psychodynamically, to look specifically at issues involved in treating violent patients with handicaps, Dr Nigel Beaill, Mrs Pat Frankish and I all agreed that fear in the therapist was a major anti-therapeutic factor and could in fact drive a patient even madder with fear.

During the fourth session a major change happened. For the first time, with his head twisted away from me, Steven held up both his hands to show me not just the difference between his handicapped and non-handicapped hand, but also the secondary handicap he had inflicted by his own banging. He held up that hand in a way that only I could see it. There was a huge swelling on each knuckle with a red bruise at the tip of each. I was aware of the thought that he had made two breasts, that maybe he was attacking his mother in fury at the handicapped body he had been endowed with, but also adding to his body at the same time. I did not feel I could make such a comment in front of his mother and worker. As that was the first private thought I'd had I felt the time must therefore be right for me to see him on his own. What I said was that he was showing me how angry he was about being handicapped and that when he banged his head he also made his knuckles larger. I then said, feeling terrified and daring, that I would see him on his own the next week but his mother and worker would bring and collect him. As usual he fell asleep fifteen minutes before the end of the session.

Fifth session: on his own

The fifth session was the first on his own. It was crucial as it would determine whether therapy was possible. After the usual banging and kicking he was put on the chair by his mother and worker, who then left quickly, looking relieved and apprehensive at the same time. Steven was in his usual foetal position. It was only in this session that I became aware that he always curled up with the normal side of his face showing and his handicapped side hidden. I looked sadly at the dark brown curls of his hair on the 'normal' side of his face. Gritting my teeth, I wondered this aloud. For a moment I sat in terror. To my amazement he suddenly sat up bolt upright and faced me. He looked proud and furious. I felt overwhelmed. A ten-year-old boy with brown curly hair and dark brown eyes gazed intently at me. The effect of the brain damage was, of course, noticeable, but nowhere as noticeable or grotesque as his twisted posture had somehow indicated.

The feelings he evoked in me at that moment made me realize that the twisted postures he took up were a terrible self-made caricature of his original handicap, so he could not be seen as he truly was. I was filled with images from subnormality hospitals and all the twisted movements and guttural speaking which I had previously taken as inevitable consequences of retardation. I found myself wondering about that. I said he was now able to show me how he really was and that he was less handicapped than he made himself look, perhaps as protection. Steven fell asleep at his usual time fifteen minutes before the end of the session and this time I was able to comment to him that he knew the time was coming to an end and he wanted to be asleep.

He would spit quietly and wake up when I spoke. I was also struck again by the unborn state he seemed to remain in where living tired him so enormously. The home staff said he spent long hours sleeping as well as catnapping. Right at the end I asked him if he wanted to continue seeing me. There was no reply. I asked him to raise a finger if he wanted to carry on seeing me. He raised a finger and he continued coming for six years with only two absences for colds, both on the last session before a holiday.

The next three months

Once long-term therapy for Steven was agreed on I arranged a meeting with the head of his residential home, his key worker and his mother. In this meeting his mother was able to make clear that although she was willing to travel with Steven for his therapy she would in no way manage his living at home with her. In addition to the work she had looking after her two daughters, one of whom required constant attention when she was at home, she was, not surprisingly, frightened of Steven and his violence. 'If he was the only child I had I still couldn't manage him.'

There was a big change in Steven over the next few weeks. In the waiting room he could be seen sitting upright or standing hugging his mother. Several therapists told me their patients were mentioning this boy in the waiting room who used to look terrible but was really nice looking. The home commented he was calm for the rest of the day after coming to see me and for the next day. We agreed that the next important stage would be for me to take him to and from the therapy room. After two months I did this, feeling extremely frightened the first time. However, he managed then and ever after apart from a regression following the death of his sister. The triumph Steven and I felt at our both managing the fear of his violence was visible in the proud way he hugged his mother and worker on his arrival back after going it alone with me. His mother even said, 'Well done, you brave boy.'

The changes that came in the next three months (after which we decided to continue therapy indefinitely) were at one level slow and yet they were immensely exciting and moving. My own affective responses were a mixture of hope and terror. The changes chart gradual movements towards closeness. Here are some examples:

Session 10: He says 'hello' and I can understand despite his speech defect.

Session 11: He asks, 'Time yet?' just before the end of the session. He already has an accurate internal clock. Also, he looks briefly at the toys. (He has not touched them yet.)

Session 12: He says his longest sentence as we walk back to the waiting room together. 'Hello, did you see my mum?'

Session 13: He looks at the toys all the time.

Session 14: His nose runs and he looks desperately at the box of tissues on the table. He cannot bear to reach for it. I offer him one. He says 'No, thank you' slowly.

Session 15: He kicks the toy bag over in order to see the toys. I comment that the table is too far away for him to be able to reach it without walking. I had moved it after our first session as a protection against his violence but now felt ready to manage.

Session 16: I move the table nearer him. He kicks the toy bag accurately so the toys fall over right near him and he can see them carefully without touching them.

Giving up self-injury

The next major change was after one year of once-weekly therapy. I was suddenly aware that when Steven banged his head he was making enormous spitting noises and sound effects but in fact he was miming banging his head. When I said he was not hurting his thoughts so much and he was thinking more about what I said, he lifted his hand to show me the bumps had subsided. I told the home staff about my observation and they then realized it was true in their environment too.

It is important to mention that I had been in a fortunate position with regard to Steven's self-injury. For fifty minutes it was tolerable for me to not restrain his self-attacks unless I felt he could knock himself out. My aim had been to understand the meaning of the different bangs. However, for the residential staff who were with him all day it was another matter. Had he been allowed to continue unhampered there was no doubt that he would have died. I therefore suggest to staff who want to think dynamically about self-injury that they find a five- or ten-minute regular observation point in the week in which they can observe without needing to restrain movement, to make room for thought when otherwise they have to take action.

In the absence of painful circumstances, such as staff leaving or shift changes, Steven's headbanging stopped except for one occasion. I was surprised to see him one week with the old familiar red swelling on his forehead. He looked embarrassed and covered it up. I could not understand the meaning of it. His key worker later embarrassedly explained to me that a staff member had kicked the television when it was not working. Steven had apparently watched this very quietly. The kick knocked the television into correct action and Steven started knocking at the interference in his own brain. I felt like laughing and crying.

I was unable to write up the session until I had written the poem that prefaces this chapter. A similar process took place in my work with Mr Johnson (Chapter 4) where a poem linked together some of the emotions I was experiencing, allowing me then to recall the session.

'Old MacDonald': the second year

After one and a half years Steven stopped falling asleep during sessions and I realized how sleeping must have been a protection for all the exhaustion he felt at being in the world, trying to control all the noises and actions around him. When I gave a comment he did not like he would mime a headbang and then mime sleeping and then open his eyes and say 'shut up', one of the few phrases he ever said to me. He was losing his secondary handicaps, his defences against meaning, and he felt very mixed and exposed about it.

It was at this point that he suddenly burst into a terrible caricature of handicapped singing of 'Old MacDonald had a farm' – or rather, I was only at that moment aware that it must be a caricature. He was singing in the guttural voice I had often felt was intrinsically linked with handicap, just as I had felt previously the twisted postures were. But there was something in the meaning he was conveying that made me say, with trepidation, that maybe he felt there was room here for the animal noises and feelings in him; but maybe too he wanted to see if I was an idiot who thought that was his real singing voice. He looked at me in a startled but proud way. I sat bracing myself, ready for a blow or some catastrophe. He whispered 'Old MacDonald had a farm' in a normal voice that conveyed just a slight slur of brain damage, and then started to cry terribly and deeply.

This pitiful crying was a strong feature for the next six months and it is difficult to put into words. It is not crying that is asking for a word or a hug. It is a weeping to do with a terrible sense of aloneness and the reality of that. Neville Symington has commented (personal communication, 1984) that weeping comes when there is a breakthrough with this kind of patient and represents a real awareness of all the meaning that has been lost in the years up to that moment as well as the aloneness of handicap. His mother and worker were very distressed to see the weeping state Steven was in. They were worried therapy might be too cruel for him. I felt worried at the pain he was in and when he desperately wept 'See Mummy, go now' on one occasion I was in a dilemma. I said that he was able to stand up and leave the room and I could help him but I thought too that he needed to know I could bear his distress. It took the combined strength of myself and Steven's drive for truth to keep him in the room at this stage.

I needed the support of my own personal psychoanalysis and the Workshop to manage emotionally and deal with the ethical issue that Shirley Hoxter (1986, p. 87) has put so succinctly with regard to physically ill and disabled children: 'we find that our methods of psychotherapy are requiring the child to confront and assimilate something which, thankfully, is far beyond that which most of us have had to experience . . . Sometimes we will ask ourselves whether it is not better to let well alone, to let these children remain in their states of non-integration, utilising the merciful defences of repression, denial or splitting, or even being excessively withdrawn, half-alive rather than painfully alive. The pains of integration may be worthwhile when they lead to "ordinary human unhappiness" but we feel guilty and cruel if integration seems only to offer the sufferance of suffering.'

However, I believe that truth is worth pain. Steven was emotionally able to move through this state and the crying stopped. It was heralded by a session in which, when I said it was time, Steven reached in his pocket and threw a toy watch at me. There was a lot of anger and accuracy in his throw but I was delighted. It was a toy he had brought from his children's home, not one of the therapy toys provided, nor could it exactly be seen as a symbolic use of time. Time was flying! And it was flying at me! But I had borne his weeping and loneliness and so had he and he also trusted that I could survive his anger.

After this, the crying stopped and Steven became more affectionate and responsive. He stopped injuring himself. However, he was still violent to staff and was more dangerous. Previously he just had to be sat in a chair and he would fall asleep; now he would stand up again immediately and attack as he did not mind physical changes so much! He was no longer startled by external noises and slept the ordinary amount for a boy of his age.

This has been a regular pattern in long-term treatment with self-injuring, severely handicapped boys. It requires discussion with the key staff or families concerned because it does not feel like an improvement to them. One father commented, at a similar stage of therapy, 'You've turned my son from a violent sleeping zombie to a violent mobile psychopath!'

After two years of therapy there was a session in which, in the silence, my stomach gurgled loudly. 'Your tummy?' he asked. I said yes, it was my tummy. He giggled. I said he knew the sound was inside my tummy. He nodded. It started raining. 'Rain outside,' he commented. There was a startled pause. A telephone rang next door. Steven put a hand to his ear. 'Outside the room,' he pronounced. From that moment there was an extra degree of hope and aliveness in the session. Steven had differentiated between inside and outside and had achieved a 'psychological birth' (Mahler et al., 1975).

Shortly after this I bought a soft toy, a bear, for the therapy room as Steven always gave me a Christmas card with a bear on it and because he had not touched the other toys. On the first occasion that he saw it, having been told several weeks in advance of its arrival, he held it to him and hugged it with his back to me, not uttering a single word or sound the whole session. He has never managed to touch it since, only to look at it wistfully.

When I commented on his fear of getting close to me, to the bear and the toys, his fear that he will be violent, he said 'stupid'. He knows the meaning of the word 'stupid' because he knows that is not what he really is. After this he started whispering to the blanket, the chair and the bear, so softly I could not hear. It felt as if he had managed to make a move to the bear and have a first embryonic transitional object (see Glossary, p. 327). From that first tentative link there was a transitional talking space he had made. At the home the staff commented that he spent a lot of time talking to all the objects in his room. He was then able to spend an hour on his own with his mother each week but his violence continued to be a problem with staff needing stitches for bites and treatment for violent kicks.

After he had been in therapy for three years his home sent a report, stating, 'Since his visits to the Tavistock, staff have noticed progress in his development. He is sometimes able to warn of his aggression and is now guilty for some of the hurt he causes. He has started to say who he will miss and asks questions about staff who leave. He has been able to get closer to his mother and sisters when he goes home for hour-long visits at the weekend. However, although he shows he can develop through understanding, his violence can be so great it is difficult to restrain him. He is 13 now and there is concern for how to manage him when he is older and stronger.'

The third year: bereavement

At this point, when Steven had been in therapy for three years, his oldest sister Mary had an acute deterioration in her condition. She had no use of her legs or arms and it became clear she was dying. There was a temporary return of his headbanging and staff reported he had kicked the television as well as a new worker. Carole also was showing signs of emotional disturbance at school.

Curiously, I found myself re-examining the poem I had written. Why had I ended the poem with the television being kicked? I was clearly frightened that when faced brutally and clearly and irrevocably with the incurable nature of his primary handicap he would not stand it and would explode. The deterioration of his sister from an incurable physical illness and disability clearly carried his pain at his own condition too.

Although he had cerebral palsy, he did not have too severe a form and was able to walk. I found myself thinking of his strong kicking legs and his sister's dying ineffectual ones for several sessions. It took a while for me to understand my thoughts. We had been so preoccupied with Steven's handicaps, his defences, his fears of speaking that his position as a sibling had been buried. At the next session Steven came in and curled up very quietly. Suddenly his left leg reached out to kick the table. It was not an aggressive act. It was as if he was wanting to show me a problem he had about why his legs could work like that when his sister's legs could not. I faced a difficult technical dilemma. Bringing in outside information could be intrusive and anti-therapeutic. However, with some handicapped patients who cannot think or speak easily I have considered it important to be the voice of these events when I think they are playing a major part in my countertransference feelings.

I said maybe it felt strange being a Steven with legs who had an older sister whose legs did not work. Steven went rigid with attention. I said he was reminding me of what a quiet baby he was when his parents were so busy with Mary and how angry that might have made him. Maybe sometimes he felt he had to sit very quietly so he wouldn't know his legs did work and then he would not be so cross with his parents, Mary and Carole.

He slowly stretched out his legs alternately. I said he was checking each of them to see they were still there and they were working. He could stretch his legs and walk and Mary couldn't, but then again, Mary did not bang her head or have a hard time getting words to come out and Carole did not have either of those problems. He looked at me alively but then banged his head.

I said he could hear my words and think about them for a bit but then they could hurt. He stopped banging and was very still. The week after, Mary died. Mother did not want the word 'death' mentioned to Steven and she did not want him to come to the funeral. She felt she had enough to cope with looking after herself and Carole. This is a regular problem in mental handicap. Sometimes the parent projects his or her own inability to manage into the handicapped member of the family, who is then denied access to something, such as the funeral in this case, so that the rest of the family can manage. I am not here, of course, talking about the mentally handicapped who are also mentally ill and whose particular behaviour would make an undertaking such as the funeral too difficult.

However, mother did not want to speak to anyone about this further tragedy in her life. The residential staff did not know what to do as they were sure Steven understood and would be in a worse state if the knowledge was withheld. Steven eventually solved their problem for them by staring avidly at a soap opera on television in which a baby died. 'Baby dead. Mary dead,' he said. After he showed he knew what had happened mother allowed the residential staff to take him to the cemetery.

A terrible period of headbanging followed. And then suddenly he became quiet in the sessions. He would come in, curl up on the armchair and hide his face in his arms or under a blanket. He did not utter a word or sound. For several weeks I interpreted the different shades of silence.

Then there was a change. At a certain moment I lost concentration on Steven. My mind had in fact gone to the shopping I needed to do before I got home later that day. For a moment I wanted to edit out cosmetically that moment of unprofessional deviation. But, of course, thinking about it was crucial. I realized that Steven was being as good as dead precisely so I could think about shopping lists, or indeed anything except him. I wondered aloud whether he was being so silent, as if he were dead, so that he would not be a burden to me. Perhaps he worried I too had a dead Mary daughter and would be angry he was alive instead of her. There was a riveting silence and then he burst into floods of tears. Unlike the lonely devastating weeping of two years ago, this was a mourning for the loss of someone else, not the loss of his own abilities.

When he then cried, 'Mum, now, please,' I interpreted it was not just Mum in the waiting room he was calling for but a longed for Mum-in-the-room who might be so upset about a dead Mary and a furious husband leaving home that she just wanted a good quiet dead baby Steven. At the end of the session Steven held his hand for me to hold. He had never done that before. As I reached for it he looked at the untouched toy bear and then said 'Arm hurts' and cried. He kicked the toy mother and father dolls lying on the floor from his earlier throw. It had taken three years to move through the secondary handicap to the trauma of the organic handicap, his hurt arm, and his family life. The hurt arm seemed to be symbolic both of the organic primary handicap that had affected his arm, the couple who had created him (see Chapter 10) and the traumatic violence of his early home life.

Fourth year: anniversary repetition

The next year was taken up with his mourning processes for Mary. Unlike his first three years of therapy, where he only had one minor cold, Steven now had severe chest and throat infections. Moving into greater humanness also seemed to make him more vulnerable to infection. The work was all connected with his guilt at being alive.

Having a handicapped sibling is painful for everyone. A child wants to beat his brother or sister in a fair fight and prove he is the favourite, the one who is really the parents' best child. Where a sibling is handicapped there has been a terrible triumph. Where the sibling dies the pain and guilt are even stronger (Judd, 1989). I was concerned for Carole and mother too at this point but mother did not wish for any family work.

For the next six months Steven was largely silent and still. In his children's home he was increasingly violent again. Around this time I decided I needed some extra supervision to help me understand why therapy was not progressing. I went to see psychoanalyst Dr Susannah Isaacs-Elmhirst (now vice-chair of the British Psycho-Analytical Society), who had been a consultant of the Child Guidance Training Centre at the Tavistock Centre. She had heard my first assessment meetings with Steven over four years ago. After hearing the description of his pale face and increased violence she wondered when the anniversary of Mary's death was. To my shock, I discovered it was only one week away.

Ready to make amends on the next session, I was extremely worried when Steven did not arrive on time. After twenty-five minutes I phoned the home to hear the car had arrived for him on time so there must be a traffic jam. Steven arrived with only ten minutes of his session left. I could hear him screaming and banging along the corridor and flinched. When I went to meet them his worker said there had been a terrible traffic jam and Steven was in a terrible mood; I might not be safe on my own with him. I said I would persevere.

Steven looked appalling. He was extremely white and his face had broken out in spots. His forehead was red and swollen again from his renewed headbanging. 'Poor Steven,' I said. 'How awful having such a big traffic jam today.' He shouted 'No!' and started spitting but I felt safe. Inside my room his worker thrust him into a kneeling position on the floor, trying to stop his headbanging. I said they should go.

Steven looked intently at me while banging his head. The sound of flesh hitting bone and flesh hurt particularly today and I wondered if that was because of Mary's painful death. I said he had felt terrible the last few weeks and only now did I realize why. Tomorrow would be the first anniversary of Mary's death. There was a riveting pause. For a moment I feared Steven would throw himself at me to attack me.

However, he carefully lifted himself so he could sit down as usual and continued to stare at me hungrily, his eyes not leaving mine for a moment. I said perhaps he had felt frightened the traffic was bad today; perhaps he was worried I might be cross he was late and then I would say, 'Why is Steven coming when Mary is dead?' Maybe he felt very bad about Mary dying when he would not die from cerebral palsy. He could hurt his head badly when he banged it and he could get bad colds, especially when he was miserable, but he would not die from it.

Steven continued to fix his eyes on mine. I said he was really looking at me today, keeping my face in sight and letting me see his eyes and face as if he especially needed to see me when I was talking about things like this. He made a sound – 'Errr'. Silence. He relaxed again and continued looking at me. I said there was a sound inside him that had wanted to come out into a word but it had not managed to. I wondered what he would want to say if he could speak.

There was a long companiable silence. I found myself recounting our joint history to Steven; how he had been ten when he first came and now he was over fourteen. How his little sister was twelve and she was two years younger than he, and how Mary had been two years older, and how in just one year he would be the age Mary had been when she died. I said perhaps his colds were his way of seeing if he ought to die to be like Mary and die at fifteen as she had done.

A couple of minutes before the end of time two workers urgently knocked on the door and came in before waiting for a reply. They were clearly expecting they would have to rescue me and were surprised to see a thoughtful peaceful Steven sitting down. When his mother came in I told them all about the anniversary of Mary's death and they, like me prior to my supervision, had all obliterated it. Since then, I have been most careful about remembering birthdays and anniversaries.

The end of therapy

For the next two years Steven faced different external difficulties. There were many staff changes and finally his home was closed, and with only two weeks' warning he was moved to another placement. That was too far away to accommodate weekly therapy, although I remained in telephone contact. After six years in therapy Steven could warn staff when he was feeling violent, could maintain relationships and ask about changes in the staff shifts. With me, right to the last session, he was largely mute. At each new blow the environment offers he returns to banging his head but stops once the situation changes. I feel he will always find life a painful experience but he is now able to gain more from his surroundings.

Summary

With Steven and Ali (see Chapter 6), had I stopped therapy after two years I would have had a far more optimistic view of what therapy could provide. Long-term work that takes in the ups and downs, especially the downs, of institutional or traumatized lives throws the individual back on her depleted resources time and time again. I came to understand that Steven would always be vulnerable to banging his head when things were bad, just as 'normal' people can return to drink, cigarettes, reading rubbish, overeating, getting headaches or catching colds when difficult circumstances arrive.

Steven's mother speaks to him loudly and affectionately and

slowly. He speaks to her, outside the therapy room, in a fast but stereotyped way. 'All right?' he will ask her, as she often asks him. As I describe in Chapter 6, I think that question carries a knowledge that the speaker himself is not all right but the listener will not bear this and will need to be appeased for being in the presence of a handicapped child. Steven's mother would ask me 'Is he all right?'

Steven was not spoken of as an individual but as a shadowy representation of the not-properly-mourned healthy twin of himself he should have been. When I commented on how he had grown after the last holidays his mother sadly said, 'Yes. He would have been so tall.' Her real speech was for the other Steven, the healthy one who never lived or died and has not been put to rest. The perpetual not-being-addressed is, I feel, a repetition of earlier non-reciprocal experiences; of being born in difficulties at the wrong time. Maud Mannoni (1967) sees in this indirect talking both the murder wish of the parent and/or the unconscious desire that the child stay ill, as I describe further in Chapter 6. If Steven continues to use words and to experience his feelings, and to make closer relationships instead of acting them out, the issue will arise of whether he can be placed with his mother. His mother does not want him. Slowly he moves to face that old, yet new, trauma.

When Neville Symington's patient Harry (1981) was able to show and acknowledge his greater internal intelligence he cried, 'I am capable of more than everyone thinks I am, but there is tomorrow and Sunday and Monday.' This means that Harry felt not just the strain of holding up the new experience of integration and intelligence without attacking it for a few days, but, I think, the meaning of the future without handicap as a defence. The fear of the murder wish of the parent has to be faced and goes back even to prenatal experience.

Many severely and profoundly handicapped patients curl up in foetal positions when they sleep. Steven, in the early stages of therapy, slept for several hours in the day as well as at night-time, as if sleep were the only time of peace for him. Pierce Clark (1933) felt that excessive sleeping and foetal postures of handicapped patients represented a return to the foetal stage to avoid the damage of handicap that would come. Neville Symington (1981) added that the patient's fantasy that he had been injured in the womb (via the creation of his handicap) was possibly based on reality. Winnicott (1949) certainly considered *in utero* experiences to be significant as well as the trauma of birth itself. He considered that birth trauma due to brain changes or the anaesthetic administered to the mother was highly significant. Steven moved from his foetal sleeping and curled-up position. He was able to face the injury his birth provided and go out into a noisy world filled with siblings and other people. That was a major remarkable step he was able to make.

Steven was born to depressed parents. He witnessed and possibly experienced extreme violence as a toddler and from the age of four lived apart from his family. His IQ is in the severe range (40) and his adverse family circumstances are handicapping quite apart from his brain damage. Steven exhausted and deadened himself, translating longings and communications into silence or blows to his head, the seat of his thoughts, to cushion his terribly impinged-upon world. He would also try to manage the helplessness inherent in trauma (Winnicott, 1949) by his violent attacks on those about him.

The American psychoanalyst Goldschmidt (1986) expresses most succinctly the stage that has to be passed through first after trauma, and the stage Steven was in when I last saw him. I am thinking of the way he would say 'Hello' or 'Time to go' quite clearly *after* his session had ended. Talking of a traumatized patient, Goldschmidt states, 'His great helplessness was something he could only show me at the end of his session – more precisely after the end, so I could no longer talk to him about it. It was as if he experienced therapy or myself as an electric cable with which on the one hand he did indeed want to come into contact in order to be brought alive but which he on the other hand must not really touch as it might kill him.'

An opportunist aspect to this defence against a terrible memory was Steven's physical appearance, handicapped smile, posture and speech. In banging his thoughts he was also allowing all means of communication to deteriorate. Where there is trauma underlying opportunist handicap, that needs to be addressed carefully. Goldschmidt (1986) writes, 'the patient must re-experience the traumatic situation bit by bit but in the presence of an object which assumes the function of a shield against stimuli.' He quotes Hayman (1957) on the need for a protecting figure. For Steven, maintaining a physical distance from him during the first few months meant I was protecting him and myself from his violence.

Steven is not alone. The Spastics Society estimate that there are 13,000 such children and adults who exhibit what is called 'challenging behaviour'. There is little treatment available of any kind. This presents an intolerable burden for parents. The Spastics Society had been given a five-million-pound donation from Asil Nadir, the owner of Polly Peck International. Although the subsequent economic problems of Asil Nadir have resulted in the disbanding of this project, it deserves attention. The aim was to open an international centre to treat fourteen young men with this problem. The Oak Tree Project, as it was named, was to pioneer a multidisciplinary assessment and treatment programme that included psychodynamic psychotherapy and behavioural therapy. A survey of 97 health and social service departments last year, carried out by the Spastics Society, identified 2,797 people between the ages of fourteen and twenty-five with mental handicap and severe challenging behaviour.

Whilst it is known that handicapped children are over-represented in child physical abuse cases (Friedrich and Boriskin, 1976), there is a question as to whether this is due to lack of attachment and bonding at the start (Blacher and Meyers, 1983) or lack of resources and support to manage children with severe behavioural and emotional difficulties coinciding with their handicap. Robin Balbernie, a child psychotherapist in Poole, worked with one mildly handicapped boy who banged his head. He found (1985) that the headbanging was a repetition of the physical attack made on him when he was little.

Steven's difficulty in speaking and his years of silence with me become easier to understand when we consider Maud Mannoni's comment (1967): 'When we are dealing with a child caught in the death-wishes of his parents it is their words first of all which must be unravelled.' Steven with his first gift of the word 'shy' was making sure his words were attended to. In considering the meaning of words in the relationship between the retarded patient and the therapist as connected with a gift, Mannoni adds, 'We have given back to himself the child walled in by terror and petrified in non-communication so that in his turn he may belong to the world.'

(p. 224) Sometimes I felt that Steven did not speak to me because he so concretely experienced his new good words as gifts that he wanted to keep them for his mother and feared using them up.

Steven yearned for contact although it felt killing, and spoke into a transitional space words that I couldn't properly hear. As Canetti says in *The Human Province* (1985) 'sometimes one says one's best and most important things to just anybody. One need not be ashamed for one does not always speak to ears. The words want to be said just in order to exist.' But in Steven's case the wish for words to exist had only developed through the satisfaction obtained from being with a therapist who could bear the meaning of non-verbal as well as occasional verbal communication. To speak directly to ears, to the healthy, seeing, hearing witness of emotional, sexual or organic violation, is to face not only all the secondary and opportunist handicaps that have followed, but the event itself and the lack of protection from the parent. Also, there is the injunction from the parent to not know (Bowlby, 1979). In addition to the widespread early fear of mother as life-giver and death-dealer there is an extra traumatic ingredient if there is a real wish, verbalized or not, for a handicapped child to die.

I. Markova and colleagues (1984), psychology researchers at Stirling University, Scotland, were surprised by their research findings that although children with haemophilia were less proficient, took less care and were more excited when handling sharp tools than the control children, their mothers did not correct their children when they used a knife incompetently and carelessly. I wonder whether the mothers were possibly unconsciously conveying death wishes by their lack of protection. It is, of course, equally possible their actions were a counterphobic mechanism to avoid being over-protective.

Even more deeply, the defence against trauma that is built up over the years is an elaborate psychotic solution. Using the obliteration of the mind, cutting off the sight or hearing, sleeping or becoming a robot, spending a vegetable life in subnormality hospitals is not a sane solution. It does not work. Thoughts would reawaken no matter how much Steven tried to beat them out of his head. The ghost of meaning still haunted him.

Steven, and other handicapped children and adults, are in some aspects of themselves stupefied, numbed with grief. But they can only so precisely know the meaning of the word 'stupid', follow its laws of speech and facial expression, and cut off eyes and ears, feelings and thinking, if somewhere else they are not stupid. In Pasteur's profound death-bed words, 'Bernard is right. The pathogen is nothing; the terrain is everything.'

6 THE HANDICAPPED SMILE: ALI'S DEFENCE AGAINST TRAUMA

> But that I am forbid
> To tell the secrets of my prison-house,
> I could a tale unfold whose lightest word
> Would harrow up thy soul . . .
>
> Shakespeare, *Hamlet I.v.13–16*

> What are the causal conditions, internal and external to the personality, that activate the shutting off process . . . ?
>
> John Bowlby, 'On knowing what you are not supposed to know and feeling what you are not supposed to feel'

Sylvia Fraser, a distinguished Canadian novelist, struggled to understand why there was violent sexuality in her successful novels. Then slowly she came in contact with another self, the young child and adolescent who was regularly sexually abused by her father. Slowly and painfully more childhood memories were returned to her. In *My Father's House* (1987, p. 252) she writes that as a child she had survived only by forgetting but as an adult 'the amnesia became a problem as large as the one it was meant to conceal'. When she first recovered her memory she recaptured the catastrophic moment of an abyss of helplessness. 'Thus I unscrew my head from my body as if it were the lid of a pickle jar. From then on I would have two selves – the child who knows, with guilty body possessed by daddy, and the child who dares not know any longer, with innocent head attuned to mommy' (p. 221). This psychic split enabled her to survive but incurred a great price, for memory, knowledge and feeling are lost to the innocent Sylvia whilst sexual knowledge, memory, guilt and triumph are given to the abused Sylvia, the self she calls 'the child who knows'.

Something of Sylvia Fraser's own constitutional gifts – gifts that allow her authentically to subtitle her book 'A memoir of incest and of healing' – protected her from further intellectual handicapping. However, for less well-endowed children, learning difficulties are a regular feature of sexual abuse as well as physical abuse (Bentovim, 1987). This is not surprising. For if surviving means cutting your head off, your intellect is destroyed. If knowing and seeing involve knowing and seeing terrible things, it is not surprising that not-knowing, becoming stupid, becomes a defence. However, it is a mad defence as it takes away the possibility of communication and gaining help or understanding.

Maria (Sinason, 1988b) was a five-year-old girl with learning difficulties. Once she was able to express more of her experience of abuse, more of her intelligence returned to her. In one session (p. 104) she tore the head off the father doll. 'Stupid daddy, I've thrown his head away. Now he is only a body. He can't see, hear or know. He doesn't know what I am doing to him because he has no mind.' She threw him across the room and laughed angrily and then did the same with the mother doll. She wanted me and her parents to know what she had felt like, deprived of her head, her sight, her intellect. Maria, however, was not mentally handicapped. It was easy to see that her learning difficulties had an emotional base.

However, my own clinical work and that of colleagues has clarified instances where mental handicap is actually caused by abuse. Sometimes, trauma evokes handicap as a defence against the memory of physical or sexual abuse. A. Buchanan and J. Oliver (1977) also point to abuse and neglect as an actual *cause* of mental retardation in certain cases. Recent American research (Cohen and Warren, 1987) also links abuse with acquired disability.

Pioneering researcher J. Oliver (1988) in fact coined the term VIMH, violence-induced mental handicap, concluding that 'ill treatment in the home accounts for such conditions [mental handicap] in 5 per cent or more of all handicapped people.' Caroline Okell Jones (personal communication, 1986), when she convened the Tavistock Child Sexual Abuse Workshop, reported an increase in referrals of abused handicapped patients. Sheila

Bichard and I, as part of our research project, have found that 70 per cent of all handicapped children referred to us have been abused or that abuse is suspected. Forty per cent of all handicapped adults referred to us have been abused. Other workers have looked at the way handicapped children are over-represented in physical abuse cases (Friedrich and Boriskin 1976; Ammerman *et al.*, 1988; Morgan, 1987) and have asked whether lack of attachment at the start of life could have a substantial negative impact.

Although these figures are new, the knowledge is not. For example, since the birth of psychoanalysis the link between trauma and handicap has been regularly examined. Pierce Clark (1933) discussed the defensive response to trauma, aided by Freud's definition of trauma (1920, p. 29) as 'any excitations from outside which are powerful enough to break through the protective shield . . . Such an event, as an external trauma, is bound to provoke a disturbance on a large scale in the function of the organism's energy and to set in motion every possible defensive measure.'

If we add to this the extra vulnerability of the baby and young child the impact of trauma becomes even more serious. As the early pioneering psychoanalyst Sándor Ferenczi so beautifully put it (1928, p. 65): 'In the early states of embryonic development a slight wound, the mere prick of a pin, cannot only cause severe alterations in, but may completely prevent the development of whole limbs of the body. Just as, if you have only one candle in a room and put your hand near the candle, half the room may become darkened, so if, near the beginning of life, you do only a little harm to a child, it may cast a shadow over its whole life.'

It is not just physical, sexual and emotional abuse that create trauma. As I mentioned in Chapter 1, the Office of Health Economics paper on mental handicap (1973, p. 13) describes mental ability as the product of three factors, 'inherited constitution, modification or injuries caused by pre- or postnatal injury or disease and conditioning and training of the intellect'. The environment itself can be traumatogenic. Child psychiatrist Michael Rutter (Rutter *et al.*, 1970) shows us that poverty, psychiatric illness, unemployment and large numbers of siblings are relevant to mild mental handicap. In fact, although chromosomal abnormality or brain damage is spread evenly across the social classes, mild mental handicap is largely located in social class V. Guy's Hospital consultant psychiatrist Nick Bouras and colleagues (1988), looking at the family background of their mentally handicapped patients, found that although only 9 per cent had a family history of handicap, 26.2 per cent had a history of family psychiatric disorders. It is not surprising that disadvantageous external circumstances should make it harder for the individual to develop or show his/her intelligence. Even with brain damage, some forms of birth injury are more common to the most deprived groups (Shaffer, 1977). For adverse external circumstances can strip whatever internal resources there might be.

Daniel Defoe (1711) understood this clearly over two hundred and fifty years ago when he emphasized that 'the man is not rich because he is honest, but he is honest because he is rich', – or even more clearly – 'Give me not poverty lest I steal.' Only the man who keeps his resources despite adversity can truly know his makeup. Confucius understood that process even further back in time when he said in his *Analects*, 'It is more difficult not to complain of injustice when poor than not to behave with arrogance when rich' (trans. D. Lau, 1986, p. 125).

When outer circumstances fail to adapt to the individual's needs or are actively oppressive, it requires exceptional gifts not to remain in a state of chronic bitterness, impotent compliance, or fake cheerfulness. Tragically, the latter way of accommodating internalized oppression is all too often encouraged and rewarded a sign of genuine good humour.

The Joker in *Batman* laughs and smiles all the time. This is not through good humour, it is through appalling circumstances. Thrown by Batman, he lands in a tub of acid and his face is deformed into a permanent smile. He accentuates this with his clown-like makeup. His smile is not one of joy or happiness. It is a manic response to terrible injury. The clown imagery is potent, for the circus clown often relies on pathos, on mimicking the awfulness of stupidity. The clown is often represented with a grotesque smile and a tear at the same time.

The writer who understands this process best is also one who has unerringly chosen to be a chronicler of oppressed groups. David Cook is an English novelist who was born into a working class

Lancashire family in 1940. He failed grammar school entrance at eleven, was sent to a secondary modern school and left at fifteen unable to spell. He experienced a range of unskilled jobs before being accepted by the Royal Academy of Dramatic Art in London. A successful actor, his own life-experiences were soon to propel him into writing plays and novels and from 1969 he has continued to produce work of a painful and powerful nature. His choice of subject matter – old age, disability, sexual abuse, mental disturbance, homelessness – is not popular. Although he has won literary acclaim for his work, the E. M. Forster Award in 1977 and the Hawthornden Prize in 1978, for example, he has still to gain the full credit his writing deserves. In the area of mental handicap, something he understood so well from his own experience of being unable to spell, he has provided us with *Walter* (1978), perhaps the most important hero with a mental handicap in current literature. Thanks to Channel 4's choosing to televise *Walter* for its opening night on British television, both David Cook's work and the experience of handicap received proper attention.

Walter lives at home with his parents. We follow his life from his birth until his adulthood when his mother dies. Like many adults with severe handicaps who live at home he receives a double blow when a parent dies. He loses the parent and his home. He is moved to a long-stay hospital. *Winter Doves* (1981) takes us powerfully through his adult life.

In *Walter*, we learn a lot about how outside insensitive behaviour is experienced. It came as no surprise to me that, at a time when many parents and professionals found it unbearable to have doubt thrown on the strange myth that 'handicapped people are so friendly and happy', David Cook understood the true meaning of the process. Walter faces early on the ridicule of his peer group and learns defensive ways of dealing with that trauma. 'If anyone looks at me, I point my finger at them and start to laugh . . . At school they would do that to me and when I told her [mother] she said "Do it back to them then." But if I waited for them to do it first I felt sad inside and couldn't laugh. So I started to laugh at them before they had time to laugh at me . . . I started laughing a lot then. I keep myself ready in case somebody who doesn't know me should point at me and laugh.'

People who are close to great grief and cannot bear it encourage 'happiness' and smiling. Old people's homes and wards as well as homes for the mentally or multiply handicapped are victims of this. Lily Pincus (1981, p. 101) described a beautifully kept hospital where the Matron said, 'And here you see our darling babies.' The old women were spotlessly dressed. 'They were all smiling because that is what is expected of "darling babies" but in contrast to babies they were not allowed to risk any attempt at independence.'

The writer Jeremy Seabrook (1989) quoted a friend who had multiple sclerosis. 'Most people think they have to be resolutely bright and cheerful. It would not occur to them that this is a form of violence against us, a denial of us; as though we could be distracted by other people's good humour.'

Someone afflicted with mental or physical pain has less reason to smile or feel happy than the rest of the population and yet there is a tremendous pressure to insist on signs of pleasure precisely because of that. 'I try to keep him happy,' said one mother about her multiply handicapped son. 'Because I brought him into the world with all his difficulties, so if I can't keep him happy what is the point?' Guilt that people exist who have to bear unfair and appalling emotional, physical or mental burdens can be so unbearable that a state of denial is brought about where those in greatest pain are asked to be the happiest.

Mary, aged twelve, was born profoundly multiply handicapped. She cannot speak, she cannot walk. She was physically abused as a baby. 'Would you like a lovely walk or shall we have a lovely story?' asks her devoted teacher. What choice is there between 'lovely' and 'lovely'? At a meeting of the APP Mental Handicap Section, we pondered on the experience of those mute children and adults whose sign languages did not provide the possibility of adequate negative language. If abused children are often found to have been deprived of proper terms for their private sexual areas, then handicapped children and adults are often deprived of negative words to express their feelings. The Makaton sign language has now added to its vocabulary more signs for sexual abuse, and Professor Sheila Hollins and I have just completed a book on abuse for handicapped adults.

Many referrals of handicapped children and adults begin 'X is a lovely young man. He is happy all the time. It is just that he bites staff'; or 'She is very happy except she hits her forehead all the time.' The discrepancy between these two facts is somehow too unbearable to bridge.

This is sometimes a *folie à deux*. It can then continue because the handicapped person wants it to. Here, for example, is an obese, severely multiply handicapped boy of thirteen at the beginning of an assessment. Andy was blind, hemiplegic and epileptic. His school said that he was very happy, he smiled all the time, it was just that he masturbated in assembly. I visited him in a small classroom the school provided for such visits. I said my name was Mrs Sinason and his teachers had asked me to come because they felt he was feeling quite sad lately. That, I am afraid, was a lie! His teachers had said he was happy. With a very guttural accent he said 'No. Happy. Happy all time.' There was a huge clown-like smile on his face as he said those words. 'Happy all the time?' I asked. 'Yes.' 'Happy when you have a fit?' There was a long pause. Then he opened his mouth, paused; the huge smile returned. 'No. But happy all the time.' I repeated that he was not happy when he had a fit but he was otherwise happy. 'Yes', he said happily, on safe ground again. 'Happy about being in a wheelchair?' I asked. Then his face changed and became more serious. 'No,' he said emphatically. He sat up in the wheelchair. 'No. Not happy. Sad. Angry. I'm sad and I'm angry.' Speech ability, language knowledge, grammatical structure, feeling, all improved immediately it was made clear the false happy self was not required.

A few weeks later there was a dramatic change. The school was short-staffed and the teachers were struggling to keep a 'happy' atmosphere. Sometimes, when they had to move children from one room to another, they just pushed the wheelchairs without saying anything and the children lay like sacks of potatoes. Just after a session the class teacher came up and without saying 'hello' just started pushing Andy. 'Heh,' he protested, turning his head. 'Oh,' she said, shocked, 'I'm sorry. I thought you were – ' She paused. I will never know if she thought he was dead or a cabbage. However, when she told me later how devastated she felt for all the years she had pushed wheelchairs without bothering to say hello, I pointed out to her that it took two to make a cabbage. Whilst the pupil colluded with being a smiling silent idiot she could continue her previous behaviour. Once he showed he was a person who could respect himself she too had to be aware of him. She has since commented on how hard it is to be a teacher for those disturbed handicapped children who are unable to learn, how it takes away all sense of professional identity. 'Going stupid', smiling and being cheerful was her way of dealing with it. She added, she was aware that doing that was not dealing with the problem.

For, of course, the main responsibility for a sane atmosphere lies with the staff. For those who are dependent on others it is much harder to show anger directly. There is the fear of abandonment or even of death.

In Michael Moorcock's *Mother London*, the heroine Mary Gasalee, a psychiatric patient, bravely tries to deal with her doctor's cheerful stupidity. She does not win but the effort matters. '"So all we need is our other prescription topped up, to help us sleep and so on." "I don't know about you," Mrs Gasalee made a crude stab of retaliation, "but I could do with some more tablets myself."' (Moorcock, 1988, p. 35)

Mary manages not to smile even though she fails to break through her doctor's insensitivity. However, for many handicapped children or adults who know they are not wanted, smiling is a way of paying to stay alive. Micheline Mason, in the pioneering *Disability Equality in the Classroom: A Human Rights Issue* (Rieser and Mason, 1990, p. 206), expresses this with stark clarity: 'A message clearly and firmly slipped into my unconscious saying that people would prefer it if I died . . . I am now 30 years old. Only now am I beginning to realise that I do not have to smile all the time, and that I can achieve mediocrity without feeling someone will come along and "put me out of my misery."'

As a defence against trauma, smiling then becomes a secondary handicap in the person and in their smiling workers or families. Behind the apparently cheery tone of Dr Bridget in *Mother London* is a sadistic non-reciprocal way of talking. Maud Mannoni (1967) sees in this perpetual not-being-addressed as a proper person both the murder wish of the parent (here the worker) and/or the unconscious desire that the child stay ill. Given the child's knowledge that the world wishes you had not been born, it is not surprising that the false handicapped smile spreads across all countries in an Esperanto of grief and denial.

Spitz (1953) shows how deprived orphanage children often succumbed to infection as a way of dying, as a way of carrying self-injury and the family death-wish to its logical extreme. Ferenczi (1929) understood this process well in his paper 'The unwelcome child and his death instinct'. He saw such children as 'unwelcome guests of the family' who quickly gained organic or psychosomatic ills in order to die. With grief of such a lethal nature hiding under the broad smiles it is not surprising society on the whole prefers to keep the smiles.

David Cook (1978, p. 101) provides us with the understanding of what happens when a handicapped person stops smiling. Walter, the mentally handicapped hero, has gone to his exploitative cleaning job after hearing his father has died. 'The conductor joked with him, as was usual, but Walter didn't respond. He was silent. The Walter who laughed his braying pointing laugh, the Walter who giggled, the Walter who made people feel good because they were not he, the Walter who comforted the unsure by showing them that not all madness is tragic, was having a day off.' At his workplace where he is usually the butt of all jokes his unsmiling face results in the manager's warning him he might lose his job. '"Do try to be more of your old self tomorrow. I can't have all my staff depressed by you. Go on then."'

It is bad enough that the normal have to face the sight of the handicapped; to face the extent of grief and depression too is clearly not allowed. The handicapped, like the fat and the old and the ugly, must be funny. Indeed, research (Yirmiya, Kasari et al., 1989; Loveland, 1987) has shown that handicapped children do smile more than others. For years I had beamed back whenever a handicapped child or adult gave me a broad smile. I had even nodded assent when a colleague commented on how friendly children with Down's syndrome were. It was only when I saw my first handicapped patient for therapy that I understood the real meaning of the smile.

In a paper on sexual abuse (Sinason, 1988b, p. 98) I felt I had grasped another meaning of the ubiquity of the handicapped smile. I had observed the development of several babies and was suddenly aware that one of these observations made of a healthy baby in a caring middle-class home offered some help. The baby was nine days old and his mother had just bathed him. She wore a towelling apron so that when she lifted him out of the bath, one hand behind his head and one under his bottom and legs, he was instantly held against the soft surface. She reached for a soft towel and gently wiped his hair, but, when she came to his mouth, she wiped it briskly. The baby's arms and legs shot into a falling reflex and he screwed up his eyes. The rest of the procedure was loving and gentle.

When the baby was 15 days old I observed bath-time again. As mother wiped his hair, her last action before proceeding to his mouth, baby screwed his eyes up and his arms and legs went completely rigid. He did not cry. At three weeks he again screwed his eyes up but moved his arms and legs alternately. At six weeks, the moment the towel touched his mouth, baby smiled and stared at his mother. 'It's amazing how he likes that,' said mother, disconcerted by the smile as if somewhere she was aware of the aggression behind her act. By three months, baby beamed broadly at this moment. At four months, to my regret now, I noted, 'Mother then wiped baby's mouth, his favourite moment.' By five months, mother no longer commented on his smile but wiped his mouth even more roughly while grinning at him. At six months, when weaning had begun, baby put his knuckles in his apple-puréed mouth. 'We don't want that,' said mother roughly and wiped his mouth sharply. He shuddered and wrinkled his eyes, reminding me of his response at one week. The following week he was smiling again.

What this observation showed me was that within the context of everyday caretaking there has been a transformation. Selma Fraiberg (1982) calls this a transformation of affect. Somehow, the baby registered he could not look or cry, and after an attempt at holding himself rigid he smiled. The difficulty I had in staying with the knowledge that a small piece of everyday abuse had been perpetrated was considerable. I had perpetuated the invitation to co-operate with the denial. The denial covered both the reality of the injury and also the earliest beginnings of a form of corruption of caretaking which involves the pair in perversion of perception to avoid unwelcome realizations.

The struggle to stay with something painful, however small, is hard enough for the worker, and often impossible for the child. I carried my own guilt for what I knew somewhere I had failed to see and it was only when I began to think of the makeup of the handicapped smile (Sinason,1986) that I was able to understand better the way the child has to process abuse of many subtle kinds, and the way the worker colludes with it by becoming stupid, losing his or her intelligence.

If it is hard to see and stay with a tiny piece of everyday abuse in a better-than-average home, it is easy to understand how much harder it is to see sexual abuse. For the really terrible effects of sexual abuse are not so much on the sane outraged child who has been assaulted once and has been able to tell and be believed, but on children who have been perniciously, secretly and persuasively corrupted over a long period in their own homes; children who in order to keep any image of a good parent have to smile or become stupid or blind to what is happening.

Spitz (1959) sees smiling as structuring perception and establishing the beginning of the ego. He calls it the first psychic organizer, the second being stranger recognition and the third being the ability to say 'no'. Sexual abuse of the body and mind affects all these crucial developmental milestones. American researcher H. Papousek (1967) found that babies smiled when they understood cause and effect, when they knew that a certain movement would make a mobile move, when they had power over their environment. However, the smile of the ordinary baby I have described who had experienced a tiny amount of everyday abuse was a manic attempt to control something uncontrollable in the parent. The abuse of body and mind can start very early and the task of unravelling it is very difficult.

The smile that is not a smile is therefore a highly significant diagnostic feature in mental handicap. It can show that something has gone wrong in mother–child relationships from the earliest point.

This is not surprising. When a child is born who is clearly 'not all right' or who is noticeably handicapped, parents receive a terrible blow. Most parents hope for a child at least as healthy and fortunate as themselves. When that wished-for baby does not appear it is hard for even the most loving, resourceful parent to feel deeply attached. When the baby is not wanted, for being the 'wrong' sex, for example, a similar transformation of affect takes place. In Rushdie's *Shame* (1984, p. 89) the handicapped Sufiya Zinobia was born normal but 'the wrong miracle' as her father wanted a son. In the mirror of its mother's eyes, the first mirror, the handicapped baby does not see beauty and joy. Covering the cracks with a brilliant simulation of joy and love is one defensive manoeuvre.

Although Sufiya Zinobia's spirit was 'parched for lack of affection, she nevertheless managed, when love was in her vicinity, to glow happily just to be near the precious thing' (p. 120). This eroticization of loss can lead to a facsimile of the real feeling or expression that is so accurate it makes fools of the intelligent.

Interestingly, just as the handicapped smile comes from loss and abuse, so Rushdie's creation of Zinobia also came from tragedy. He explains that the idea for her came from the true case of an East London Asian girl who was killed by her father because she slept with a white boy. 'My Sufiya Zinobia grew out of the corpse of that murdered girl' (p. 116).

Now that I am aware of the loss behind such smiles I have become very aware of the extra intensity they carry, the pressure they convey for a response. In one session, after a severely handicapped boy of nine stopped his smiling, he intensely demanded, 'Please, please, we are going to play going to the seaside now. You will make me a picnic. You will. Just for me. You must say, here is a special picnic for you my darling son.' The longing for what should be said revealed in equal proportions what was not said. I now see the shadow of the smile forms the shape of loss in exact proportion to the excess of the upward curve.

Sometimes the smile is to keep the depressed parents happy, sometimes it is to prove that no intelligence is alive. While Walter looked happy everyone could feel that he did not know he was handicapped and knew his place in the world. Bowlby (1979) has shown how children cut off their knowledge in order to uphold the family need or wish for a secret to be kept.

In a poem written nearly twenty years ago, 'Charity Children', I observed something of the sadness in the smile:

Sometimes the tide goes out and doesn't bother to return
Sometimes it only comes back to dump old shoes and tins
And when the off-peak sun reddens out at opening time
The charity children jump up and down and shriek and smile
As if they knew how they were supposed to look happy

Their parents need a smile. American child psychologist and psychotherapist Mary Sue Moore (personal communication, 1988) notes that abused and handicapped children are the two statistically significant groups who produce big smiles on their drawings. In the London *Evening Standard* (12 September 1989), in a report on the British Association for the Advancement of Science, Dr Paul Harris of Oxford University was reported as commenting on a survey of boys who had entered boarding school. He found many struggled with hiding their homesickness by smiling. One eight-year-old said, 'If you smile and act cheerful, it doesn't show that you are actually afraid and worried.' Every year, of course, upper-class children face their own culturally accepted act of abandonment in being sent away from home and having to smile about it.

Whilst the smile leads us back to loss, trauma and fear of death it can be used to serve an aggressive purpose too. If we believe the smile is a smile we are being stupid idiots and are therefore being laughed at precisely at the moment we feel sympathy or pleasure. Sometimes we are aware of aggression in the inappropriate nature of the smile. Thomas Szasz (1973) spoke of a schizophrenic woman in her fifties whose husband had died and whose children had left home. She came to tell him her extended family were poisoning her and she smiled. He comments, 'A fleeting smile remains on her face. The so-called inappropriate affect – what psychiatrists consider the classic symptom of schizophrenia – is perhaps the poorly suppressed amusement of the con man, secretly laughing at his mark.'

Those living a good moral life are expected to be happy. People who show they are damaged in any way evoke fears of immoral or dangerous activity in the onlooker and a smile smooths over this fear.

Cicero was concerned to show that a wise man could not stay happy if he was afflicted by internal or external catastrophe. 'I refer to poverty, failure, low birth, loneliness, bereavement, physical agony, exile, slavery. All these states of affairs, and others besides, may easily befall even the wisest of men, since they are the products of chance, from which no man, however wise, enjoys immunity. If therefore, they really deserve the name of evils, it is quite impossible to maintain that a person who is wise will always be happy – because, however wise he is, any of these happenings may very well overtake him at any moment; or indeed every single one of them, all at the same time' (Cicero, trans. M. Grant, 1982, p. 68). Cicero was one of many enlightened voices who tried to keep hold of a concept of randomness, a sense that 'there but for the grace of God go I'. Fear of damage, of handicap, of illness, of madness, evokes a desire to blame the victim. Someone dying of AIDS can therefore be dismissed as causing his own agony, similarly a smoker dying of lung cancer. Blame enters the area of disease with a vengeance.

ALI: 'BEING STUPID IS BEING MAD'

Ali was a beaming dumpy boy of eight, whose notes said he had been handicapped from birth. He spoke only in two-word sentences, could not recognize his name or write it, and could not concentrate for more than a few minutes in the classroom. From the interpreter I learned that he was just as handicapped in his native language. His parents were mildly handicapped and had health problems as well as economic ones. His father had one grown-up son from his first marriage but Ali was the only child of this marriage. He was premature and was kept in hospital after his birth. On being taken home he was unable to feed and was readmitted and drip-fed. His parents visited him but did not stay in the hospital with him.

At nursery school Ali was experienced as violent and disruptive. On being moved to a special school his violence decreased but he then took on the role of village idiot, beaming at everyone and asking strangers and teachers, 'All right? You all right?' His parents, unable to maintain any consistent environment, nevertheless shared a worry with the teaching staff about the indiscriminate way he could approach strangers. There had been an incident at school when he complained about an older boy, John, assaulting him in the toilets. This was investigated but then dismissed as Ali frequently lingered smiling round the toilets annoying the older boys. At nine he had a circumcision for religious reasons, which had also disturbed him.

For the first year in which I saw Ali for once-weekly therapy he would speak of television programmes and superheroes in a confused disjointed way. His sentence structure was faulty and his vocabulary was extremely simple. 'I Hulk. I wake. Angry now. Sleep.' There were moments of free play where he enacted a tea in which he was poisoned and fell to the floor needing ambulance and hospital. However, he would quickly move on, in a smiling way, to other activities, impervious to any comment of mine.

After a year, I introduced some new toys into the therapy room (Sinason,1988a, pp. 340–63), including bears, dolls and a clown doll. There was a dramatic change in Ali.

Session 42: first session with new toys

Ali looked at the dolls. He looked at the clown doll and then at me. The clown doll had a huge smile on its face on one side. But if you turned it round there was a crying face. Ali examined these different expressions carefully. His huge beam dropped and then he showed me a devastatingly sad face. After a second, his usual broad beaming smile returned. Only this time I knew, for the first time, that it was not an authentic smile. In that one moment I understood how I had misread this expression for years in my handicapped patients. Ali had clearly noted the shocked expression on my face for he said 'Yes. I sad. I am Ali with sad face. Clown knows sad face.' Already in those few sentences a verbal change had equalled his emotional change. He had moved from his usual two-word sentences – 'I sad' – to a grammatical sentence with a subject, a verb and an adjective.

He looked at the clown again. 'It is not just my circumstar that is sad.' ('Circumstar' was his word for circumcision and linked to his wish for a 'star' penis.) He looked frightened. 'Doctor say if I did not have injection properly he would cut it off [his penis]. But all right now. I man now.' (His fake beam returned.) 'Everything all right.' (He beamed again.) He lifted the clown to show me the happy face and then the sad face. I said he was showing me that although he was saying everything was all right he was sad because everything was not all right. He frowned and then looked frightened. 'Circumstar,' he began hesitantly. 'Circumcision. Your language is hard.' I said perhaps he meant what I said to him as well as the fact that I spoke English.

'Circumstar, circumcision,' he practised. He then showed me on his face sad and happy expressions. He was no longer scanning my face anxiously and I understood he did not now feel he had to worry about my response.

From Ali I have since understood that every patient who asks 'All right?' is actually telling me that they are not all right and they do not know if I am all right enough to bear them not being all right. There is also a class factor involved in the linguistic code of address. Basil Bernstein (1972) has postulated a restricted code for working-class communication and 'All right?' is very much a working-class version of 'How are you?' Although the latter form of address may be token in its wish to receive a real response, it does not restrict the answer by stating how the other person should be, which 'all right' does. Simply by refusing to say 'yes' when Ali and other patients asked me, I was removing some of the leaves of mild secondary handicap and making it clear that it is possible to have room for sad and angry feelings.

Ali then put the clown down and walked to the table, where there were two teddy bears (one large, one small), two teenage dolls and three baby dolls. 'Look dolls! Hello dears! Want a fuck?'

It is hard to convey the shock I felt. Ali had never sworn. Nor had he spoken in that leering yet fluent English accent before. He had moved from nursery-school English ('Look dolls!') to sexualized slang fluency via the iconic power of the word 'look'. Something had happened that he had had to witness and now he had to show me, I had to be the looker. He turned to me and nervously said, 'I am not talking to you, Mrs Sinason. Only to the dolls.' I said he was talking to the dolls but to me too. I was not able to say at that moment how amazed I was to hear a complete grammatical sentence. Before, he would have said, 'I not talk to you.'

His new-found sense of language, albeit in a sexual context, continued. 'Hello dearies! Wanna try something, heh? How about a little suck? You like that, don't you? You love it. How about a few of you together, that would be good.' He gathered the dolls with a world-weary sigh and sat on the armchair facing me, with the dolls facing his penis. He stretched his arms and put them behind his head, then he sighed and concentrated like a middle-aged man at a pornographic movie. He unzipped his trousers and placed the dolls on his penis. I felt sick and unable to speak.

'Look what I'm doing,' said Ali seriously. 'I'm having a good time with the girls. I'm giving them a good time. They all like a suck.' I was doubly shocked. Not only was he showing me in this sudden way the grammatical knowledge and memory he had hidden in his handicap; he was also the first child I had worked with who had shown sexual abuse in a session. I was unable to reply therapeutically. I said I knew what he was doing but his penis was private to him. Obviously, it wasn't. He was showing it to me but at that moment I could not bear the knowledge he was offering. I was the one who became stupid.

Luckily, Ali was able to continue. 'Penis? That's not the word in my language. Do you know my language? In my language you say "sick" for "fuck" and now I'm going to be sick.'

Ali had correctly understood that for a moment I had been unable to bear the language of his emotional experience. The Roman orator Cicero, understanding that deafness did not have to incapacitate a wise man, pointed out, 'and indeed every one of us is deaf to all the innumerable tongues we do not understand'. Tragedy can certainly make the victim as well as the worker lose her usual senses and capacities. Unsurprisingly, Ali was also correct about his native language, as an interpreter later made clear. However, I did not need the interpreter to know that my countertransference feelings of sickness were linked not only to the terrible abuse of Ali's body but at the same time to his bi-lingual learning. I felt that an adult must have said, 'I'm going to make you sick,' knowing that an English person would then misunderstand what had really happened.

My intelligence had returned and I slowly said, 'Perhaps

something made you sick, Ali.' Very seriously he replied, 'I'm a baby. I just go to sleep. But the dolls like it. They have gone to sleep.' I said perhaps something made him sick when he was a tiny baby Ali and he fell asleep because he did not want to remember it. 'Want to suck my wally?' he asked, earnestly. He walked towards me, knocking the dolls off his lap, his penis erect. I was not able yet to discuss his expectancy that I and all adults expected sexual contact with him. However, what I did understand easily and pointed out to him, was that he had called his willy 'Wally', trying to make 'it' stupid, so 'it' would not know something bad had happened. For a moment he looked devastated and then he put back the beaming smile that I used to think was natural.

'Want to look at my circumstar?' he asked brightly. I said he wanted me to tell him his penis was all right after the circumcision as well as wanting to be a man with a star penis. Those comments may have been partly right, but what I was still unable to deal with at that moment was his wish for me to be the abusive adult interested in his penis. I was understanding more about the link between stupidity and trauma through my own cowardice than through what Ali was actually saying and doing.

Ali put his penis in a girl doll's bottom. 'You like that,' he insisted. 'It doesn't hurt. There's a good girl.' He made one doll suck his penis while another was placed behind that doll. Then he sank back into the armchair like a seedy pimp with all the dolls and bears at each other's orifices. When it was time for the session to end he said he wouldn't go until all the dolls had had a fuck, a sick. I said the new dolls, my new babies, had made him remember something about a new baby Ali who was hurt a long time before his circumcision and before the incident with John (an older boy he had accused of assaulting him years ago), and who wanted to leave all his bad memories in me.

When he left the room I scrubbed and disinfected the dolls, the floor, the chair, the table. I went to the staffroom feeling pale and sick. It was not just his bad memories he had left in me. His abuse of the dolls and room had also been an abuse of me. The supportive psychiatric team and school staff discussed the session with me. We were agreed that a series of meeting with the parents should be arranged but that Ali was not yet ready and able to have a forensic meeting with the psychiatrist. His sudden fluency in the therapy room might take a while to generalize to the classroom.

Session 43

Ali was beaming when I came to get him, repeating 'Thank you, thank you, thank you.' But the moment we entered the therapy room his smile went and he urgently pulled his trousers down. 'Want to see my circumstar?' I said he was very frightened about his penis at the moment, what had happened to it in the circumcision and what had happened since. 'You can suck it if you want,' he insisted. His grammatical language had stayed with him. He moved behind an armchair and pressed himself against it, just showing me his face. He gave an awful leer, then a wink and then a fake beaming smile. 'You can suck it,' he said seductively. He picked up a teenage girl doll, stripped her and pressed his penis into her bottom. 'John sucked my penis. It was lovely.' He stroked the girl doll's hair. 'She likes it nice and easy, that's all right, isn't it.' He turned to me seriously. 'She likes it.' Then he slapped her viciously round the face. 'Look – her cheeks are red, that's what she gets if she won't suck.'

I said he had a pretend smile on his face before and now he was pretending the doll was enjoying it. But he was showing us that people could pretend something was lovely when they were frightened. He again asked me to suck his penis, this time more insistently. I reminded him of the way he had said 'Thank you' when I came to get him. Perhaps he felt frightened that I was a dangerous doctor who would hurt him so now he felt he had to offer himself to me. There was a pause and then he desperately asked, 'Mrs Sinason, how do you remember things? How do I remember?' When I said how painful it was to remember things that hurt he commented, 'I try to go to sleep.' He stroked the doll's hair and said in a mournful voice, 'Close your eyes. Go to sleep. It doesn't hurt. You don't remember.'

I said he was put to sleep for his circumcision and he did not know what had happened to him and maybe he was remembering other times, with John as well as someone else or other people, when he tried to go to sleep to not know something terrible that was happening.

I said there were a few minutes left. Ali asked desperately if he could look up my skirt. I asked if he thought he might find a bit of his penis there. He nodded and explained, 'Yes – the bit they took away.' He picked up the teenage doll, imitated intercourse and said, 'Maybe it is there too.' He then looked terrified and beamed and said, 'All right Miss Sinason?' I said he was worried a bit of his penis was inside mummy and if he went back to get it daddy would be angry so he had made me into a Miss Sinason. Maybe when he was very frightened of a daddy being cross he felt he had to say everything a daddy did was lovely.

It was time to go. 'I'm going out with my willy out,' he announced. I said he could not leave the room like that and he angrily pulled his trousers up.

This time, when Ali left the room, I felt heartened by the stirring of his anger and his ability to have retained his voice as well as concern for the still untold story which was beginning to be enacted before me. Something in Ali was not being allowed to tell its story. Freud (1893) felt that the 'psychical trauma [of abuse], or more precisely the memory of the trauma, acts like a foreign body which long after its entry must continue to be regarded as an agent that is still at work.' Freud was aware of the repetitive nature of abuse, and Klein's later comments (1932) that guilt itself heightens sexual desire and causes further disturbed sexual behaviour is also linked to Freud's idea (1923) that guilt itself can cause a crime. This I later felt (Sinason, 1988b) could be compared with some theories of allergy which state that the patient's body is dealing with an allergy by taking in even more of what is poison to it.

Attempts at symbolizing

Session 44

Ali brought a game of Snap with him. He gave us six cards each and whenever he had a matching card he used the sexual slang 'I'll have ya'. He looked more worried each time he said this. Winning the card game was not symbolic for him, the cards for him were what

Hanna Segal has called 'symbolic equations' (1957), where the substitute for an original object, instead of becoming a symbol, can pathologically be equated with it.

He looked round the room frantically. The struggle to maintain even a symbolic equation, let alone a symbol, was too much. 'I've got to see the dolls – the teddy,' he added, still trying. He paused, took a deep breath and then reverted to the playacting he had done prior to the advent of the new dolls. But this time it was with language and intelligence both in him and me. 'You make me a cup of tea Mrs Sinason because I am JR coming home in *Dallas*.' He put on a cowboy hat, mimed knocking on the door and announced woodenly, 'Hello, I'm JR back from work. Can I have a cup of tea?' I said 'yes' and he thanked me, specifying he wanted milk and sugar. He then said I was to be Pam (another character from *Dallas*) and he would make a cup of tea. With us both symbolically having drunk the same drink he took the drama a stage further. 'Now only pretend, Mrs Sinason,' he said reassuringly, 'but this time you are going to put poison in my tea and I will drop dead and you must say "Poor Ali is dead". You are watching television while I get poisoned.' A painful feeling was building up in me that this was leading to an image of public or filmed abuse. 'I'm watching television,' I announced, 'and you clearly want me to be someone who doesn't care what happens to you.' Ali then ordered me to put the poison in his tea. I announced, 'This is me pretending to put poison in Ali's tea so he will die while I watch television.' Ali mimed a collapse and a death and I said, as he had requested, 'Poor Ali is dead.'

Ali then turned into a popular television character, the Incredible Hulk, a man who, when threatened with danger and made angry, turns into a creature of enormous strength. Breathing deeply, Ali transformed himself before my eyes and I became the frightened victim. 'Don't be frightened,' he said. I said he was perhaps telling me that if I did not care what happened to him something terrible could happen and he would need to be a superman to escape from it. Ali then said he would now poison me and the same scene was re-enacted the other way round. 'Now we are the same,' said Ali seriously. I said he felt that only if I knew what poisonous experience he went through could he feel better.

'Now,' he said thoughtfully, 'You sit back on your chair.' As I returned to my usual chair by the door Ali undid his trousers and made for a baby boy doll. 'I am sorry but I have to fuck you,' he said. He looked at me anxiously, as a theme of remembering and the struggle with traces of memory continued. 'Tell me again, like last time. What does private mean?' When I said it meant parts of him that no-one should touch except him and asked him if he knew what his private parts were, he blurted out 'dead bum' and then changed it quickly to 'the bum', adding on his former stupid smile and handicapped voice. 'What did I say?' I said maybe he felt bums could only be private if they were dead.

I thought of how horror films understood the nature of 'undeath' – a state of wished-for but unsuccessful repression. In a poem on Lilith I considered how:

> Her cries never change but only retreat
> to recharge their hoarse voices
> with fresh news from the angry dead

A little while later, buggering a baby doll behind two armchairs 'so I am more private', he suddenly pleaded, 'Please don't tell. Don't let the films go in the assembly hall or everyone will laugh at me and smack me.' I asked what he meant. His eyes filled with tears. 'I don't want them to see it in assembly. They will laugh at me.'

I dealt with his fear that maybe I was filming what he did in the therapy room and then added that it sounded as if he had done something sexual on a film and people could laugh at him or hit him. He screamed in terror, 'Cut my ears off, please, please cut my ears off! I don't want to hear them laughing at me.' He rushed across the room to pick up a pair of scissors, which I quickly took from him. He reverted to his broken-up speech – 'What did I say?' – but we both knew what he had said. Something about the need to cut off his ears in order to not know or hear something terrible was in the process of being understood. At the same time we could both see how cutting off his ears meant depriving himself of words and knowledge that could have helped him.

Ali looked at me desperately and then ran for the baby boy doll. Before I could say or do anything, although I still do not know what

I could have done, Ali urinated into the doll's open mouth. I felt sick and told him he had to use words, he could not do that again but I added he was showing me how poison was put in his mouth and now he was wanting to put it in mine. When it was time to go, he became frantic, sticking his penis into all the dolls. I said he found it unbearable to leave without pouring all his horrible feelings into the dolls' orifices and, through them, into mine, but he had to go. He refused and I said we would have to end earlier next time if he did not leave properly. He left, snatching a doll, shouting, 'I'll kidnap it.' I grabbed the doll back. He left, adjusting his trousers. Again, I scrubbed the floor and the dolls and disinfected the doll he had urinated in. I also had to remove that doll from general use and I reserved it just for Ali.

Session 45

Ali came in looking very alive and thoughtful. To my astonishment he went straight to his private toy-box; he had never done that before. He took out an action toy called 'Six-Million-Dollar Man' or 'Bionic Man'. (I find it useful to add toys based on figures from popular culture to the basic psychotherapy toy kit that has hardly changed since Melanie Klein (1932) first described her choice of little figures, male and female, adult and child, cars, trains, animals, bricks, houses, drawing material, paper, scissors and glue.) He called the toy 'Fall Guy', making clear there was a pun. The guy was a 'fool' who could 'fall' on a baby and fool with him. Having his ears restored meant he could use and understand a pun. 'Did you see? Do you understand what I am saying?' he asked, before adding with exhilaration, 'These are good toys. Why couldn't I play with them before?'

However, touching them rather than playing verbally with them was hard. 'Can I take his shoes off?' he asked nervously. 'He has trainers too. I think it is hard to take his shoes off. Will he break? Will you help?' I said Ali was worried the man might break when he was undressed and he wanted my help so he wouldn't break. He agreed and I gently took the boots off. I was aware that I had never assisted in undressing any of the dolls before as that involved me in an abusive task. However, this was definitely different and not perverse. I was also aware that Ali had not yet needed to undress himself.

When the shoes were off Ali carefully picked up the toy trainers. 'These are so small, like a baby's, will they fit?' I said he was wondering what size things were right for a man and which for a baby and maybe too what was the right size for a boy. He agreed and asked me to put them on. He gingerly practised dropping the toy. Then he picked up a toy motorbike with a tiny superhero, 'Streethawk', on it. He forced Bionic Man into a position where he kneeled on all fours and made Streethawk ride the motorbike up between his buttocks. 'Bad Fall Guy.' I said Streethawk was small but he could do to Fall Guy what had happened to him. 'Yes. Watch.' This time he was more explicit, riding the bike over the doll's genital area. 'Do you see? Do you understand?' I said he wanted me to see that a little Ali Streethawk knows how to spot a dangerous man who fits together things that shouldn't fit like a big grown-up penis and a little boy with a little hole in his bottom.

Ali then took another linguistic leap forward. Each item in his toy tray he picked up and told me both the English word and his native word. 'This is a dog. That is the English word. In my language we say. . .' He repeated this seriously with each item, moving from simple words to complicated adjectives. I felt I was seeing several years of language development in two languages before my eyes.

However, when he knew it was near the end of his session he pulled his trousers down and said he had to fuck the dolls. This time, however, he asked if he could pee in a doll's mouth and when I said he couldn't, he didn't. His sexual desperation was less.

Session 48

Each move forward in his sane development brought further signs of the perversions he had accommodated. Just before his session Ali came to find me to tell me, 'Mrs Sinason, there is shit on the door. It's lovely. I licked it.' There were several encopretic children in the school at that time and I knew the act was not Ali's. Sure enough, faeces were smeared on the door handle to the therapy room. I told Ali I would go and get some disinfectant to clean it off and would add some time on to the end of his session so he did not lose any of his time. I asked him if he really had licked it because if he had I would find an antiseptic mouthwash for him.

Once the cleaning-up was accomplished and I had procured mouth-wash for Ali we entered the room. 'That shit was lovely. I have got to have a fuck now.' He pulled his trousers down and instantly urinated. 'I can't stop it. I can't,' he screamed in panic. 'I'll clean it. Will you fuck me now? Will you make me sick now?'

I said seeing how someone had treated the door to my room had stirred him. There was an Ali who wanted to make my room and me a dirty invaded body but there was also an Ali who was terrified and despairing at all the dirt.

'I'll get the disinfectant,' he screamed. 'But don't tell the secretary. Will you fuck me? My mother does. I do it with her because she loves me. That's why she does it.' My heart sank at this information, which I duly passed on to the psychiatric team, having told Ali I would need to do so.

The development of language

Session 49

The sickening nature of the last session paved the way for the next step forward. In this session Ali concentrated on the toys in his box. He used a tiny robot to represent himself in battle against Six-Million-Dollar Man. The Robot was called Ro-Bot. 'Bot – do you understand?' He had managed another pun and his free symbolic play continued. A little knight with a detachable sword was helping the robot fight. The sword fell down and Ali asked me to pick it up. When I asked why he couldn't he painfully said he could not bend. I felt the terrible meaning of the word 'bend' and picked up the sword. Ali thanked me as the Knight. 'Thank you, thank you, I have my sword back. How wonderful.' He turned to me with a genuine beaming smile. 'Did you see? Do you understand? The knight thought he had lost his little sword but you gave it back to him and now he is safe.' He stroked the cow. 'Oh you good cow! thank you, cow, thank you, Mrs Sinason, thank you President Reagan and everybody. I have my sword back'.

As the session came to an end he sat on the floor on the place where he had urinated the week before. He looked frightened. 'The sword is pretend but it could still hurt if I pierced you. Last week I peed on the floor and that was real so I thought you would do something real to me that hurt.' I repeated that last week he was scared I would do something to hurt him. 'Fuck,' he whispered. He then put back his old ESN accent – 'Who said that? I don't know that word.' I gently said he did and his intelligent voice returned. 'Yes. It means sick and it makes me sick. It's putting your willy in a hole like I do.' He then walked towards me with a fake seductive expression but looking desperately sad. I commented on this. His sexual manner disappeared and he picked up a puppet and said very simply and powerfully, 'This poor puppet has lost his voice. He has lost it. He used to have something inside him that made a loud squeak and now it isn't there.' I said perhaps he was telling me that he used to have a loud voice that said how he felt and it was hard to find it. 'It is inside him. It must be still there. But it has been cut.'

The sword he felt I had returned to him, concretely and symbolically, was the pen and the penis as well as the sword. The return to sexual autonomy had allowed his voice to grow louder and more confident. The repetitive moving language made me think of the Seafarer and the Wanderer, figures from the Anglo-Saxon epics. There, the lone voyager has stored his lonely story inside himself for years, not knowing if anyone would ever share it. Ali had somehow kept intact within himself the words of the witness, the words of the healthy seeing child who would keep witness for the future when it was safe. It was at this point that I did not have to be the degraded impotent voyeur.

His anger now grew hand in hand with his intellect and memory.

The growth of anger and intelligence

Session 50

In this session, when all the toys were crowded in a line to watch television, the little Robot knocked over Six-Million-Dollar Man and said in a strong, loud voice, 'I do not want to sit on your lap to watch the video, Six-Million-Dollar Man. I do not want to sit on your lap, Mummy Cow. I want to sit all by myself. I don't want to sit on anything.' There was a terrible painful silence and he looked at me expectantly. I said that now he realized I was a mummy cow who would give him his sword back, then he could remember painful things and he wanted to make sure he did not allow them to happen again.

A few minutes later he picked up a baby boy doll and said, 'This . . . doll is so little. Such a little baby. Such a tiny bottom-hole. But look what the man did.'

Over the next few weeks, memories of an original trauma grew closer. He acted scenes of death and dying and being rushed to hospital, beginning with the doll mother and father asking worriedly, 'Can our darling boy survive what has happened?' He lost his dumpy girlish look. He began to wear more male clothes. In the classroom he showed improvement but was still nowhere near the verbal fluency he displayed in the sessions.

Session 72

One day Ali came into the room looking particularly angry. He lined all the toys up and made the Robot say to them all, loudly and forcefully, 'Get the hell out of my arse.' For the last time in therapy, his old dimwitted expression returned as he asked bemusedly, 'What did I say? I mean out of my house.' I said he wanted all these thoughts out of his head. He thought for a moment and then acted his dying scene. This time, however, a new ingredient was added. 'My brother collapses like that when he drinks too much.' I felt a sudden lurch in my stomach, thinking of the 'fall guy' and the poisoned cups of tea. 'I drink too when I am at that party where the English lady does belly-dancing.' He then looked white-faced and terrified. His memory of an actual event.

His teacher reported progress with Ali that day, saying he was no longer the most demanding and childish member of the class and was able to concentrate more.

Session 73

The next week Ali made it clear why he so often asked me 'Do you see?' when he meant 'Do you understand?' It was not just his ears that had been cut off. He savagely whipped the boy doll whose hair was being washed by him. 'I had to hit him because, look, he is watching. He is seeing what has happened. Stupid boy. Close your eyes! Please don't look.' Ali had to close his eyes to the healthy seeing boy who had seen something unbearable and that meant not seeing his name when it was written down, not seeing colours and shapes, not being able to draw.

Session 74

A week later Ali made the Robot walk upside down. 'See, his bottom-hole is showing and he is upside down but he has strong arms to stand on and I have just come from the gym and I walked upside down and Mr R said I had strong arms.' I said there were ways of being upside down that were good even though he might still be exposed. He was only then able to recount his first dream. 'I had a dream last night. I want to tell you it. It was raining, raining, raining. It was dark. I was so frightened. I was out in the dark and the rain and I was frightened of the drunk man, the drunk man who called "Where are you going? Come here." And I shouted, "None of your business, it is none of your business!" I shouted loud and I woke from it.'

He was only able to differentiate a dream from the nightmare of his daily fantasy after this amount of work. His unconscious had joined him in saying no. After this session he did his best picture at art. It seemed clear that he could only be creative in visual movements when it was possible to be in a position that did not just convey a sexual meaning. I was also particularly grateful to the gym teacher who had been so sensitive.

Because of the split that we make between mind and body, teachers who are given 'the body' are often marginalized, left out of normal staff meetings or any intellectual or emotional considerations. Sometimes there is self-selection for this position and sometimes it is imposed. It inflicts great damage on sexually and physically abused children, for whom bodily positions are icons of abusive memories. Mr R's willingness to wait for Ali and the staff structure of the school which saw gym as something intrinsic helped Ali at this point.

Session 78

Only now could he speak occasionally in his classroom in the fluent way he had shown me in the therapy room. The connection between sexual fears and learning difficulties was made even more clear when, five weeks later, he came happily to the therapy room to tell me how good his reading was. He asked me to tell him how to spell 'sex'. He then flung his pen towards me and said urgently, 'Smell it.' Instinctively, I said, 'No.' He had used it as an anal assault weapon only two weeks earlier, making me painfully aware of the verbal connection between pen and penis. 'Please,' he said desperately. 'Smell it. Help me. I mean spell it.' I said smell and spell seemed mixed up as if he could not spell unless I knew the smell. I then smelled the pen and told him how to spell sex. He wrote it on a piece of paper and threw it out of the window. He said there was a hurt boy in the stinging nettles outside and he had to throw him the books so he could spell. I said there was a hurt boy in this room too but he could not throw things out of the window.

He picked up his diary to throw it out. He said he wanted to throw it out because he did not like the words. I said he wasn't sure how to throw out bad sexual memories and thoughts and feelings without losing good words and dates too.

It was time. He said he was angry, relishing the sound of the word 'angry' as if it was an new entitlement. His teacher said he did addition by himself that afternoon. Things were beginning to add up.

Session 80

Just before this session an important meeting was held with Ali's parents. A psychiatrist and social worker had been visiting regularly since I first passed on my concern about abuse. Because of their lack of boundaries and their mental limitations it had taken time to build up the relationship sufficiently to investigate what was happening. We were all certain that nothing was happening in the present and that allowed the team the time to proceed carefully.

After pointed questioning they slowly remembered an occasion when Ali had been left with his half-brother babysitting. When they returned they found him bleeding on the pavement. He had thrown himself through the lounge window, saying, disjointedly, he was frightened of his brother locking him in. The hospital had discharged him without any investigation, apparently thinking that a four-year-old handicapped boy might easily not see a window and go through it. Nothing further could be elicited at that stage except the fact that the brother concerned no longer lived in England.

After this, we felt as a psychiatric team that Ali was ready for an external forensic interview with the school psychiatrist. I was fearful he would cut off his ears and speak in the meaningless television/superhero babble he still used for most of his classroom time. However, he showed my colleague the same high level of mental functioning he had allowed me to witness in the therapy room. My colleague, who had assessed him nearly three years earlier, was as startled as I had been by his linguistic and emotional transformation. He was able to tell her his birth fantasies as well as details about John but anything about his brother or any other sexual activity was completely unavailable for recall.

Session 85

In this session Ali looked at me very seriously and said something that devastated me. 'Do you know something, Mrs Sinason? There is something I know. Being stupid is being mad.' I felt tearful. I said he was telling me that now he did not have to cut his ears off he realized that when he used to look stupid he was really mad. He nodded and made the toy cars travel along a toy road, humming a tune like an ordinary latency child.

He looked at me again. 'I am not stupid,' he said simply. 'What John did must never happen again because I say "None of your business" and it hurts.' A little while later he looked at me most sharply. 'You saw my parents when they came here. Did you tell them I fucked the dolls?' I said it was private what he did in the room; I had told his parents just what I had said I would, that I felt someone had done something to his bottom-hole as well as whatever John had done.

His nose was running and he wiped his nose on his sleeve. I felt sick and knew it was not the wet nose but a link to the buggery.

Suddenly my nose felt wet and I reached for a tissue. Ali watched in fascination and then he took a tissue and blew his nose. 'Close your eyes', he said urgently. He wrapped the tissue into a tiny ball with great disgust. 'You should not see what comes out.' I said he was letting me know about the horrid feeling he had about what could go in or out of him. 'Like drink,' he added. 'I have a girlfriend now. Her name is Tracy. On television last night a girl ran away from home and when her parents found her, mum hit her across the face because of what she did when she was lost.'

I wondered aloud whether he was frightened of what his parents and I would do to him when he was lost in other people's business. Again, I had the feeling his memory was getting closer.

The fourth year onwards: from victim to abuser

The first three years of therapy slowly restored Ali to more of his intelligence. His inappropriate smiling, approaches to strangers and learning difficulties were all clearly linked to the trauma of abuse. Had therapy stopped at the moving point where he was able to help me understand that being stupid is being mad I could have been left with an unrealistic picture of what therapy could do. As with Steven (Chapter 5) truly long-term therapy gives a more extensive understanding of the internal difficulties.

In addition, with Ali, I was watching the painful move an abused child can make, from being the victim to being the aggressor.

Session 90

Here is the transition, some details of which are written about elsewhere (Sinason, 1988b). After three years, just after a half-term holiday, Ali came for his first session back in the therapy room and asked where the robot was. 'Here's the little boy,' he said happily. He picked up the Robot and said his hands were cold. He went to the gas fire to warm his own hands and then held them out to me. 'My hands are so cold.' I touched his hands, aware of the pleasure at that rare event, a non-sexual touch. I agreed that his hands were cold and added that maybe he felt cold all over at half-term.

He touched his face and said it was cold. He touched it

wonderingly as if it was his own body for the first time. Then he bent the Robot over and aimed a powerful kick at its bottom. 'Now I'm warm again and I can go back to the table.' I commented that being back with me made him feel warm again but then he felt I was warming him in a bad way. He nodded and picked up his abuser-figure, Six-Million-Dollar Man. 'That's his willy and he hurts the dead bum with it. Now I remember everything again.'

A despairing sexual expression crossed his face as the session came to an end. The ending represented my abuse of him as well as loss and always stirred up perversion. 'Come on, suck me, Mrs Sinason. You want to.' He put a sickly leer on his face and walked towards me. I said he did not have a real smile on his face because he knew it was not something friendly he was offering. I added he had missed me over the holiday and was angry he had to leave. He nodded, looked clear but then shouted angrily, 'If you don't let me I'll fuck you.' I said it was time for him to leave and he did manage to leave easily.

Session 102

A few months later he showed me a plastered finger. 'I hurt myself on the school bus. I made my hand go whoosh along the seat and there was glass there and everyone laughed and I laughed but it hurts. It hurts.' He repeated the word, sounding surprised. 'I did not think I hurt. I thought I was a robot.'

To keep the abused mind and body numb often means not knowing differences in temperature or pain and I have found that one effect of therapy is to make children very sensitive to all the infantile senses of heat and cold, dark and light, seasons and pain.

Session 107

The school setting where I saw Ali was a difficult one as the head teacher was ill, and morale and numbers were low. The fabric of the building itself was failing – the therapy room had a crate in it to catch rainwater from a leak in the ceiling. Casual violence was high. Ali, even when he was not being actively perverse, was an easy and obvious target for gratuitous bullying. On one occasion a terrible incident happened. When the playground was momentarily unsupervised some older boys tied his hands, pulled his trousers and pants off and forced him to walk round the playground. He came to me white-faced and tore his clothes off.

'This is how I am. This is me,' he declared. I said what a terrible thing to have happened; how awful he must have felt not being able to stop them and now he wanted to pretend this was how he always was. Ali rushed round the room, berserk, shouting, 'I'm going to fuck the door, the teddies. They love it.' He inserted a pen in his anus and then smelled and licked it. 'It's lovely.' I was feeling sick and I apologize to the reader for the feeling of nausea that will be passed on. I said he had been forced to eat shit by the big bullies and he was pretending it was lovely. Ali threw himself into the plastic crate with its layer of water. 'Suck me, for God's sake, no-one will know.' He anally masturbated again, licking a brown finger. He walked towards me. I felt sick. I said he wanted me to feel as sick as him, treated just like a piece of shit and he wanted to pretend he was one and he liked it. It was time to go and I felt sick for several hours afterwards.

Session 108

Next session he came in and lunged at my skirt. Instinctively I shouted 'No!' Ali was startled and frightened and backed away shouting, 'Fuck off! how dare you!' I had calmed down by then and was able to understand what was happening. 'That's right,' I agreed. 'You're saying to me what you wish you had said to the boys and when you behaved to me the way the boys behaved to you and I shouted "no", it reminded you of what you wished you could say.' Ali then quietly said, 'I'm eleven and I'm getting bigger.' I agreed that he was getting bigger and braver and cleverer and stronger, but the boys were older and stronger and he couldn't stop them even though he wanted to. 'But,' I emphasized, 'it matters that you want to stop them.' 'Even though I'm bigger?' he asked. 'Yes,' I replied. 'Even though you are bigger there will always be people who are stronger, but it matters that you say no, even if you can't stop them.' There was a pause and then he spoke with great difficulty and surprise. 'I'm angry.'

Session 110

Two weeks later the outside world struck again when a violent teenage girl kicked his bottom when he walked past with me. Ali ran to me for protection and I took him to the therapy room while the girl called, 'Slag, slag, don't say excuse me.' When I said what she had done to Ali she denied it but Ali, to everyone's surprise, shouted clearly, 'She kicked my bottom.'

Inside the therapy room he stabbed the baby doll and masturbated violently, shouting that in his dream I had burned his bottom with stinging nettles. I said sometimes my words hurt him a lot and today it was his bottom that Alice had kicked and maybe all the things from me that hurt felt like they were hurting his bottom.

There was a period of improvement between sessions but a social work visit to his home brought further fury. 'I don't need protection. I love being hurt. I love being shit.' The visit revealed that Ali was given an enema frequently as a toddler and up to the age of five. When he couldn't sleep at night he was allowed into the parental bed. At the end of the visit the father slowly said that they had come to England because his son, Ali's half-brother, had been gang-raped by a group of men in their village when he was only four. Very slowly the couple tried to consider if Ali's half-brother could have perpetuated that ordeal on him. After saying that the brother had been involved with a group of bad men they then announced he had left the country several years ago and would not come back. The subject was closed.

Session 111

For the next few weeks Ali sexually ravaged the room but I slowly became aware of something more healthily angry and less despairing. I became confident that I could now bring in behavioural limits. When Ali lunged at me at the end of a session I said, 'Come on now, Ali. You have intelligence.' He stopped for a moment and said, 'I can't think now. Stupid bitch. I don't want to remember. I don't want to think.' But when he started to pull his trousers down I said, 'No, you don't need to do that now. You are an older Ali. You can talk.' He looked astounded. 'You mean you won't let me do my sexy things?' I said no. He started to undress and I said the session would end if he did. 'But what can I do?' I said we would see. 'But what did I do last week?' I said he had hurt me and my Ali in front of me by sticking things in his bottom and he had done it enough. The rightness of this decision and its timing were shown a week later when he symbolically, although only temporarily, managed to bury his perversion.

Session 112

Ali took Six-Million-Dollar Man out of his box. He had not played with him for a while. He looked at him carefully. 'Six-Million-Dollar Man. Six-Million-Dollar Man. What a long time since I saw you. I was only little. Now I'm eleven. I'll put you in the water but give you shoes and gloves so you won't be cold, and a breathing tube.' He then started singing a beautiful lullaby. Oliver Sacks (1985, p. 183) describes how some retarded individuals can become transformed in their love of music. Martin, for example became 'a man in his wholeness wholly attending.' Similarly with Ali. I had never heard him so fluent and expressive.

When he finished he said to me gently, 'It is my language and it is what you sing when someone goes to God.' The premature baby, complete with breathing tube (Ali was in an incubator as a baby) is returned to the bath and not tortured.

Just as each loss sends us back to the one before and backwards and backwards until weaning or birth trauma, so each abuse travels a similar path. Ali had unconsciously completed his journey back to the birth injury he had suffered and his intensive care period as a tiny baby.

Frankenstein, and the end of therapy

Because Ali's disturbed behaviour had diminished he was moved to a school for children with mild learning difficulties. I was extremely concerned about that move as there was no provision for psychotherapy in the new school. However, as the previous school environment where Ali was placed had deteriorated even further,

I explored the possibility of Ali's gaining an escort so he could continue therapy.

Although the new head teacher was sympathetic he was also concerned about Ali's losing educational time. It proved useless for me to argue that Ali had only become able to read anything because of his therapy and that he was still so handicapped that two hours away from school once a week could hardly make a difference. The head teacher could not see the emotional determinants of handicap in Ali. If he had he would have had to see disturbance in the hundreds of other children in his school. 'Problem' children were those whose violence to themselves or others posed a management problem. Ali was certainly a noticeable target for sexual teasing and he also hung about the toilets watching smaller children, but he could only be allowed therapy for a term.

Ali's family were not able to act as escorts and Ali himself could not manage the journey. A term it was to be. I did agree with the school that after-school therapy would be the ideal solution but a dying Inner London Education Authority had no escort available. In his new school Ali regressed to his smiling stupid behaviour but his writing and reading did not deteriorate.

His disturbed sexual behaviour continued, of course. He brought me information about small children he watched in the toilets. He did not want to do anything to them but was scared he could. At the same time, a concern for his abused and handicapped self was growing.

Session 120

Ali was excited about telling me the difference between a dream and a film. The film was *Jaws* and the dream was about Frankenstein. 'Frankenstein has a hole in his head and so did Jaws have holes from where they shot at him. Frankenstein had drill holes in his head. The man drilled holes in his head, terrible, terrible holes that should not be there in a head.' He covered his eyes in agony. 'Drill, drill, drill in poor Frankenstein's head.' I commented on these terrible holes that were made in the wrong place.

Session 121

In the next session he told me that while in hospital for a throat infection he saw a little girl who was a friend of his. 'Now she was handicapped and she had a hurt tongue and could not speak and there were tubes all round her face and into her nose so she had to whisper. I said "Hello Tracy" and I thought she would say "Hello Ali" but she could not speak, only murmur the words with her lips. So my dad and my mum and me were sad to see a friend like that, all handicapped, with tubes.' He wiped a tear from his eye. 'My mum cried too. So sad to have a friend like that unable to have a tongue to speak.'

I said he too had been a poor sick Ali who did not have a tongue to speak and he knew what that felt like but today he had all his thoughts and feelings and could speak them. He had compassion for his handicapped self, not loathing or despair, and the good wishes of both his parents.

Session 122

Ali looked round the room. 'Such a lot has happened. Now I am older and we are back in your room.' He walked around. 'Last time I was talking about the poor handicapped girl and she is still in hospital.' He picked up a teddybear and sat in an armchair and wiped a tear from his eye. I said he was an older thinking boy and he felt sad for the poor little handicapped Ali who had no tongue but just horrid things done to him like the girl in the hospital. He hugged the bear and looked at me with a truly loving expression before his expression became sexualized and he was asking me to suck him.

Session 123: penultimate session

Ali spoke in a long monologue for almost the entire session. 'Can I tell you something, Mrs Sinason? I watch all the Frankenstein films, all of them, and I want to talk to you about them. Frankenstein has this bolt in his neck. If it was a human person's neck they would die but he doesn't. But when he wakes up and lives his neck hurts and he puts his hands round his neck [Ali demonstrates], and then he strangles someone.' Ali demonstrated again. I felt deeply moved as Ali had unsuccessfully tried to explain this to me in our very first session five years ago.

I said he had always been worried about strangling. He agreed. I asked if he remembered that the reason why Frankenstein felt his neck was because he had been put together from the body of a hanged man. 'Yes, hanged and strangled,' said Ali. 'And poor Frankenstein he cannot speak at the beginning.' I reminded him of Tracy in hospital and the little Ali who could not speak at first.

'Ah yes,' he agreed. 'Well, poor Frankenstein has this terrible bolt in his neck and he cannot speak easily and he runs to the priest who is blind and nice and the priest helps the handicapped Frankenstein to speak and it was all nice but then the people come and warn the priest about a monster and the priest gets scared of Frankenstein. But he shouldn't because Frankenstein is kind to children and people who are kind to him. Sometimes they scream and run away but they don't have to because he is only cruel to adults, not to children.' I said he wanted me to know that a monster me could not hurt him because monsters were nice to children but also he wanted me to know monsters could be sad and lonely and he was going to miss me next term.

I added that maybe I seemed like a stupid blind priest. It was fine while I did not see what a monster Ali I had but now I really knew him I was running away. He knew very well that I hoped to find a way of getting an after-school escort but that it was unlikely. In fantasy though, he saw me as running from the wounded monster just as he had learned to speak and just as some little children might be in danger.

Last session

Ali looked pale and awful and said he was going to the toilet to be sick. He came out a few minutes later looking even paler and told me he felt sick and ill. Inside the room he asked if I had an aspirin. I said it was no wonder he felt sick and ill. It was our last session in school time and at the moment there was no hope of an escort for a later time next term. He put his head in his hands. 'I might as well leave now and go swimming,' he said angrily. The head had made clear he did not like him missing swimming in order to come to therapy. I said he felt the head was stronger than me and when I said Ali needs more therapy it had not worked so what was the point. 'He is stronger,' said Ali sadly.

I reminded him of when he was at his last school and he managed to say 'No' to bullies. I reminded him of how even if he did say no there could be someone bigger and stronger but it mattered saying no. I said even if I was losing when I said 'Ali needs therapy,' and the head said 'Ali needs school most,' I was still sending letters and trying to find an escort. 'I need my therapy,' said Ali, 'but they will never let me come. I feel sick.'

I said if we really could not find an after-school escort then he could come himself in a few years when he was older and did not need an escort. He lit up. 'Yes. Because when I am older I can get a bus pass.' He brightened up and took a game of ludo out. He had only learned to play games in the last couple of months. He threw the dice and burst out crying. 'How can I play? How can I move without therapy? I can't.' I agreed there were further moves he could not make without therapy but a couple of months ago he could not play at all and a couple of years ago he would not have been able to say what he just had.

He cried and wiped his eyes. 'I will fight. I will say I need my therapy.' I said he could and it still might not happen until he was older. His face went thick and his stupid smile returned. I said, 'Poor Ali, this is sad for both of us, because we know it is not the right time to stop. So it gives you that sick and stupid feeling you used to have.' He nodded and wiped his eyes.

Two months later, as I had arranged, I visited him at his school. He was smiling stupidly and was very demanding to his teacher. She told me that she was concerned by his sexualized behaviour and the way he approached the little children. I was pleased she understood the situation and gave her further details of his background. However, therapy is still ruled out for the moment, until Ali is old enough to travel by himself.

Summary

Shortly after this visit, I watched a Frankenstein film on television and was struck by the rich symbolism of the hurt neck. The abused creation has a hurt neck and cannot speak because it carries the history of a hanged man. Similarly, the abused child has carried into itself a dead and deadly part of the abusing adult. A gang of men, grown-up abused children, had abused a small boy who grew up and abused his half-brother. A terrible history had been evacuated into the small and fragile receptacle of Ali.

However, in the process of six years of therapy, Ali had managed to identify this handicapped injured baby and to feel compassion for it. He had found a tongue and speech for it, even though he had to learn most painfully that even finding a language and a tongue and saying 'No' does not stop abusive things from happening.

Ali had an IQ of 45 when he first came to see me and spoke in two-word sentences. He used the word 'stupid' a lot. When Melanie Klein (1932, p. 115) looked at the material of a young boy abused by an older brother, she commented: 'He would threaten me with a wooden spoon, wanting to push it in my mouth and calling me small, stupid, weak. The spoon symbolised his brother's penis being forcibly thrust into his own mouth. He had identified himself with his brother and thus turned his hatred of him against his own self. He passed on his rage against himself for being small and weak to other children less strong than him and incidentally to me in the transference situation.'

Ali too is now bullying smaller children in his secondary school though struggling against it. Melanie Klein shows us clearly the process involved in moving from abused to abuser and she takes up every word except 'stupid'. I feel however that 'stupid' is a very important word and that adult and child are inevitably to be seen as stupid for sharing a blind concentration camp of a world where all normal values are turned upside down. The spoon that symbolizes the brother's penis is also the first feeding shape after the nipple. The child is thus hurtled back to the earliest images of abuse, of things being thrust into his mouth.

There is a further infantile strand I wish to bring in here that helped me understand my feelings of being nauseous in the countertransference. M. Woolridge (1986) points out that the mother's milk ejection or 'let-down' reflex causes the active expulsion of milk into the infant with little or no involvement on the part of the infant. He argues that after let-down the expulsion depends on the baby's sucking, but not during. There is still debate amongst scientists as to how voluntary swallowing is. However, it is clear that when fluid in the oral cavity reaches a certain volume swallowing has to occur due to either the quantity of milk or a specific tactile stimulation. The way 'swallowing' has entered our vocabulary perhaps puts more emphasis on the involuntary aspect. However, it is clear that the baby sometimes has to deal with getting more of a flow than it wants and will then feel forced to swallow to some extent. Where everything else in the environment provides the baby with time and good holding care and the baby's constitution is also equable, this will be resolved. But where the environment is not sensitive to the baby's needs then clearly 'swallowing' the indigestible and smiling or grinning to bear it is a short-term solution that starts to build up long-term problems.

Where the worker feels nauseous in the transactions with a child the child may have managed to project into the worker the terrible experience of something that was forced into it and can be swallowed down no longer. This is a frequent experience of clinical staff working in situations of concealed sexual abuse and has some diagnostic significance.

How can we deal with the terrible effects abuse has ? Firstly, by holding in mind the possibility of abuse. As the American child abuse specialist S. Sgroi has pointed out (1982), 'recognition of sexual molestation in a child is entirely dependent on the individual's willingness to entertain the possibility that the condition may exist.' A child knows only too well what its parents can tolerate it knowing, as Bowlby (1979) has shown in his paper 'On knowing what you are not supposed to know and feeling what you are not supposed to feel'. A patient is as hampered by the terrors and unresolved struggles of its therapist as it is by the same process in its parents.

It was a year before I was able to entertain the possibility that Ali had been abused and even then I felt I was mad to think it. With no medical proof (when the forensic examination took place) and no ordinary kind of disclosure the solidity of a professional sense of 'knowing' is easily battered. However, once Ali knew I was understanding his first communications and did not go stupid then he could begin to conceive properly what had been done and to explore his feelings about it.

Just as importantly, the adult has to stay with the repellent raping child who will become the raping adult and bear losing the tragic former victim of abuse. The mentally handicapped child victim who grows up into a mentally handicapped offender finds little help. English psychoanalyst and consultant psychiatrist Dr Mervyn Glasser works at the Portman Clinic, which specializes in outpatient psychoanalytical psychotherapy for sexually disturbed adults. He is one of only a small though influential number of workers who offer psychoanalytically orientated treatment to such adults. Work with adult abusers, HIV positive children or adults, geriatric patients and handicapped patients remains the least popular area of work.

I hope that understanding the process by which the abused child can become the abuser helps us see the legacy of abuse which will follow if the child sufferer is not helped to overcome the injurious identification with the process.

When Ali angrily called me 'stupid' he was showing he knew that word, not because it had been said to him and he was parroting it back but because, very deeply, he knew the meaning of the word. He was indeed mad with grief but he could only say that because he knew he was not stupid. As Myshkin asked in Dostoevsky's *The Idiot* (1869, p. 71): 'But can I be an idiot now, when I am able to see for myself that people look upon me as an idiot? As I come in I think: "I see they look upon me as an idiot and yet I am sensible and they don't guess it."'

7 THE SCRIBE FUNCTION AND CHILD DEVELOPMENT: TOMÁS

The flowers of the cherry tree
How they wave about!
It's not that I do not think of you
But your home is so far away.

Confucius commented, 'He did not really think of her. If he did, there is no such thing as being far away.'

Confucius, *The Analects*

Boys and girls come out to play
I call you up now
I am marking the register
of broken nursery rhymes
Are you there?
Are you truanting dear dead ones?
Where is Eddy, Eddy
with his Brylcream Ever-Ready?

Valerie Sinason, 'Round Up'

When a severely disturbed and mentally handicapped patient is referred for psychotherapy the exploration process is twofold. The therapist is exploring whether she thinks she can offer anything and whether she thinks the patient could make use of the process. The patient is similarly exploring whether she can bear the two-person process and whether she thinks the therapist has something useful to offer. In some cases, such as that of Maureen (Chapter 9), the first meeting in itself decides the issue; in others, like Steven's (Chapter 5), the exploration takes longer.

Drawing up guidelines for assessment is complex in a new area.

As I showed in Chapter 3, when psychoanalysis began Freud did not consider psychotic or handicapped patients suitable for psychoanalysis. In 1979, when the Tavistock Workshop was founded, no formally trained psychoanalytical psychotherapist considered that a profoundly multiply handicapped child or adult would manage therapy. Providing treatment for adults with mild mental handicaps was revolutionary enough.

However, although all practitioners, hopefully, improve through learning from their experiences, there will always be a mismatch to some degree between need for treatment and ability to use it – either with the practitioners available or indeed with anybody. When Ann Hithersay of the Spastics Society's pioneering but sadly now defunct Oak Tree International Project brought together exponents of cognitive and psychodynamic ways of working (Castle Priory College, April 1990) we considered this most carefully. With the benefit of a joint assessment and treatment evaluation process (as was being planned for the Oak Tree Project) it would be possible to refine our understanding of the best programmes for different individuals. It would be possible to evaluate who would benefit most from a behavioural approach and who from a psychodynamic. It might also shed light on those disturbed individuals who have such a terror and hatred of communicating that they would find any kind of treatment intolerable.

It is extremely important for workers to evaluate their own work and learn from errors. Tomás is the subject of this chapter for two different reasons. Firstly, although Tomás managed a year of once-weekly psychotherapy he could not really use it. He was the only patient with a handicap who did not manage the normal fifty-minute hour. I had the hope that it might be possible slowly to feed him more time, bit by bit. And indeed, the time slowly did increase. However, the pain of his inner life was too much for him to bear.

The second reason for basing this chapter on Tomás is to discuss what he showed me about the developmental processes involved in dealing with absence and the meaning and power of writing. Traumatic early experiences of deprivation and abandonment had damaged his sense of continuity. Not surprisingly this affected all his activities. He could not stay still long enough to think or learn. Although the environment was now relatively stable, inside himself he perpetuated the system of precipitous indiscriminate moves. He was unable to learn to read himself, but he wanted me to be his scribe and write his words down for him. Using me as a scribe meant that I was his communication organ, something important that he did not want to spoil. Nevertheless, using me in that way meant I could not have a function of thinking for him or about him. It raised many issues for me about the developmental tasks of reading and writing.

TOMÁS

Tomás was referred at the age of fourteen. A severely mentally handicapped adolescent, he lived in a residential home where there was realistic concern about his violence. His father was mildly handicapped and his mother was mentally ill and frequently in and out of hospital. They found themselves unable to look after Tomás, or his older brother, though they had tried. The children had not come to the attention of their local social services as babies or toddlers.

Tomás was a difficult baby for his already burdened parents. He cried a lot and did not respond. He was placed with an unregistered child-minder who was alcoholic and abusive. On one occasion his father went to collect him and found him eating food from the dustbin while the minder lay in a drunken sleep. They then sent him out of England to be looked after by the paternal grandparents. Nothing is known of those early four or five years. From some of Tomás's actions and words we suspected that he spent many hours locked up in a farm shed. His uneducated grandparents lived in primitive conditions in a society with no proper provision for handicapped children. When Tomás was returned to England because his grandparents were too old to manage him any more, the nature of his mental handicap and increased emotional disturbance meant that he came to the attention of the authorities. Then began nine years of varying short-stay and longer-stay placements, until Tomás finally found a resting place that would see him through until chronological adulthood.

On his referral there were many notes about Tomás's behaviour that could be passed on but there was no real history. This is a familiar tragedy in the world of mental handicap. Loss follows loss: loss of normality, loss of family, loss of history. Brendan McCormack (1989), a consultant psychiatrist in mental handicap at Harperbury Hospital and a member of the APP Mental Handicap Section, found that of 70 handicapped patients transferred to his area when a large hospital closed, in not one case was there a full history to be found. Given that so many of this client group can find it hard to speak or think, this is a double deprivation.

Tomás's new key worker, Anne, was very aware of the impact of his not having a past history and was building up a photograph album and a diary with him to compensate. She had referred him to me because of cumulative concern about him, capped by two recent violent episodes. In both of them, an argument had triggered off an uncontrollable state in which Tomás inflicted enormous damage on the environment and those around. He had, for example, thrown chairs through the window, kicked the side of a car in and hurled heavy pieces of furniture at the female staff present.

When male staff or Anne were on duty he was calmer, but violence could still occur. However, the staffing ratio meant it was impossible to ensure even moderate safety. In addition, Tomás could not concentrate on anything for more than ten minutes. Trying to keep him content, the staff quickly found themselves exhausted. If they did not accede to an activity he wanted or if they could not find him a new one they faced the fear of his increasing violence. He was already tall and strong for his age and there was concern for how manageable he would be when older. Football was the only activity that could hold him for any time. He had no friends but was content to go out in a group. He went to discos and a club at his school but danced on his own, never really relating.

First session

When I came into the waiting room to meet him I saw a tall muscular boy with a frightened expression on his face, shuffling his legs and moving his head whilst turning the pages of a comic very quickly. As I introduced myself the expression turned into a stupid smile (see Chapter 7 for the meaning of that kind of smile). I suggested Anne come to the room with us to begin with. With many handicapped patients who do not live at home I have a first meeting with the key worker present. Where it has taken a child a long time to trust the residential staff I have found it helpful to show that I am a part of that extended family team.

Inside the room I showed Tomás the drawing materials and toys available and said we would see if he liked coming today and if he did I would be able to see him each week. I asked Anne to explain why she had referred Tomás and she gently described how concerned the home was with his increased violence and their feeling that he found it hard to express himself. When she described his violence Tomás smiled stupidly and jerkily got up from his seat to move next to her, clinging onto her arm, fear eventually breaking through the smile. I said it looked as if Tomás was very frightened of how violent he had been and could be and that the very mention of the word frightened him. I added that he might also be frightened we would be cross with him because of his violence. Tomás nodded and moved back to the table where the toys were. Even when he sat down, parts of his body kept up a movement.

I suggested Anne wait downstairs and I would meet with Tomás for fifteen minutes. With every other handicapped patient assessments have taken the standard psychoanalytic fifty minutes. However, I could see that Tomás would not manage that and I had yet to ascertain the nature and level of his violence. With Anne gone, Tomás looked nervously at me. I said he did not know me yet and he was frightened of me without Anne there. I repeated my name and the fact that he could use any of the toys or writing material on the table. He reached quickly for a crocodile and made it bite a little boy's legs. His face looked anguished as he did this. 'Dad,' he said, pointing to the crocodile. I said the father crocodile had hurt the boy's legs. He nodded and pointed to his trousered leg. 'Hurt.' I found myself wanting to see his leg. I said he wanted me to know his leg hurt just as the boy doll's leg did. He nodded. He gave a stupid smile. I said he was smiling when he was hurt to hide the hurt, just as his trousers hid his hurting leg, but he could tell me with words or show me with the dolls.

'Go,' he suddenly said, terrified. He got up to walk to the door. I said it was very frightening for him but he had only been here a little time and I thought he could manage longer. I said he was frightened now he had shown me his leg hurt. Perhaps he felt telling me would make it hurt more. I wondered aloud too whether his father had hurt him when he was little and lived at home.

He came back and urgently picked up the exercise book on the table. 'Write,' he ordered, pushing a blue felt-tip into my hand. He then grabbed my wrist to pull me to the table. It hurt. I gently told him to let go of my hand. I said he had used words to ask me and they were enough. I did not feel anger at his use of force although I was quite certain he knew his own strength. I was reminded of the handicapped Lennie in Steinbeck's brilliant *Of Mice and Men*, who was supposedly innocent of his strength.

It was hard for Tomás to let go of my wrist but I did not move or speak until he had. I walked to the table, drawing up a chair. Tomás urgently sat beside me. 'What do you want me to write?' 'Name. Valerie. Name. Tomás. Tomás frightened.' I wrote my name and then Tomás's. He seized the pen and copied the shapes of the letters. 'Now – Tomás frightened.' He thrust the pen in my hand again and pulled my wrist onto the paper. I said he did not want his words to do the work. He did not want me to respond to his words. He felt I would be useless and unwilling to help him if he did not pull me into action. He let go of my hand. I said he could hear my words. I wrote, 'Tomás is feeling frightened the first time he is in the room with Mrs Sinason. He asks her to write his name and her name and he copies it. He asks her to write down in the book that he is frightened.'

'Read,' ordered Tomás. I read it to him. For the first time he relaxed. 'That's right,' he marvelled. I said he was pleased with the words I had written. They said what he wanted them to. 'Leg,' he suddenly added. 'You want me to write down that your leg hurt and your father hurt it and it felt like a crocodile bite.' 'Yes,' said Tomás. I wrote it down. Tomás watched carefully and then snatched the book the moment I had finished. 'Tomás's book.' I said yes, that was his book and if he wanted to see me each week it would stay locked up so no-one else could touch it except him. 'Good.' He relaxed in his chair and in that one contrasting moment sharply showed me how tense his usual movements were. 'Go,' he suddenly said, quite terrified. I said he had managed to have something important written down and that had made him feel better for a while but now he felt he had to go. 'Have to,' he underlined. I agreed. We went downstairs. He had been with me for fifteen minutes.

When I told Anne by phone later that Tomás had mentioned his leg hurting she said he had a scar across his leg which they felt was a whipmark. No-one had been able to get an explanation of it from him. She added he was also terrified of the dark and of keys and they felt he must have been locked up in a dark room or cupboard as a small child, as well as whipped.

Tomás was to end up coming once weekly for a year. Both were at his limits of tolerance. His sessions initially lasted fifteen minutes. After three months they increased to twenty minutes and after six months they lasted for half an hour. It was quite clear that anything longer than that was intolerable.

What I now want to look at in relation to Tomás are two regular themes in his therapy, a game of hide-and-seek and the use of myself as a scribe. After the first few months of fifteen-minute 'scribe' sessions Tomás played hide-and-seek for the first time. The two activities then happened each session forming something in the borderland between obsessional ritual and comfortable habit. Only then could the space and time become bearable. Only with the time so ordered could the different shades of his feelings and my responses be tolerated.

Session 12: the first game of hide-and-seek

Tomás has covered himself with the blanket on the couch in the therapy room. 'Find me,' he calls. 'I wonder where Tomás is?' I ask wonderingly, as if to a toddler. I am aware my voice is soft. 'Is he under the table? No. He is not there.' I start the search slowly with the table furthest away from him. I am aware that he needs distance. Unlike the normal child who wants a build-up of excitement in the adult's voice as the prospect of finding becomes closer, Tomás needs unexcitement. My voice stays slow but questioning. 'I'm here,' he suddenly screams, crying desperately, throwing the blanket off himself and throwing himself onto the floor sobbing uncontrollably. I wait a moment until his crying has quietened. A touch would have been an intrusion to him. Then I say, 'You found it hard to be found and hard to hide.'

'Write,' shouts Tomás, pulling me to the table. 'The word worked,' I say. 'You do not have to use your hands too. Perhaps there is a Tomás who does not like the fact words work as well as a Tomás who likes words to be said and written.'

We sit together by the table, Tomás hovering insistently over me. 'What shall I write?' I ask. I feel like a mother about to feed a baby. Only for this writing experience does Tomás find me safe to be near and then he is very close. Winnicott (1962) shows how good-enough mothering allows a child the 'brief experience of omnipotence.' I felt that allowing Tomás to see the way his words could be thought by him, spoken, understood by me and then written by my hand furthered this; similarly the expansion of his two-word sentences into my lengthier sentences. 'Tomás sees Mrs Sinason every Tuesday except holidays. Why doesn't he see her on weekends and other days? This makes Tomás cross. Cross and frightened. Tomás told Anne he did not like people shouting. Shouting makes Tomás angry. Sorry. Tomás misses Mrs Sinason.'

Tomás copies the letters although he cannot read. Then he relaxes. Then he asks me to read the entry to him. He nods his approval. Then he becomes frightened and cannot be still. He wants to leave the room. The last strand of the session is the inability of his sane self to withstand attack on the peace he found earlier.

Tomás's first words that he wants recorded after our names are our connection, our meeting and then our separation. Our meeting clearly conveys true 'we-ness' (Alvarez, 1988) for him. He is aware that I am pleased to see him just as much as I am aware of his pleasure in seeing me, even though there are risks involved for him being in touch. However, 'our' separation is not a joint decision. Tomás is aware that I have defined the rhythm of our meeting even though his needs have partially defined the time. For example, he was aware that our initial meeting time of fifteen minutes was in response to his needs and that it expanded to twenty minutes when he was able to manage it and, had he been able, it could have expanded further.

This session is a typical one, and was repeated every week with subtle differences and refinements. Over the year, the book was used to record a mixture of important social events in Tomás's life, practical details and fears. Whatever the difference in the details, the extract would usually include loss, anger and then further loss. Similarly, even if occasionally Tomás allowed the hide-and-seek game to continue a fraction longer it never reached a position of safety. The only two objects he was able to touch after the first session were a Jack-in-the-box and a musical clock.

Tomás could barely play, because the prerequisite for play is being able to hide and find, being able to bear absence because you know presence will come and because presence means someone you are attached to who will not be abusive.

Early developmental theory

Psychoanalytic theory and psychological theory agree that in the first two or three months of life, a child's visual universe is made of fleeting images. The baby attempts to follow an object until it passes out of its line of vision and then the baby abandons the search. Any new toy or object can capture its attention. Similarly, the baby can be held by a variety of different people without protest. However, from three months the child can co-ordinate its arm and hand movements and its vision. It can reach for objects that it sees, but would not search for a hidden object. According to Piaget, at this stage the infant behaves as if an object out of sight has lost its permanence and no longer exists. At nine months a baby can find a hidden object if it has seen it being hidden.

Emotionally, a similar journey is being made. When a mother leaves the room for a moment and a tiny baby cries the baby does not understand the mother will only be away for a few seconds. For the baby the mother has gone forever. The baby feels it is dying. That is why we all turn in the street anywhere when we hear a baby cry. It is a powerful sound that we recognize emotionally because a baby could actually die if we did not respond. Babies in orphanages died when they were tended physically but not responded to emotionally (Spitz, 1953). However, by six to nine months the baby who has had a good-enough experience will have some preliminary sense of object permanence; he will believe his mother will return and will manage to survive a little while on his own resources.

At the same time as this sense of permanence is being developed, other means of communication are growing. Smiling grows after eight weeks, often directed to the mother. Its appearance is often linked with important sounds, renewed babbling. Early views were that the baby was attached primarily to the mother for the satisfaction of instinctual hunger. However, the Harlow experiment (Harlow and Zimmerman, 1959) changed this. Professor H. Harlow of the University of Wisconsin placed infant monkeys with artificial 'mother' monkeys made of wire mesh. A feeding bottle was attached to the chest of the wire-mesh 'mother'. A similar 'mother' was constructed but the wire-mesh was covered with soft terry-cloth. As one part of the experiment the soft mother had no feeding bottle attached. The infant monkeys stayed with the soft mother for most of the day only going quickly to the wire-mesh figure when they needed food. This showed that attachment needs were linked to something more than just feeding. The terry-cloth also gave the infant monkeys the confidence to explore, to leave home base, whereas when they were with the wire-mesh mother the space was threatening.

A background of safe-enough attachment is therefore an important prerequisite of play. Playing peekaboo, using a Jack-in-the-box, lifting up beakers to see what is hidden inside, can all only be done if there is enough safety and pleasure in permanence to test out in play the experiences of departure and arrival. When all goes well a child slowly manages more time away from its parents without disintegration. This is a lengthy process, however. For some children and adults, absence wipes out all links.

A tiny baby is beset by powerful forces and anxieties with which it is not yet equipped to deal. A means of survival is found which is also a communication. As described first by Melanie Klein (1946) and later by Wilfred Bion (1959) it manages to split off and projects what it finds unbearable into the mother. The baby then faces those frightening forces in the person of the mother. If the mother is capable of responding sensitively to the fears of her baby by her physical and emotional holding (Winnicott, 1952; Bowlby, 1958; Bick, 1968) or her thinking, reverie or containment (Bion, 1962), the baby will see its terrors have been modified. The mother has not confirmed the baby's fantasy and this has transformed the baby's emotions into a tolerable experience. If the baby is lucky enough in its own unique constitutional personality it will then take in this modified experience. In healthy development the child will allow the absent object to stay good and to return when needed.

Such a baby will then find small manageable absences becoming a spur to thinking and emotional development. Bion (1957) sees thought as a link between a preconception and frustration. For example, if a baby has somewhere the preconception of feeding and that preconception is not joined up immediately with the actual experience of feeding, that gap in time can become a thought if the baby tolerates the frustration.

However, this was not the experience for Tomás or for many of the other children or adults I write about here. What happens, then, when the baby's cry is not answered and its terrors are not modified? Bion (1957, p. 105) thinks that all aggression and envy in the baby are exacerbated when the mother is unreceptive. The fear of dying is not dealt with and turns into a 'nameless dread'. The infant's consciousness is too fragile to bear this. Where the baby's projections to the mother are not received or are retaliated against, thinking cannot develop.

For example, a baby starts to cry. It is lying in its cot and nobody is there. If someone comes quickly enough and calmly soothes the baby, the baby, if it is temperamentally lucky enough, is likely to be comforted and stop crying. The baby is able to build up a sense that its communications and its distress are manageable. Let us change the scenario. Another baby wakes up and starts to cry. Someone comes rushing in, grabs the baby roughly and shouts at it for crying. That person is not able to bear the baby's grief because the cry has set off his or her own infantile memories of unmet needs. The baby then experiences that its terrors cannot be managed. Not only that, the terror it experienced internally is all too cruelly reflected back by the outside world. There is no safe space. What happens when a baby is left crying for hours, with parents who have disassociated themselves from the experience? Such a baby, left unattended, might not continue crying. It might give up all hope of communication and become quiet, sleep a lot, and become deeply depressed. For although a small amount of frustration leads to thinking, too much frustration and deprivation destroy it. If nobody is thinking adequately for you or feeling for you, how can you take in such concepts?

The absence of a thinking mother and a feeling mother are not experienced as a neutral absence. Psychoanalyst and child psychotherapist Edna O'Shaughnessy showed (1964) how an absence is never just an absence – it becomes a frightening, persecuting presence. A baby in this situation is then haunted by the bad presence of absence. One way of surviving this is to get rid of all emotional baggage. However, this has problems. If the mind is permanently emptied to avoid being annihilated from within, nothing can be experienced as good. Anything taken in, words, or thoughts, or learning, becomes instantly transformed into something dangerous and annihilating.

No wonder Tomás could not keep still. He was haunted by this active malevolent ghost of present absence. He not only met an unreceptive response from his mentally ill mother, he was also provided with equally traumatogenic caretakers elsewhere. Tomás could not keep still because he had no solid preconception of finding any sane home base. Being still put him at the mercy of unbearable feelings. Moving about was exhausting and depleting but not annihilating.

Mary Main (1981, 1985, 1986) and other attachment research theorists have graphically shown the predicament of the baby whose needs for attachment and physical contact are rejected. A video Mary Main showed at the birthday conference for John Bowlby organized by John Byng-Hall in 1986 showed a frightened baby moving towards his mother and then away. If the person who cannot deal with your feelings is also the person from whom you need reassurance because of your own attachment needs, you are in a terrible predicament.

Psychoanalyst and autism researcher Peter Hobson, professor of developmental psychopathology at the Tavistock Clinic, has shown how organic impairment (as in autism) has implications for symbolic development and language development (Hobson, 1983). It is not surprising that words and feelings were dangerous for Tomás with the combination of his traumatized environment and his handicap. If you develop words because you are involved in a reciprocal relationship where feelings and meanings can be understood, children with a background likes Tomás's face extra developmental difficulty.

In trying to understand the experience with Tomás with these theoretical issues in mind, I became fascinated with the light shed on it by my work with Mandy, an eight-year-old who was sexually abused by her mother and stepfather. She was not organically handicapped but her experiences had substantially reduced her intelligence. She was in short-term care, not knowing where her permanent placement would be. Her approaches to me were either sexualized or avoidant.

Here is the first session in which she tried to play. As with Tomás, it was preceded by her using me in a different way, by her having me tell her a story.

She came into the therapy room and cried. She walked towards me crying and then ran away to the couch, where she curled up sucking her thumb and sobbing. I said she was really sad and she wished she could trust me to help her with it. She nodded. There was a long silence broken by sobs. 'Story,' she whispered. I asked if she wanted me to tell her a story. 'Yes.' I was sure that was what she meant but I was checking that single word did not stand for a story she had just heard that had frightened her. I asked her what story she would like and she asked for 'The Three Billygoats Gruff'. This is the story of three billygoats who want to get to the green grass on the other side of the bridge but have to face the angry devouring Troll to do that. I felt this choice linked to her longing to be on the green grass on the other side of short-term care, but was also a geographical way of expressing how, to gain a caring parent, she had to first deal with the violent abusive one.

I told her the story. As in playing hide-and-seek with Tomás, I was aware that my voice was soft and unexciting and I was very careful to herald the frightening parts of the story, inviting her participation. After the story she put the blanket over her head so she was hidden from view. 'You can't see me but you have to look for me,' she announced. 'Where's Mandy?' I wondered. Again, as with Tomás, I started by checking the furniture furthest away from her, the table and chair and slowly and untantalizingly went round the room until I came to the couch. I paused. 'You can't see me,' she instructed. 'OK,' I agreed. I returned to my chair.

'Where is Mandy?' I asked. 'I have looked everywhere for her and I can't find her.' There was a pause. 'That's because she is naughty and she ran away,' whispered a shy voice. 'Well,' I replied, 'she might have run away and she might be naughty but I am the grownup here and I didn't keep a good eye on her or she wouldn't have been able to run away, even if she wanted to.' There was an electric pause. 'Ask the bed where she is?' came the voice, a little stronger. 'Bed,' I asked, 'have you seen Mandy?' 'Yes.' 'Where is she?' I asked. 'She is on me and I am the good bed.' I asked if it was hard for the bed to be a good bed. 'Yes, because there is a bad bed and that is when people do bad sex on you.' I said, 'Poor Bed, it must be hard being a bed if people do bad sex on you.' 'Yes. You just have to lie there and put up with it.' Mandy's voice was getting stronger and I felt ready to get closer to her experience directly. 'Maybe that is what happens to Mandy,' I wondered aloud. 'Maybe she feels like a bad bed putting up with bad sex on her and then she feels she has to run away.' There was a long silence. Then Mandy sat up, removing the blanket from her face. 'It is smelly and sweaty and noisy and no-one wants you.' She quickly covered her face again. 'Find me, but you mustn't look at me.' I again went through the routine of 'Where's Mandy?' and when I came to the couch I asked, 'Can I find you now if I don't touch the blanket?' 'Yes.' 'I wonder if Mandy is under the blanket?' I asked in a matter-of-fact tone. 'She is,' replied Mandy, and then sat up. Unlike Tomás, she was not in terror, but this first game, which has since been repeated weekly for two years, has never reached the moments of pleasure or excitement that most children take for granted.

The rejecting parent heightens the baby's need for attachment and its sense of being tantalized. Where the rejecting parent is also abusive a delusional system is sometimes the only means of survival. As Shengold (1979) comments, 'If the very person who abuses and is experienced as bad must be turned to for relief of the distress that parent has caused, then the child must out of desperate need register the parent delusionally as good.'

There is another theoretical strand I find helpful in thinking about Tomás. Esther Bick's (1968) depiction of the infant needing a psychic skin equal to the actual physical skin helps us understand how at times of absence and in fear of spilling out, the baby tries to hold itself together. Some babies whose proud parents say 'Isn't he active' are thrashing desperately around with their bodies to hold themselves together. Tomás's incessant physical movement was at times a flight from persecution and at times a bodily way of keeping intact. Elsewhere I have written (Sinason, 1987) of the way some forms of dancing and physical activity are an attempt at creating a 'second skin' (Bick, 1968) in the face of primitive loss.

When a baby faces separation it can hallucinate its mother's presence. There is a fine distinction between internalizing the missing person so that they stay with you and hallucinating the missing person so you deny they have ever gone. Sometimes a teddy or dummy, far from being a transitional object that allows separation to happen, is in fact experienced as proof that no separation has happened. Annie, aged one, shows no sign of noticing her mother leave the room. There is a dummy in her mouth and as far as she is concerned she is still connected to her mother.

The longer a baby or child has had to deal with separation and abandonment the more powerful this facsimile non-relationship becomes. Rushdie expresses this process powerfully in *Shame*: 'There is a thing she has inside that has never happened anywhere else; her mother skips with her, Bilquis holds the skipping-rope and the two of them jump together . . . It tires her out to play with this toy, not because of the skipping but because of the difficulty of doing things inside that you haven't brought there from the outside' (Rushdie, 1984, p. 213). To keep internal control of the powerfully hostile and rejecting outside mother depletes emotional space and energy. And yet to pause and stop means seeing that mother will not skip with you or be with you.

The Jack-in-the-box is a very powerful toy of absence and presence. Most have two outside functions. One button allows Jack to emit a squeak whilst staying hidden. The other allows Jack to spring out, forcing the lid open as well as making a sound. The best parenting in the world cannot prevent the primitive processes of splitting and projective identification (although it can modify the timing and nature of them). The baby has an experience of sending something negative and hostile to inside the mother, inside her breasts especially. He then fears her as damaged and when she shows she isn't damaged and has survived there is joy at her safety and strength. This early experience is reinvoked when weaning occurs and then again at each new developmental stage involving separation. The Jack springing up after he has been shut away inside the container and attacked can similarly symbolize these powerful primitive processes. Patients who have experienced multiple separations are amazed each time that Jack is not damaged by what has gone on inside the box. However, the sound he makes does justice to the aggression he has borne whilst suffocated and pressed inside a small inhospitable space.

A child that unconsciously understands the nature of its aggressive attacks and who has had good-enough mothering can enjoy the representation of absence and presence that the toy offers. For the child whose experience has been more traumatic the toy is not a symbol. It is what Hanna Segal calls (1957) a 'symbolic equation'. The substitute is treated as if it were the same as the original object.

The scribe

Tomás not only did not have a receptive mother, he had an abusing one. While frustration of a certain amount within a context of understanding allows thinking to develop, intolerable frustration and abuse of any kind attack thinking. With those concepts in mind I would like to attend now to the actual words Tomás wanted me to record and to consider the meaning of the link between the experience of absence and presence and writing. I will start with extracts from a poem by James Berry, a quotation from the Bible and a poem of mine.

> She say you sign your name with X
> you show no paperwork
> but you have your workings

with pencil and paper in your head
Gal I say the printed page is
a spread of dead things: insects
what stares at me
doin notn saying notn
but turn dark night
an bother me an bother me
for time I hear prints-a-talk
like voices of we children

James Berry, 'Thinking Aloud'

He [Aaron] will do all the speaking to the people for you, he
will be the mouthpiece and you will be the god he speaks for

Exodus 4:5

Light streams
through the shuttered windows
The ward lies
in the shadow of words
Men and women warp
into the shape
of broken sounds
Tongues loll
in leaden bells of skull
All faces are gasps and gutturals
For the zoo
I bring the sentence-keepers
the joined-up writing
the clash of consonants
and the joyous anguish of vowels
Such a price to pay for a name
For the skeleton-key of a letter
I learn
the animal pre-alphabet
A bestiary of grief
For the cut flowers
I bring the universe of a tear

> the rooted visiting cards
> of tombstones

Valerie Sinason, 'Subnormality Hospital',
Inkstains and Stilettos

For every single session I wrote an entry in Tomás's exercise book
which he dictated. He never spoiled this activity or destroyed a page
or attacked the pen. He sat close to me while it was done. Whilst
engaged in writing I was clearly experienced as safe. The moment
he took the pen from me and writing was over I was dangerous
again and so was the room and so was being still. Although in the
first couple of sessions Tomás took the book in order to copy a word
or even a sentence, he did not need after that to make the words
his by copying them. They were allowed their separate existence
on the page. The words were clearly good parents.

In his residential home, the staff tried to compensate for
complicated shift-work and staff shortages by keeping careful notes
on the residents. At handover time the notes were handed over. The
words represented the continuity in thinking of the adults. Sidney
Klein (1985, p. 38) feels that the infant sees the normal separation
of parents as caused by its own splitting processes, 'which in turn
leads to primitive guilt and fear in relation to the excluded parent'.
I think the act of writing brings together these splits, and reduced
Tomás's guilt.

Session 14

'Tomás went to hospital because he cut his leg kicking a window.
When his leg is better he will have the plaster taken off. He kicked
the window Saturday. He missed Mrs Sinason. He did not see her
last week because it was the bank holiday. Tom made me kick the
window because he shouted. Tomás is hurt by the noise.'

Session 15

'Tomás pretended to phone Mrs Sinason. He went to a disco. Tomás
wants a drink after school. Tomás wants his plaster taken off. He

wants to ride a bike again. Tomás went out for coffee with Anne. His leg hurts. Steven was shouting last night. It hurt Tomás.'

Session 24

'Today the hospital are taking off Tomás's plaster. No needle or stitches. Better now. Tomás can move his leg. Tomás is protected by Ghostbusters. Tomás feels like dancing because his leg is better. Tomás wants to leave the room because Mrs Sinason is dangerous. Tomás remembered his therapy today. Everyone else forgot.'

Session 28

Tomás walks in holding out a Lion bar of chocolate. He offers me a bite. Although it is in its wrapper, untouched and unopened, I feel repelled and am unable to deal with a poisonous projection.

'Tomás went out to get new clothes. He is going to join a club at his school. There will be dancing. He has new shoes, new gloves and a jacket. Mrs Sinason has not seen him in it when he went to the disco. Tomás has a Lion bar to eat. He is going to the cinema tonight.'

Session 29

I am allowed a second chance. Tomás brings another Lion bar and this time I am able to pretend to eat it. This satisfies Tomás, who then eats it before playing hide-and-seek.

'Tomás brought a Lion bar last week because he was too frightened to eat it. He offered it to Mrs Sinason but she said "No thank you". Today Tomás brought a Lion bar again because he was frightened last week and Mrs Sinason ate it. Tomás ate it and he can go to the disco if he says sorry to Anne for biting her.'

Re-reading his words I was struck by Tomás's clear understanding of my previous inability to help him be a 'Lion' and take in sustenance. I was helped by Juliet Hopkins's comment (1987) that the avoidant child's feelings and projections of being untouchable, repellent or contaminated 'need to be traced to their origin in the parents' treatment of their child, and not ascribed only to the hatred and guilt which the child inevitably feels'.

Session 30

Tomás touches two toys, the first he has touched since touching the crocodile on his very first session. He winds up the musical clock and listens to it. He holds it to his ear and then his heart. Then he presses the button on the Jack-in-the-box to hear the Jack make a noise. He cries. Then he presses another button to make Jack come out. He screams and throws it away. 'Poor Jack,' he says. He goes back to the clock. For the first and only time he manages a couple of minutes of hide-and-seek with the clock. He hides the clock under the blanket instead of himself and asks me to find it. He watches me nervously but allows me to find the clock. Then he hides but nothing is different. He is just as terrified.

For a while he could not think of anything to write. He looked terrified and said 'Go.' I said to him we could manage; if we stayed there together a thought would come that I could write down for him.

Anne-Marie Sandler (1985) has usefully commented, 'Too many analysts, because of their fear of giving reassurance to the patient (which is not an appropriate measure in psychoanalysis) are afraid to give interpretations which have a reassuring effect (which is not only legitimate but also very appropriate in the analytic work).'

Anne Alvarez (1988) has also shown most forcefully that some deprived and disturbed children need to have presence mentioned as much as absence. She looks first at Freud's (1920) description of his grandson's game with a wooden reel and string, the first such psychoanalytical observation. In this observation Freud saw the one-and-a-half-year-old throw a wooden reel with a piece of string attached to it into his curtained cot so that it looked as if it had disappeared. When this happened the toddler made an expressive 'ooo' sound. He would then pull the reel out of the cot again and hail its reappearance with a joyous 'da'. Freud saw this as the child learning how to deal with absence with joyful return being an essential ingredient of the game. Alvarez comments (p. 3) that all too often pleasure in the joyful return of the object is mainly seen as a defence against the unpleasure at its loss rather than as an entity in its own right. She points out that coming to terms with gain is the other half of the story!

Then the writing began. 'Poor Jack is locked up. Jack cries. Tomás went to the club. Tomás ate fish and chips. He shouted at Steven and kicked him. The noise hurt. Tomás found that 9 o'clock [his therapy time] on his musical clock is a special sound'.

Session 34

This was before a bank holiday.

'Tomás wants the time to go quickly so he can go. He is worried Mrs Sinason is cross and the musical clock is dangerous and can kill him. He wants the musical clock to go fast. He thinks it is stupid. He wants Mrs Sinason to come to tea and see him in his house.'

The musical clock has been an object of pain and relief for many handicapped patients as the clockwork action means that at a certain point the tune slows down. This can represent symbolically the point where handicap begins.

Session 35

'Tomás is going to the club tonight in his new shoes. He has to say sorry first. He will dress up smartly for the disco. He likes dancing. It is for boys and girls. Tomás likes the plane and fire engines even though it is a rescue plane.'

Session 38

'Tomás had to move somewhere for the holiday because there were not enough staff to look after him in his home. Why?'

'Tomás does not like his red shoes. He wants to change them now. He wants Mrs Sinason to shout at Anne. He wants to go back to the shop. He never wanted red shoes. Why? Why did they get them?'

This was the last session he attended.

Session 39

I waited. He did not come. I rang the home and was told he had refused to come that morning.

Session 40

He did not come. A message came that he had refused again. After that Anne rang up saying he did not want to come any more. When this happened I followed my usual procedure. I wrote a letter making clear that I would keep his place open for a month to see if he wanted to come and think about what had happened. Through his worker Anne he made it clear that he did not want to come. I then wrote to say I was no longer keeping that time open for him but if he ever wanted to come back in the future he was welcome. Through Anne, I asked him if he would like to come for a goodbye meeting. He did not want to come to my room again but did want to see me. I decided I would go to his residential unit to say goodbye to him. Home visits always pose a difficult technical problem (see Chapter 4 for more complex ones); however, I considered that if I did not visit Tomás to say goodbye he could be left with frightening fantasies of damage.

I visited the home and saw him briefly with Anne to say goodbye. 'Show, show,' he said, tugging at my arm and clearly wanting to show me his environment. With Anne's agreement I then spent half an hour following Tomás's manic footsteps. He moved from the kitchen to his room to the garden to the football pitch to a shop to the garden to the kitchen at lightning speed. When a group of adolescents indicated they were going to a club with one of the resident workers Tomás ran off with them, waving a quick goodbye. As I watched the group make their way to the bus stop Tomás stood out by his unceasingly active and frenetic physical movements. He darted in and out of the group, across the road and back and in and out of shops. At no moment was he at peace.

Back in the home with Anne, I could now understand more fully the difficult management problem he represented for staff. Anne was able to shed further light on why Tomás had given up coming at that point. He had always come easily to therapy and been relatively peaceful afterwards. However, whenever there was a staff shortage in the home, especially at or near a holiday time, he would keep demanding of Anne that I should be called for to come and stay at the home. The fact that I did not was intolerable to him. Anne added that after his last session he had done something most unusual. Politely and clearly he had explained he did not like his new red shoes and would like to go back and change them. She had agreed and then he had become violent. Thinking together, we were able to see that therapy had helped Tomás express his own wishes more clearly. However, if the outside world showed it could respond to that he was left with anger and hurt that his own family had not. The moment his sane self could see it could change the outer reality, an internal civil war took place. As Freud has expressed so clearly (1909, p. 223), 'During the progress of a psycho-analysis it is not only the patient who plucks up courage, but his disease as well; it grows bold enough to speak more plainly than before.'

The meaning of the written word

Words have a sound, a meaning and what L. Ehri (1978) calls 'a graphic identity' when they are written. Nor is the meaning a simple unitary concept. There is grammatical meaning as well as emotional meaning. Written language requires conscious work 'because its relationship to inner speech is different from that of real speech: the latter precedes inner speech in the course of development, while written speech follows inner speech and presupposes its existence (the act of writing implying a translation from inner speech)' (Vygotsky, 1983, p. 265). Vygotsky was interested in the lag between the ordinary schoolchild's oral and written language, which could not be explained by such concepts as the mechanical difficulties. He found that the development of written language did not repeat the development of spoken language and concluded that the conscious abstract nature of written language was the main feature of its difference.

The French psychoanalyst and professor of linguistics Julia Kristeva (1981, pp. 13–25) points out that writing acts in the absence of speaking subjects. It uses space to indicate itself by defying time. It is also symbolic as it replaces or represents something that is absent.

However, those who can never learn to write much or at all do not manage to reach the symbolic level of the sign. In looking at a child with a severe learning inhibition, Melanie Klein (1932) pointed out, 'Arithmetic and writing symbolised violent sadistic attacks upon her mother's body and her father's penis. In her unconscious, these activities were equated with tearing, cutting up or burning her mother's body together with the children it contained and castrating her father. Reading too, in consequence of the symbolic equation of her mother's body with books had come to mean a violent removal of substances, children . . . from the inside of her mother.'

Even where emotional problems are not so severe, teachers notice the impact of emotional meaning on the written word. In one school for emotionally disturbed children where I worked a girl wrote of a visit to the zoo: 'the mother monkey was busy with the baby so the little monkey banged on the class.' She had meant to write 'glass' but her identification with the displaced monkey broke through the containing structure of the word showing how she acted out her displaced feelings in the classroom. Similarly, in an infant school, a little boy could not write zero in mathematics. There had been a death in his family and the concept of nothingness was too raw for him.

Daniel Stern, professor of psychiatry at Cornell University Medical Center (1985, p. 163), looking at the origins of a verbal self, feels it causes a split in the child's emotional experience. 'It also moves relatedness into the impersonal, abstract level intrinsic to language and away from the personal immediate level intrinsic to the other domains of relatedness.' I believe a similar further split can occur with the development of written language. It strips the musical inflection of voice and mood away and the satisfaction of a relatively fast response.

Tomás could only write his own name and copy a few shapes, sometimes correctly and sometimes incorrectly. He was unable to learn to write more than that. Nevertheless, he appreciated the writing function in me and in his caretakers. His violent outbursts destroyed furniture, cars, ornaments, and clothes and hurt people. But he never destroyed paper or books or pens and pencils. He could trust that, despite the speed with which feelings persecuted him and made him need to move about, the written words would stay still and hold his thoughts. They represented the best way he could deal with absence and perhaps their very abstraction meant they were safer than the physical flesh.

I wondered too if keeping me writing kept me doing something that he did not find dangerous. I could not, for example, speak so much if I was busy writing and saying his words. I also could not think separately to myself about him in the actual moment of writing. At different times I raised those possibilities aloud to Tomás but they did not seem to be so important to him. What was far more important was the receptacle that the book and the writing mother made together, which was far more precious and safe than any other activity. In the hide-and-seek that preceded the writing Tomás was trying each time to trust that I would find him without hurting him. However, it never became possible. It is worth noting, though, that his tears and terror decreased slightly over the year. Something about the repeated proto-play that never quite became play allowed the development of the writing connection. He and I could be linked together via the intermediary of the writing.

Jenny Sprince and Judith Usiskin (1987), in their group work with handicapped women, set out to offer a 'scribe' function. The two group facilitators wrote down whatever the women said, typed it up during the week, and gave each woman a copy for her own folder the following week. Each group began with a read-through of what had been said before the current week's new thoughts arose. At an open meeting of the Tavistock Clinic Mental Handicap Workshop in 1988 when they presented their work, Jenny Sprince commented, 'Re-reading the transcripts of the first weeks of our group, what strikes me most strongly is how concretely the women experienced the containment we offered through this [writing] process. It becomes clear that having their words written down, a concrete form of being listened to, has a quite physical meaning for them, which is the same as warmth and food.'

Tomás could slowly bear more time over the year. The extra minutes were like extra food. However, although the hide-and-seek and the writing extended his ability to bear time and space they caused further problems too. The rise of curiosity in Tomás, the questions he managed to ask as a result of therapy, were good food for his growing developing self but poison for his disturbed self. Bion (1957) points out that the disturbance of the impulse of curiosity makes normal development impossible, as it is the impulse of curiosity on which learning depends.

I was not allowed to be more curious about Tomás. It mattered that I should try and look for him but it was important that I should not be curious about where he was hiding. Those communications to me that came unconsciously from Tomás helped me understand his internal organization. There was an object that did allow him to survive and know something but that blocked any real curiosity or liveliness and did not want to receive his feelings. Tomás could therefore only show excitement moving between activities, being in limbo. Once in residence, there would be danger. By using me as the writer of his words, Tomás was disarming me temporarily. However, I did not succeed in helping him understand the process further.

If every baby fears some kind of dying or annihilation if it is not responded to, then a baby or child who faces a real death-wish or death-threat and/or concrete abuse experiences a double death. If a baby is born organically handicapped and receives a 'stupid' response from its parent, who is not able to receive its projections, then its first proto-thoughts will boomerang back doubly damagingly.

Writing and story-telling involve the co-operation between different parts of the body. Writing involves a thought that is then allowed to be uttered by the mouth and linked to the hand's ability to manoeuvre an object into a shape known by the brain. Story-telling involves the memory of something heard or written similarly being allowed to pass through the mouth and become speech. Where people are lucky they are unaware of the trade-union agreement between different parts of the body required for such activities to occur. Breathing, walking, speaking can occur almost on auto-pilot. But once there is an obstruction all the components that make up each action that is taken for granted suddenly show their myriad parts and chaos looms. When an adult lends her senses to the child's wish, an experience is being offered of healthy omnipotence. When a parent carries a non-swimming child in the water the child is given the experience of what it will be like in the future when he is able to keep himself afloat by his own movements. The handicapped child may never be able to do certain tasks for himself but still needs the emotional loan of them.

Tomás was the only patient who did not manage the normal psychotherapy time of fifty minutes and the only child patient of mine who left after only a year's treatment. The thinking he provoked in me about the nature of writing and language has served me well for other patients, but I remain regretful that my exploration with him was so truncated. He has since been moved to three more units, finally ending in a special hospital. His physical violence was too much for the short-staffed community homes and hostels he was placed in. His fear of intimacy and his experience of closeness as killing might well be relieved by his placement in a large hospital. For some children and adults for whom 'home' was a place of terror, an institution can offer greater symbolic safety. Whether a point will come in the future where he feels able to contact me remains to be seen. However, the advantage of being attached to a particular workplace and not intending to move means that the chance of concrete contact remains. When I worked at a school for disturbed children in the East End of London, the head teacher, Sean Foley, was proud of the number of former pupils who would come to see him and show him what had happened in their lives even twenty years later. One of his biggest regrets when the school was closed in 1988 was that it deprived all former pupils of one real physical proof of their past history.

8   THE SHOCK OF INTELLIGENCE REVEALED: HOUSE M

And those that did see me, enacted their business with me, plied their trade as it were, did they ever pause to wonder at this flaky receptacle that passed for a body, to ask themselves if there was any kind of a soul inside, bearing witness to the suns and moons that passed before its eyes?

Paul Sayer, *The Comforts of Madness*

> . . . Only the mouths that talk
> get attention!
> Only the mouths that talk
> Give a direct kick up the arse
> to those who listen
> Sometimes the world must realise
> that life inside is dark and difficult
> Physique gets in the way
> The world understands only talk,
> Maybe the world is blind

Pia Mentallyhandicapped, House M resident

The scene was a private old people's home. It was a sunny day and the bedrooms and large dayrooms were empty. Filipino assistants were disinfecting the floors, windows were open but a smell of urine was still noticeable. Music was coming from the large garden to the rear and I made my way there. Outside, at a distance, the scene was reminiscent of a seaside photograph. Tables sported bright parasols, there were striped deckchairs for visitors and the flower beds were full of colour.

It took me a while to realize the lack of human sound. For underneath the blaring of the loudspeaker no-one was speaking. The old people sat in their fixed spaces. No sound came from the nurses or the auxiliaries. Unlike some hospitals, where depressed nurses band together to look after themselves in the nursing station, here the staff were too depressed to make contact with each other. They just stood like hot sentries.

Assistants were the only people who moved. Carrying trays of tea and plates of biscuits, they made their way in and out of the tables, but they did not pause to speak. The assistants and the nurses were not English. They too seemed dispossessed. Suddenly, there was a burst of noise and movement. A volunteer visitor weaved her way in and out of the tables stroking cheeks, giving hugs, speaking loudly. Everywhere she passed faces began to move into life but she had already finished her rounds before real contact could be made. It appeared she made this flying visit each week. The nurses remained impassive but the residents showed the potential for contact. A few were demented, most were not. They were affluent enough to be in a private home with good staff numbers. However, turning off their brains was, as is the case with handicapped patients in thoughtless institutions, a way of existing.

I wrote:

Sun streams through the tall windows
and the dayroom is empty
Filipino assistants are disinfecting the floors
scrubbing at shadows of loss and incontinence
While the owners of the shadows
are wheeled into the garden
to dry

Round bright tables and under the parasols
loudspeakers are blaring an end-of-pier song
No-one knows that no-one is talking
The nurses have lost their native land and tongue
The residents have lost.

This particular scene is international. It is happening right now in mental handicap hospitals and institutions and old people's homes and some hospital wards throughout the world. It is also happening in some schools for the profoundly multiply handicapped. Children and adults are sitting in wheelchairs, on chairs and beds with only fleeting interaction with staff. Someone comes in and washes, toilets, feeds and dresses another human being. This is done, on the whole, quickly but carefully. There are others in the ward waiting their turn. Keeping people clean and alive matters too. A couple of hundred years ago they could have been left to fester and die. But without meaningful human contact another kind of death occurs.

In *The World is a Wedding* the Jewish poet and novelist Bernard Kops (1963, p. 45) describes how, as a child with rheumatism, he was sent to hospital away from his family. When fear of his new surroundings caused a return to bedwetting, nurses rubbed his nose in his wet sheets and hit him. They also stuffed the food he could not bear down his throat 'and when I was sick they made me eat the sick.' Despite the family's initial awe of the hospital, his older sister took one look at him and told their mother he had to be got out immediately. The experience did not last long but, even so, 'as the ambulancemen carried me into the ward something died within me.' Many ordinary children who were not allowed parental visits, let alone parents staying with them, were subjected to these scarring experiences in addition to the primary blow of separation. It is thanks to the work of pioneers like James and Joyce Robertson and John Bowlby from the 1950s onwards that such experiences are now known to be damaging. The National Association for the Welfare of Children in Hospital (NAWCH) came into being as a result of their work.

Incontinence, the lack of control of one's bodily orifices, from dribbling, spitting, vomiting to defecating and urinating, unites the experience of the very young, the very old and the profoundly handicapped. Fear of such loss of autonomy, the unprocessed memories of childhood helplessness, can turn into hostility, too often uniting the workers, from nurses to residential workers.

In the old people's home I mentioned first, residents' urine was treated like rain, something that was inevitable and happened every so often, the results of which could be eventually mopped up. There was no direct hostility to the patient, who was regarded as a grey cloud in an impersonal sky doing what it had to do.

Witnessing one such incident I wrote:

A stick woman seated on a chair
a pool of water spreads beneath her
the only sign of movement
A nurse enters with a mop
an assistant enters with food
together they keep her alive

However, cleaning people's mess continuously as a way of not
managing to stay with their emotional experience is only the flip
side of shouting at them aggressively. Being close to something that
has gone wrong is a permanent reminder of the frailty of the human
body and mind. Where staff are not helped to deal with that there
is no possibility of an attempt to link the incontinence to any
emotional disturbance or to anger or depression. There is no
attempt to think of a behavioural programme or provide such
facilities as art or music or drama therapy.

In her important book *The Empty Hours* Maureen Oswin
documented the hours a child was left in an institution without any
meaningful contact. Her book evoked concern for the plight of the
hospitalized child but not enough change has happened since. Like
Spitz (1946, 1951) and the Robertsons (1952) she showed how
originally useful ideas about hygiene were abused into creating
sterile environments where children sat 'bright, intelligent,
physically disabled, bored, lonely, no toys, no occupation, nothing
to reach out to or touch through the bars of their cots. Like battery
hens, void lives in cot cages' (Oswin, 1971, p. 10).

If the mentally fortunate can deteriorate so rapidly in a setting
where there is no thoughtful personal contact, it is not surprising
that the chances of psychic survival are lessened with each
additional handicap. The profoundly multiply handicapped individual can exist in a double vacuum where his or her own sense of
bereavement and isolation is matched by the outside world's
indifference, fear or hostility.

The reasons for this state of affairs vary. The depression of the
powerless, speechless patient can pass into the medical or social
work hierarchy hardly touched. Poor pay and conditions can mean
that the most deprived are tended by the almost equally deprived,

who are then envious of the 'care' their clients get. 'No-one mops up after me,' protested one nursing assistant. 'These dummies have the time of their life just sitting down eating, pissing and shitting knowing that I have to clean it all up.' In one unit I observed, staff rushed the 'residents' through their unchosen lunch to make sure of their own free time. The unit was small and was supposedly a first step in the 'return to the community'. However, the kitchen was clearly for staff only and so was the right to change television channels and set the time for bed. The idea that the handicapped were 'just like children' was a historical advance on the idea that they were 'just like animals'. However, this attitude reveals what cruelty still exists in our treatment of children. As A. Tyne showed (1979), although large units can restrict patients' privacy and development, some small units can be equally inflexible and sterile.

In 1984 Film Australia launched *Annie's Coming Out*, based on a book by Rosemary Crossley, a teacher who specialized in teaching children with multiple handicaps, and her former pupil Anne McDonald. It was the story of a teacher's growing awareness that a handicapped child possessed intelligence but had hidden it inside her handicap because of the painful institutional experiences she had to face, including a Matron who removed all colourful posters that offended the clean sterility of 'her' ward. The teacher was treated as if she was mad or dangerous for holding such a thought and since the child Annie needed her arm supported in order to write there were accusations that she was directing the movements. At the end of the film the child was able to show her intelligence to other people, vindicating her teacher's understanding, and finally they both left the institution together.

The disbelief Rosemary Crossley faced in trying to make friends and colleagues begin to consider the child's intelligence was similar to responses to child sexual abuse work and mental handicap work in England too. In both cases thinking the unthinkable means accepting a child's knowledge of terrible experiences. A child or adult living in an unsupported and unsupportive institution has witnessed the worst caretaking behaviour. 'Just to remember how I used to wash them makes me squirm,' said one charge nurse who had been given the chance to see that his patients had feelings when the hospital regime altered. 'When I think of the conversations we had on our shift I dread to think what they made of it.'

Where staff are not helped to take in the meaning of their client group, where they are short-staffed and there is no leadership, it is easier, as I have said earlier, to deny the emotional reality of the residents and to adopt what at best is what Joan Bicknell calls a 'horticultural' approach, involving only feeding and washing. At worst there is systematic physical and emotional abuse, theft, and sexual abuse. Only now that we are beginning to be able to see the extent of sexual abuse in the ordinary population are we able to look at the abuse of the handicapped. I suspect that we will then be able to see more clearly what is happening to the elderly.

Shortly after the film came out, I gave a talk at the Royal Free Hospital's Child and Adolescent Psychiatry Department in London on the link between mental handicap and abuse. A staff member, Helen Peto, approached me. She said she had a friend, Ian Johnson, an English residential social worker who now worked in Denmark, who was facing similar issues. She told me of House M in Denmark, where a change in the way staff worked and a new management system had led to a sequence of shocking revelations of intelligence. The shock to the system that happens when internal or external injury handicaps a child is reflected almost in mirror image by the shock that ripples to workers and parents when the process is reversed. I was fascinated to hear of this and gave her copies of some articles to send and soon Ian Johnson and I were in contact. He had previously worked with children in care at a therapeutically run school, the Mulberry Bush, and at Barnardo's. He had also worked with blind and partially-sighted adults with other handicaps at the Royal School for the Blind in Leatherhead. Now he was working in House M.

Run by Copenhagen County Council, House M began life in 1966 as one of nineteen connected residential units for multiply handicapped patients. Its particular residents were aged 5–24 and suffered severe epilepsy. After a while staff agreed the age-range was too wide and from January 1985 House M became an adult unit. Most of the residents have no speech and all are wheelchair-users. Half have epilepsy as well and many have emotional problems. There was a consensus that their level of functioning lay between 0 and 3 years.

But then a major change happened. Within one year of the new regime, with greater attention by workers and a smaller age-range, by 11 August 1986 all fourteen residents revealed that they could understand language and could point out letters or type with their arms or wrists supported. Amazingly, since only two had ever received tuition, most had a correct written language, whilst a few spelled words phonetically. In addition, the content of their writing in all cases corresponded to their age level. Hanne, aged twenty, would sit all day sucking her fingers, becoming drenched with saliva. Up to the age of seventen she had to be fed and was totally physically helpless. However, one teacher knew Hanne had more potential. She started teaching the Bliss communication system to Hanne. Other teaching staff saw their colleague's actions as deluded. Only when Hanne was in her last year of school was the teacher able to convince Hanne to share her knowledge with her key worker at House M. Hanne was clearly made to understand that with her schooldays coming to an end, if she did not show her ability she would be left with no communication. House M staff were able to add that she needed to show her intelligence to gain a place in adult education. At first Hanne was only willing to communicate with her key worker when they were alone, arousing doubts in the rest of the staff. However, as new staff joined, Hanne was slowly able to increase her communicating radius. Some of the old staff could not bear the implications of Hanne's change and resigned.

The second catalyst was twenty-year-old Catja. After she had shown her key worker that she could write she said other residents could write too. The new philosophy in the staff group meant that this was taken very seriously, and alphabet boards and typewriters and communicators were begged and borrowed. Catja also sent a letter to another resident, Maja, telling her to write. With a staff member supporting her hand, Maja wrote 'Say hello to Catja' and then 'It's my secret' – meaning her ability to write. Then the other residents followed. The group had given permission for writing to be shown. Unlike Hanne and Catja, the other residents had not been taught and psychologists are struggling to understand how they taught themselves.

As other residents showed they somehow possessed, untaught, written language, parents also needed help to deal with the new situation. Other professionals, outside the centre, reacted with disbelief, accusing workers of a mass psychosis and saying it must be their hands pushing the fingers onto the right letters.

Despite the startling events that were happening in House M there was little supervision or emotional support to help the staff deal with the dramatic changes, although the change in the residents was itself a reward. However, there were important new problems too. As long as residents were just physically tended and deemed unable to communicate the staffing levels were manageable. Knowing that everyone could communicate if only there were adequate time was a painful responsibility. To hold someone's arm or hand while they slowly pointed to letters takes a long time. Staff had to take on board the fact that they were surrounded by people needing to communicate who would have to wait a long time for their turn. House M has still not received the technological electronic aids that would make communication easier and faster. Ian was helping colleagues by translating their reports into English and seeking feedback from others working in this area. In England, the Tavistock Clinic, St George's Hospital, MENCAP, the Royal Free Hospital and Community Care were quick responders.

The media in Denmark were particularly helpful. In July 1987 Danish television made a programme on House M, which Ian brought to London to show us at the Tavistock Clinic Workshop. When he next wrote he was clearly pleased with the continued helpful media interest within Denmark. Newspapers were not exploiting the stories of the House M residents. One newspaper especially impressed the residents by submitting in advance the questions for which its editors wanted answers. It had properly understood both how long it took for an answer to be signed and how much time the residents might need to discuss how to explore their situation publicly. While most agreed with Mark, who commented, 'I hope it can help other mentally handicapped in institutions,' Maja's wry realistic rider was 'It sounds good, but I don't think we'll get extra staff. The council aren't likely to give us more money.'

Among other articles, I suggested that Ian and his colleagues should read *Annie's Coming Out*, the book on which the film was based. They not only read it, they traced Rosemary Crossley and Anne McDonald in Australia and are now in regular contact with them. They also sent details of the Tavistock Clinic Mental Handicap Workshop to them. Rosemary Crossley is now the project co-ordinator of DEAL Communication Centre, in Victoria, Australia. DEAL is an acronym for Dignity, Education And Language for people without speech. It was established in 1986 to promote the welfare of people with severe expressive communication disabilities, to seek out systems of communication for them, to provide counselling for the clients and their families and to 'advocate their cause to the general community'. DEAL has estimated that just within the State of Victoria there are 6,000 people in need of such help of whom 5,000 receive none.

The major package this provides has produced important changes in the client group. As well as joy for the individuals and their families there has also been distress at realizing the years of ignorance. In DEAL's annual Newsletter we learn that 'Amy's father described how he had cried on the way home that day at all the years wasted' (1987). Similarly, formerly silenced clients are providing memories both of good and appalling experiences. In a letter I received in January 1989 Rosemary Crossley commented, 'Several of our clients have reported physical or sexual abuse once communication has been established. We suspect their severe communication impairments rendered them more susceptible to abuse in that they could not complain. Once given a means of communication (usually typing) their complaints were direct and forthright. Some of the anxiety about communication therapy undoubtedly results from concern by some staff and parents as to what the previously mute person might say – not necessarily about abuse, but also about things they have seen, such as petty thefts in an institution, for example, or what they have heard or about their overall treatment.'

Similarly, Ian Johnson wrote to me, 'One very important development in the last few weeks is that one of our female residents has been able to start telling us about the abuse she was subjected to by her mother over many years. It has really bowled us over and makes some of her behaviour and various remarks more understandable.' The connection between abuse and handicap is as international as the emotional experience of the handicap.

What causes the return to life and potential? In working with ordinary children and adults I find that if I do not entertain the possibility of trauma it is then harder for the client to think it and share it with me. The space within the worker to consider what the client may have gone through allows that memory to return. In working with the mentally handicapped, we know we are dealing with trauma. However, there is another unthinkable thought. It is that they have emotional intelligence: somewhere they know and understand what is happening within and around them. Once that thought is bearable to the client, the client senses that growth is possible. In a similar way, if an institution provides privacy clients will know that they have the possibility of such space. The emotional space in a worker is matched by the architectural space of the building.

This idea has been well documented by researchers into institutional life in general (Goffman, 1961), but, like many important pieces of understanding, it has to circle round and round again historically until it meets the right circumstances to be put into practice. While there are still hospitals in this country that do not have provision for parents to stay with their sick children it is not surprising that thinking for the demented and the mentally handicapped lags further behind.

What, then, promotes change? Rosemary Crossley had first to know that Annie had understanding. Then she succeeded in helping Annie express herself. She had to bear being seen as deluded by friends and colleagues. Apart from the guilt evoked in other workers, disbelief could be sustained because of Annie's inability to show her intelligence widely. For a while this teaching process remained dyadic; it did not generalize to other staff or social contacts. Then a point came when Rosemary Crossley's support for Annie so threatened other staff that her job and reputation were in jeopardy. The situation culminated in a court case to decide whether Annie had the right to leave the hospital. Everything hinged on whether Annie had the intelligence to make such a decision. Rosemary knew Annie did privately have the intelligence but the question was whether she would dare to show it publicly. In the same way that Ali (Chapter 6) was able to show to my psychiatrist colleague the same level of fluency he had shown in the therapy room, Annie was able to show her intelligence.

The shock of intelligence is painful then as well as rewarding. Ian Johnson and his colleagues are facing problems. Achieving meaning does not mean that there is a 'happy ever after' any more than disclosing sexual abuse means that all distress is over. Some residents are more emotionally dependent, scared that their newly recognized ability will create an expectancy they cannot manage; most residents require staff to come to them first before they begin to communicate, placing quite a resource burden on staff. Outside the institution, disbelief creates one kind of pressure whilst within House M belief causes another. Parents of House M residents are now ringing all the time making sure further stages of help are available for their children. But House M has been given no extra staff to deal with this, and talking to parents means giving up time that the residents need.

There is also another response to deal with. Some workers in mental handicap have dealt with the changes by stating that no-one at House M was really handicapped, so more sympathy, time and resources need to go to the 'truly' handicapped. This is a regular response here too. In the last few years I have seen some powerful videos produced by the self-advocacy movement. Originating in America in the mid 1970s with the creation of an organization called People First, the self-advocacy movement is for people with learning difficulties to get together and speak up for themselves. Sometimes they are facilitated by advocates, sometimes they perform this function for each other. In 1984, when the Washington People First group held an international conference, British self-advocates and their professional supporters who attended decided to start a branch in the UK. One main professional facilitator of self-advocacy groups is John Hersov from the City Literary Institute. At several conferences he has shown videos of his clients speaking up for themselves; at other times his group take themselves on tour. There will always be some professionals who comment, 'Oh, they could not have been that handicapped to begin with.' There can be envy of any step forward. Anna Freud, in her lecture notes for teachers (1930, p. 129), gave an example of a governess who brilliantly taught a boy who was behind in his work so that he eventually did well. The moment he did well the governess lost interest in him. Her emotional investment was in the ugly duckling, not in the swan. The fact that some ugly ducklings grow into ugly swans and cannot bear any change for the better shows that this identification with illness can be inside the handicapped as well as outside of them.

Indeed, for Ali, Steven and my other patients, the experience of moments of wellness was as frightening as it was transforming. For some, moving to wellness meant leaving behind some unmoving handicapped injured self; it meant an act of betrayal. For others it meant facing lethal envious attack. In 'I Have Longed to Move Away', Dylan Thomas understood the backlash that could face one self that wanted to move:

> I have longed to move away but am afraid;
> Some life, yet unspent, might explode
> Out of the old lie burning on the ground,
> And, crackling into the air, leave me half-blind

The residents of House M know their staff are catering both for their highest functioning and their lowest. No-one is denying them their right to be alive and feel and think. This means they are faced with their own internal enemy. Nietzsche (1886, p. 74) understood this interplay well. 'Under conditions of peace the warlike man attacks himself.'

What is the nature of the internal enemy that makes showing intelligence a fearful process? Now the residents are processing their experiences into poems and comments. As with Tomás and myself, the act of creative writing offers the possibility of integrating many levels of experience. I want to look at four short poems by House M residents that help to throw light on these issues.

Everything in moderation
Know your limits
Sleep your life through
The train has gone for you
But you've started up too late
Hellish difficult to live in this world.

Catja

Cowardly Jesper locks up his
body and soul
Can't open up himself
But with help I want one day
To choose my own life

Jesper

I have lived many years and seen
many things and I thought that
I could neither do anything nor
think anything. Nobody and
nothing, they thought of me.
I wonder if I'll come to know a
life of happiness.

Hanne

Hope have I!
Jesus how I hope!
Ought to give up!
Can false hopes weaken me?
the world can/must be lived in

Pia Mentallyhandicapped

The poems poignantly describe two different states. One is a state
of secondary handicap in which it feels so impossible to manage
the 'hellish' difficulty of life that it is better to be dead. To sleep your
life through or lock up your body and soul, to avoid thinking and
to know nothing offers some safety. The safety lies in avoiding
experiencing too keenly the trauma of loss. This means trying not
to know that the train has gone, the train of normal life that has

passed the residents by. However, there is another state. This state is one of truth and sanity. There is a non-handicapped self that knows locking up body and soul is cowardly. That self has hope that there is always time to start up again, even though there is fear of what happiness or hope are possible.

Jesper beautifully differentiates these two selves. There is 'cowardly Jesper', who stays locked because he cannot unlock himself, and an 'I' who wants to manage with help. He helps us understand another predicament of the profoundly multiply handicapped. Ian Johnson makes it clear that for many physical tasks residents remain at a three-year-old level. Their physical handicaps are incurable. Even though mechanical aids can make transformations there is always the fact of the physical limitation. This blow to independence can make it even harder to develop the life that is possible. If the help of an other is needed for unlocking communication it is not surprising that so many thus handicapped clients stay in an omnipotent state of non-living.

If thinking in the head is a hard task for speaking clients it is made harder when a helping hand has to become an aid to thinking. In order for most residents to write, physical contact with staff is emotionally necessary even when it is no longer physically necessary. A staff member holds the resident's hand so the forefinger points and the resident then points to the letters. Where the resident is suddenly incapable of continuing, Ian Johnson has found that a 'shake' to the hand sends the brain working again. This, of course, was not true for Steven when he tried knocking his thoughts into shape.

It seems that it takes two people physically touching before the thoughts can then be expressed by pointing to letters or typing. This takes us again to the psychobiological origins of thinking. It takes the connection of mother and baby with a good-enough relationship for thinking to occur. If the mother does not receive the feelings of the child and transform them into something manageable the child will be left with nameless dread (Bion, 1957). Similarly, if the child has hope that his preconception of taking in something good – food and love – can be met, then the absence of that happening will create thought. Where the child is always frustrated there is no proper growth.

Rosemary Crossley's centre has a computer consultant individually tailoring communication equipment for the clients, a
technician, an occupational therapist and a physiotherapist, as well
as speech pathologists. As a result of these resources they can slowly
phase out direct physical support so that clients end up typing on
their own. However, even there, 'generally they like to have
someone near them, perhaps with a hand on their knee, for
security.' Similarly, with individuals who have more strength to
spell when standing, 'a hand on the shoulder is often necessary at
the start, both for confidence and to stabilise their physical
condition.'

In House M, physical contact for writing is universally needed
still and Ian Johnson is aware of a fear clients have about taking
responsibility for writing. Spelling out, pointing to, or saying a word
provides a piece of communication between two people. Where an
external or internal response has been to kill off meaning, the first
communications can carry a naked feeling of fragility, like a tortoise
peeping its head out from its shell. The dyadic link with the staff
member means the function is shared. One person speaks for two.

Also, of course, we are back to the fear of knowledge as original
sin. When Moses goes up the mountain to receive the tablets of
stone, the laws and commandments, it takes forty days. He is the
only one invited into God's presence. By the time Moses returns,
the people have turned back to heathen gods because it was such
a long time to wait. Moses is so angry he destroys the tablets, which
were 'God's writing' (Exodus 32:17). God tells Moses to come
again, insisting that no-one else can be present or be anywhere in
sight, and He says He will write on new tablets. As it happens, Moses
writes the words of the covenant down at God's dictation and this
also takes forty days and nights. If we consider that the writers of
the Bible felt God could create the world within a week, it is a
curious material projection of the meaning of writing that it should
take nearly six weeks to write the laws. Also a fearful privacy is
required for one to dictate and the other to write. To carve into
stone is to create a new life of meaning, and once there is meaning
of value there is also awareness of death.

During a visit to Prague this combination made me write:

> On Charles Bridge the statues ache heavenward
> – God's braille
> And in the Jewish cemetery they thrust up their
> stone samizdats
> A library of life

9   FINDING MEANING WITHOUT WORDS: SELF-INJURY AND PROFOUND HANDICAP

> The Master said, 'I am thinking of giving up speech.' Tzu-Kung said, 'If you did not speak, what would there be for us, your disciples, to transmit?' The Master said, 'What does Heaven ever say? Yet there are four seasons going round and there are the hundreds of things coming into being. What does Heaven ever say?'
>
> Confucius, *The Analects*

> Thou hast no hands to wipe away thy tears,
> Nor tongue to tell me who hath martyr'd thee.
> Shakespeare, *Titus Andronicus* III.i.106–7

House M was initially established as a home for children with profound mental and physical handicaps who then grew into young adulthood there. With the advent of a different staff culture it became clear that most of the residents were only physically handicapped. The experience of House M is a salutary reminder of the ways that some severely physically handicapped individuals are being wrongly diagnosed. With shortage of trained staff and lack of adequate communication resources, physically handicapped individuals can give up wishing to show their intelligence. Sometimes the neglect is due to lack of external interest rather than to inadequate financial resources – to a failure to notice, for example, that a child is deaf. In a report in the *Guardian* newspaper, Dr Jack

Piachaud, a consultant psychiatrist from Harperbury Hospital, a long-stay hospital for mentally handicapped people, estimated that there were 3,000 deaf or hard-of-hearing people being kept in long-stay hospitals because they had been wrongly diagnosed as mentally handicapped. The struggle different physical handicaps cause, the difficulty in saying a word that can be heard, the difficulty in having the mobility to point to a letter: all these hurdles are enormous. Thanks to the contribution made by computer technology and engineering some mechanical gadgets can alleviate some pain and difficulty, but too many individuals are having to survive in appalling circumstances.

However, despite important links with the physically handicapped, I am concerned here with the plight of those handicapped individuals who do not have an intact brain to help them. The heroism of some gifted individuals imprisoned in damaged bodies has been satisfyingly documented in the last few years in star-studded films, plays, books and television. The emotional climate has been changed not only by people like Helen Keller but by works such as *Annie's Coming Out*, *Walter*, *Children of a Lesser God*, *Mask*; autobiographies such as Christopher Nolan's *Under the Eye of the Clocktower* and Al Davison's *The Spiral Cage*; and portrayals like Dustin Hoffman's Raymond in *Rainman*, Daniel Day Lewis's Christy Brown in *My Left Foot*, or John Hurt in *Elephant Man*. I am indebted to Jenny Allen of the Tavistock Clinic for pointing me to William Horwood's *Skallagrigg*, which is a first-rate thriller having the search for identity and dignity in handicap as a base. It should be borne in mind, however, that not only are the majority of physically handicapped people no more gifted than anyone else, but that those who are multiply handicapped have even less of a chance to be so.

The burden of severe or profound multiple handicap leads to an increased rate of psychiatric illness and self-injurious behaviour (Oliver, Murphy and Corbett 1987). Too often, unsupported workers, despairing over such clients' chronic self-destructive attacks, give up trying to understand what is happening. Faced with six clients who knock themselves out by the extent of their headbanging, they might find it easier to think that it is due to the handicap rather than consider that each act has its own inner meaning. It is not surprising that some workers defend themselves against the pain of their clients' meaning, as the following example shows (Sinason, 1989d).

It is lunch-time in a residential home for severely and profoundly handicapped adults. Steve, a young man with cerebral palsy, sits banging his head rhythmically. His forehead is bruised and swollen. A staff member approaches him and restrains his arm. There is a moment's pause. The worker moves away and the banging starts again. Next to him, Sara, a woman with Down's syndrome, is picking pieces of fluff off her jumper, her skirt, her arm. When she sees no more left she starts picking pieces of flesh off her arm. Every few minutes she bites her arm. There are fresh teethmarks visible from across the room. On the other side of the table Laurence is rocking up and down and muttering gibberish. A line of dribble falls down the side of his mouth. A woman next to him, Susie, is picking up food with her fingers and smearing it over her face. This is only one table. There are several. There is food on the floor. There is a clattering of cutlery. There is muttering and shrieking.

At first sight, this could be Dante's Inferno. It looks as if there is no intelligent life, no meaning. Indeed, at such moments staff and visitors can find themselves wishing there was no meaning. For of course there is. It is precisely the weight of meaning behind every gesture that we can find unbearable. Des Pres (1976, p. 44), talking about concentration camp survivors, comments, 'Insofar as we feel compelled to defend a comforting view of life we tend to deny the survivor's voice. We join in a conspiracy of silence. . .' However, managing to be in touch with the meaning offers a way of helping the client group and ourselves as professionals faced with such sights. Sarah, a residential social worker and Steve's key worker, had left the home a week before after having been there for eight years. When she first took on Steve he was a violent headbanger. After several years this stopped. Now, as he takes in the tragedy of her going, after she has left he reverts to his headbanging. The loss of Sarah is just the latest in a whole lifetime of losses. Sara had always picked pieces of fluff, real and imaginary, from her clothes and body. However, this biting behaviour has not been seen before. The loss of Sarah seems to have activated memory of her early loss of her mother when she was abandoned at the age of one. Like Spitz's deprived children (1953) she seems to be in a state where the difference between her own body and food has lost its meaning and in a state of emotional starvation she feeds on herself. Laurence has rocked up and down ever since he entered the institution. He has no formal language, no history. Susie cannot speak and was physically and sexually abused by her parents. Sarah had worked hard to create a sense of choice for Susie by offering her an alternative lunch when she could, allowing Susie to nod a 'yes' or 'no', what Spitz calls the psychic organizers. No other worker did this. Now Susie is left for the moment with her unchosen lunch smeared across her.

Michael Friedman and colleagues (1972), looking at adolescents who self-mutilated or attempted suicide, found that abandonment or threat of abandonment was an invariable feature prior to such attacks. One way of understanding the timing of such suicidal actions was to see them as turning the passive position (being left) into an active one (leaving). For in the mind of the adolescent, it is then the family or friends who are bereft.

Children and adults are hurting themselves cruelly every day. A lot of self-injurious behaviour in the form of excessive drinking, eating, smoking or promiscuity is accepted as normal. As psychoanalyst and consultant psychotherapist Michael Sinason has commented (1989), such behaviour has to be taken to extremes before it is seen to be disturbed. We are not therefore witnessing anything new as clinicians when we see individuals condemned to hurting themselves. However, when the methods of self-attack vary with the mentally ill, and those mentally handicapped people who are also mentally ill, we can for a while feel we are dealing with something alien and lose our own intelligence.

For example, we have a clinical understanding that masturbation in a public place is one of many symptoms that can be linked to sexual abuse. Yet, faced with the sight of mentally handicapped children and adults masturbating in public, many workers say, 'they are mentally handicapped, that is why they do that'. Similarly, although we know most clearly that the majority of handicapped patients who injure themselves do not have a syndrome that causes this (Oliver et al., 1987), there is a widespread assumption that 'handicapped people bang their heads because of their handicap'.

Certainly, the burden of any long-standing illness or handicap would deplete anyone's resources and make the individual more vulnerable to disturbance. However, it does not cause the disturbance.

There are two other general comments that I want to make about self-injury in severely or profoundly handicapped individuals. Bion (1962) makes it clear that thinking is an activity required in order to process a thought. Where there has been organic damage to the brain or trauma, the actual apparatus for thinking has been affected and I consider that a thought then becomes an uncomfortable physical sensation. Some headbanging, for example, is a way of knocking a bad feeling out of the head; sometimes it is a desperate attempt to knock a thought into shape. As I have described in Chapter 5, Steven watched his housefather kick the TV when it wasn't working and sure enough the interference went. He then bashed at his head violently and it was quite clear he hoped that would get rid of the awful exhausting disturbance inside.

We therefore need to examine very carefully each instance of violence to understand it. Is it suicidal, depressed, a response to pain or an infantile way of dealing with difficult feelings? Small babies can show their anger not only by their looks and sounds and by displacement activity: from 7–12 months they have a range of aggressive communications available – biting, hitting, scratching and pulling. They employ these methods on people and inanimate objects. This process not only requires mastery of eye–hand or eye–leg co-ordination, it also helps differentiation between self and other, alive and inanimate. Spitz (1951) shows how aim-directed aggression is needed to achieve mastery of grasping and walking, needed to move out of the confines of the cot or playpen. This development requires not only the physical skills but also the mental skills of having a thought, a memory, bearing to wait for something to be achieved.

This ability is aided by having a parent who responds, who engages in dialogue and helps the baby know the difference between human and toy. Useful aggression can be directed at a person or can be a quite separate way of experimenting with the environment.

It seems that the human baby (or indeed adult) cannot be still or comfortable for long. Infant observations, a part of all psychoanalytically informed trainings, show that an inner disturbance resulting in the need for movement happens regularly. Some of the sentimental paintings of babies asleep owe their power to the fact that only then is there any real cessation (although movement occurs in sleep too of course). Something disturbs us and our sense of peace.

Klein shows us how basic functions in babies and young children such as wetting can be experienced as 'cutting, stabbing, burning, drowning' and psychiatry has long made use of her understanding that 'burning' feelings of urethral sadism can be involved in bedwetting. Hellman and Blackburn (1966) found that eneuresis, firesetting and cruelty to animals formed a particularly disturbing constellation in childhood that could indicate the likelihood of future violence. Violence, however we understand it, is universal in small children although it is trivialized by the use of such words as 'tantrums'. As children age, screaming, kicking and biting transform more into whining or sulking and physical outbursts of anger become rarer. With violent offenders that also holds true. P. D. Scott (1977) comments, 'the resort to violence does in general diminish with age even though offences continue.' Oliver *et al.* (1987) found SIB (self-injurious behaviour) cases were more prevalent in childhood, adolescence and the early twenties. In aggressive behaviour we are therefore witnessing something infantile or from young childhood located in an older body.

The point of greatest active physical violence in young children is in two-year-olds at the point where they are having to give up their sense of being the most important and powerful members of the family. Babies often look at little children as if at amusing mobiles. They are the ones carried about by the adults and they are identified with adults. However, once they start walking they face a different perspective on their position. Restraints and rules suddenly come into being which they can find intolerable. Freeman (1970) postulates that the rages that Goldstein called 'catastrophic reactions' in patients with cerebral palsy and which he attributed to brain damage might in fact be related to the guilty permissiveness and over-protection that some parents adopt with a handicapped child. Where there is a recognizable omnipotent child inside a violent handicapped adult it is very hard to be the grownup who sets limits. Workers in one mental handicap hostel sat in despair while residents smeared food or threw it. 'They don't understand – they're just being like little children,' said one worker hopefully. Whoever said little children didn't understand? Little children will gustily attack their mother's mothering function by their treatment of food but a kick from a small child is quite different from one from a large adult.

Another aspect of this stage of omnipotence is that the choice available is very painful. You are either the King of the Castle or the Stupid Rascal. The two-year-old is murderously desperate to be King because otherwise he will have to face the fact that he is only tiny. The omnipotent adult or child with a handicap will fight even harder because being the stupid rascal is even more unbearable. The healthy child knows somewhere that he or she will grow up and be an adult; the severely or profoundly handicapped adult will always be dependent.

Nevertheless, if the primary caretaker thinks enough about the baby or handicapped adult she can provide what Stern (1985) calls 'attunement'. This is the way mother and baby find a healthy reciprocity. Where there is handicap and a delay or an injuring to the bonding process, this attunement process can be missing in both parents and workers with damaging results. For example, in one secure unit a worker said to me, 'If you see me run follow quickly.' I felt bemused as I followed her round her lockings and unlockings of different doors. A tall young man with cerebral palsy walked up and said 'Hello'. As I started to reply the worker started running. I followed her nervously and she quickly locked the door against the inoffensive young man. He then banged violently on the glass window pane. 'See what I mean?' she said. 'He's really violent.'

Understanding or trying to understand meaning does not necessarily make disturbance and aggressive behaviour go away, but it can lessen the extent of the damage to our clients and make us and our colleagues feel more able to bear the difficulties. Every improvement, however small, helps. When Maureen, one of my patients, stopped spitting and screaming and biting her workers so much, she was able to appreciate more what they could provide for her and they were happy to cater for her more because they were less hurt. There is a spiral upwards as well as downwards. However, with some of our most handicapped and disturbed clients, too much damage is done, organically and emotionally, for treatment to make major changes.

MAUREEN

Maureen was a profoundly mentally and physically handicapped young woman who was abandoned by her parents at five. She had no verbal language, hardly any sign language, no mobility. She was referred for eye-poking, gouging her hands and arms so that they required stitches, and non-stop weeping and wailing. After a series of short- and longer-term residential placements she was now in a permanent home, a residential hostel catering for a mixed group of young people. The referral letter was particularly moving because her key worker had noticed that her outbursts were worst around Christmas, which was when her family abandoned her. It has taken a long time for the importance of anniversary repetitions in ordinary experience to be understood, let alone their importance for the severely and profoundly handicapped. Maureen was incontinent, had no use of her legs and was a wheelchair-user. She was seventeen when she was first referred. The final note in the letter was that the key worker would be able to provide an escort and driver if we offered Maureen a treatment vacancy.

Assessment

I arranged an exploration meeting with Maureen and her key worker Teresa. With clients with little or no verbal speech and few signs I find it useful to have the worker in the room for a short time. As I see both children and adults in the same room the normal child psychotherapy range of toys and drawing materials is there, including paper and pens, plasticine and glue, scissors and small doll and animal families. Some adults with severe handicaps find it aids communication to draw or show me situations or fantasies using the small dolls. I have added a musical clock, music box, Jack-in-the-box, typewriter and a large mail order catalogue. I have found all these useful for handicapped children and adults, clockwork musical toys being especially useful for those without speech. Having the power to make something else make a sound or move can help some patients express their feelings about their own inability to control these activities in their own bodies. Some of my colleagues who work only with adults have been concerned that 'toys' might be offensive for handicapped adults. However, I have found that adults as well as children take and use whatever they find of meaning.

Despite a two-hour journey, Maureen and Teresa managed to arrive on time and I left my room to meet them by the lift. As the lift doors opened I felt a sudden shock. On the wheelchair, covering her eyes with twisted fingers, a mass of black hair looking the only healthy sign of life, sat Maureen. Her back was curved, a breast was falling out of the loose T-shirt/dress just under her neck and her useless legs had thinned into matchsticks. Maureen had clearly registered my shock as she was now covering her eyes with both hands. For a moment I had a stupid cowardly wish to cancel that knowledge. Then my intelligence returned. After I had introduced myself to Teresa and Maureen I commented to Maureen that she had come out of the lift with her eyes covered, perhaps because she knew that when new people saw her for the first time they got a shock at how handicapped she was. Her hands then came down, and two brown eyes, one very vivid and one dull from self-injury, looked at me. I knew in that moment that Maureen possessed a high level of emotional intelligence.

Inside the room, Teresa gently pushed Maureen next to a table full of paper and pens and various objects. Maureen did not look. I asked Teresa to say why Maureen had been referred. Teresa gently said that everyone was very proud of Maureen for being so brave when she had gone through so much: having no use of her legs, not being able to speak. However, Maureen cried for hours and was clearly very distressed and nobody had been able to do anything about that and that was the main reason why she had been referred. I said that Teresa had mentioned those things in her letter and she had also mentioned one other matter, that Maureen was most distressed at Christmas-time because that was when her mother had abandoned her.

To Teresa's surprise and my own Maureen reached out quickly

from her wheelchair and picked up a baby doll. Then she picked up a mother doll and made it knock the baby doll away. She quickly covered her eyes again. I said she was showing us her key worker was right – she was sad at being rejected and now she was seeing a strange woman – would I knock her away too? Without any further exploration I let her know that I had a once-weekly vacancy and it was hers if she would like to come. She smiled, her eyes still covered. I said that the Easter holiday would start next week so we would not be able to start meeting regularly for another three weeks.

I asked her if she felt able to be in the room on her own with me now. There was no response. Teresa said she felt it would be all right. Maureen smiled. I was aware that Maureen needed to know Teresa did not mind sharing her before she could show her interest. I asked Teresa to show me Maureen's main signs and once that was done Teresa left.

On her own with me Maureen kept her face down so I could not see her. She sat completely still. I commented on how shy she felt about looking at me now that Teresa was not in the room. I wondered if I seemed different with Teresa not there. We spent twenty minutes, largely in silence, with me occasionally venturing a comment on her non-moving. A minute before the end of the time I told her Teresa would be back in a moment and I needed to know from her if she would like to come again. There was no response. I asked her to raise her little finger if she would like to come, which she did. Then she looked at me directly, grinned warmly and covered her face again.

There was a gap of three weeks before we could start meeting again after the Easter holidays. Teresa told me that Maureen had placed all her few precious photographs on her bed each Monday (the day she came to see me) of the holiday and cried when she was told it was not the right Monday yet.

First meeting after Easter

Teresa wheeled Maureen into my room. Both women looked particularly attractive. There was a connecting glow about them both. Unlike the last visit, Maureen was well-dressed. She was wearing a bright green dress and a green necklace and was clutching a photograph book. 'Maureen has brought her photos to show you,' said Teresa meaningfully, letting me know how important an act this was. 'She has been waiting to come all through the holiday. Each Monday she had her photograph book ready on her bed. It took me two weeks to understand it, then I told her we didn't see you for another week.' Maureen covered her eyes. I said she was embarrassed to let me know she was pleased to be starting. 'Ooh – she is,' said Teresa. 'She has been choosing her clothes very carefully for today. She didn't bother last time because she didn't know if you would carry on seeing her. Us women, we only dress properly for friends!' She gave Maureen's shoulder a squeeze and left.

When Teresa left, Maureen lifted the album up with difficulty for me to look at. Inside was Maureen's tiny known history in her excellent new hostel. The first photograph showed Maureen in the dress she was wearing, smiling and pointing to a birthday cake. I asked if she was wearing her birthday dress for her first session and she smiled and nodded. Also on the page were photos of Maureen and her key worker, Maureen and her room, Maureen in the garden. She turned the page. There was nothing. She turned the next page. There was nothing. I felt awful. Maureen turned the pages faster and faster, her teeth making a terrible clicking noise, tears falling down her face, and before I could speak she began poking her eye violently.

It was unbearable. I said how painful it was for her to see all the empty pages and the empty years where no-one knew what had happened to her. She pointed to her birthday photo and poked her eye again. I said how unbearable it was to see her life, to think of her birth and everything that had gone wrong. She could not listen. A high-pitched animal screaming began together with headbanging and eye-poking. Then she started charging her wheelchair at me, intending, I felt, to smash my legs. I could not bear what was happening and asked her if she would like me to phone for Teresa to come up. She calmed instantly. I felt a terrible pang of uselessness. Maureen had been referred because her crying was unbearable. The residential home had spared a staff member for the whole afternoon to bring her and I could not bear it either. Teresa was not reachable. She had gone out for a walk. However, the fact that I had shown I needed to be part of a couple to deal with that grief had its effect. Perhaps too, the infantile self needed to know I would not keep her away from the mother she needed.

The weeping diminished into sobbing and then subsided. There was a moment's quiet and then a look of utter pain crossed her face and she started poking her eye again. Rather like a desperate mother with a crying baby I reached for a musical clock, wound it up and stood it on the table. The moment the music sounded her crying stopped. She was entranced. She signed she wanted the clock. She held it to her ear and then against her heart and kissed it. Tears poured down her face. I said she wished I could wind her up and make a sound come out. She wished she could speak. When the music slowed down Maureen listened intently and then wound it up again. Each time she listened for the moment when the music slowed. I said maybe she was trying to find the moment where the music was all right, before it started to slow down. Maybe she was wondering where she went wrong, what had made her go slow. Tears continued to pour down her face. The self-injury stopped. The music was about the grandfather clock that stops when the grandfather died and something of the sadness in the music calmed her.

In Shakespeare's *Titus Andronicus*, Lavinia is raped and then mutilated. Her tongue and her arms are cut off. When her uncle Marcus sees her he cries, 'Come, let us go, and make thy father blind, / For such a sight will blind a father's eye'. When Titus sees her he is overwhelmed with grief. 'Thou hast no hands to wipe away thy tears, / Nor tongue to tell me who hath martyred thee.' Those words apply to many of our multiply handicapped patients.

The sight of the horror stories that pass for family histories in many of our client group blinds the workers as well as the clients. Far easier to think that Maureen is 'seeking attention' than to feel the weight of her personal tragedy, because sometimes, as in that moment with me, the tragedies are unbearable. Shakespeare expresses powerfully the inability to contain great grief in *Titus Andronicus* (III.i.229–32):

> Then must my earth with her continual tears
> Become a deluge, overflow'd and drown'd;
> For why my bowels cannot hide her woes,
> But like a drunkard I must vomit them.

Second session

Maureen arrived brightly dressed and brown and looking openly at
me. She had been on a five-day holiday and travelled on a plane for
the first time. Teresa said there had been less crying in the week
and that Maureen had been looking forward to coming. This time
we had arranged that Teresa would sit in a chair outside the door
so that she would be easily accessible if Maureen needed her.
Maureen nodded at this arrangement and Teresa left the room.

This time, Maureen looked carefully at the table and picked up a
felt-tip pen. Very carefully she then drew line after line of what I
thought of as proto-numbers and letters. They were half-shapes,
tantalizingly familiar but never a complete letter. The only complete
shapes were the zero and a plus sign. I commented on this but
Maureen did not seem interested. When she got to the end of the
page she pointed to the bag that hung over her wheelchair. I asked
if she wanted me to get something for her and she nodded urgently.
Inside her bag was an envelope full of holiday photographs. It was
painful to see her lying topless and deformed on a beach next to
normal-bodied care staff. She started jabbing her eyes. I said she did
not want to see the photo right now. That was really to buy time
for what I was finding painful to say. Then I did say it. I wondered
aloud if it was painful for her to see the difference between her body
and mine and hers and the other women on the beach. She looked
sad and turned the other photos over one by one. She clearly liked
the photos of herself dressed and I commented on this. Then she
put the photos away and gestured for me to put the envelope back
in her bag.

She then turned to look at the doll's house. She picked up a baby
doll and made it walk into the parent's bedroom. Then the baby fell
down and Maureen started sobbing and crying and clicking her jaw
by biting her teeth savagely. I said she had come back into my house

and felt hopeful, but then something had gone wrong and she did not feel she could express it. Never mind. We had time. We could sort it out.

She carried on crying and then began smashing her wheelchair up and down. I did not feel despair, like the last time, but I felt she might need to know Teresa was still available. I asked her if she wanted Teresa and she nodded. I opened the door. Teresa, of course, had heard all the screaming and crying but had professionally waited to see if I would invite her in. As soon she came in Maureen held her hand and stopped crying. I commented on the speed of this and Teresa and I had a few words about the desperate nature of Maureen's crying. I asked Maureen if she was able to manage without Teresa and she nodded. Teresa left and we had a further fifteen minutes of silence.

Third session

Teresa sat outside again after bringing a hot drink for Maureen. Maureen held the cup gently and made it touch her mouth sensually. She took a sip and I could almost feel the warmth trickle down her. Her eyes closed, her matchstick legs moved slightly. She put the cup down slowly. Then she picked it up and touched its rim. Then she put it down again. I was reminded of Shukhov in Solzhenitsyn's *One Day in the Life of Ivan Denisovich* (1963) who remains human in spite of his circumstances because he can find pleasure in food for survival. As he sips his soup, 'filling his whole body with warmth, all his guts begin to flutter inside him at their meeting with that stew. Goo-oood!' Workers with the elderly and the handicapped have spoken of the comfort food provides (Sprince and Usiskin, 1987).

Over twenty minutes passed this way. I was observing the meaning and sequence of the movements. Then there was a moment when the experience turned bad. It was somehow depleted of any pleasure and there were only the repetitive movements reminiscent of a character's physical self-immersion in Beckett's *Stirrings Still* (1989): 'There had been a time he would sometimes lift his head enough to see his hands. What of them was to be seen. One laid on the table and the other on the one. At rest after all they did. Lift his past head a moment to see his past hands. Then lay it back on them to rest it too.' Then she touched a doll's hair, then the cup, then the doll's mouth. She repeated the process faster and faster until she seized the cup with both hands and poured its contents down her mouth, faster than she could manage. Liquid poured round the fold in her neck, over her dress, everywhere. It felt sticky and awful. I asked if she wanted a tissue but she gave no response and I realized it was I who wanted the tissue, I who wanted to wipe that sticky mess. She was not feeling the discomfort herself, she had passed it to me. I would not understand the meaning of the fast drinking for several months but I did note and comment on the fact that she did not cry or need Teresa.

Fourth session

Teresa was not able to bring Maureen so someone else brought her. I wondered how she would manage without Teresa. When the new worker arrived I looked at Maureen. She looked awful. All life and spirit had left her features, making her handicap take on an ugly form. She suddenly lifted her skirt up, showing she wore an incontinence pad underneath. 'If you need to go to the toilet you can give the proper sign,' said the man. Maureen started tearing at her pad, throwing pieces into the corridor, while the man continued his harangue. 'If you don't do the Makaton sign and stop doing what you are doing right now I won't take you to the toilet.' (Makaton is a major sign language.)

I did not know the man and did not feel free to intervene. However, I felt angry on behalf of Maureen that, as a young woman, she should have to make a specific sign to answer a basic need when he clearly knew what she wanted without it. As it was, he took her to the toilet probably because he would be the one to have to wipe her up if he didn't. A child can be tantalized by being made to say 'please' first before a treat. But what must it feel like to not be allowed to urinate unless you are in a good enough mood to make an appropriate sign? Similar situations crop up all the time in 'homes' for the handicapped. Twenty-six-year-old Martin was forced to get up and wash and dress at 9 a.m. on a Sunday. Why?

Lazy or depressed adults get up when they want at the weekend and choose whether to flop around in dressing-gowns or get dressed. Is a home really a home if residents are not allowed their choice?

Then, while waiting for them to return, I thought of the predicament of Maureen's young escort. He was probably the same age as Maureen, had received little training and had the delicate task of taking a young woman to the toilet. At least the Tavistock Clinic now had a ground-floor disabled toilet. Buildings without such facilities are providing handicapping environments. An important political initiative has yet to be taken in insisting on ramps, disabled toilets, wheelchair access.

After a few minutes they came back. The mood was calm and they had both righted themselves, as had I. He wheeled her half-way into my room and said he would wait outside. Maureen nodded and he left. She wheeled her chair near to the table and pointed into her bag. She had brought her large photograph album. She deliberately opened it back to front, turning the empty pages laboriously. I said she wanted me to see her photos and she wanted me to see the empty part of the book. She continued turning the pages slowly. I was aware of feeling irritated, of estimating it would take twenty minutes for her to turn all the pages. Then I realized we would be coming to the holiday beach photographs she had shown me last week and that was why she was delaying. I said nothing but no longer felt irritated and something changed in the way Maureen turned the pages.

I said maybe she wanted me to see all the pages of her life that had no photos, no photos of her mum and dad, her brothers and sisters, no photos of a baby Maureen. She listened intently while turning the pages and then pointed to her bag. Inside it was an envelope with a single photo. It was Maureen planting some bulbs. I said she was planting bulbs, growing new life and she felt that even with the terrible empty pages she could still have hope for new life.

And then she came to the holiday photo of her deformed topless body lying next to a topless helper. She looked at it but this time she did not cry. I felt awful but I did not feel it was necessary to repeat my comment of last time. Instead I spoke of the forthcoming summer holiday and her wish to know when I was going away. She nodded. She put the album away and made a sign for a drink. I said we had fifteen minutes left and she could get a drink after that. She urgently repeated the sign and wheeled angrily to the door. I said it was not the end of her session. To my surprise she paused there. I said if she really could not manage more time I would phone her escort but I thought she perhaps could. I said she wanted a drink because she felt empty looking at her holiday photos and thinking of the next empty space, me going away without her. I then wondered aloud whether she worried how different our bodies would look on the beach. She gave a huge grin, but I knew from Steven and Ali (Chapters 6 and 7) that it was not real. I said sometimes there was a Maureen who smiled mockingly at a Maureen who felt sad at being different.

She then wheeled herself back to the table. She started going through the photographs again and I noticed for the first time the bite marks on her hands. This time, as she looked at the photos she looked at me. I said she was looking at me to see if I minded not being shown the photos but getting the empty pages instead. Maybe she felt that she had years of empty pages and she wanted me to know what that felt like. She grinned genuinely at that. I said it was time and commented on her courage in staying.

Session 9: first session after the summer break

A new temporary worker brought Maureen. She pushed her aggressively and angrily stated that Maureen had ripped her catheter out and wanted a new one. She asked if she should wait outside and I said that Maureen was able to manage now. Something of the loud sounds coming from the worker had meant I did not properly see Maureen. Only when the worker left did I see she was holding a beaker of coffee and had a hand over her face. At the table she took a tiny sip and held the cup tightly. Then she gave further little sips. Her hands started to shake. I said she was terribly thirsty and the coffee was very hot so she could not drink quickly. Maybe she was especially thirsty after the summer holiday.

After a few more sips she poured the coffee down her throat so that it spilled all around her neck and over her dress. I felt awful and sticky and unconsciously moved my hand to my neck as if to dry it. Then Maureen put the beaker back and covered her eyes. I said I wasn't sure if she was doing that so she couldn't see me or whether it was so that I could not see her after she had soaked herself. She smiled a sadistic smile. I said sometimes she felt sad for the Maureen who got things spilled over her and sometimes she felt triumphant.

She sat still and then pointed to the typewriter. She signalled for me to put paper in and then she typed, but not hard enough, so no letter came out. I held her finger to show how hard she had to press (it was a manual typewriter) and I pointed to the 'M' for Maureen. She then typed four Ms in a row and when I said she had managed it she quickly typed lightly so nothing would show. I said she was not sure how much she wanted to communicate clearly with written words. She then typed a 'C' that came out clearly. I said 'C for Coffee and Cup'. She smiled genuinely and then pointed to a pad and a pen. She then wrote a back-to-front C. I wondered if she was trying to do a C for Coffee. She nodded and then filled five pages with zeros and back-to-front C's. I said she was now filling the empty pages as desperately as she had filled an empty space in herself with coffee.

She felt her right breast. I said she was holding her breast, maybe to mother herself, a place where a baby got milk. Then she poked at her rib-cage. I said maybe she felt empty, as the page felt empty without the writing, and she did not know if it could be filled up properly.

Supervision

After three months Maureen had stopped crying and biting. A new stage had been reached in therapy. She would come in with a coffee, spend twenty minutes drinking it, trying very hard not spill it and eventually managing. She would then obsessively draw, largely in a non-representational way. I felt I had reached a plateau of understanding and needed more help to take the therapy further. At this point I went to psychoanalyst Dr Isaacs-Elmhirst, who had given me help with my treatment of Steven.

I was to go for a weekly supervision for a year, bringing a session of work with Maureen and one of work with Steven. I would type up my memories of the sessions and make a copy so that we could go over the sequence in great detail. This made an important impact on my work then as well as providing me with some ideas that could continue percolating inside me long after supervision ended. It also reminded me again of how important it is for professionals working in this field to receive support and further learning opportunities.

On 18 June 1988, Dr Helen McConachie and I co-organized a one-day workshop on the emotional experience of multiple handicap. Helen McConachie is a psychologist at one of the few major assessment and treatment centres for multiply handicapped children in this country, the Wolfson Centre. We decided to include psychotherapy supervision by Dr Isaacs-Elmhirst of my work with Maureen to demonstrate the insight and support gained through reviewing strategies and assumptions with an outside person.

When I first went to see Dr Isaacs-Elmhirst I brought Session 15 to supervision. The start was the familiar sequence of Maureen's twenty-minute coffee time. Although she now managed to take longer and spill less, she had continued in a desperate buildup of speed. I had tried all sorts of hypotheses: perhaps she was scared of finishing the drink because then there would be none left and she feared it would be irreplaceable; she did not think it would wait for her and cool down so she had to swallow it hot. All these respectable but uninspired interpretations washed over her.

Dr Isaacs-Elmhirst told me to think of Alice in Wonderland and the bottle that says 'drink me'. 'Perhaps,' she wondered, 'Maureen has to drink the coffee quickly because otherwise it would drink her up.' I thought she could be right but it felt mad! It was, after all, an infant's view of the world which was rarely verbalized by adults. I would never have thought of such an interpretation myself and wasn't sure if I could put it to Maureen clearly.

Session 16

Maureen came drinking her coffee as usual. I thought of Dr Isaacs-Elmhirst's words and could not manage to say them. I felt stupid thinking them. Meanwhile Maureen continued sipping, but building up speed. Then I knew I had to say it to see if it was right. 'Perhaps you feel you have to drink the coffee up quickly because otherwise it will drink you up.' There was a pause. I felt tense and stupid. Then Maureen looked at me with a knowing happy smile on her face. There was a speed in her development over the next few months, including the development of sounds. First she gave a sneeze, then, a few weeks later, a burp. This was very important. Then came a fart. With many other patients a fart is a smelly attack on the therapist and the room but with Maureen it was quite different. It was as if only now could she re-explore in a safer setting some aspects of infantile development. When she farted she looked round to see where the noise had come from. I described it to her. Similarly when she sneezed or coughed.

Session 20

She sipped slowly and suddenly made a gulping noise I had never heard before. Although her speech therapist had informed me that if Maureen ever did speak her sounds would include a severe speech defect, there was no known organic reason why she could not. I found myself thinking about that. I listed all the noises I had heard her make and suggested maybe, if she wanted to and tried, she might be able to speak, because if she could let those other sounds come out of her maybe a word could. I emphasized that it did not matter if she never spoke but I would like her to have the choice if she wanted to. She listened very carefully. I wondered whether she feared words could hurt her if they came out. Maybe sometimes she felt my words hurt her. She spilled not even a drop of coffee and listened intently.

I pondered on the state in which a word, like a thought, is experienced as a physical object. Where there is a speech defect (and we knew that speech would prove very difficult for Maureen even if she wanted to speak) the experience of uttering a word is far more physical. Golding's *Darkness Visible* (1980, p. 19) describes this perfectly. 'Not only did he clench his fists with the effort of speaking, he squinted. It seemed that a word was an object, a material object, round and smooth sometimes, a golfball of a thing that he could just about manage to get through his mouth, though it deformed his face in the passage.'

The move to continence

Over the next few months Maureen continued to make more sounds. She also started tearing her incontinence pad off and exposing her vagina before her new regular activity of drawing. Dr Elmhirst had suggested giving her 21 pages of drawing paper each week, one for each year of her life, to aid her symbolic development. Maureen treated the paper in the same way she had treated the coffee initially. She would start by making a representational drawing that was at a four-year-old level. Then she would attack that clear communication and rush through the pages, scribbling on each.

Gradually, the connection between pulling off her pad and writing became clearer. Like a baby not knowing what went in or out of each orifice Maureen was struggling with an infantile zonal confusion. She did not know if the ink from the pen that went onto the page would come out of her vagina or if her urine would come out of her mouth. As that was interpreted Maureen grew clearer about when she needed to go to the toilet. There was one other theoretical strand that supervision helped me with. The way Maureen covered her eyes after she drew something was not being dealt with adequately by me. I knew that I had been correct at the start of her therapy in commenting on what she wished or did not wish me to see. But that was no longer right. In supervision I was put in touch with Bion's concepts of the jealousy different parts of the body could have for each other. Once I had realized the importance of that, Maureen was to develop further. For example, on one occasion, after she had drawn a representational wheelchair and then covered her eyes I commented that perhaps her eyes would be jealous of what her hand could draw. Her face lit up at the correctness of the comment.

Session 31

A smiling Teresa wheeled in an attractively dressed and beaming Maureen. I thought how pretty they both looked. 'I don't know how to say this, but Maureen is marvellous and I am so proud of her. Do you know she has been amazing, she has transferred herself from her chair to the toilet and she has not cried and I don't know what's being going on here but things have really been changing.'

When Teresa left Maureen wheeled herself to the table to draw. She undid her incontinence pad without exposing her vagina. I said she wanted to uncover herself to draw but she did not need to expose her private parts. Perhaps because she had not wet herself and had managed the toilet herself, she felt safer at being covered up. After a few drawings she suddenly reached for some of the figures. She picked up a toy aeroplane and placed it in a fallen-over position. A baby calf, lying down on its side, was placed nearby. Then a picnic table was brought in and a lying-down mother doll. Finally, she picked up a cow and made it lie down with its bottom touching the mother's face.

I said the aeroplane was crashed and could not fly, the calf was lying down and could not walk. There was a table set for two but could the mother and the cow eat or would they hurt or excite each other? I said the cow had its bottom in the mother's face. Maureen laughed. I said perhaps she wanted to be close to me, as another woman, but then something angry happened and she wanted to stick her bottom in my face. She listened, riveted. I said maybe the crashed plane and the lying-down people and animals represented her, unable to use her legs. She was interested in that and made an odd sound in her throat. I wondered aloud if there was a word wanting to come out.

However, the next thing to come out was a tear.

Session 40

In her first session after Christmas Maureen arrived with Teresa, looking alert and well-dressed. She looked out of the window and round the room checking they were all the same. She spent fifteen minutes slowly checking each item of furniture. Then and only then could she look at me. It was as if the things, the objects represented permanence more than the people. In her case that was certainly true. Her furniture would now stay with her long after her key worker left.

She looked at me and then the sky and round the room again. Suddenly a tear appeared in her right eye. I commented on it, and she touched it slowly and softly. I said now she knew that was a tear. She was pleased the room and I were the same because she had missed us.

Loss

Over the next few months there was a deterioration. Teresa, Maureen's excellent key worker, was leaving. Like Steven and Ali, when faced with a new external blow Maureen reverted to her old modes of false comfort. Her crying returned and her biting. She started spilling her drink and the only toy she touched was the fire engine. She was full of burning feelings about this loss. Teresa's thoughtfulness extended to her leaving plans. She was carefully handing over care of Maureen to a sensitive young man, Tom.

He told me that although Maureen had been wailing and biting there was a new quality of sadness that had never been there before and he thought it was very good because it meant she really valued Teresa and knew she would be missing someone good. With Tom understanding Maureen's grief so well she began to recover and, not only did she recover, she made a further step forward.

Session 44

Tom brought Maureen. She was wearing a new green two-piece suit. Her black hair was in a bun with a green ribbon round it and she had green slip-on shoes. Tom told me that he had taken Maureen shopping with a female staff member and she had pointed out what she wanted to try on and it had been extremely successful.

When he left Maureen looked at the coffee and then her two-piece and then her hand. She held the coffee towards her mouth and then away, towards and away. I said she was showing me her new green suit and the coffee and how hard it was to let her hands bring the coffee to her mouth in case something went wrong and the suit got spoiled.

The whole session was full of threes: Maureen, Tom and I; her eyes, her two-piece suit and the coffee; her hands, the coffee and her mouth. An oedipal triangle was being worked out with her own body parts.

Session 45: the triangle continues

There was a knock on the door and Tom the escort wheeled Maureen in. He was beaming with real pleasure and so was she. I said they had managed to get here exactly on time. The last few times the minicab had let them down or there had been traffic jams. He smiled and said yes, he had been determined to arrive on time. Maureen continued to beam. 'Bye then,' he said to her and went out. She was sitting on her chair in the middle of the room holding a coffee and grinning. A small giggle came out and she covered her eyes. I said she and Tom were both really pleased to get here on time this week. I added something was so funny about that that a sound had to come out of her to show her feeling, and she had covered her eyes so as to not see me hearing that sound. She put her hand down and beamed again and then another giggle came out.

She covered her eyes again. I said she and Tom had come together smiling and laughing while I was sitting here on my chair and now her smile and her laugh were coming together. She put her hand down again and another giggle came out and she covered her mouth. I said first it was her eyes that must not see or hear her laugh and now her mouth must not open to let that sound out. She had a quick look at me and then started drinking her coffee. She then charged to the table, bounced up and down on the chair, and then she started drawing fast.

I said her eyes had been full of laughter and that had been all right, and then her mouth had smiled – that was all right. But when a sound wanted to come out and be part of that laugh something had to be covered up, her eyes or her mouth. Only two things could feel the same. And then when her mouth wanted a drink and her eyes saw the drink and wanted it the coffee could not just come comfortably out of the cup into her mouth. She looked at me, most interested. I said two things could happen at the same time but when there was a third thing it was either shut in or poured out.

Session 50

Maureen was wheeled in by Tom, looking very pleased. She had coffee. She sat peacefully drinking. Then something quite different happened. Each time she sipped she breathed out making an exhaling sound and at the same time as she breathed out she moved her right hand out as if – in my thoughts – pushing a breast away. I watched this several times and then I said, 'Isn't that interesting – have you noticed that each time after you sip you are making a sound and moving your hand in time as if you want to make sure that nothing comes into your mouth at the moment you are taking your breath – as if you are scared something might try to get in?' She listened but continued fending off with her right hand.

When her incontinence pad was off she started drawing. Nothing representational and all very similar. I don't think I said anything useful here about the shapes or colour. As soon as she had finished she charged away to the other end of the room. I said she wanted to be right away from me, as far away as she could go. Perhaps she was worried the drawings would come back at her when she finished them. She lifted her hands as if fending off an attack. I commented on this, how she expected something to get inside and disturb her just when she was looking after herself with the coffee and now looking after her knees. She smiled and covered her eyes. Then when she moved her right foot she lifted her right hand at the same time like a marionette. I said she wondered how her arm worked – what made it go up and down and could her arm teach her leg what to do? She smiled again and covered her eyes and then burped and covered her mouth. I said today it felt she was in all different bits and pieces – there was a bit that burped and another bit that moved and she wondered if they could all work together. She then giggled. There was a pause. I commented on the new movement in her leg and wondered if it was a cramp or real feeling coming back.

Session 60: first session after a holiday

Maureen was wheeled in by a new staff member. She held a coffee in one hand and partially covered her eyes with the other. I could see her lips curled into a big smile and said 'Hello Maureen.' Her smile got larger and she tried to cover her mouth but that meant her eyes showed and she grinned more whilst struggling with which bit of herself to hide. I said she was pleased to be back and to see me again although she wasn't sure she wanted me to see that. She grinned.

Then the worker left. Maureen sat absolutely still but looked out of the window and round the room – very slowly. I commented that she had a new summer skirt on and she smiled. I said she was looking to see what was the same and what was different here. She continued sitting still and then began to sip her coffee very slowly. In fact it took over fifteen minutes for her to drink it. She sipped, paused, covered her eyes, uncovered her eyes, looked around. I said she was taking her time with the coffee – she was not in a rush and the coffee was not in a rush. Although she had not seen me for two weeks she had been able to wait and she felt I could wait.

When she came to the last sips she poured the coffee down her mouth again, spilling it on her clothes and then she rushed to pull off her incontinence pad. After that she charged her wheelchair to the desk but then drew slowly and thoughtfully.

Her first drawing was clearly representational and I commented on this, but the rest was very much as usual. After the drawing she did not reach for a toy but charged to the other end of the room, covering her eyes. I said today she did not want to do anything with the toys. She wanted to be as far away from me in the room as she could. She partially uncovered her eye. Then she very noticeably began to stroke the bare knee of her right leg. Just as I started to comment on her preferring her own body her leg suddenly lifted in the air. She looked at me and grinned, partially covering her eyes.

I said, goodness, her leg had moved. Was that a spasm or movement she could control? She stroked her leg again and again it lifted. Then she did it five times in a row so there was no mistaking what had happened. I said it looked as if there was some real feeling in that leg today. She grinned and then a giggle came out of her mouth.

I commented that was a sound coming out of her mouth. She giggled louder and tried to stop the sound by covering her mouth. I said it was like before when she did not want me to see her smile or her eyes. She didn't want me to see her smile now or hear the sound coming out of her mouth because that smile and that sound showed she was happy that her leg could move and she was happy that a sound could come out of her mouth; and if those things could happen – would she want to be able to talk or walk? She continued grinning and giggling. When her worker came in he grinned at the giggling Maureen and I said Maureen had moved her leg. Maureen demonstrated. The worker was amazed and congratulated her.

She will not regain use of her legs, just as she will always be profoundly handicapped, but she has the chance now of psychic movement and that is a major liberation. Nevertheless, there was some return of feeling and this brought pain as well as hope.

Session 70

After drawing, she moved her wheelchair to the other end of the room. Only twelve minutes of the session had gone –this was much quicker than usual. I was just about to say that when she started stroking her knee and it was clear her foot had gone into a cramp. She made a guttural noise. I said her leg was hurting – some of that was good because it meant that leg could feel again, but some of it was very painful and perhaps today her leg hurt more than usual. She hid her eyes and grinned. I said I wondered if she was wanting her leg to hurt. She grinned more. I added perhaps she wished it was my legs that hurt so I couldn't walk away for my holiday. She continued to stroke her knee and her leg kept contracting painfully. She then suddenly went to open the door and I hurried to sit by her near the door saying she was free to leave with Tom but not by herself because she would not be able to just quietly wait.

She then quickly touched her leg and, sitting close to her, I could see how rigid it had become from cramp. She made a painful sound and in answer I eased her toes for her. She smiled gratefully and the cramp subsided and I said how hard and tense the cramp made her leg. When I let go of her leg the cramp returned and she looked at me for help. I then moved her toes again. This happened three times. Her cramp was horribly chronic and her leg was painfully rigid. She looked at me intently both thankfully and vulnerably. I said she was pleased I understood how much her leg hurt. I sat back in the chair and she continued attending to her leg, which stayed constricted. I wondered whether she had moved so quickly there in order to have a space for her leg as if she couldn't attend to her leg when she was at the table with the paper and everything else.

When there was a minute to go I told her and asked if she would like me to put her shoe and sock back on and she nodded. Her leg was still painfully stiff but the act of putting the sock on relaxed her foot for a moment. When Tom came in I said Maureen's leg had been painful and he said Maureen had had a very painful morning with her leg but was very brave about it. Maureen smiled.

Session 90

As soon as she had finished drawing she charged as usual to the other end of the room to tend her legs. As soon as she was in that position she snorted inwards, a painful mixture of a sniff and a groan. I said she was taking a sound back inside herself – it sounded painful and perhaps she felt the sound could go into the pain and help it. She looked at me and then back at her leg that had contracted again. For the rest of the session her leg seized up and relaxed and seized up and relaxed. Then she made a painful guttural exhaling sound several times when her leg dramatically seized up. I said the pain was so bad she wished it could go out in a noise. I was aware of not feeling a need to assist her physically so it was clear the sound had helped. I then said the pain had needed her to tell me how bad it was and when she could do that so I could hear, it felt easier to manage. There was then a quiet pause. She rested her head against her shoulder. I felt she was exhausted but peaceful. I said it was really tiring having her legs hurt like that and cramp like that and that when she was able to show me how they hurt she was able to rest a bit. She smiled and then covered her eyes. I said again she was pleased with me, and so was her mouth, but then her eyes did not want to see. She put her hand down. Another long peaceful silence.

Then both legs seized up awfully and her sounds were different. She needed attention and I went across and bent her toes for her. Her leg softened and I went back to my chair. I said the pain was so bad then that her sound had been different and she needed me to move her leg with my hands, words were not enough. She rubbed her knee so hard to try and control the next cramp that a red mark appeared and I then saw there was a bruise from past rubbings. I said 'Poor Maureen, that looks really painful. Maybe you moved from the pictures to there because you felt you needed lots of space for your legs.' She then made her new noise, like a snort. A backwards sniffing sound. I said she was making a noise for her poor legs to show that they hurt. She looked at me most intently and made a painful guttural noise again and then as her legs seized up started to rub her knee again. For the rest of the time her legs contracted, relaxed and contracted.

I said it was very hard for her to think of anything when her legs hurt so much. I commented on how once she could walk with them and now she couldn't, after the operation. I reminded her of how there had been no feeling and now there was some feeling but it was painful too. Maybe seeing me again after the holidays also stirred up life but painful life too. She nodded.

Tom, Maureen's new worker, is now leaving for a more senior job elsewhere. He has not told Maureen verbally yet but she has picked it up emotionally. There has been a return to crying, biting and wetting. The residential staff include new members who have never known how Maureen was when she first came. They see her crying and biting and feel despair. However, there are still enough continuous staff with a history of Maureen's ups and downs to make the transition work. Mary, another worker Maureen has been attached to for a long time, has also just left for maternity leave.

Session 100

Maureen was wheeled into my room by a new escort. She tore off her shoes and socks and then threw her incontinence pad. It was wet with urine and emitted a strong smell. She then covered her eyes and sat still. I felt a great sense of distaste and for a few seconds could only think of disinfectant and how I could word my wish to throw the pad away. I said she had a wet pad – perhaps she was uncomfortable with it but I wondered why she had not shown her worker she needed a new one. Perhaps she wanted me to see and smell how she was when a new worker went out with her who did not know her signs so well.

She took her hand down and looked at me. I said her hand did not have to cover her eyes now – we could both see better what had happened and I would fold the incontinence pad up so the room would not smell so much (which I did).

She wheeled herself to the table and picked up a toy cow. Then she picked up a man and woman doll. Then a calf. Then a baby. She threw them away. Before I could comment on her feelings about couples and babies she pulled her dress up, then wheeled her wheelchair back and started putting her finger in her vagina. She wailed and then held her stomach and a trickle of urine and menstrual blood came out onto the floor.

I felt immensely sad and said, 'Maureen, it is your period and, do you know, all the months you have seen me you have never wanted me to know when it was your period.' Her wailing stopped and she wiped her eyes and looked at me. I said, 'Perhaps Teresa and now Mary going on maternity leave have made you think about your stomach and your period and how babies are made and whether you could have one.' She nodded and then she cried. She wheeled back to the table and picked up a little baby doll and stroked its hair. Then she cried and dropped it. I said she was feeling awful, like a baby whose mother had left it because her own mother did leave her and now her favourite worker had left; but also like a woman without a baby who knows she is handicapped. She looked at me really sharply then pointed for the baby doll. I gave it to her. She put it down. Then she signed for a musical clock and listened to that and hugged it. Then she drew her wheelchair. Then she looked out of the window and looked round the room and looked at me and smiled. I said she enjoyed her music and being here with me and being able to see and draw and sometimes that made up for not being a mother with a baby or a baby with a mother. She nodded.

One worker had wanted Maureen sterilized – as a profoundly handicapped young woman without verbal speech she is vulnerable to abuse. However, the idea that Maureen would not understand the concept of pregnancy or sterilization is clearly crazy. For further understanding on this subject, Sandra Baum, head of the psychology department at Leytonstone House, has written a moving chapter on work with a pregnant severely handicapped woman which will be in Ann Craft's forthcoming book, *Practice Issues in Sexuality and Mental Handicap*.

There are particular issues in working with patients with no verbal speech and little symbolic play or communication. It means working far more intensively with countertransference feelings and checking them out by the response of the patient. These intuitive responses are clearly honed and deepened by training, analysis and supervision. However, they do pose difficulties. Sometimes, a patient can provide a nod which might be compliant rather than a sign of real agreement. When I am unsure I comment, 'I wonder if you are feeling — when you do that. Maybe it is hard for you that I do not know why you are doing that. Perhaps you imagine I can guess properly. Well, sometimes I do think I know and sometimes I might guess and then I could be right or wrong.'

Long-term therapy can help the profoundly multiply handicapped who face such regular external losses. Maureen knew that when someone goes, something remains inside her, but with the amount of loss she had suffered this inner experience was not solid enough yet. There was no time limit on therapy with Maureen. The commitment from her residential home was sterling. There had also been backup from her local hospital, which was willing to take her in when depression ground her down to a high level of self-injury. When we face severe handicap and severe emotional disturbance no one treatment provides the total answer. It matters even more that we are multidisciplinary in our approach, so that behaviour therapists can say 'We can't do any more with this patient, can you?' without feeling attacked; so that I can reciprocate to them or to the acute in-patient unit. We face yet again the new round of grief, but with a difference. We know and hold the hurt. As I wrote in 'Night Shift':

> Collecting and changing the dressings on cries
> See how in our hands
> the white sheet holds like a glacier
> the skeletons of pain

Those words of mine were to be prophetic. I thought I had finished writing my chapter. But just at that point Maureen faced the loss of another key worker and a renewed outburst occurred. This time her self-injury was far more physically dangerous. She poked her anus to the extent of making herself bleed as well as becoming regularly infected by the faeces with which she was surrounded. She slowly recovered in her usual way, only to die suddenly of renal failure. She was clearly unwell for the two weeks before her death but we did not expect her to die. Only later did I learn that many people who are so multiply handicapped have a severely shortened lifespan.

Maureen's death had a profound impact on me and everyone who worked with her. There were forty people at her funeral, including her speech therapist, occupational therapist, psycho-therapist, psychiatrist, key workers past and present, other residents from her home and her former Adult Training Centre. There were huge bouquets of flowers. The level of genuine loss testified to the attachment everyone felt for her. Handicapped and non-handicapped cried together and celebrated together. I had written a poem for her.

FOR THE FUNERAL

(i)

A young woman without words
is singing hymns through our mouths
a young woman without legs
has moved us here

a woman without words, legs, hardly any family
a woman with one ear and one eye
she made us hear her, see her
held us together
as between us we held her
her damage and her great heart

we the professionals
at the funeral

(*ii*)

This woman who has just died
who sent her spirit out to us
for safety
she broke and entered
her own smashed house
again and again

she carved graffiti on
the inside and outside walls of herself
poked an eye
bit an arm

stuck a fist up her bum
and found nothing there
but pulled the gathering ruins
down down

This woman who tugged at our hearts
tore out the lining of herself
made an abortion of herself
Left heartprints and shit-stains
and tear-stains

and all the kings horses and all the kings men
wept
Because she was in pieces right from the start

(*iii*)

This broken jigsaw woman
she tried to make her wheelchair
hum like a bird
on the small branch of my room

her one good eye bright as a beak
such a small time she stayed perched
Her wheeled soul
longing for wings

(*iv*)

Week after week
loss after loss
she arrived dead and again dead
waiting by the coffee machine her mother
her incubator

while we circled like plastic cups
trying to hold her leaks

Each week, each coffee, she revived
Our Lady Lazarus
with something else missing
something else stored inside

this woman, this patient
longing to be in-patient
She pulled the plug out of herself
and left us all drained

(*v*)

There is only so much anyone can take
with an eye and an ear, no words
and a broken brain

There are only so many leavings
with no working legs and a
damaged heart
There is a limit even for Lazarus

I knew her for the last quarter of her life
So here I am for a woman who gave herself
and was given no quarter

but whose one eye, one heart,
could shine above the coffee cups
the ransacked shrine of her self

After the service we all returned to Maureen's home to look in her room, talk together and share memories and thoughts. One mourner was moved to hear she had managed to come for therapy and when he heard she was the only such multiply handicapped woman in therapy with me long-term, he commented, 'Then there really was something special about her that made people look for the right treatment for her. She has made history in her own way. She is a survivor and we won't forget her.'

10 MALE SEXUALITY AND HANDICAP

There is Terry
The frog the Princess did not marry
The beast that beauty did not kiss
He was never allowed to be a prince.

Valerie Sinason, 'Round Up'

The child seemed to be smelling right through his skin, into his innards. His most tender emotions, his filthiest thoughts lay exposed to that greedy little nose which wasn't even a proper nose, but only a pug of a nose, a tiny perforated organ, forever crinkling and puffing and quivering.

Patrick Suskind, *Perfume, The Story of a Murderer*

Sheila Hollins, professor of the psychiatry of disability at St George's Hospital, London has aptly termed the 'three secrets' of mental handicap the handicap itself, sexuality and death (Hollins and Grimer, 1988). It is the link between the first two I want to concentrate on here. Firstly, as a culture we find it hard to look at difficult sexual areas within the ordinary population, witness our late ability to see sexual abuse. Secondly, there is an even greater fear of looking at sexual issues and handicap together, although there has been important progress since 1981 when the Crafts (1981) linked the philosophy of normalization to the increasing provision for sex and social education.

The concept of normalization was developed in Denmark by Bank-Mikkelson and enlarged by Bengt Nirje of Sweden. In 1976 it was taken up in the USA by the President's Committee on Mental Retardation. Basically, it is a process which uses means as culturally normative as possible in order to establish, maintain and support patterns of behaviour which are as near normal as possible. It is not intended to force normal expectations on those who cannot manage them. On an important practical daily level it means, for instance, using a minicab or taxi rather than a special bus which has noticeable logos or words on it.

The philosophy of normalization aided the move of returning people from long-stay institutions to smaller community homes. Instead of being artificially segregated sexually, there was the possibility of normal peer contact, privacy and the possibility of developing sexual and emotional relationships. This is still not easy.

As I have written elsewhere (1989b) the connection between mental handicap and sexuality has been a painful one for several hundred years. At the root there is unresolved anger and fear in some societies that the sexual and procreative connection between a man and a woman could lead to a damaged offspring. In the same way that the illegitimate have had to carry social and cultural fantasies about wild unlawful sexuality, so the mentally handicapped carry, stamped on their features, the mark of what is feared as bad sexuality. This is relevant to the fantasy life of both the parents and the child. In their work on perinatal bereavement at the Tavistock Clinic, psychoanalysts Emmanuel Lewis and Sandy Bourne found (1989, p. 938), 'Adult ideas about the reason for a malformed baby link up with unconscious memories of childhood fantasy about how babies are made and unmade,' and stir up feelings of shame.

Class issues also come in here. Binet's turn-of-the-century IQ scores showed that most prostitutes and minor criminals belonged to the deprived group who made up the mildly mentally handicapped range. The Victorians were largely as unwilling as we are today to end cycles of deprivation and preferred to blame the victims of the process instead. We have seen one logical outcome of that view in the enforced sterilization of a handicapped young woman that was permitted last year.

However, it is not just 'normal' society that contains these fears. It is mentally handicapped people too. For we all carry a sense of biological hope for future generations and sadness when the hoped-for new arrival is not healthy. Then fears of 'bad' sexuality enter and handicapped and non-handicapped share a range of infantile fantasies about the meaning of this. A pregnant woman has many fantasies during her pregnancy which she may completely forget afterwards: for example, fears about the nature of what she is carrying, is she really a woman, is the baby hers or is it stolen, is she allowed to have a real baby, was the act of love-making that caused the child to be conceived the best one, does it matter, what about that extra glass of wine or cigarette or active housework? When a healthy baby is born all of this can be forgotten. However, when the baby is noticeably handicapped these primitive fears return. The damaged baby can then sometimes be seen as punishment for unhealthy sexuality.

There is a reciprocal effect on the child. Most children do not think of their parents as sexual beings except in terms of their own conception! Parents live a life of spotless celibacy otherwise, only spoiled when they foolishly add on a sibling. However, a child who is severely handicapped from birth can link itself to the procreative moment. If two people coming together produces something experienced as damaged, then sexuality is indeed dangerous. This fear paradoxically makes the handicapped more vulnerable to sexual exploitation and increasingly to abuse (Sinason, 1988c).

In therapy, many handicapped patients have expressed the fantasy I have just described: that they gained their handicap because of bad sexual activity between their parents. They feel part of something sexual that went wrong. Handicapped patients feel even more silenced and guilty than others when abused. They are visual proof that something is wrong and went wrong, so how can they speak, especially if it is somebody non-handicapped who has abused them?

Sol Gordon (1972) makes it clear that handicapped children have the same emotional and sexual drives but are given less knowledge, a factor leading to exploitation. Other workers (Buchanan and Oliver, 1977) point to abuse and neglect as actual causes of mental retardation in certain cases. In Chapter 6, I showed how mental handicap can become a defence against the memory of sexual abuse.

PROBLEMS IN CHILDHOOD

Mothers, fathers and other primary caretakers have the task of tending to their child physically as well as emotionally, socially and intellectually. Washing, wiping and drying sexual areas of the body are part of this task, especially when the child is very young. However, there is a problem here that increases with the level of the disability. With ordinary children a point is reached where they can carry out private caretaking functions by themselves, or with the help of the same-sex parent. This enables a sense of autonomy and bodily privacy to be built up. However, if you are not able to do your own toilet, there is a very delicate joint task to negotiate that can have a great impact on psychosexual development.

For example, Mrs Bannister cares for her multiply handicapped son Brian largely by herself. He needs her help in feeding, dressing, washing and toileting. 'In the beginning, it was not so bad. It was just a continuation of what I had always done. But when he was eleven he started having erections when I washed him. He was embarrassed and angry and I was embarrassed and angry. I hated my husband for going out to work and leaving me with this problem and I hated the world for not providing me with extra help.'

Mrs Bannister wrote asking for an appointment. At our first meeting she made it clear she did not want her husband involved in any follow-up meeting as it would be embarrassing for her. Further exploration showed that she was perfectly capable of discussing sexual matters with her husband. However, her own sense of sexual shame that she had produced a handicapped child made discussion of Brian's sexual feelings more difficult. When her husband did come to the next meeting, he was extremely supportive to his wife, although shocked that she had not come to him first with concerns about their son's development. 'I thought you would say it was all my fault we had him anyway so I shouldn't bother you,' cried Mrs Bannister.

After this meeting the parents went home to find their own answers and a few weeks later they wrote to tell me what they had done. Mr Bannister had a long talk with his son first and then all three of them sat together. Mrs Bannister apologized for getting angry and told her son she had been taken by surprise by his erection. She said it must be very hard for him to be growing up and not be able to do those private things himself. Other sons would have erections and their mothers would never know when. It was because he had his disability that he had lost that privacy so they had to do their best to manage.

Mr Bannister needed to maintain his employment and no male help was possible in the day. However, airing the problem openly together made it possible for Brian's development to stay healthy. This issue could have had a very different conclusion.

Many young men with disabilities are referred for violent disturbed sexual behaviour when their mothers unconsciously excite and stimulate them. Nick, aged 20, attacked female staff and students at his Adult Training Centre. He viciously pinched their breasts and buttocks. Although, unlike Brian, he had the use of his arms, his mother still bathed him in a most lascivious way. 'He loves his bath, it really calms him down and I can make sure his little private parts are all nice and clean.' I pointed out that she was trying to call his private parts 'little' to diminish the fact that he was an adult male with adult genitalia. However, she insisted that he was only a little baby, her own little baby with a sweet little body.

It is not surprising that mothers, on whom the largest burden of caretaking still rests, infantilize their adult handicapped children. If your child is not going to grow up and leave home in the usual way, one way of staying attached, albeit not age-appropriately, is to keep your child as a Peter Pan. However, there is a heavy price to be paid for this. It crushes emotional and sexual development. To try and develop sexual and bodily autonomy in such a context is very difficult.

Nick, in addition to the internal fear of attack for progress, was facing a real external attack too. A mentally handicapped boy, sexually abused by his mother, said, 'It's like the dolls inside the dolls. They want to come out but if they do they will not be inside a mummy and they won't have a mummy' (Sinason, 1989). Where parents or workers need and/or demand a symbiotic attachment it presents one mode of survival; staying unborn and fighting against any real separate life can be chosen rather than facing the internal and external attack (Sinason 1990).

PETER: NINE MONTHS OF ONCE-WEEKLY PSYCHOTHERAPY

Peter was a mentally handicapped boy referred by his mother at the age of twelve because of his emotional problems and the way he was always bullied at his school for children with learning difficulties. His teachers revealed another story. Whenever they tried to help him achieve any independent stance (like learning how to use public transport or go shopping) his parents would complain and then he would too, becoming sexually violent to girls and female teachers in the school.

As I went into the waiting room Peter, a tall lanky boy, leaned forward suggestively and intrusively. 'Hello Valerie . . . ' He beamed falsely. I said my name was Mrs Valerie Sinason and he could call me Mrs Sinason or Valerie, whichever he liked, and we were going to go to my room. This was rather a delayed response as he already had called me what he liked but even a retrospective boundary seemed useful! Peter rushed ahead, pausing at each set of doors as if surprised he did not know the way. Inside the room he sat on my chair, out of the reach of the toys and drawing materials. I commented on this but he quickly replied, 'Why do you say that? Why don't you ask me about television? Do you like Cilla Black's "Surprise Surprise"?' I said maybe he felt surprised at his parents deciding to send him here to meet me. He sighed and nodded, scratched his leg and penis and looked more handicapped. 'When is your birthday? How old are you?' I asked what he guessed. 'Twenty-six.' I wondered why. 'Because my mum is thirty.' I said he wanted me to be a Valerie younger than his mum, not a Mrs Valerie Sinason who could be older than his mum. Pause. He asked if we could go now. I asked if it was hard for him. 'Yes. I am bored.' Then he looked terrified. 'Don't tell my mum I said I was bored.' I said what we said in the room was private. 'What does private mean?' Like Ali (Chapter 6), Peter had a 'stupid smile' that concealed both his trauma, his terror and his intelligence, but the hint of intelligence he had shown led to further intrusive behaviour.

Five minutes before his second session I came upon him in a different part of the clinic, looking inside every room. I called him firmly and brought him back to the waiting room. When it was his time to come he was exceptionally polite. I said perhaps he felt he had to be polite to me because he was worried I'd be angry at him for going where he shouldn't. 'How did you know?' he asked, rubbing his penis desperately. I commented that when I stopped him from going where he shouldn't he worried about his penis. He looked most alert and then asked 'Are you thirty-nine?', getting much closer than the week before. I said once he was less afraid of me being cross he was able to use his eyes more intelligently. He then asked if I was fifty. I said that now he would like to turn me into a grandma and make me older. He giggled. Child psychotherapist Juliet Hopkins has suggested that perhaps he was afraid of being sexually needed and masturbated by a mother-aged woman and that turning me into grandmother was therefore making me safe as well as punishing me.

On his thirteenth birthday Peter said he had had a bad day. He had been taken to his parents' friends for his birthday and they said he was so handicapped he shouldn't have been born. Tears poured down his face. He pointed to the Jack-in-the-box. 'He is really sad. It is stupid to be sad. You have to be happy.' I said it was stupid pretending not to know when you were sad and he was showing us how sad he felt on his birthday about what was wrong with him. 'Don't cry, Jack,' he cried. 'He's hidden away.' I said maybe he had cried hidden away from me on his birthday. He nodded and tapped on the box. 'Is he all right in there? Is he damaged?' I said he was very aware of what was damaged in him on his birthday. He grabbed his penis. I said it seemed he felt his willy would fall off if he did not check. 'Yes. But I have not been touching myself so much.'

After five months he touched another toy, a musical clock. He wound it up and listened as the tune got slower. 'Where does it start to get slow?' I said he was hurt by his slowness. He wanted to know where or how it happened; did he start all right and then slow down or was he wrong to begin with. Tears fell down his face. 'I think I will clean up the room. I do not have to have an untidy room. I can change the order.' I said he could change the order even if he could not change the slowness.

After six months he lost his handicapped voice and started nervously voicing his worry that his mother still washed him, something he had never mentioned before that threw some light on his sexual disturbance. It emerged his mother was bathing him, not just washing him. And his father approved of this because Peter was so 'slow'.

Peter started sounding angrier and clearer in his sessions. He was also angrier with his parents and had sworn at them when they handled him in an infantile way. Social services rang the week after this saying a neighbour had phoned to say a child was being hurt. He had been heard crying for help. He said he had called his mother and father 'stinking' parents. Their immediate response was to beat him and change his school yet again. For a while there was talk of a boarding school and Peter had hopes of this. However, the parents made clear they wanted him at home for good because no-one else would understand him. A colleague made a home visit and found that the flat reeked with unwashed plates, rubbish and old food. It made her ill just walking in. It certainly made clearer why, when his eyes opened, he used the term 'stinking'.

At his next session he was very sad and quiet. 'You see . . . you see . . . my flat is a dirty flat. My flat stinks. My mum and dad won't put the rubbish out. They don't clear up. My flat stinks. There is nothing I can do.' I said maybe having Mrs X coming to his flat meant he saw his flat with the clinic's eyes. 'Yes. You should not have a flat stinking like that.' Then he smiled excitedly.

I said sometimes, he, like a moment ago, felt really sad thinking of what spoiled his flat and his mind but then he had smiled as if he also enjoyed how spoilt everything was. The next session he spoke with his old handicapped voice. 'Hello Valerie. You have made me worse not better. My Mum and Dad and I agreed I shouldn't come to you any more. You are as bad as my silly school. I wrote to my girlfriend. I hoped she would get measles and have a handicapped baby. I hope she has a poo baby. It is funny what I wrote.' I said he was worried about what sort of handicapped baby he had been and what babies he would produce and now that we had met for nine months he wanted his bad feelings towards me to give me a shitty baby. His mother rang to say he did not want to come any more and since she could not force him to come, therapy had to stop.

Further letters from the school revealed extensive sexual harassment of the female teachers. Peter was expelled after he tried to rape a teacher anally. His mother said all he needed was a cold shower. 'It is natural for a handicapped boy of his age to be sexually frustrated.' His mother's continued bathing of him, with his father's assent, made it harder for him to grow as normally as he could. To be the handicapped baby who was washed and toileted allowed him safe attachment. Where he tried to be a young man he faced a real outside death-threat that he shouldn't have been born because of his handicap. He could recognize the external sanity available in his therapy and in himself but I was not strong enough to help him fight those abusive attachments. The family was in desperate need of help, but, unlike the Bannisters, could not use it. Peter, as the baby–husband of his mother, was also fulfilling his father's own unresolved infantile longings. His fear of having a damaging penis that could create handicapped babies was in identification with his father's own damaged authority.

Peter's predicament is a painfully common one for boys and men with disabilities and handicaps. The male oedipal fantasy of marrying your mother and killing your father has an extra twist. You marry your mother by becoming her sexualized baby, her toy, and your father is killed off by the powerful effects of your handicap.

SEXUALITY AND EDUCATION

Before 1980 there was little normal appreciation of the handicapped as sexual beings. They were either monsters with animal appetites or they conveniently did not feel anything. The little sex education that existed was largely concentrated on the mechanics of intercourse. In other words, at a time when schools were understanding that sexuality was connected with emotion and formed part of human relationships, sex education for the mentally handicapped, where it did exist, was largely reverting to the old pattern of school sex education, the birds and the bees, basic biology and soulless procreation.

Although major progress has been made in the last decade there is a long way to go. The Canadian representative of the APP Mental Handicap Section is a social worker, Wai-Yung Lee. She is director of the Surrey Place Centre in Toronto, a pioneering counselling and sexual education service for handicapped people. She is also involved in sexuality training for the staff who run group homes. She has pointed out that when staff refer a handicapped individual for sexual counselling or education their hidden or not-so-hidden agenda is still all too often the wish for such behaviour to stop. She has shown very clearly the way a question by a handicapped individual is often dealt with in a brusque fact-providing way linked sometimes with a moral lecture or statements about hygiene. As she reminds staff in her training manual (1988, p. 24), 'The purpose of sex education is to offer your client factual information so that they can make an informed decision about their actions – but there is no guarantee that they will make the decision according to your standard.'

It is no good for a hospital or home to be proud of its libertarian attitude to residents' sexuality if is does not provide individual rooms or privacy for personal relationships. Similarly, proclamations that handicapped people have the same sexual rights as others are invalidated if the staff group also believe their residents do not understand anything that is being said to them and are like six-month-old babies. How can you provide factual sexual education or groups to facilitate discussion about feelings for six-month-old babies? Either the staff perception of the residents is correct, in which case sex education is completely inappropriate, or the staff need support in realizing that however infantile their clients are some of the time, they are also, sometimes, their chronological age in terms of emotional insight.

Ian, aged 17, asked his key worker if it hurt to have a willy up your arse. She read him a lecture on AIDS and perversion whilst another colleague furiously argued Ian's right to be gay. Ian was only asking a question. He did not need a lecture on either morality, AIDS or gay rights.

Some education programmes are therapeutic as a byproduct. For example, in one home, a male residential worker showed the male residents different condoms and walked in to a chemist shop with them so they could see the process of selecting and buying. He thought he was providing a social education experience because 'they wouldn't know what a condom was or how to see one in a shop'. In fact, they all knew very well what a condom was. What he had provided for them was permission to think of themselves as males who might at some stage need to buy such an item and who had a right to walk into a shop and pick one up and buy it.

Sexual and emotional development can proceed if the staff can bear it. However, sometimes all the euphemistic words about education and programmes are cover-ups for concern about the mentally handicapped who are mentally ill and perverted. Malcolm, aged 34, is mildly handicapped and manages a cleaning job. He spends all his money on pornographic magazines of a violent kind. He pins them all over his walls and spends most of his free time masturbating. True, what he does in his own room is private and there are thousands of individuals all over the country doing the same thing without anyone noticing. However, because Malcolm can't manage on his own, it does not stay private. He is impervious to staff requests for him to keep his collection to his own room. He also tells female staff his fantasies and sexualizes any contact, physical or mental. Police have interviewed him a couple of times because of the way he hangs round playgrounds watching small children. The staff feel his masturbation, his fantasies and his pornographic literature all reinforce each other and he is unable to control his actions. There is no sexual education programme that will help him. Nor will a liberationist view of 'everyone to their own thing'.

I have found it useful to examine the commonest adolescent and adult male difficulties through Shakespeare's portrayal of Richard III (who bears little resemblance to the real Richard III) and the Greek divinity Hephaestus.

Richard III

> Then, since the heavens have shap'd my body so,
> Let hell make crook'd my mind to answer it.
> I have no brother, I am like no brother;
> And this word 'love', which greybeards call divine,
> Be resident in men like one another,
> And not in me! I am myself alone.

Richard in 3 Henry VI, V.vi.78–83

> But I, that am not shap'd for sportive tricks,
> Nor made to court an amorous looking-glass;
> I – that am rudely stamp'd, and want love's majesty
> To strut before a wanton ambling nymph;
> I – that am curtail'd of this fair proportion,
> Cheated of feature by dissembling nature,
> Deform'd, unfinish'd, sent before my time
> Into this breathing world, scarce half made up . . .'

Richard in *Richard III*, I.i.14–21

Richard III is of royal birth and education, unlike most of the mildly handicapped we see today (Rutter *et al.*, 1970; OHE, 1973). Nevertheless, his response to the organic handicap he is faced with is highly relevant to the mentally and multiply handicapped and their families and carers. He has an objectively quantifiable organic damage. As portrayed by Shakespeare and chronicled by Sir Thomas More (1557), Richard was born prematurely, lame and hunch-backed. That, as with any organic or environmental handicap, is clearly an added burden to the normal difficulties of life. However, as we have seen, what can be far more crucial to the final quality of life is the use made of the primary handicap. Hatred at the difference between handicapped self and normal ('I am like no brother') can help to create opportunist handicap (Sinason, 1987), which can cause even greater human distress and destruction than the original handicap.

Shakespeare's portrayal of Richard III reveals how bearers of a handicap feel 'rudely stamped' by the sexual act that created them. Whereas ordinary children often try to deny that their existence is really due to parents' lovemaking or, at best, imagine that it might have come from one deviation in an otherwise spotless celibate life in order to create them, children born with a handicap feel linked to that sexual act. The hatred of parental sexuality is then often displaced onto others. Shakespeare makes Richard speak of 'wanton ambling nymphs'. Richard's warped sexual feelings are projected onto the court women, who are then seen as wanton and ambling. They have the luxury of normal limbs. While there is such raw hatred of the parental couple the word 'love' becomes impossible.

According to Thomas More (1557), on 13 June 1483, as part of his campaign to seize the crown, Richard accused his mother, the queen, and Jane Shore, the late king's mistress, of trying to murder him by witchcraft. Regardless of historical truth, the emotional truth represented by Thomas More's account is important. '"Ye shall see in what wise that sorceress and that other witch of her counsel, Shore's wife, with their affinity, have by their sorcery and witchcraft wasted my body." And therewith he plucked up his doublet-sleeve to his elbow, upon his left arm, where he shewed a withered arm and small, as it was never other. And thereupon every man's mind sore misgave him, well perceiving that this matter was but a quarrel for well they wist that the Queen was too wise to go about any such folly. And also, if she would, yet would she of all folk least make Shore's wife of her counsel, whom of all women she most hated as that concubine whom the King her husband had most loved.'

The sexual disgust and fear of the parental coupling that had produced Richard extended to all the sexual relations of his parents. Luckily, the emotional linking together of mistress and wife was clearly seen as disturbed. A madman with power, invoking witchcraft, was able to cause many deaths and the dark ages of English history are full of the mentally ill and handicapped being burned at the stake because of the sexual fears of others (see Chapter 2 for further historical details).

Hephaestus

Hephaestus was the only Greek god who was not perfectly formed. He was ill-made and lame in both legs (Burkert, 1985). His stumbling gait made the gods laugh. Hera, ashamed of his ugliness and handicap, as he was a child she made herself, tried to hide him from the Immortals. She cast him from Olympus into the sea, where he was looked after by Thetis but spent nine years hidden away. This is painfully familiar – the shock of having a handicapped child leading to abandonment and rejection. Hera, interestingly, felt she had created him by herself. She took all the blame. Hephaestus grew up to become a blacksmith and superb craftsman. He was linked with fire.

Hephaestus built palaces for the gods and lived in a dwelling of glittering bronze. Most of the time he would be by the hot furnaces, poking the fire. To punish his mother for her cruelty he sent her a golden throne which gripped her with invisible hands when she sat on it so she could not extricate herself. Force (Ares) could not move her. When Dionysus made Hephaestus drunk he agreed to free his mother in exchange for a beautiful bride. He was given Aphrodite, goddess of love, fertility and seafaring, the perfect woman dreamed of by handicapped men. His wife was unfaithful to him and he dealt with his humiliation by snaring her with her lover Ares in a magic couch he had invented so that they are exposed to the gods, who laugh. Hephaestus made the gods laugh one other time when he pretended to be a beautiful youth, Ganymede, and hobbled round a banquet pouring out wine.

Hephaestus and the myths about him make us aware of the secondary defence of laughter to control the public humiliation of handicap. Both situations where he evoked the laughter of the gods involved displacing sexual humiliation onto others. The fear of being seen to be ugly and sexually distasteful is widespread among our client group. It seems that if the first mirror of mother's eye registers distaste, as Hera's did, and as most parents' do when initially faced with the shock of a handicapped child, a sense of not being the wanted beautiful healthy child builds up. Hephaestus has to ensnare the most beautiful desired goddess, Aphrodite, and Ares the swift and powerful, as a means of dealing with this. 'The race is not always to the swift,' is the proverb that came from this (Burkert, 1985). The handicapped child or adult also feels he or she has caused powerful destruction by becoming handicapped, and this can mean enormous attempts are made at repairing the destruction by the development of other talents. The superb skills of Hephaestus can be seen (Klein 1932) as an unsuccessful struggle to atone for damage.

It was Freud (1909) who first understood the childhood fantasy that babies came from the anus and that an aspect of children's interest in their faeces was the fantasy of faecal babies (Little Hans). Hephaestus, by being deprived of feeling the product of a normal marital relationship, needed to stay working in the dark, hot furnace area, manufacturing golden robot-like women. I feel there is an extra developmental burden on handicapped children that makes it harder for them to resolve oedipal issues.

Although Hephaestus later protects his mother from his father's wrath, his retaliation against her, consisting of sticking her to a golden throne, is, I believe, sticking her down by her bottom to join in a mock coupling. With those forced into wheelchairs by the nature of their handicap there is further meaning. Nature has not let them separate and walk away, they have to remain stuck down. To rise courageously above this takes constitutional and environmental gifts. Not surprisingly, some will try and stick themselves down like an albatross on their families, forbidding any movement.

HOWARD/HEPHAESTUS

Howard is an eighteen-year-old handicapped man who lives in a hostel as he had proved unmanageable at home. There is certainly an increased family burden for the parents of a handicapped child (Friedrich and Friedrich, 1981), and the divorce rate for such parents is three times the average (Sternlicht and Deutsch, 1972). His parents had been in care themselves as children and the blow of his abnormality – 'I knew he wasn't right at birth' – which was formally recognized as cerebral palsy and mental handicap at two, was too much for them. Howard's increasing violence made it all the harder for them to manage.

He was referred by his hostel because of headbanging, masturbating in public and his furious attacks on staff who 'weren't giving him a woman'. The staff group, themselves only a few years older, were struggling with the different social/sexual attitudes that are directed towards the mentally handicapped. On the one hand there was a feeling that he had a 'right' to sexual fulfilment almost regardless of any emotional relationship, whilst on the other hand there was worry that his negative behaviour meant that any link with another person would automatically be doomed. He only agreed to consider therapy, I later learned, because of a bribe: his workers suggested that it might help him 'get a woman'.

When I saw Howard he was wearing a short-sleeved T-shirt that revealed his well-proportioned torso. He held his head at an angle to try and hide the side that showed effects of brain damage. His eyes fixed themselves on mine strongly as if to prevent me from seeing his wasted legs in the wheelchair. I introduced myself to Howard and his worker but the worker was then sneeringly dismissed by Howard, who was only a couple of years younger. 'Go now.' The worker turned and left. It was clear the worker was seen only as 'legs' – an otherwise useless appendage that helped to get Howard about. The worker felt guilty at having legs and being able to push a handicapped young man in his wheelchair and was therefore receiving this hatred without comment. Struggling with feelings of guilt at being normal is a very big burden for those who work with the handicapped, as well as a wish to deny that handicapped people have any envy or hatred for their carers.

In my room I explained to Howard that his workers had referred him because they felt he was unhappy about himself and getting violent because of this, and that not having a girlfriend seemed a part of this. 'Crap. Crap. Talk, talk.' I said it was very easy to turn talk to crap. 'Crap, crap,' he repeated, an uncertain echo of himself. I said he wished some talk did not turn to crap. He was quiet for a moment and then said, 'Talk. Talk. I can talk. I don't need talk.' I said he could talk and he couldn't walk and it seemed he was hurting the area where he could manage because it was so painful that he could not walk and at the moment it also felt so painful he did not have a girlfriend.

'I don't want the ugly ones. That's all I get. The ugly ones no-one wants. The ones in the wheelchairs, the ones with no proper faces. The ones that can't speak. What are you going to do for me? Kiss my arse?' I said he had come to see a woman to talk about his problems and not only was she a Mrs but she was normal too. And as long as he saw close contact as only to do with kissing arses and crap he would not be able to enjoy the normal relationship of love whatever his handicap was.

He was quiet again. 'I can go.' I agreed he could. There was a long silence. 'I'm stuck in the chair.' I said he was stuck in the wheelchair because of his handicap but he had the freedom, because of that chair, to move in or out of the room. However, maybe it was deeply hurtful that he could only get that freedom because of the chair.

'I'm thick.' I said we knew he was mentally handicapped too but maybe he was using that rude term about himself just now by way of an apology to the chair and me that we had not restricted his freedom.

'I don't want a girl thicker than me.' I said he seemed to be worrying that I expected him to. 'And if she is in a chair and not as thick as me how will we do it?'

There was a long silence. I said that was an important thing to think about. It might indeed be physically hard to make love. He might need help. It might not be possible. But it seemed as if fear of needing help or of being humiliated had made him avoid all the steps for actually meeting and learning to care about someone.

'I did meet someone. She couldn't use her arms and I had to do all her lifting.' He looked ruefully at his strong arms. 'It went on and on.' I said he did have strong arms and maybe he was proud they could do strong work but he did not want to have to use them all the time.

'No.' Long silence.

I said it was almost time and we could have another exploration the week after to see if he would like to come and meet me regularly.

'Talk. Crap,' he said, girding himself up for the outside. 'I'm leaving now.' I said I would write. He did not turn his head round but whizzed his wheelchair out, almost knocking over the young man who had brought him. I wrote a letter offering a second appointment if he wanted one but he did not. I have not heard from him since. However, that one assessment meeting brought home to me most powerfully the opportunist uses of handicap, as well as the painful self-assessments that all young men and women have to go through at adolescence, and the realization of how much worse that experience is when a handicap is present.

Like Shakespeare's Richard III, Howard had turned the relationship of love into a degraded sexuality. The opportunist aspect of his handicap meant that all sadism, envy and destructive feelings have found a home in it. His hurt at his non-working legs and, to a lesser extent, his mind had meant that he attacked what was healthy in himself and in others. Art therapist Simon Cregeen (1988), running a group for mildly handicapped young men on sexual issues, commented, 'It often felt that the men experienced a permanent frustration at our inability to provide them with sexual partners. I believe that this largely unspoken demand on us was rooted in envy.'

This secondary handicap protects Howard from the unbearable awareness of his difference. He can only bear to reach it a few times. 'I don't want the ugly ones. That's all I get.' Every adolescent is aware of the hierarchy of selection that is caused by levels of attractiveness. Howard cannot accept his handicap and his self-hatred is then directed against other handicapped people, especially young women.

His oedipal struggle for his mother is made harder by the fact that she is not handicapped. As H. B. and H. Robinson (1976) point out, 'A particular source of psychopathology in the mentally retarded is the slowness of their passage through and their poor resolution of the stages of psychosexual development. Fixating at early stages of development maintains the immature defence mechanisms.'

Like Hephaestus, Howard has strong arms to help him take on restitutive work, but it seems as if using his omnipotence to tackle big tasks only makes him more aware of the destruction he feels he has caused and therefore he inhibits even what he could do.

In 1977 in America, eighteen profoundly retarded men were tested for mirror and photographic memory and recognition of themselves (Harris, 1977). Nine were given mirror training but there was no improvement in recognition. I wonder whether there was such terrible narcissistic injury at not looking like their own families that it was easier altogether to give up on looking at the self in the mirror. Howard faces it only by displacing it onto handicapped women. Adolescence, as we know, is painful, but it is even more so for the physically and mentally handicapped (Roger Freeman, 1970), as peer differences are acuter and there are fears about not finding a partner or a job.

For Hephaestus not to entrap the beautiful and swift, for Richard not to use his hunched back to exacerbate his hatred, means blocking ears to the siren call that some of the handicapped cannot bear to resist. That is the call that takes them back to the womb unhurt yet by the handicap that will afflict them. It means going back to an auto-erotic state, finding sexual pleasure only in their own bodies. To give that up means having eyes and truly facing the extent of the handicap. But the reward is the possibility of real relationships, sexual and emotional.

However, it is important to keep in mind that although the mentally and multiply handicapped have these problems to deal with, some manage to surmount them. Janet Mattinson's work (1975) and that of the Crafts (1979) found that handicapped couples who got married clearly considered their marital experience successful. The experience of mentally handicapped parents is not one that I am going to examine in this book. However, it is worth noting that despite some clear difficulties there are also successes, similar to other parents in deprived circumstances. Also, with our new knowledge of the extent of abuse across all social classes, it is clear that some severely mentally handicapped parents manage better than their non-handicapped counterparts.

11   FEMALE SEXUALITY AND HANDICAP

> Sleeping Beauty burps
> under mountains of fat, rivers of gin
> Her flesh cries out for silk and jewels
> Her flesh cries out for the mouth of a king
>
> Valerie Sinason, 'Round Up'

Carol, a thirteen-year-old girl with Down's syndrome, sat in the therapy room and picked up a toy mirror. She looked at her face carefully. She put on a toy crown and looked at her face. She took it off. Then she put a necklace on and looked in the mirror. She took it off. I said she did not look pleased with what she saw in the mirror. She did not appear to hear me. She was deep in her own thoughts. Then she picked up a black veil and wound it round her head. She took it off. Then she covered her face with it. She took it off. Then she covered the mirror with the veil. Then she threw the mirror. It was unbreakable and held in a plastic frame, otherwise it would have broken, the way she felt broken at that moment. She sat and cried.

I said she did not think she could look at herself without adding something, a crown, a necklace, a veil. Perhaps she did not think I would care for her unless she were a princess or a queen. But then that was no good, because she felt a useless princess. She wished she could cover her face up to hide her Down's syndrome or throw it away. 'Why doesn't my Down's syndrome go away?' she asked. 'Why is it here? Each time I look in the mirror it is still here.'

Adolescent girls often look in the mirror wanting to know how their inner picture of themselves matches the outside picture. Worries about sexuality and the growth of sexual characteristics are often displaced to the face – to the nose that sticks out, to spots, to strands of hair that are felt to destroy the whole sense of self. It can be a painful time where 'face' values can overtake more integrated ideas about the worth of what is behind a face, inside a person. It is much harder to deal with these issues when there is something permanently showing on your face or in your speech or behaviour that marks you out as noticeably different. And you are not fantasizing that you look different. You really are. And it will not go away. And you wished it would and so did your family, your friends, your community. You were not going to be the frog that turned into the prince, you would stay the frog. You would not be the Cinderella who becomes the princess, you would stay by the cinders.

Carol's experience came to my mind when I was preparing the Annual Pam Smith Memorial Lecture for the Women's Therapy Centre and the Polytechnic of North London, on sexuality and the plight of the severely handicapped young woman. She made me think of the meaning of mirrors for all of us. Our first mirror, as Winnicott has pointed out, is our mother's eyes. As babies we look up into the eyes of our primary carer and in that shiny mirror we see how loved we are. We do not ask, 'Mirror mirror on the wall, who is fairest of them all?' That is when rivalry begins or when the mirror tells the tale of those not loved for what is inside them. No, the first mirror tells us whether we were wanted, whether there is a real space there for us; whether we are thought to be the most wonderful new thing in the world.

If we see that then we thrive under that mirror, we take back into ourselves a reflection of love, of being wanted, of being thought lovely. The mirror is not passive. It very actively sends messages to us. And it affects our internal image of ourselves. When a child (handicapped or non-handicapped) is not wanted it sees a very different message in its parents' eyes. There is no gleaming light or twinkle that says 'You are lovable'; there is coldness, hurt, shame, hate, fear, anger. That unloving mirror actively sends into us at a most vulnerable age the message that we are not wanted. The mirror does not have to be a visual one. Blind children who cannot see the look in their parents' eyes can hear the tone of voices, feel the response of bodies and receive back an image of worth or worthlessness.

However, I am concentrating here on the mentally handicapped young woman who is not visually impaired. (I am also not talking here of the painful plight of the parent or parents who hoped their child would be at least as healthy as they are and see instead a fragile new being whom they find damaged in some way. They are supported far too little at such a crucial time.) I am concentrating on what it is like for the handicapped baby to see hurt and grief and other feelings in its mother's eyes but not a reflection of its own inner beauty.

For some children bonding is eventually achieved with parents and a sense of inner worth returns, but for those where it does not the inner sense of being unwanted is exacerbated by the period of adolescence and makes psychosexual development even more difficult.

Mary, aged seventeen, was severely mentally handicapped. She belonged to a club that offered facilities to handicapped and non-handicapped teenagers. There was a disco, plenty of outings, a coffee bar and a wide range of activities. Mary's hostel encouraged her presence there and were very proud that she had access to normal mainstream activities, such as going to club. Mary never missed a meeting. She went regularly, angrily and despairingly whilst displaying a 'happy smile' to the youth workers. In a group she boasted of her club nights. After a few months she came in a very quiet and depressed state. 'There are not enough boys there,' she complained. When another group member asked what she meant, she gruffly explained that none of the boys had asked her out. There was a painful pause in the group. 'The boys are all normal,' she added. 'And the boys like me want to go out with normal girls.'

There was an unbearable tension in the group. One of the most painful aspects of integration had been touched on. All of us had to face in our teens the hierarchy of attractiveness. There is an unrealistic stage in which narcissistic adolescents fantasize that different pop stars or film stars are just waiting to see them. Thousands of young men and women feel certain that Kylie Minogue and Jason Donovan would be the right partner for them. After a while, those fantasies diminish. We recognize the limited range of options available to most human beings and we find someone like or not like a parent! However, where there have not been the reality-testing experiences to help them make realistic choices (because some of the aspects of their reality are so painful), some handicapped young people stay in a fantasizing state longer, and this is deeply damaging to them. It means seeing a world in which certain people are deliberately depriving them of partners rather than the reality of limited choice. In one consultation to the staff of such a youth club a worker expressed her own anger with normal adolescents for not choosing someone mentally handicapped as a boy- or girlfriend. I asked why she should expect such a thing to happen. She looked shocked. I pointed out that most people, heterosexual or homosexual, choose partners of roughly the same background, intellect and level of abilities. People noticed when there were wide discrepancies of age, wealth, intelligence, and so on. This is not to say that an average man or woman who is emotionally handicapped might not find a fair swap with a mentally handicapped peer who is emotionally sound, but that on the whole will rarely happen. However, because workers feel guilty about not being handicapped they sometimes feel they are responsible for their clients' lack of boyfriends or girlfriends. Who amongst us, as of right, gets a partner found for us? None of us has sexual rights – even within a relationship. It is a matter of choice and reciprocity. However, the guilt of non-handicapped people can make us sometimes not help handicapped young people with their realities.

It is very painful to speak truthfully. Dana, for example, worked as a part-time cleaner in a college. In a women's group she mentioned how sad she was that she would never find a boyfriend at her work. I agreed with her. 'Why?' protested Evelyn angrily. 'Why did you agree with her? There are men teachers, aren't there?' 'Yes' said Dana. 'Then why can't she go out with them?' There was a painful silence. 'Why won't she find a boyfriend at the school

where she works?' Gritting my teeth, I said that it would be very
unlikely that a college teacher would want to go out with a young
woman who was severely mentally handicapped (Sinason, 1991).
There was a terrible pause and I felt a brute, but then there was a
big sigh of relief. I could then add that on the whole people wanted
to go out with someone quite like themselves and that was very
painful and some teenagers found it so painful that, for example, a
pop star wouldn't go out with them, that they even formed fan clubs
in order to share the experience.

Tragically, like the black societies where 'white' is seen as
beautiful and shades of colour nearest to white have highest status,
the handicapped community can also internalize hatred and disgust
for its own condition and handicapped men and women can fix
their fantasy hopes outside their own peer group.

I would like to explore another area particularly relevant to
female sexuality: the fear of abandonment. All female children have
to face dealing with a frightening inner and sometimes external
mother when it comes to negotiating independence and separation.
Where severity of handicap makes dependency greater, fear of
invoking the anger of this mother imago is even more damaging.
Hence June, aged thirty, arrived in white socks because her mother
wanted to see her as a sexless little child and June was terrified of
being abandoned if she asked for tights and older clothes.

Fear of punishment from a mother takes on a different meaning
if we look at the myth of Echo. Echo, the mountain nymph, could
only echo back the last few words of what was said to her. She fell
in love with Narcissus but was spurned and died heartbroken.
Narcissus was punished by falling in love with his own reflection.
There is also an earlier aspect to this story that merits attention.
Echo used to chatter to Hera in order to distract her attention from
Zeus's infidelities. It was for that behaviour that Hera, the queen of
the gods, punished her by taking away her full power of speech.

Victoria Hamilton (1982) points out that Echo is like the young
child trying to copy older words. She cannot initiate or sustain
dialogue. In this way she mirrors the parental couple who cannot
sustain dialogue. Her sexuality is affected by the example of marital
adult infidelity.

The echolalic female patients I have seen have largely been

sexually abused by their fathers or stepfathers. In these instances, the mothers could not bear sexual dialogue with their husbands and allowed them to turn to daughter. Daughter was then punished by an angry internal mother. The phrase 'Has the cat got your tongue?' was mockingly used by all these women about their inability to manage clear speech. For me, that phrase represented their predicament. Struggling with their fear of the furious internal mother, whilst feeling fury for the external mother's collusion, their own words become a meaningless echo. Clearly, there is a great deal of echolalia without concrete abuse having occurred but I think that in these cases there can be a sexual problem in owning language.

EVELYN/ECHO

Evelyn was a severely handicapped young woman of eighteen referred for therapy after a series of minor thefts, such as stealing *Woman* magazine (a rather symbolic theft!). The persistence of her stealing and the fact of her handicap made the court want to provide treatment and led to her referral. Her parents had met in a subnormality hospital and her mother had frequent psychotic episodes and admissions. There was a multiply handicapped sibling two years older than Evelyn, who was boarded out from the start and has, according to Evelyn, a mental age of two. Evelyn was fostered from babyhood and moved from place to place until her mother decided to have her back when she was dying of cancer. At sixteen, Evelyn took on a nursing and cleaning role at home and on her mother's death stayed with her father. She kept complaining about eye problems which had no known physical cause.

On our first meeting I saw an institutionalized-looking teenage girl, institutionalized, that is, to the waist. She wore a short institutional hairstyle, dowdy cardigan and had a dimwitted expression. From the waist down she wore a miniskirt, black fishnet tights and high heels, as if there were some vital though promiscuous life going on below. The probation officer, Evelyn and I shared some preliminary introductions. It was explained why she had been referred and also that social services would subsidize her treatment for six months by providing an escort (the clinic was a two-hour journey away). After six months she would be free to continue seeing me if she could manage on her own. It was clear that the probability was of a short-term six-month treatment. The echolalic aspect of her handicap was very prominent. 'My dad says I should come because why get into trouble and my probation officer says why get into trouble and I thought I might as well go to the clinic because I mean why get into trouble.'

A sexual link appeared shortly after: when I commented that she was full of other people's words but did not seem sure of her own opinion, she stated in a normal cockney voice, 'My father touches my sister up.' I felt an instant shock at the intelligence and clarity of her voice when talking about abuse. This is an experience I have had each time a handicapped patient reveals her intelligence when disclosing abuse. She continued: 'He did it when she was very little and she can't speak anyway and although she's older than me she's only got the brain of a two-year-old. I went and told the police last year but they did nothing because she was so handicapped and couldn't speak and the lady next door saw and she went to the police and they didn't listen to her either.' I said she really hoped that I would listen to her with her lesser handicap and not avoid dealing with what she had told me by using her handicap as an excuse. She wiped her eyes. I said I would have to tell her probation officer. A few moments later her handicapped voice returned and her echolalia but we both knew that was not the whole story. When I phoned her probation officer the story was checked and it turned out she had complained several times but had not been listened to. The probation officer said she would contact social services. Meanwhile, therapy continued.

For the first couple of months the main themes in therapy were the strain of 'being good' and not stealing versus the excited desire to steal and spoil. Issues connected with intelligence or handicap did not appear directly but via the person of her severely handicapped boyfriend. He lived in a small group home with three other men and had occasional violent outbursts. Over the weeks, a clear image of Evelyn's picture of him emerged. He would turn up at her house haphazardly, with unerringly accurate bad timing – 7 a.m. on a Sunday morning or 2 a.m. on a weekday. He would expect her to accompany him to his hostel immediately and clean or cook for him. He would be violent if she refused. As this picture built up we had an identikit of Evelyn's handicapped, delinquent personality that would snatch objects illegitimately and suddenly invade her intelligent thinking in a threatening way.

Evelyn loved her 'engagement ring', although she thought it had come from a Christmas cracker. She wanted to be married like normal women even though she worried more and more whether her boyfriend was the right vehicle to that state. She made it clear she was due to marry him on her nineteenth birthday, which was just a few weeks before the end of therapy. In the first four and half months she stole twice, once during a holiday break and once when she learned her probation officer was pregnant and would be leaving for maternity leave in a few months.

The other major theme to appear was her loss of her mother. This was not only the grief at her mother's dying and death but also her awareness that she had not received adequate mothering and that her mother had only wanted her at home so she could be the unpaid cleaner and cook. Whenever a criticism of her mother appeared, however mild, she would become terrified and revert to an image of her mother as a courageous martyr. The only dreams she could remember were of her mother, persecutory or idealized. Her increasing anger with her father, regardless of his sexual behaviour, seemed to have a function of keeping her mother 'good' for it was clear that her father did look after her in certain ways.

Session 20

As soon as I saw Evelyn she sprang up asking, 'Awright?' She followed me up the stairs saying how bad the weather was and what a struggle she'd had to avoid being late because if she had missed the fast train she would have been late for the next connection. I said she had gambled about whether she would be on time or not and then she wondered if I was all right. She giggled and spoke of how she had got into the lift just as it was closing so that her escort had to wait for the next one. 'So when I got in the waiting room I could see her coming out of the lift late.' She giggled again and I said it seemed that the Evelyn who had managed to get the fast train and the fast lift sneered at the slow part of herself. 'Yes,' she giggled. 'And when I'm slow the fast bit laughs at me. But I know it is not good to be late here. And I'm being good because as my dad says it's not worth getting into trouble and I've been good for three weeks now and my probation officer is pleased with me because she says I should not get myself into trouble.'

I said nothing to this familiar refrain. There was a long silence. Then she began again. 'My friends think I have lost weight. They say to me I have lost weight. My father said I should watch it or he will call the doctor because he thinks I am not eating enough.'

I felt she was being angry with my silence, seeing it as not feeding her, but commented instead on the way there were always 'other people' who said whether she was good or not, or eating enough or not. She did not seem to know for herself what she thought. She pondered that for a moment and then seriously commented, 'Well, I put on a skirt and it fell down. And then I put trousers on and they fell down. So my dad said I was losing too much weight but I don't think so.' I repeated that her clothes were falling down but she did not think much had happened. 'No. But my friends and my dad say I look different. I eat with my friends when I am out so my dad worries because he does not see me eat.' I asked her what she did eat at home. 'Well, just cups of tea really.' A story was beginning to clarify itself. 'So your dad eats on his own?' I asked. 'Yes'. 'Did you used to eat with him?' 'Yes. And I cooked for him.' I wondered aloud then whether eating out with her friends was trying to worry her father because she was cross that nobody looked after her. She did the work and she was cross with me that she had to come on a long journey to see me and then be rewarded by me saying how good she was to be out of trouble for three weeks.

'I saw my probation officer and she said I had lost weight.' I commented that her probation officer was pregnant and would be leaving soon and maybe she felt like a tiny hungry baby that was not looked after properly, especially as I only gave her one meal a week. She looked serious and intelligent. 'Yes. And inside me I really know I have lost weight.' In the pause that followed I noted how well she had understood my previous metaphor – the one weekly session being described as one meal.

'Do you know,' she began, with her familiar phrase but a serious tone, 'my sister is staying with us and she has not said anything else about Dad touching her up so he may have stopped doing it.' I wondered whether she had especially not felt like cooking for her father or eating with him while there was a new baby – her sister – in the house. I wondered, but did not say at that point, whether she saw her intelligent state as being one that was not 'touched up' by an abusive intrusion. 'Do you know?' has also seemed to be an important concept in the language of handicapped people. To ask the state of someone's knowledge means, of course, that you do have a sense of what knowledge and knowing are. As Confucius commented, 'Shall I tell you what it is to know? To say you know when you know and to say you do not know when you do not know' (*The Analects,* p. 23).

Evelyn sat thinking. There was a frown on her face and a pleasurable concentration about her. I had the sense of a physical sensation as thoughts passed through her head. 'Do you know, I have an interview for a job today. It is making sandwiches for workmen. I would like to get the job but I am scared of an interview. I do not mind making food for money.' She giggled in embarrassment. I said she felt she should be paid for feeding her father and he should pay for what he had done to her sister, just as I got paid for seeing her.

Her giggle stopped. There was someone who did not think she had the right to have a job or earn money or be respected. However, when she spoke again, it was not that self who was speaking. 'At the weekend my boyfriend came round early without phoning and he asked my dad where I was and my dad said I was in my room studying and he laughed and said "What does she want to study for?"' Now the mocking, attacking voice could be heard, but it had found a home in her boyfriend. Once her intelligent self was allowed a space she understood very well the meaning of intrusion: her boyfriend's coming round early without phoning and her father's letting him in automatically. They mirrored the way her intelligent mind could be interrupted.

Then followed her longest train of thought. 'I was reading a book about Elizabeth I. I like trying to read more and now I am not at any school and I did my literacy course at college I want to learn more. And last week I went to the library with my friends and they were all laughing at me saying "Why are you going there?" And I said I wanted to read a book by a man called Charles Dickens and it was called *Oliver Twist*, but they laughed and they made me laugh and then I said, "This is a library. You will have to sit away from me or you will get us thrown out and I won't be able to study."'

There was a long painful pause with her twisting her hands. I felt very moved.

I said the fast train her wanted to add to her knowledge – as she also did by coming to the clinic – but then she had to face this sneering, mocking gang that could say, 'What does she think she's doing trying to learn? We don't need to learn. We just take what we want.' She looked at me intently. I added that Queen Elizabeth was a powerful queen and Oliver Twist was a poor little boy and maybe that showed us the struggle going on in her between a powerful queen who could take anything and a deprived boy who faces terrible danger in asking for more.

'I haven't taken anything for three weeks,' she said concretely. I said she had not been taking food either, but bits of her body had been taken away from her. I did not add that bits of her brain were regularly stolen and taken away by this arrogant Queen Elizabeth I. Indeed, the return to concrete thinking at that point, was, I felt, in terror that the omnipotent internal mother would attack her for wanting to know more or eat more. For Evelyn to learn more she had to take both Elizabeth I and Oliver Twist to the library. She could not feed Oliver without Elizabeth's permission or giggling would appear. To keep one self happy, the other had to starve.

All those thoughts about Evelyn's predicament were running through my mind while Evelyn sat looking at me and then at her hands. Her eyes were thoughtful again, as if my silent communing with my thoughts had provided an ally against concrete thinking.

'It is a long way to the station,' she said sadly. 'I have to walk or get a bus.' Then her voice tone and expression changed and she returned to her echolalic speech and manner. 'And my dad says the walk does me good. He says it is good to get out and walk and take your mind off things so maybe next time I will walk or I will get the bus back some of the way and then I will be able to get the train. I will ask my dad and the probation officer. They are good at knowing the directions.'

I said we were coming to the end of our time and that she knew this and had got involved in complicated repeating of directions when we came to this moment. I said the end also made her suddenly lose her sense of knowledge and independence and returned her to what her father and her probation officer thought.

As she stood up to leave I watched her deteriorate before me. Her posture and expression transformed and the intelligent light went out behind her eyes. The girl walking out of the room down the corridor to greet her escort was not the same girl who had spoken just a few minutes earlier.

Session 21

Three weeks before the end of the six-month period something new happened. Evelyn's escort was ill and the probation office rang to say Evelyn would not be able to come. I said the time was open to her if she could manage to come by herself. She came, early, dressed in bright colours with highlights in her hair. There was no sign of anything institutional about her. 'Do you know, I came here all by myself today. I came on the bus and it was really quick. My escort couldn't come and they didn't think I'd get here but I knew the bus was quicker and cheaper so I've saved social services five pounds in fares.' I was dumbfounded; the stupidity passed into me and she was the clearsighted one! I said she was showing how when she used all her intelligence she could be more clearsighted than the others around her. She went on to talk lucidly about having arranged an eye appointment, a meeting with her GP for a pill prescription and a job application. There was no echolalia.

'I always thought the bus would be easier and so it was, so very easy. I decided to go further and look in Hamley's for a present for my sister. She wanted this game where you press buttons and a sound comes out. She was home because of the teachers' industrial action but she goes back tomorrow.' I said it looked as if all the adults were not working and she had to be the only one who could manage things and look after the child who could not speak. She smiled. 'They didn't have what I wanted so I got a doll for my collection. Did I tell you I collect dolls? I have over a hundred. There was a life-size doll in the display window and all the children looked at her and wanted their mums to buy it for them.' I said that although she was proud at being independent she wished her mum was alive and would do something for her like that, or that I would.

'Yes,' she agreed simply. 'Because my probation officer will be on maternity leave soon and it is Mother's day soon and I will put flowers on my mother's grave.' There was a pause. 'You know, it was strange on Sunday. My boyfriend came round at 10 p.m. just as I was going to have a bath. I just had a jumper on. My dad yelled upstairs "There's a visitor for you" and I said I couldn't come down because my dressing-gown was stiff on the washing-line. So I poked my head round the bathroom door and it was my boyfriend. We laughed and I pulled my jumper down a bit and we chatted but he and my dad said I should put my trousers on because he wanted to show me the house he was going to share with his friend and he wanted me to see the plans at his place. I said I was going to bed. I went to my friend's wedding last week and she cried all the time and her mum and me. I will be scared of laughing or crying on my wedding day. When I get married.'

I said maybe she felt in and out of being married just as she had been half in and half out of her clothes. 'Yes. I said I will be 64 before he really gets round to marrying me.' I said maybe she had felt hurt that he came round so late and had wanted her to get dressed. I was silently wondering if she had dealt with his intrusive unannounced late visit by trying to eroticize it but this too had failed.

'Yes. You see he has a friend and they are getting this house together. I say to him "You know you have to leave him when we marry" but he wants his friend to stay and they want me to do all the washing and cooking and cleaning and I can't do that. My dad says I am not to be their skivvy.'

It was her father's words that expressed her anger, but in expressing her anger her former pleasure in herself returned. 'Did I tell you that I have filled out a job application by myself and sent it off? And I have sorted out an eye appointment for myself because I don't think I am seeing so well in my right eye. My dad did not think I could do the form myself but I knew I could.'

I commented on the changes between last week and this, how she is so clear about what she knows and what she can do and what she thinks this week. 'Yes. This week is different,' said Evelyn reflectively. She twisted her hands together. 'I had a cold at the weekend and I knew if it was still there this morning I would not be well enough to see you. But then I cried all weekend and I knew I would come to see you anyway.' I wondered aloud whether her sneezing was another way of crying.

'I went to the doctor to get a pill.' I asked her what sort. 'You know.' I said I did not know what she did not tell me. I could guess but I did not know. She seemed taken aback with that thought and then informed me, 'A contraceptive pill. My dad says why bother but I say to him that if I get pregnant he will be left with the baby and he wouldn't like that. So I am doing lots of things.'

I agreed she was indeed doing lots of things and was proud of what she did know and could do. But I wondered if I felt to her like a lazy kind father who noticed her do things but did not really want to help so she had to manage everything, especially as therapy was coming to an end unless she managed to come by herself each week, as she had done today. I said it was also her birthday in a few days and perhaps she was worried her boyfriend and I would forget it as she had hoped to be married on her birthday.

'My friends forget,' she said bluntly. 'They always forget things like birthdays and then they laugh and go out and get an old card. We all laugh.' She giggled falsely. 'My boyfriend forgets. He forgot Valentine's day too.'

I said she would be getting a new probation officer next week and in three weeks this term of therapy would come to an end. Those were a lot of changes. I had told her that there was a space for her to continue with me after the holiday break but her local authority would not be able to provide an escort then. She had managed to come today but maybe she did not know if she could every week. Maybe too she did not know if she was really about to get married. She had not mentioned any of the procedures that usually have to happen before people marry.

She looked shocked and then thoughtful but said nothing. There was a long silence. Then a light returned to her eyes. 'When I was in the West End I ate a steak and chips. I had a really good meal. I did not want rubbish.' I said she was rewarding herself for her journey here by taking in something good that showed she knew what she really needed. 'Yes. Not like any old wimpy you can have anywhere.' It was time. She got up slowly saying the weather looked warmer than when she had arrived and she was sure she would find the bus stop on the other side of the road easily.

As she walked out, upright and not looking handicapped, I felt a moment's wish that she could stay like that. The words of Neville Symington's patient Harry came to mind (1981, p. 195): 'I am capable of more than everyone thinks I am but there is tomorrow and Sunday and Monday.'

Session 22

Evelyn's escort was still ill and the new probation officer did not know if Evelyn would make it again on her own. She came, just as her session time was over, on the dot. She needed £1 more for her fare back. I did not have any free time as another patient was due for her regular slot in just ten minutes. However, the quality of the lateness was so exceptionally accurate that it needed to be acknowledged. Adding on time, even if I had had it available, would have damaged the understanding of that form of accuracy.

Session 23

Evelyn was sitting in the waiting room with her escort. Although she looked less intelligent than two weeks ago she looked much smarter than she usually did. In a long T-shirt worn over black ribbed tights she looked like an ordinary teenager. On the way to the room she gleefully announced that her escort had wanted to come by train and had not believed her that the buses were quicker. 'My escort said she didn't like hanging round bus stops waiting when trains came every minute. But she nearly missed the train because I rushed in as the doors were closing and she was locked out, but then the doors opened again so she could get in.'

Inside the room, she sat down and relaxed. I said she was annoyed that the escort did not believe her; that the escort did not think a slow woman knew a faster way. So she had wanted to shut the escort out and make her slower. And last week she had shut me out by arriving only when her session was due to end. She nodded.

I silently wondered to myself about how she felt coming with an escort instead of on her own but said nothing.

'Ooh – my escort said I should show you these.' She held out a bag meaningfully. I asked her what it was. 'I've been to the doctor,' she said sharply, angered at my slowness. I said she seemed to think I magically knew what was inside the bag or what she had said to the doctor and she felt I was really stupid being so slow. Her sharp expression hovered uncertainly and then went. 'I have been having terrible nightmares and seeing my mum and thinking about her every night since last week so I went to the doctor and he gave me these pills and my escort said you should look at them.' I said I would look at them if she wanted me to but I was not a doctor so the name of the pills would not mean much to me. There was a long pause. 'I have been feeling really terrible with these nightmares of my mother.' I asked her if she could remember any. 'I can remember last night's. I went into the kitchen to get water and my mum was sitting in the kitchen smiling happily and I screamed and I screamed. My dad came in and I told him what I dreamed and he said I was stupid.' There was a pause. 'So my escort told me to tell you about the pills.'

I commented that she was very angry she had come all the way to see me last week and, even though she knew she had missed her time and only arrived in time to say goodbye, she was angry I did not look after her. She looked intently at me. I said perhaps I was like her mother. Her mother only said hello to her when it was time to say goodbye because she was ill and dying and wanted a cleaner. Perhaps I was a ghost in the kitchen, who offered nothing but just smiled and looked after myself. And perhaps I had turned into a ghost in the last week because she had angrily killed me.

There was a long pause. She looked at her hands as she twisted them. There was no ring on her finger. I commented that her birthday had passed now and she was not wearing her ring. 'I've broken off with my boyfriend. He got another girl pregnant so he will have to marry her instead.' I felt shocked but she looked very casual. 'I saw him last week and he was still all cross I did not go and look at his stupid plans in the middle of the night before. He forgot my birthday too. So did my dad. So then I went to visit him and he was rude and I said to his flatmate, "What's up with him" and his flatmate said he was ashamed because he had done something wrong. I asked what he had done and his flatmate said, "Don't you know?" and I said "No" but I thought he had got my birthday wrong and my wedding ring. Then his flatmate said, "He has got Josie pregnant so he will have to marry her." But I don't care because there are plenty of fish in the sea.' She giggled excitedly. 'My dad said I shouldn't take the pills and he was worried my sister would take them but they have a special top so they are too hard for her to open.' She giggled excitedly again.

I said she had some big knocks in the last couple of weeks. She was losing her boyfriend, her father and boyfriend had forgotten her birthday, she did not get a present from me and therapy was coming to an end. Sometimes, when she got such knocks, she got excited so she would not have to feel how sad she was. She was excited about the pills and the thought of their harming her or her sister.

There was a painful silence. 'I get lots of knocks, you know. My mum said I was in and out of hospitals when I was little. She did not know how I survived. I took my cat to the vet yesterday, it got knocked over crossing the road, and I have to feed it by spoon because it is too ill to come out of its basket. I said it was a basket-case to my dad.' She giggled, but there was no excitement in her giggle.

I said she wanted to be looked after by me because she had received so many knocks, but she still did not know if she was able or willing to continue seeing me after the holiday, and perhaps she was scared of being a basket-case.

'Cars knock me down a lot. When I was seven I got knocked down and my mum said the hospital had to sew me up. And when I was thirteen. A car knocked me down first and then a lorry.' I said they were painful knocks and they hurt her a lot even though she felt there were lots of other fish in the sea.

'My dad said it was bad what my boyfriend did.' I said she was returning to saying what other people thought. 'Well, I don't care. I gave him back his ring. It was only a ring from a cracker. He thought I did not know the difference. I told him I did not want to see him again and I told my dad not to let him in and my dad agreed. My boyfriend said, "Why? I have not married Josie yet".' There was a long silence. 'The cat just sits in the basket. Oh, my eyes are fine. I don't need glasses.'

I said the cat had got very independent and crossed the road too fast and maybe she felt she had shocked herself the week before last, coming so easily and managing so much. It was hard to do so especially as she was seeing so clearly that she was not about to have any real marriage. It was as unreal as her engagement ring or her boyfriend's feelings for Josie.

Penultimate session

The following week, the penultimate session, she came with her escort looking drab and subnormal. 'All right, are you all right?' I said maybe things were not all right with her today and she only had one session left with social services support and then the summer holidays. 'Well, I am not all right. Things are bad, very bad.' She looked miserable, pale and excited. 'Something bad happened on Sunday. My dad touched me on Sunday morning and it is bad.' I felt the full impact of that statement and my mind went to her comment about her father and her sister on our very first meeting. I repeated that her father had hurt her by the way he had touched her. 'He touched me when I got back from the bathroom and I told him to stop and he didn't and it is not right and my friend said she knew a girl who got pregnant like that and then her dad threw her out.'

I was very aware that her experience of my having agreed to a short-term contract that was about to end was here represented as abuse. Michele Elliot (1988) has commented that many calls about abuse come in a school at 3.30 p.m. on a Friday. That is no coincidence. It is precisely because partings are experienced as abandonment. I said she was worried, not just about his doing something when she said no, but about his throwing her out if she got pregnant by him, and maybe she felt I was abusing her and then throwing her out after six months just when she felt more fruitful about things. She agreed.

I said maybe it was not just Sunday it had happened and maybe it was not just touching – because just touching couldn't make someone pregnant. There was a long painful pause. 'No,' she said in absolutely intelligent and clear language. 'But since my mum died he went onto my sister too. I told you that before and the police did not care and he should not have got away with it. My mum would be furious if she was alive. She would not have let it happen.' There was a pause. I said I had been alive all these six months and it had still happened that we had come to this end. Maybe her mother had been alive when it happened. There was a long painful pause. Suddenly, her nightmares about her dead mother and her desperate attempts to idealize her made sense. Not only had she called for Evelyn to nurse her in her last days, not having much interest in her earlier, she had failed to protect her from long-standing abuse.

Evelyn then spoke even more lucidly. 'If I think, if I really try to think and have a memory then I will have to say it goes a long way back as far as I can remember. He always touches me, touches me when I come out of the bath. He says "Can I feel you" but I did not like it on Sunday and I said "Go away" and he didn't. He shouldn't do it to me. But I know he will lie and deny it just as he did over my sister.' I said maybe she felt too that I would lie and deny I was hurting her by our stopping.

'Maybe,' she reflected, 'but I haven't stolen for ages now.' I said she had not stolen but she had been stolen from, by her father. He had been taking something that he should not and our finishing date made her want me to know this. 'Yes. I don't know why I suddenly said I didn't like it. It was just suddenly very obvious.'

Her language was not only not handicapped now. It was eloquent. 'I had another dream that frightened me. I dreamed my mother was outside the window calling me and she called "Evelyn, Evelyn . . ." She had grey hair as if she had aged since she had died and she looked sad and happy and she was calling me. I screamed and the girl next door came running in and I said, "I think it was a dream. My mum is dead and she called me at the window but she couldn't get in." She said it could have been my mum's ghost and at the convent a nun told me my mum's spirit watches me all the time.'

She looked frightened. I said maybe she was scared her mum and I would be angry that she had been doing things with her father; maybe there was an Evelyn who, despite knowing her father was wrong, enjoyed it sometimes and maybe that Evelyn was scared her mum would be angry and she was angry too because we both knew her mum did not look after her.

After that session I had several phone calls from her social worker and probation officer. It turned out that in the files Evelyn had complained of her father's touching her when she was eight. Nothing had been done. This time the police decided to visit Evelyn's father. As soon as they told him what Evelyn had said there was no denial. He immediately responded, 'I would have stopped it years ago if she had said she didn't like it. I thought she liked it. I'll never do it again.' Because he was mentally handicapped, there was no physical cruelty involved and Evelyn was over the age of consent, they decided not to prosecute and Evelyn was moved into a sheltered hostel.

Last session

Evelyn was early, with her escort, and dressed very attractively. 'Well, a lot has happened to me. I have a room all for myself. I was moved in just one day and it is in a house not far from my sister so I can see her in her home. It is not too far to see my father. He visited me yesterday. I have my own rent-book. And the DHSS will send me money separately from my dad, so it is lots of new things to learn and I have more money than I had before. I have a nice big room with a fridge, a cooker, a bed and a wardrobe. It is a house with lots of flats in it. I met a boy and his dad there. Their mum burned their house down.' She giggled. 'It is not nice to laugh but it did sound funny the idea of a mum burning a house down.'

I said maybe she was worried I was a bad mother who had burned her house down by not managing to provide escorts to bring her and that she also had a bad mother inside her who attacked her ability to come on her own.

'My dad said I was grown up so if I wanted a place of my own that was fine. When he came here I left the door open to protect me and when I went to visit him he left the front door open. I don't want it to happen again. My dad went out to visit friends when I went to see him. He still left the door open even after he left.'

I said it was very hard for her and her dad to see how to be together without touching. It sounded rather lonely. 'He is my only family,' she mused sadly. 'I am glad he is not getting into trouble. But he should. He should have been put away for what he did but I do hope he stays all right.' I said her stealing had been linked with her fear and wish to be put away. Maybe she had been looking for a way to be put away from him so he could not touch her, and put away so her mother would not be angry with her.

'I wish I was not stopping,' she said. 'I wish I could carry on. It will be strange not coming here.' I said the door here was still open but without me having an escort to bring her it sounded as if it was a meaningless invitation. She looked sad, but then bright again. 'Do you know in the six months I have known you I had a boyfriend and was going to be married and that stopped and I went to court for stealing but I stopped stealing and I didn't get put away and then my dad did this and then my probation officer went on maternity leave and then I get a new home and now you go off.'

There was a peaceful silence. 'Do you know, I have other family. My mum told me but I don't know if I will ever find them.' I said she really felt she needed family at this point when so many new things were happening; she also wanted to understand her family history.

There was a long silence. I asked her what she was thinking. 'I was thinking of my mum calling me at the window but not getting in.' I did not know if she was getting more in touch with the need for a mother as she had moved away from her father or if she was worried her mother would be angry she had said 'No' to her father. Sadly, I would never properly understand, because after the holidays, despite two letters from me repeating the fact that a place was still open for her, she did not feel able to come.

There have been several occasions where the importance of the 'escort' service has been underlined for me. Even for people like Evelyn who could sometimes manage the journey, it mattered having provision for the days when she could not.

I had offered some joint sessions for Evelyn and her father but neither wanted any further help. Both grew increasingly lonely. It then emerged that Evelyn was pregnant with her father's child.

The key words that came from Evelyn's simple, moving and intelligent statement were 'think' and 'memory'. It is thinking and memory that are attacked when they lead to a knowledge of trauma and guilt.

Summary

For a child, a parent is like Zeus, the father of the gods. To obey a parent feels essential, otherwise there is a risk of abandonment or death. Only when the active mirror of psychoanalytical psychotherapy reflects back and comments on the false echoing can Echo get her own speech, her own tongue back.

Evelyn was above the age of consent, living with a non-violent, mildly handicapped father who nevertheless abused his daughters. Abuse was not uncovered by me but revealed by Evelyn when she was faced by my having a time limit for therapy. By not being a good mother who would look after her indefinitely I was bad enough to be allowed to see what had happened. Evelyn herself was blind, deaf and dumb before.

Evelyn was sad and lonely when she understood her real situation. She had lost her smiles and giggles in the main, and she understood what it meant when echolalic speech and extra handicapped behaviour returned. It was a high price to pay for giving up stupidity and Evelyn did not want to carry on paying it. I hope that the abilities her true internal knowledge gave her continued to compensate her for the pain.

Evelyn's eye difficulty righted itself. The connection between 'seeing' and illegitimate sexuality has been understood from the myth of Oedipus onwards. In recent times Weil (1989) showed that in an examination comparing children's dream content with their symptoms and reality experiences, eye-poking, psychogenic blindness and eye difficulties were linked to exposure to adult masturbation, hard-core pornography and intercourse. In 1937 Oberndorf linked eye problems and episodic stupidity with the relationship between intellectual and sexual development.

Evelyn's situation also raised questions for me about the plight of the adult mentally handicapped who live in incestuous situations. She was over the age of consent and whatever force was used on her as a child was no longer in action. At many conferences there has been concern as to whether police involvement is necessary.

Something that is clearly seen as abusive to a child seems to be wiped out when that individual crosses a line which apparently divides childhood from adulthood. But I believe that where something corrupts, however lovingly it corrupts, it continues to destroy truth and sanity. Evelyn's relationship with her father was not aggressively ferreted out. She was able to bring it because she realized that she did not want it to continue. Plenty of adults, handicapped and non-handicapped, avoid situations where insight could flourish because they wish to make sure they never face such truths.

12   Sexual Abuse, Psychosis and Legal Redress

My preoccupation with Babette and other such cases convinced me that much of what we had hitherto regarded as senseless was not as crazy as it seemed . . . through my work with these patients I realised that paranoid ideas and hallucinations contain a germ of meaning. A personality, a life history, a pattern of hopes and desires lie behind the psychosis. The fault is ours if we do not understand them . . . Although patients may appear dull, apathetic or totally imbecilic, there is more going on in their minds, and more that is meaningful than there seems to be.

Jung, *Memories, Dream, Reflections*

Children and adults with disabilities are particularly vulnerable to sexual abuse. If their communication difficulties are severe they cannot be properly understood and that provides the abuser with more power. Where they have unworked-through feelings of guilt about their disability they can be more vulnerable to pressure from their caretakers. 'I knew I shouldn't be alive anyway so I thought no-one would care,' said Kevin, a young man with cerebral palsy who had been abused by his key worker.

Legally, their problems are compounded. They may not be considered to be competent witnesses in the eyes of the law and similarly, the evidence provided by workers they trust can be discounted on the grounds that leading questions were asked.

Some abused children and adults heal slowly in their own way and do not require any treatment. For others, the law and possible legal action are the only therapeutic agent required. For others still, referral to psychotherapy can be a denigration of the actual level of the real crime that has been committed. A treatment model is only necessary when the trauma has excited disturbance on a level that makes supportive contact with friends and carers unuseable. Increasingly, children and adults are referred for therapy when workers are too frightened to deal with the legal issues involved. The therapist is then asked to untangle the mess. This marks a historic change in the way therapists are perceived. We were previously seen as workers who denied the reality of abuse. Now we are sent cases where social services networks are denying the abuse.

However, there is a group who do need specialized treatment and are especially vulnerable. Where there is also fear of confusing actual sexual abuse with psychotic fantasy, what happens when someone psychotic is sexually abused or has a painful tale to tell?

ELAINE

A mother rang up in distress to say her eighteen-year-old daughter had been sexually abused. Elaine was blind, partially deaf and severely mentally handicapped. Despite medication she was prey to major epileptic fits. She was also, in her mother's words, 'quite mad', hearing voices and seeing invisible people. 'But she wasn't mad before. He has driven her mad because he won't tell the truth about it.' Elaine had accused a male residential worker of raping her. There was, in this case, no difficulty in proving that she had been abused. Her local doctor could validate that. However, when it came to naming the abuser it could only be Elaine's word versus the worker's. The police were sympathetic to her but made clear that Elaine would not be competent to give evidence. Even if she did her best there was no proof whatsoever so they dropped the case. A letter from the social worker involved explained Elaine was now masturbating all the time, putting herself further at risk. She provided further family details.

Elaine was born multiply handicapped. It was known during the pregnancy that the baby would be handicapped, as the mother had contracted measles. However, both parents were adamantly against an abortion and felt that as they 'were blessed with two normal children they could manage this child'. The family were affluent and middle-class. Elaine was the youngest of three and, apart from special holiday camps and occasional respite care, had always lived at home. Six months ago, Elaine's parents had needed to go abroad for six weeks as Elaine's grandmother, who lived in Europe, was ill. They had clearly also needed a break from the 24-hour care Elaine required. They were not happy with the respite care provision found for Elaine but felt it would be viable. When they returned they were shocked to find her thin, ill, terrified and hallucinating. The staff just reported that she was 'homesick' and consequently did not manage to eat.

Elaine could not speak but had terrible nightmares. She would wake up screaming and crying. She clung to her mother and would not go anywhere without her. She slept on a camp-bed in her parents' room for two weeks. She screamed so hysterically at night-time that they could not leave her. It took three months before she could say what had happened.

She said Mr X had come into the bathroom to check on her because there was no woman worker on duty. (Because of her epilepsy she was not allowed to stay in the bathroom on her own.) Then he had started touching her and poking his fingers in her vagina. She had screamed but he had just laughed at her. That night she woke up to find a hand across her mouth. He raped her.

At this point, her shocked parents phoned the sympathetic family doctor whom she had seen when she was first brought home and who had failed, like them, to understand the meaning of her dramatic deterioration. The doctor now examined her and found bruising consistent with her story. Her parents then called the police and the worker was questioned. He denied the accusation and there was no proof. It was his word against Elaine's so they would not prosecute. At this point Elaine deteriorated further and hallucinated all through the day. There was no local counselling or therapy. Although their distance made ongoing therapy a highly unlikely possibility, I decided to offer a meeting. There have been an increasing number of referrals like this where long-term therapy is not available locally. I have found that one way of providing a therapeutic exploration is to make a video. Where the patient is too handicapped or mentally ill to make a statement that would stand up in court I have found that nevertheless providing a context for a formal statement has therapeutic meaning.

Mother, Elaine and the social worker, Mary, arrived promptly despite a three-hour journey. Elaine was a thin, almost camouflaged creature. Wearing a long shapeless brown coat, the same colour as her mother's, she seemed to disappear into her. I could not see her face or any expression because her long fair hair was like a veil over her face. Her mother was an attractive, distressed-looking woman in her fifties. I introduced myself and asked how they would like to be addressed – by first names or formal titles. Mother emphatically asked for first names.

I said we would spend the first hour all together and asked Elaine if she knew why she was here today. 'Don't know,' she said in a handicapped way. 'Don't know?' I asked. 'No.' I said maybe it was hard meeting a stranger today and thinking about painful things but I had the feeling that somewhere she did know why she was here. 'Yes,' she said, in a clearer voice. I asked if she would like to say why. 'I can't remember.' I asked if she would like me to say why we had arranged the meeting. 'Yes,' she whispered. Her voice was very hard to understand. I said her mother and her social worker both felt things had not been the same for her since she had been abused in the X Home while her parents were away. They felt she had been very different since that happened. 'That's true,' she said and lifted up her head. Her mother and Mary looked pleased she was able to speak then. I repeated, 'It's true that you have been different since then.' 'Yes. Hard time.' I said it was a hard time. 'Yes.' I said her mother and worker had told me she had been sexually abused; what had happened?

'Bath.' 'You were in the bath?' I asked. 'Yes. Came in.' She covered her body with her arms. I said she did not like him coming in when she had no clothes on. 'No.' I said that was hard because I knew that with her epilepsy they did not let her have a bath on her own. 'Touch. No.' She wrapped her arms round herself again. I said she didn't want him to touch her. She nodded. 'Look,' she said. She lifted a hand and then pointed between her legs. 'In. He put it in and I said go away.' Her speech was hard to decipher because of both a speech defect and secondary handicap but it was charged with feeling. I said 'How horrible.' For the first time she looked fixedly in the direction of my voice. As if able to be less handicapped now that I had agreed that such an event (whether historically or emotionally true) was horrible, she commented, 'Yes. It was horrible. It was very horrible.' Her whole manner was alert and animated and her sentence structure became more complex. 'Do you know, do you know, I woke up. I woke up and I can't see and there was a hand over my mouth and his thing inside me. Do you know. In my bed. In the night.' Her mother started crying and I repeated how horrible, what an awful experience.

I said I had heard that nothing had happened to the man because the police had said there was no proof. 'That's right.' I said that must be very hard. 'It is because I hear him all the time now.' I asked what she meant and her mother said since that event Elaine hears his voice all the time. I asked if she had heard any voices before the event. 'Yes,' she said, 'but only in the street. Now everywhere, all the time, day and night in my room.' I asked if she heard him here in the room. 'Yes.' I said maybe she heard him talking all the time because nothing had happened since she had told her story. 'That's right,' said her mother, 'and I want to take it further because it is awful to think he is still there.'

'Yes,' said Elaine, 'he put his thing in me and hurt me. Hurt me.' I said again how horrible and she said forcefully, 'It was horrible. It was. I remember. I remember all of it. I don't forget.' Her mother and worker agreed that her memory was vivid and what she had told me was exactly what she told them over six months ago. After a bit more talk I suggested I now speak to Elaine on her own and then we would meet together again.

On her own Elaine turned her face towards the sound of the door closing. Her face then lit up, the flat or sad expression going. 'The voice,' she said. I said maybe at times the voice seemed to be company for her when she was on her own or without her mum. 'Yes,' she agreed, 'he's here now.' She underlined the word 'he' to let me know that her absent abuser was now here in the present. It was clear he was like an imaginary friend as well as the absent man present in her mind in a bad way and as a hallucination. I asked about other things, like her sight, and she told me she used to be able to see when she was a baby but then her eyesight started going. There was great grief over this loss. 'But I won't lose my memory,' she said emphatically, in a completely fluent sentence. There was silence for a moment and she then added sadly, 'But I have.'

I asked what she meant. 'I can't remember before I went to school. I have only one happy memory.' I said it sounded as if she had more painful memories. 'I do,' she said emphatically. She then said when she told Mr X to stop he said, 'Don't you worry, I wouldn't go near you again with a barge-pole,' in a sneering way. That sexual rejection had clearly hurt as much as the physical attack. His imaginary presence felt a concrete way of dealing with his verbal rejection. He was having to go near her again.

We decided to make a video of Elaine stating what she had told me as clearly as she could with her mother and Mary in the room. It would not go to court but her local police officer could see it. We felt that Elaine had been hurt by the lack of legal follow-up and a formal recording of her statement would have some ritualistic strength.

When the time came, however, Elaine could not do it. Each time she was about to make her statement her eyes would light up and she would say, 'I can't, he's here, he will go away if I say what happened.' I said she was frightened that if she said what had happened and the police saw it Mr X might go away to prison, and for punishment the Mr X she kept seeing would also leave her. 'Yes. Then I'd be alone with nothing . . . Because he comes to my bed and when he doesn't frighten me and give me nightmares he is nice. He's here now. He is the one who hurt my eyes and took my eyesight away.' I asked if she felt it was because of him she was blind. 'Yes. He took my eyes away. There was a prick and lots of blood everywhere . . . and the doctor puts a big needle in me and it hurts and there is blood.' I said every incident where someone had to put something inside her hurtfully was now in her mind and perhaps having the video here when I and her mother and Mary could see and she couldn't felt hurtful to her.

Those were the moments she could listen to me. At other times she would suddenly stand up as if to follow the man or giggle and move parts of her body that were being touched by him. From time to time she would whisper to him so no-one else could hear. Her mother was crying and very distressed that Elaine could not tell her story while being videoed. Michael Gunn (1989), who has specially concerned himself with the legal difficulties of the handicapped, comments that if a handicapped person is unable to take the oath or affirm, he or she will not be able to give evidence. Even if the handicapped person is competent to give evidence in court, will she manage to maintain her story in the face of cross-examination? Clearly, Elaine's situation is not just to do with mental handicap. Where there is just one person's word against another's and no proof, the law can do little. However, where one person is not seen as 'competent' the scales are even more weighted.

Elaine has continued to deteriorate. Her local psychiatrist has struggled to find local psychotherapeutic provision, to no avail. The family feels very bitter that no further legal redress is possible.

TONY

I first saw Tony when I was asked to observe a ward in an adult unit. It was agreed that after the preliminary observation I would make three half-day visits to offer appointments to particular patients. Concern for Tony was one reason for the referral. Aged 24, he was mentally ill and mentally handicapped. His mother had died when he was five and he was brought up by his father. When his father died, two years ago, he was admitted to a short-stay unit and was now in a long-stay hospital. As for many handicapped people, death had produced a double loss, loss of family and loss of home.

Tony had a prodigious memory for geographical detail and for train times and lines. His self-injurious behaviour, different 'voices', public anal masturbation and depression were of concern. When I saw him, he sat rocking on the side of his bed, talking to himself incessantly. Every so often he would bang his head as if the words or thoughts hurt. As I walked closer I could hear that what he was saying to himself was the name of all the Underground stations on the Northern Line. He said them in accurate order followed by the Metropolitan and Circle Lines. 'Oh, he knows all of them – and British Rail too – and timetables and the prices of the tickets,' said the nurse. 'It's not the sort of thing that will make you famous, like that autistic artist or the pianist, but he is brilliant. Listen. Tony?' He looked up for a moment. 'How long to get to Aberdeen?' Staring blankly at her, he recited: 'King's Cross to Aberdeen is seven hours twenty-six minutes. Aberdeen is in Scotland. King's Cross to Dundee is six hours ten minutes. Dundee is in Scotland. King's Cross to Edinburgh is . . .' he continued, no longer looking at the nurse. He was rocking up and down reciting Scottish facts. 'See?' she turned to me, pleased. He started banging his head and moaning painfully.

Suddenly he stopped. He turned to the nurse and asked, in a completely normal tone, 'You have to live to breathe, don't you?' Rather taken aback the nurse tried to alter that statement. 'No, it's you have to breathe to live.' 'But you have to live to breathe,' he repeated. I said yes, if you killed yourself or died you would not be able to breathe. He sat still for a moment.

When I saw him for the first time on his own we were given a small staff cubicle. 'Valerie,' he stated. I replied that was my name and he remembered it. 'Valerie's come from London. From Tavistock Clinic, 120 Belsize Lane. Valerie came by car along the . . . or she went by . . . bus to . . . and then got the train from . . .' In fact he had completely accurately worked out my journey and my setting-out time. I commented on this. 'Valerie,' he said. I commented he was using my name to try and keep it and me in his head because once he had worked out my journey he did not know if there was any other way of being in contact with me. 'Valerie,' he tried the sound again. I said he knew my name and he was satisfied that if he said it I would be concentrating on him but then he did not know how to let it go.

'Mmmm.' He started gouging his fist in his mouth. I asked if he was hungry. 'Mmm. Yes. See Valerie.' Stuck it in his mouth again. I said he maybe felt hungry for me since he hadn't seen me for a week and would only see me two more times. He smiled and looked at me and relaxed. Then he spoke in a completely different voice. 'Stupid Tony, stupid boy, shut up, get under.' I said there was a Tony who thought Tony was stupid.

'Valerie.' I said nothing. 'Valerie. Is your clinic Finchley Road Frognal British Rail, Jubilee Line Swiss Cottage station, Metropolitan and Jubilee Line Finchley Rd station?' I said he could correctly place where I had come from because he did not feel able to place himself and me in a conversation right now.

He put a hand inside his trousers to touch his bottom and began a whispering litany. I said something had happened that had sent him away from me. Then I realized I was being a stupid coward and he was telling me something sexual but I could not bear it. As I thought this he stood up and jumped, which frightened me a little. His harsh voice returned – 'Stupid Tony, get under' – and then he quickly returned to train lines. I said maybe he kept travelling on train lines because if he didn't he would have to think about more painful kinds of travelling in his bottom that made him jump. He shouted 'No!' and then went through an ear-splitting litany of train timetables.

On the second meeting he went through his litany of my name and my journey and when I was silent he started banging his head and moaning. I said how awful he felt when he moved from what he knew to what he could not bear to know. He looked at me intently for a moment and then started rocking and moaning again. 'Dad on top' he suddenly said. Then he began keening again, even louder. 'Dad under.' I said his father was dead, was that what he meant by under? He nodded. I asked what he meant by 'on top'. I had a horrible feeling I already knew. 'Bunk beds. Dad on top. Tony under.' He started whispering and banging his head and punching the wall. I said maybe when he slept underneath he felt dead, as if he was buried under the ground. He started crying loudly. 'Dad on top.' I said maybe his dad did not just lie on top of the bed, maybe he lay on top of his body too. He nodded. 'Stupid Tony, piece of shit. Piss off. Pyjamas off. Filthy piece of shit. Get under.'

After this meeting he spent several days crying and was put on anti-depressants. Staff then thought of other comments he had made which corroborated the idea of his father abusing him, although nothing could be done now that his father was dead.

On the third meeting Tony looked white and tired. He did not say anything when I saw him. I commented how tired he looked at the memory of being under his father and now his father was under the earth and it was hard to know what to do with his feelings. He sat looking intently at me, wanting me to speak. I said when his father had died he had lost his good father as well as his bad father and he had lost his home.

He cried again and then stood up and assumed his harsh voice. 'Get those pyjamas off, you piece of shit. Think you're going to mess up the sheets when I am on duty. I'll give you something to mess the sheets with, you arsehole.' He stood up, put his hands in his trousers and ran round the tiny room screaming and crying. I felt awful. I said it sounded to me that when his father died and he had been moved to a hospital, the one before this, or this one, a male staff member had done what his father did. He collapsed crying and whispering and returning to train maps.

With great difficulty, I told the psychiatrist who had made the referral. He told me that there was suspicion about abuse in the particular short-term unit Tony had previously been placed in, but no residents had ever been able to hold to their story. He did not feel the abuse was happening now.

I had a meeting with Tony and the psychiatrist and it was arranged that Tony would have a weekly session for the next six months. I learned that Tony was too frightened to name the staff member but he did name the unit and the day and times abuse occurred. In trying to take the case further the psychiatrist met the difficulties described with Elaine's case. Staff closed ranks in total denial. Tony's experience with his father was seen as the only abuse and everything since then was dismissed as a fantasy. Legal opinion was clear that Tony could not be a competent witness, and he had not named anyone.

TRACY

Tracy is 33. She had been neglected, then abandoned by her family and was hospitalized from the age of five in psychiatric hospitals. She had been returned to the community last year and it was found she had been sexually abused by staff. She was referred for her self-injurious behaviour, compulsive public masturbation, violence and pica (the way she ate anything – hair, rubbish, or paper).

She was thin and very handicapped-looking and tottered unsteadily on her feet. She did not look at me and had to be carefully supported. In the room she sat on the couch next to her worker and kissed her hand desperately. I introduced myself and asked the worker to stay in the room today so Tracy would not be frightened. I asked Tracy if she knew why she was here. There was no response and then she pointed to her worker. I asked if she would like her worker to speak for her and she nodded. The worker told me the traumatic life story of Tracy, adding self-injury of a quite violent kind. She also made it clear Tracy only said about eight words. 'Oh dear,' said Tracy mockingly. I said there was a Tracy who felt sad at difficult things in her life and a mocking Tracy who said 'Oh dear, who cares about any of that.' She turned a fake handicapped smile on me. I said again that was not a real smile.

The worker agreed and went on to talk of Tracy's sexualized behaviour and how she sought abuse and went too near to people and how nervous the male staff felt. 'Oh dear, oh dear,' said Tracy, patting her head.

As we discussed the traumatic life history she has experienced, her smile went. 'Oooo,' she said. I said she would come another time to be with me on her own. She listened. She held her own file and pointed to it. 'You want me to see your file.' She touched a blank space. 'Look.' I said that was a space. 'Look,' she pointed making a shadow. I said she had made a shadow. 'Doggy.' I said the shadow was a doggy. 'Look.' She repeated the words without any visual purpose. I said she didn't want me to think any more, she just wanted to catch me with one word said again and again because it was so painful to think of her life.

When I told her worker it was nearly time to stop, she started crying and I said how endings were hard for her. The worker spoke of her self-injury, how she gets black eyes and throws herself down stairs and does not seem to register any pain at all. As they left she tripped on her unsteady feet, crashing her head against the wall. 'Oh dear,' she said tokenly.

Second assessment session

This time, after a brief talk with the key worker, I had the session with Tracy on her own. It was immensely painful. She tottered to the table to look out of the window and touch the objects on the table. Then she crept under the table and bent her head down and started breathing deeply. I could not see if she was asleep but felt she was. After a while she came up to pick up her comb and touched the hairs on it.

Then she came up again and stood by the table. She could not sit down and I felt there was some sexual fear in the act of sitting. She picked up my hand and kissed it and said 'kiss' wanting me to kiss her. When I said she wanted me to kiss her but made it clear I was thinking about her but not kissing her, there was a terrible outburst of headbanging worse than any I had seen. I interpreted that if I would not be someone to kiss she was going to attack herself. She kept trying to kiss me with her teeth sharply ready, and I commented it was not a real, friendly kiss, it was a bite. I found myself thinking of AIDS and contamination too.

She looked out of the window and her only words were 'Where's pussy and doggy?' When she drew, she made a two-year-old's doodles and she said 'doggy' and 'baby'. She tried to kiss me again and when I said that was not helpful for her she bashed her head on the floor. When I commented on her attacking herself when I would not be kissed, she said, 'Oh dear.' Only when her worker came in was she able to sit on the chair and relax. When it was time to go she was screaming and crying and bashing her head against the wall.

Third session

Tracy was holding a magazine, saying 'Oh dear,' and could not let go of it so she carried it up with her. Inside the room she sat down. 'Ki–,' she said to her worker, who reluctantly let her kiss her hand. Then the worker left.

Tracy stood with her back to me, rocking, next to my chair. She looked at the objects on the table but could not move near them. I said there was a Tracy who wanted to use things and a Tracy who could not. 'There,' she said, 'there' – her head facing a doll. I said yes, there was a doll there and it looked as if she wanted it.

She looked on the floor and very slowly knelt down. She picked up a piece of hair and then a piece of dirt and ate it. I said she did not think she had a place on the chair. She felt her place was on the floor with the rubbish. She turned to look at me with excited eyes. I said there was a Tracy excited at being rubbish. She looked at the shadows on the floor and then bashed her head. 'Ouch,' I said. 'You wanted to look at the shadows, at a different shape, and you were not allowed to.' She looked up at the toys and then banged her head again.

Then she sat very still. I could not see her face or what she was doing. Then she turned and scratched my arm sharply with her fingernails, which were dirty. I said no, she could say she wanted to scratch me to bleeding pieces but I would not let her scratch me. I said perhaps she sat with her back to me because she felt she was disgusting and no-one would want to be near her. She turned round and pointed her nails at me again and I held her arm to restrain her. 'There,' she then said, pointing to the doll. I said she really wanted it. Perhaps she wanted me to get it. She nodded. I moved it near her. She looked at it. 'There, there.' I said yes, it was. 'Baby. Pussy. Doggy.' I said it seemed as if a very little Tracy remembered those things. I reminded that her worker would come in two minutes. She came in and to my surprise Tracy stood up easily to leave. As she got up she pinched my leg and went 'didididi', an exaggerated tickling noise, posing her body in a sexual way.

Summary

Elaine, Tony and Tracy, like many other abused handicapped children and adults, now sit masturbating for hours each day. Sometimes the masturbation is linked to a relationship with the missing but present man, sometimes it is a way of keeping the body memory of what happened. Eileen Vizard (1988, 1989) has shown how, in this population, body memories can be enacted in the form of psychosomatic symptoms which may mimic or re-enact certain aspects of the abuse. By entering themselves with their own fingers Elaine and Tracy are also trying to be in control of the entering against which they were helpless. Similarly, Tony's anal masturbation takes control of being under. But it is a mad way to take control because it also hurts, as does his headbanging.

I have looked at the impact of trauma more fully in other chapters. What I have wanted to concentrate on here is the way handicap, mental disturbance or both compound the problems of legal redress. To put a painful experience to rest internally takes a lot of therapy; but there is also an external component. To have the law of the land stand up for you as a citizen and say you have been unlawfully treated is in itself therapeutic. Now that we are trying to make it easier for children to give evidence I think we need to consider seriously the issue of 'competent' or 'incompetent' witnesses. As Hilary Brown and Ann Craft state (1989): 'They [handicapped people] are minimally protected at law and may be additionally handicapped as witnesses by the prejudices of others. Nonetheless, the service ought to use the legal safeguards which exist while exploring additional structures such as protective guardianship or specialised advocacy to enhance the rights of individuals with learning difficulties and signal to the general public that these are people whose rights will be respected.'

In 1986 an application was made to the Family Division of the High Court by Sunderland Borough Council for the sterilization of a handicapped young woman. Her mother supported this application and so, in the end, did the court and the House of Lords, despite the opposition of the Official Solicitor as guardian *ad litem*. Those supporting the sterilization considered that a young woman with a cognitive ability of six years and an expressive ability of two years would find pregnancy and childbirth traumatic.

An ordinary two-year-old is not capable of being sexually active in the same way as a young woman. Whatever this young woman's measureable abilities were at the time of testing they do not reflect the life history of her body and mind. Sometimes, the idea of a pregnancy or a baby is more traumatic to the environment than to the individual concerned. If a handicapped adult could not in any way help to bring up a baby without the 24-hour aid of other agencies, and if those agencies were not able or willing to help, then there is an important issue that needs discussing from ethical, emotional and financial angles. However, the idea that a young woman capable of a sexual relationship has no possible concept of the meaning of pregnancy, childbirth, menstruation or sterilization is a stupid one.

Michael Gunn is a lecturer working in the Department of Law at Nottingham University who has specialized in legal issues and how they affect people with handicaps. He collaborates extensively with

Ann Craft on these legal and ethical issues. He makes it clear (1989) that English law provides no completely satisfactory answer if a person is not capable of making treatment decisions. In a personal communication he also made it clear that in America the courts have decided that a person with a handicap has both a right not to be sterilized and a right to be sterilized. All options should be flexibly open as they are for other people. However, he added that it was extremely rare now for American courts to authorize sterilization. He considers the guardianship functions in America and Australia as a useful model from which to balance the interests of the individual, staff and society.

Assessment interviews to explore possible abuse

The sexual abuse of children, handicapped and non-handicapped, is often a crime without legal proof. Not more than 30 per cent of abused children show any medical signs of abuse (Bentovim, 1987, p. 296) and even where they do, that does not necessarily aid in finding out who the abuser was. Most of the proof is in the mind, memory, emotions and behaviour of the child. An exploratory interview, often with the aid of anatomically correct dolls, can sometimes help the child to recall traumatic memories.

Where the child, handicapped or non-handicapped, is in an optimum environment, the impact of abuse can be lessened by the response and attitudes of parents, care workers and others. Here, there may be less long-term emotional problems.

SUZANNE

Suzanne, aged eight, was severely mentally handicapped. After a neighbour babysat for her she complained to her mother that she did not like his rude secrets. Her mother ignored her comments, thinking Suzanne was saying that to prevent her and her husband having a night out. The following weekend, after the babysitter came again, Suzanne had nightmares and started bedwetting. This time her mother listened carefully.

When Suzanne was brought for a therapeutic exploration of

abuse there was no need to use dolls or other play material. Suzanne repeated, 'I told Mummy. Bad David. Hurt my fanny. Bad willy. I told Mummy. Bad Mummy didn't listen.' She slapped her mother's knee and her mother said, 'I am so sorry darling. But I am listening now.' Suzanne's mother had believed her and Suzanne was able to state clearly what had happened. The police also believed Suzanne and interviewed the babysitter. He denied any inappropriate behaviour and claimed he would not babysit for her any more as she kept trying to sit on his lap. Although there was medical evidence that penetration had occurred the prosecution was not successful.

This scenario is at one level a necessarily familiar one. The implications of an innocent person's being convicted by one other person's uncorroborated testimony are appalling. Gillian Douglas and Christine Willmore, two lecturers in law at Bristol University, point out (1987) that 'these are easy allegations to make but difficult to prove or disprove . . . allegations of abuse can never be proved or disproved with absolute certainty.' However, D. P. H. Jones (1987) estimates that only two per cent of children give fictitious accounts about the occurrence of abuse. In my experience, I have never come across a fictitious account. In the relatively small number of cases where I have experienced doubt it has been over the identity of the abuser rather than the existence of abuse. In a couple of cases, a traumatized child has displaced the experience of abuse. This indeed highlights the need for caution.

Legal difficulties are therefore inevitable if innocent people are to be properly protected. However, all too often they militate against the innocent and the most vulnerable, children. Children with disabilities are the most vulnerable and, for them, legal difficulties increase when they are so traumatized that they cannot spontaneously provide evidence in the way that Suzanne did.

TERESA

Teresa, aged ten, was severely handicapped and had Down's syndrome. She lived with her parents and older sister and attended a day school for severely handicapped pupils. When a new head teacher was appointed, he was shocked at the level of sexual disturbance that had gone unchecked in the school. He provided time and support for the staff to consider the issue of abuse and Teresa's class teacher, Joyce, was able to voice guiltily the fact that Teresa had been excessively masturbating with soft toys in the classroom for over two years. The school decided to speak to her parents.

The parents were extremely angry at the school's concern, stating this was normal behaviour for a handicapped girl worrying about puberty. However, the mother did take her to the family doctor. A vaginal infection was found, which the family doctor and the parents dismissed as due to Teresa's masturbating. Teresa's disturbed behaviour continued and the school finally gained the permission of the parents to take the matter further.

When Teresa came for the first time with her class teacher and her parents it was clear there were going to be difficulties. She sat with a huge false smile, like Ali's, tossing comics and pencils up in the air to make her parents laugh. When I introduced myself they both aggressively said that Teresa was a lovely happy child, so whoever had abused her had not hurt her. It was Joyce who had to point out that abuse always hurt but could be hidden by smiles.

Unlike Suzanne's mother, it was clear that Teresa's parents would not bear to be in the room to help facilitate their daughter's interview. However, the class teacher willingly came.

Teresa was happy to play in the room, but the moment any verbal response was requested from her she froze. This time the anatomically correct dolls were needed. For children with limited language they provide an important means of non-verbal communication. After playing with them dressed for a while I asked Teresa if she knew what the different parts of the body were. She did not reply so I suggested her teacher might reply for her. 'Yes!' exclaimed Teresa clearly, despite a speech defect. The moment her teacher began to mention the names of innocuous body parts, like arms and legs, Teresa was quickly able to join in herself. This allowed me to gain an understanding of her language and comprehension.

She suddenly undressed a male doll, put his penis in her mouth and began sucking lasciviously. The teacher and I were both aware of feeling sick at that moment and in the presence of a re-enactment of an actual experience. I commented that she was putting the doll's willy in her mouth. Reluctantly, she nodded. 'Who is the doll?' I asked. There was no reply. She continued sucking, this time placing one hand between her legs. I asked again. 'Daddy!' she replied. There was a painful pause. 'Who has his willy in your mouth?' I asked. 'Daddy,' she agreed, nodding her head. I said that was a daddy doll and his willy was in her mouth – and maybe her real daddy also put his willy in her mouth. She put her hand over her mouth and dropped the doll. I said she did not want her mouth to say who did things like that. She nodded.

Clinically, Joyce and I were aware of the power of Teresa's non-verbal and verbal communications. However, there is a big difference between a clinical understanding and a legal one. As Arnon Bentovim comments (1987), 'If responses are reluctant, however, and through agreement to suggestion, with little additional material, this may convince the clinicians, but a legal view may see the interview as biased, and confirming the expectations of the examiner. Therefore the interview may be discounted and the child left unprotected.'

A handicapped child who has been chronically and lovingly corrupted by a parent is even more at risk here, because many are not able to be verbally forthcoming to any extent except in answer to a question that is legally considered to be a leading one. For example, later on in the interview with Teresa, we were able to establish that her father abused her when he took her to the toilet. I asked Teresa if Daddy took her to the toilet once, twice or lots of times each day. She replied it was lots of times. Legally, that could be called a restricted choice question. In other words, from the legal viewpoint, I, as interviewer, could be seen as forcing her to provide one of those answers and thus restricting her choice in order to fabricate a confession of my own design. However, clinically, I was using a multi-choice question. I was offering her permission to say that something appalling happened more than once. I was giving her, by those choices, proof of my willingness to conceive that awful things happened to her regularly.

This case, like Suzanne's, could not be properly taken further. Unlike Suzanne, however, Teresa is not likely to be able to tell until she is an adult and has left home or her parents die. She will then join the large numbers of mentally handicapped women and men who give up their false smiles and reveal the emotional damage that has gone on throughout their childhood. However, thanks to the courage of pioneers like Arnon Bentovim, Marianne Tranter, Margaret Kennedy, Eileen Vizard, Judith Trowell and Beverley Loughlin, the law is changing and is helping clinical practice to change.

CONCLUSION

> *Prospero*: Dost thou hear?
> *Miranda*: Your tale, sir, would cure deafness.
>
> Shakespeare, *The Tempest*, I.ii.106–7

We are facing [in the USA] a conservative estimate of 200,000 deaths a year of handicapped and other devalued people whose lives have been taken either directly or indirectly, and at the very least by readily preventable abbreviations of life motivated by social devaluation or outright death wishes. Canadian figures can be assumed to be about one-tenth of that i.e., 20,000. Thus, the term 'genocide' seems warranted, and in order to give such genocide its proper historical context and recognition, it may deserve a special name, such as 'Holocaust II'.

Wolf Wolfensberger, *The New Genocide of Handicapped and Afflicted People*

In April 1989 I went to America to speak at a convention organized by Dr Randi Hagerman on the Fragile X syndrome. Fragile X is a relatively recently discovered chromosomal abnormality which can lead to mental handicap. We had met at the International Scientific Study of Mental Deficiency conference in Dublin the year before and I had learned for the first time about the needs of children and adults with Fragile X syndrome. Randi Hagerman told me there was a strong interest in psychodynamic work with handicapped children and adults in America and a growing counselling programme pioneered by two psychotherapists, William Sobetsky and John Brown.

At immigration control I had to fill in a visa waiver form. This informed me of some of the grounds for exclusion from the United

States. In order to protect the welfare, health safety and security of the USA it seemed reasonable that those seeking to engage in criminal activities should be excluded. However, the first grounds for exclusion that met my eye were 'Afflicted with contagious diseases (e.g. tuberculosis) or mental illness, or who are mentally handicapped'. As an English visitor making my first visit to America in connection with mental handicap it was a stirring moment of feeling devalued and unwanted. What is it like if that experience does not just last for a few seconds but is chronic?

An unwanted baby, for example, unheld, unthought about, unfelt-for, is exceptionally gifted in itself if it manages not to die an emotional death or succumb to real physical death too. Some partial survivors of this experience might face the physical abuse that results from lack of early bonding, die in childhood or adolescence, become injured in fights, drug abuse, motorbike or car accidents, or join the legion of international teenage runaways, becoming prey to other forms of exploitation. In the USA alone more than 1,000 children and adolescents attempt suicide each day and up to 1.5 million children and teenagers run away from home each year (Wolfensberger, 1987, p. 69).

Thanks to the work of psychoanalysts, child psychologists and others the impact of poverty, deprivation, separation and rejection is well known, despite the appalling gaps in provision and practice. An unwanted baby represents a core human tragedy involving loss and damage to the man and woman who created the new life, the vulnerable baby itself, and the wider society that failed to support the primary unit or the survivors of the primary 'nuclear fallout'.

Perhaps unsurprisingly, there has been a far bigger gap in psychoanalytic literature, psychological literature and general understanding when it comes to considering the emotional experience of a child with multiple mental and physical handicaps. If an unwanted 'normal' baby needs extra personal gifts to survive, what about an unwanted handicapped baby or, for that matter, a wanted baby that is born handicapped? For most parents all over the world, there is hope that a new baby will be at least as well-endowed as its parents. Regardless of the innate courage, talent, potential (or not) of the handicapped baby and its parents, its arrival will initially usually be a moment of shock for parents, professionals, friends and relatives. However much some parents will later be able to say that their child has brought all kinds of personal gifts, in the initial period there has usually been a loss. If this cannot be acknowledged and supported then denial will set in (Bicknell,1983). Parents are still not given adequate emotional support early enough, causing even further delay to the life-saving bonding process.

After twelve years of work with mentally handicapped children and adults who have been overwhelmed with different kinds of emotional disturbance, it seems clear to me that one reason why the history of counselling and therapy for this client group is so truncated is the pain of the life-experience of many of those who refer themselves. Children and adults with mental disabilities not only have to deal with the limitations to their lives in terms of thinking and speaking, they also have to deal with familial and societal death-wishes that come powerfully towards them all the time. Just listening to current discussion about embryo research is experienced differently when you have heard patients who were thought to be 'ignorant and blissful' straightforwardly talk of their knowledge that people wished they were dead and that no-one else like them should be born. Young women with disabilities courageously consider their own attitudes should they become pregnant with a handicapped child. They have as many differences of opinion concerning abortion as there are in the general population.

Some of these histories, these life-stories are extremely harrowing and the process of recovering them has made me understand why their authors numbed their memories and minds for so long. However, the courage some people possess in bearing both handicaps and the horror that often accompanies them is inspiring. Those facilitating self-advocacy groups and those working hard to ensure that there is as much access to the best of ordinary living as possible are in danger of becoming traumatized themselves as they hear, without support, what their clients or students have experienced.

It must be understood (see above, Introduction) that my knowledge comes largely from treating clients whose mental handicap co-exists with severe emotional disturbance, largely linked to the experience of trauma. There are, of course, people with disabilities who are not in need of any psychological treatment and are in far better emotional shape than some people without mental disabilities who are emotionally handicapped. There are also a few children and adults with disabilities referred for treatment whose problems are not to do with their disability but with the usual range of emotional problems that life throws up. It will be a sign of major social progress when most of our referrals come from that category instead of those who are multiply traumatized.

It must also be understood that the actions I take and the points I raise are within the context of psychoanalytical psychotherapy and might not be appropriate out of that context. For example, when I treat a patient with self-injurious behaviour I am free, within the context of a fifty-minute session, to not restrain my patient unless he is in danger of very severe damage. A care worker who is with that patient for over eight hours a day has to make an intervention or the patient could be concussed. The nature of the worker's intervention can be informed by psychoanalytic thinking but it is, of necessity, a different intervention. At a conference in Amsterdam, John McGee, the pioneer of Gentle Teaching, and I became interested in the different actions our different functions and roles imposed on us. When I spoke of Tracy picking up dust on the floor and eating it I commented that my interpretation was that she felt like rubbish. John McGee, in his role, would have got down on the floor with her. We were able to clarify to each other the difference between our actions and how it was important to understand the meaning of the relationship, function and context. What was shared was the unconditional valuing of the client and the knowledge that there was meaning needing to be restored.

There are several points I would like readers to take from this book. There is the important need to understand how all people fluctuate between their most and least integrated states throughout the day. We all need expectancy for our highest level of functioning and provision for our least able. We need social changes and financial and emotional resources to ensure that handicapping processes are not intrinsic to our culture. While we do the best we can to meet people's external needs we also need simultaneously to press for treatment resources for those whose disturbance is of an internal nature and cannot be addressed otherwise. We need to understand the difference between emotional understanding and cognitive intelligence and the way we all enrich or abuse our own unique psychic inheritances. Most importantly, we need to understand and respect what is similar and what is different without denigration, denials or stupidity.

Those of us who are therapists and analysts need to reconsider our inability to use some of the theory available to us. If we are depriving people of treatment for fear of their psychotic selves, what does that say about us or leave open to them? Michael Sinason (1990) comments, 'If there is no-one willing to take the patient on when the extent of the psychotic hatred for non-psychotic relationships is recognised, then the non-psychotic personality of the patient has few options left. One is to go elsewhere and try to get into treatment by concealing the extent of their illness. The only other will be to try to resign themselves to the impairments and impoverishments that internal co-residency with a psychotic personality entails.'

Prisons, secure units, psychiatric hospitals, mental handicap hospitals and units are full of people living depleted lives, worn down by the ravages of their coexisting, untreated twin. Their families and workers struggle, often unsupported.

Over 200 years ago, Pinel freed the mentally handicapped and mentally ill from their chains in post-revolutionary Paris. A hundred years ago, Freud freed us from mental chains of non-understanding. We now have it within our theoretical grasp to extend that freedom. If we fail to do so, we will be adding to the handicapping processes in society.

GLOSSARY OF PSYCHOANALYTIC TERMS

Child psychotherapist A child psychotherapist is a graduate, usually in his or her late twenties or early thirties, who undertakes a six-year postgraduate training in child psychotherapy. In addition to treating intensively (3–4 times weekly) a child under five, a junior-aged child, an adolescent, and less intensively a family, perhaps a group, and a range of other cases, as well as taking theoretical classes and work discussion groups, trainees have to fund their own psychoanalysis. Although child psychotherapists work almost entirely within the National Health Service, they have to subsidize their own lengthy training. The theoretical and clinical foundations of the training are psychoanalytical. There are similar child psychotherapy trainings in Europe but not in the USA. Child psychotherapists work with children, young people and families. Training can be undertaken at the Tavistock Clinic, the Anna Freud Clinic, the Society of Analytical Psychology, the Scottish Institute for Human Relations or the BAP (British Association of Psychotherapists). All these trainings belong to the professional organization, the Association of Child Psychotherapists.

Countertransference The conscious and unconscious reactions and feelings of the therapist who is responsive to the transferred feelings of a patient and uses her understanding of those feelings to further the work. When faced with a patient with no words, countertransference is a crucial tool to understanding. When Ronald, aged six, banged his head, I would learn from my countertransference response what the meaning of his action was. One time when he banged his head I felt immensely sad for him and could speak of his longing to bang out the bad thoughts that hurt him. Another time, I felt angry and knew he was attacking me by hurting himself in front of me.

Ego-splitting Starting with Freud, then developed further by Rosenfeld and Bion, the term describes the process by which the self does not exist as a unitary entity but can be split either coherently or into fragments.

Omnipotence A state of mind (especially in infancy and childhood) in which the child fears that its thoughts and phantasies can alter the external world. Children in this state can feel especially guilty if their destructive thoughts and phantasies are mirrored in what actually happens in their external life. For example, David, aged eight, was severely mentally handicapped and was prone to banging his head at times of distress. At the point in his life when he had the most destructive thoughts about his father, his father died in a car accident. David's headbanging then accelerated to a dangerous level. Therapy revealed David's fear that the bad thoughts inside his head had killed his father. He was bashing his head to stop other potentially dangerous thoughts. Children with handicaps can be more troubled by this state of mind when they keep up omnipotent thinking as a defence against realizing their own limitations.

Projection Ascribing to someone else a state of mind in ourselves that we want to disown. Moses Maimonides, the twelfth-century Jewish philosopher, understood this process beautifully. 'If a man always casts aspersions on other people's descent – for instance if he alleges they are of blemished descent and refers to them as bastards – suspicion is justified that he himself may be a bastard.'

Projective identification As with projection, part of the self is split off and projected into the external object. However, it then becomes 'possessed by, controlled and identified with the projected parts' (H. Segal, 1973, p. 27). For example, one deprived woman battered her baby when it cried. She could not bear the cry because she felt it was her own. Everything dependent and fragile in her that she could not bear had been projected into the baby. The baby's cries were then intolerable.

Psychiatrist A medical practitioner who, after the five- to six-year basic training, specializes in the study and treatment of mental illness.

Psychiatry A branch of medicine concerned with mental illnesses, such as dementia, schizophrenia, organic psychoses, manic–depressive illnesses. While the Royal College of Psychiatrists now recommends some psychotherapy training, very few psychiatrists are also psychoanalytically trained.

Psychoanalysis A method invented by Freud in the 1890s to investigate unconscious mental processes, to provide treatment and to build up a new body of knowledge. In Britain, it is practised by psychoanalysts who have trained at the Institute of Psycho-Analysis.

Psychoanalyst In Britain, a graduate who has undergone a training at the Institute of Psycho-Analysis, seeing two patients for psychoanalysis (five times a week), having their own psychoanalysis, and attending a range of theoretical seminars, work discussion and supervision. Although some psychoanalysts work in the health service the training is a private one. The detailed and intensive work of psychoanalysts informs psychoanalytical psychotherapy and thereby enriches public sector treatment. Psychoanalysts also support health service psychoanalytical psychotherapy by taking on trainee therapists as their patients. There are about 400 psychoanalysts in the UK and 2,560 in the USA.

Psychodynamic Refers to movement in the psyche; theories of the mind that allow movement.

Psychology The study of the mind or behaviour. It looks at memory, learning, child development, animal behaviour. After a basic three-year degree, graduates can specialize in clinical, industrial, social, educational or human psychology. Different thought systems can also be studied, such as behaviourism, psychoanalysis, Jungian analytic psychology, and so on.

Psychotherapist All practitioners who call themselves this! There is no compulsory registration in the UK and trainings vary enormously.

Psychoanalytical psychotherapist Someone who uses psycho-analytical theories as a basis for her understanding but who has not necessarily been in psychoanalysis herself or been trained by a psychoanalytic institute. Child psychotherapists, BAP psychothera-pists, Tavistock-trained adult psychotherapists all call themselves psychoanalytical psychotherapists. However, others also use that name without equally rigorous trainings.

Splitting This describes the way young children, especially, divide the world and individuals into wholly good or wholly bad. As they develop, children are more able to integrate these opposites.

Transference In the postscript to the case of Dora, Freud (1905, p. 116) provides a major definition of transference, a crucial tool in treatment. 'Transferences are new editions or facsimiles of the impulses and phantasies which are aroused and made conscious during the progress of the analysis; but they have this peculiarity, which is characteristic for their species, that they replace some earlier person by the person of the physician . . . a whole series of psychological experiences are revived, not as belonging to the past, but as applying to the person of the physician at the present moment.' The ramifications of this in daily life are very clear. When an autonomous adult phones a dentist to make an appointment he or she can sometimes be aware of sounding like a nervous, tentative child. Towards the harmless dental receptionist have gone transferential pieces of behaviour that are to do with dealing with authority figures in the past!

Transitional object A term introduced by British psychoanalyst Donald Winnicott for any object of special value to a little child, often a blanket or a teddybear. Winnicott saw these objects as entities that allowed a child to make the move from its oral relationship with its mother.

Trauma A shocking experience that breaks through the protective shield of the psyche and cannot be processed. Freud saw it as a 'foreign body' within the self.

For a detailed historical account of major psychoanalytical processes, see R. D. Hinshelwood, *A Dictionary of Kleinian Thought* (Free Association Books, 1989); J. Laplanche and J.-B. Pontalis, *The Language of Psycho-Analysis* (Hogarth/Institute of Psycho-Analysis, 1973); and Charles Rycroft, *A Critical Dictionary of Psychoanalysis* (Penguin, 1972).

BIBLIOGRAPHY

Place of publication is London unless otherwise indicated.

Alexander, F. and Selesnick, S. (1967) *The History of Psychiatry*. George Allan & Unwin.

Alvarez, Anne (1988) 'Beyond the unpleasure principle: some preconditions for thinking through play', *Journal of Child Psychotherapy* 14 (2): 1–13.

—— (1989) 'Development towards the latency period: splitting and the need to forget in borderline children', *Journal of Child Psychotherapy* 15 (2): 71–85.

Alzheimer, A. (1906) 'Über Eigenartige Erkrankung der Hirnrinde', *Allg. Zeitschr. f. Psychol.* 64: 146.

Ammerman, R.T. *et al.* (1988) 'Maltreatment of children and adults with multiple handicaps', *Journal of the Multi-handicapped Person* 1 (2): 129–39.

Angelou, Maya (1969) *I Know Why the Caged Bird Sings*. Virago, 1984.

Balbernie, R. (1985) 'Psychotherapy with an ESN head-banger', *Br. J. Psychother.* 1 (4): 266–73.

Balint, Michael, ed. (1955) *Sándor Ferenczi: Final Contributions to the Problems and Methods of Psychoanalysis*. Hogarth.

Bargh, J. (1987) *Play Back the Thinking Memories*. National Children's Bureau.

Beail, N. (1989) 'Understanding emotion', in Brandon (1989).

Beckett, S. (1989) *Stirrings Still*. John Calder.

Bennett, G. (1989) *Alzheimer's Disease and Other Confusional States*. Macdonald Optima.

Bentovim, A. (1987) 'The diagnosis of sexual abuse', *Bulletin of the Royal College of Psychiatrists* 2 (Sept.): 297.

Bernstein, B. (1972) 'Social class, language and socialisation', in P. Giglioli, ed. *Language and Social Context*. Harmondsworth: Penguin, pp. 157–78.

Berry, James (1984) 'Thinking Aloud', in *Gallery* 5: 29, Gallery.

Bick, E. (1968) 'The experience of the skin in early object relations', *Int. J. Psycho-Anal.* 49: 484.

Bicknell, J. (1983) 'The psychopathology of handicap', *Brit. J. Med. Psychol.* 56: 167–78.

Bion, W. (1957) 'Differentiation of the psychotic from the non-psychotic personalities', in Bion (1967).

—— (1959) 'Attacks on linking', *Int. J. Psycho-Anal.* 40: 308–15; republished in Bion (1967), pp. 93–109.

—— (1962) 'A theory of thinking', in Bion (1967), pp. 110–20.

—— (1963) 'Elements of Psychoanalysis', in Bion (1977), pp. 1–107.

—— (1967) *Second Thoughts*. New York: Jason Aronson.

—— (1977) *Seven Servants*. New York: Jason Aronson.

Blacher, J. and Meyers, C. (1983) 'A review of attachment formation and disorder of handicapped children', *American Journal of Mental Deficiency* (Jan.), pp. 359–71.

Blum. H (1983) 'The position and value of extra-transference interpretations', *J. Amer. Psychoanal. Assn.* 31: 615.

Bouras, N. *et al.* (1988) 'Mental handicap and mental health: a community service', NUPR.9.

Bourne, H. (1955) 'Protophrenia: a study of perverted rearing and mental dwarfism', *The Lancet* 2: 1156.

—— (1989) Talk, Tavistock Clinic Mental Handicap Workshop.

Bowlby, J. (1958) 'The nature of the child's tie to his mother', *Int. J. Psycho-Anal.* 39: 350–73.

—— (1969) *Attachment and Loss*. Hogarth.

—— (1979) 'On knowing what you are not supposed to know and feeling what you are not supposed to feel', *Canadian Journal of Psychiatry* 24: 403–8.

Brandon, D., ed. (1989) *Mutual Respect: Therapeutic Approaches to People who have Learning Difficulties*. Surbiton, Surrey: Good Impressions.

Brenman Pick, I. (1985) 'Working through in the counter-transference', *Int. J. Psycho-Anal.* 66: 157–66.

Broadbent, J. (1982) 'That melodious noise: DUET (the Development of University English Teaching project)', *Studies in Higher Education* 7 (1).

Bromberg, W. (1954) *The Mind of Man: A History of Psychotherapy and Psychoanalysis*. New York: Harper Torchbooks.

Brown, H. and Craft, A. (1989) *Thinking the Unthinkable: Papers on Sexual Abuse and People with Learning Difficulties*. Family Planning Association.

Buchanan, A. and Oliver, J. E. (1977) 'Abuse and neglect as a cause of mental retardation', *British Journal of Psychiatry* 131: 458–67.

Buckley, A. (1989) 'Unconscious imagery', in Brandon (1989).

Burkert, W. (1985) *Greek Religion*, trans J. Raffan. Oxford: Blackwell.

Burlingham, D. (1963) 'Some problems of the ego development in blind children', *Psychoanal. Study Child* 18.

Burt, C. (1935) *The Subnormal Mind*. Oxford University Press.

Canetti, E. (1985) *The Human Province*. Deutsch.

Castell, J. H. *et al.* (1963) *Bulletin of the Brit. Psychol. Soc.* 16:53.

Chatfield, A. (1986) Unpublished discussion at EBD Day Schools Conference, 21–23 March, Merchant Navy College, Greenhithe.

Chidester, L. and Menninger, K. (1936) 'The application of psychoanalytic methods to the study of mental retardation', *American Journal of Orthopsychiatry* 6: 616–25.

Cicero, Marcus Tullius, 'On the State' and 'Discussions at Tusculum', in Cicero, *On The Good Life*, trans. Michael Grant (1982). Penguin.

Clark, P. (1933) *The Nature and Treatment of Amentia*. Baillière.

Cohen, S. (1986) 'A sense of defect', *J. Amer. Psychoanal. Assn.* 34: 47–56.

Cohen, S. and Warren, R. (1987) 'Preliminary survey of family abuse of children served by United Cerebral Palsy Centre', *Developmental Medicine and Child Neurology* 29: 12–18.

Conboy-Hill, S. and Waitman, A. (1992) *Psychotherapy and Mental Handicap*. Sage Publications.

Confucius, *The Analects*, trans. D. C. Lau (1986). Penguin.

Cook, D. (1978) *Walter*. Harmondsworth: Penguin.

—— (1981) *Winter Doves*. Harmondsworth: Penguin.

Corbett, J. A. *et al.* (1975) 'Epilepsy', in J. Worris, ed. *Mental Retardation and Developmental Disabilities*. New York: Brunner/Mazel.

Cotzin, M. (1948) 'Group therapy with mentally defective problem boys', *American Journal of Mental Deficiency* 53: 268–283.

Craft, A., ed. (in press) *Practice Issues in Sexuality and Mental Handicap*. Routledge.

Craft, A. and Craft, M. (1979) *Handicapped Married Couples*. Routledge & Kegan Paul.

Craft, M. (1979) 'Classification', in Tredgold (1952).

—— (1981) 'Sexuality and mental handicap: a review', *British Journal of Psychiatry* 1181 (139): 494–505.

Craft, M., Bicknell, J. and Hollins, S. (1985) *Mental Handicap: A Multidisciplinary Approach*. Baillière Tindall.

Cregeen, S. (1988) 'The sexual needs of handicapped people', talk given at BIMH conference, Barnsley, 26 September.

Crome, L. (1960) 'The brain and mental retardation', *British Journal of Medicine* 1: 897–904.

Crossley, R. (1984) *Annie's Coming Out*. Penguin.

—— (1987) *DEAL Newsletter*. Victoria, Australia.

—— (1988) *DEAL Newsletter*. Victoria, Australia.

Danquah, S. A. (1976) 'A preliminary survey of beliefs about severely retarded children in Ghana', *Psychopathologie Africaine* 12 (2): 189–97.

Defoe, Daniel (1711) *A Review*, vol. VIII, entry for Saturday 15 September 1711. Quoted in J. T. Boulton, ed. *Daniel Defoe* (Batsford, 1965), pp. 130–1.

De Mause, Lloyd (1974) *The History of Childhood*. Souvenir Press, 1976.

Des Pres, T. (1976) *The Survivor: An Anatomy of Life in the Death Camps*. Oxford University Press.

Dixon, H. (1989) *Sexuality and Mental Handicap: An Educator's Resource Book*. Cambridge: Learning Development Aids.

Doll, E. A. (1953) 'Counselling parents of severely retarded children', in C. L. Stacey and M. F. Demartino, eds, *Counselling and Psychotherapy with the Mentally Retarded*. New York: Free Press.

Dosen, A. (1984) 'Experiences with individual relationship therapy within a therapeutic milieu for retarded children with severe emotional disorders', in J. Berg, ed. *Perspectives and Progress in Mental Retardation*, vol. 2, Baltimore, MD: Union Park Press/Baltimore University Press.

Dosen, A. and Menolascino, F. J. (1990) *Depression in Mentally Retarded Children and Adults*. Amsterdam, Leiden: Logon Publications.

Dostoevsky, F. (1869) *The Idiot*, trans. C. Garnett. Heinemann, 1975.

Douglas, G. and Willmore, C. (1987) 'Diagnostic interviews as evidence in cases of child sexual abuse', *Family Law* 17: 151–4.

Ehri, L. C. (1978) 'Beginning reading from a psycholinguistic perspective; amalgamation of word identities', in F. B. Murray, ed. *The Recognition of Words*. Newark, Delaware: International Reading Association.

Ferenczi, Sándor (1928) 'The adaptation of the family to the child', in Balint (1955), Chapter 6, p. 65.

—— (1929) 'The unwelcome child and his death instinct', in Balint (1955), Chapter 9, p. 105.

Fisher, L. A. and Wolfson, I. W. (1953) 'Group therapy with defectives', *American Journal of Mental Deficiency* 57: 463–76.

Foucault, M. (1967) *Madness and Civilisation*. Tavistock Publications.

Fraiberg, S. (1982) 'Pathological defences in infancy', *Psychoanal. Q.* 21: 612.

Frankish, P. (1989) 'Meeting the emotional needs of handicapped people: a psychodynamic approach', *Journal of Mental Deficiency Research* 33: 407–14.

Fraser, S. (1987) *My Father's House: A Memoir of Incest and of Healing*. Virago, 1989.

Freeman, R. D. (1970) 'Psychiatric problems in adolescents with cerebral palsy', *Developmental Medicine and Child Neurology* 12: 64–70.

Friedman, M., Glasser, M., Laufer, E. and M. *et al.* (1972) 'Attempted suicide and self-mutilation in adolescence: some observations from a psychoanalytic research project', *Int. J. Psychoanal.* 53: 179.

Friedrich, W. N. and Boriskin, J. A. (1976) 'The role of the child in abuse', *American Journal of Orthopsychiatry* 46: 580–90.

Friedrich, W. N. and Friedrich, W. L. (1981) 'Psychosocial aspects of parents of handicapped and non-handicapped children', *American Journal of Mental Deficiency* 85: 341–9.

Freud, A. (1930) 'Four lectures on psychoanalysis for teachers and parents', in M. Khan, ed. *Introduction to Psychoanalysis*. Hogarth, 1974, pp. 73–121.

Freud, S. (1893) 'On the psychical mechanism of hysterical phenomena: preliminary communication', in James Strachey, ed. *The Standard Edition of the Complete Psychological Works of Sigmund Freud*, 24 vols, Hogarth, 1953–73. Vol. 2, pp. 1–17.

—— (1904) Loewenfeld, 'Freud's psycho-analytic procedure', in *S.E.* 7, pp. 249–54.

—— (1905) 'Fragment of an analysis of a case of hysteria', *S.E.* 7, pp. 3–122.

—— (1909) 'Notes upon a case of obsessional neurosis' ('The Rat-Man'), *S.E.* 10, pp. 153–318.

—— (1913) 'On beginning the treatment (further recommendations on the technique of psycho-analysis)', *S.E.* 12, pp. 121–44.

—— (1912) *Totem and Taboo*, *S.E.* 13, pp. ix-162.

—— (1920) *Beyond the Pleasure Principle*, *S.E.* 18, pp. 1–64.

—— (1923) *The Ego and the Id*, *S.E.* 19, pp. 1–59.

García Márquez, Gabriel (1967) *One Hundred Years of Solitude*, trans. G. Rabassa. New York: Harper & Row, 1970.

Gath, A. (1977) 'The impact of an abnormal child upon the parents', *British Journal of Psychiatry* 13: 405–10.

Glasgow, D. G. (1980) *The Black Underclass: Poverty, Unemployment and Entrapment of Ghetto Youth*. San Francisco: Jossey Bass.

—— (1982) 'Labelling: effects on the black mentally retarded offender and the black community', in A. Harvey and T. Carr, eds, *The Black Mentally Retarded Offender*. New York: United Church of Christ Commission for Racial Justice.

Goffman, E. (1961) *Asylums*. New York: Anchor Books.

Golding, W. (1980) *Darkness Visible*. Faber.

Goldschmidt, O. (1986) 'A contribution to the subject of psychic trauma based on a course of psychoanalytic short therapy', *Int. Rev. Psycho-Anal.* 13: 181.

Goldstein, K. (1948) *Language and Language Disturbances*. New York: Grune & Stratton.

Gordon, Sol (1972) Sex education symposium, *Journal of Special Education* 5: 351–81.

Greenacre, P. (1933) *Trauma, Growth and Personality*. Hogarth.

Grünevald, K., ed. (1978) *The Mentally Handicapped: Towards Normal Living*. Hutchinson.

Gunn, Michael (1989) 'Sexual abuse and adults with mental handicap. Can the law help?', in Brown and Craft (1989).

Haley, Alex (1978) *Roots*. Picador.

Hamilton, V. (1982) *Narcissus and Oedipus: The Children of Psychoanalysis*. Routledge & Kegan Paul.

Harlow, H. F., and Zimmerman, R. R. (1959) 'Affectional responses in the infant monkey', *Science* 3373 (130): 421–32.

Harris, L. P. (1977) 'Self recognition among institutionalised profoundly retarded males', *University of Texas Bulletin of the Psychonomic Society* 3 (4): 229–39.

Hayman, M. (1957) 'Traumatic elements in the analysis of a borderline case', *Int. J. Psycho-Anal.* 38: 9–21.

Heal, M. (1989) 'In tune with the mind', in Brandon (1989).

Heaton-Ward, A. (1977) 'Psychosis in mental handicap', *British Journal of Psychiatry* 130: 525–33.

Hellman, D. S. and Blackburn, M. (1966) 'Eneuresis, firesetting and cruelty to animals: a triad predictive of adult crime', *American Journal of Psychiatry* 122: 1431–5.

Hinshelwood, R. D. (1989) *A Dictionary of Kleinian Thought*. Free Association Books.

Hersov, J. (1985) *Let's Work Together* (video). Mencap.

Hobson, P. (1983) 'Origins of the personal relation and the strange case of autism'. Paper presented at the ACPP, London, 00 May.

Hollins, S. (1989a) *When Dad Died*. Silent Books.

—— (1989b) *When Mum Died*. Silent Books.

Hollins, S. and Bicknell, J. (1990) 'Behaviour disorders', in Conboy-Hill and Waitman (1992).

Hollins, Sheila and Evered, C. (1990) 'Group process and content: the challenge of mental handicap', *Group Analysis* 23 (1): 56–67.

Hollins, Sheila and Grimer, Margaret (1988) *Going Somewhere: People with Mental Handicaps and their Pastoral Care*. New Library Of Pastoral Care, SPCK.

Hollins, S. and Sinason, V. (1992) *Jenny Speaks Out*. St George's Hospital Mental Health Library.

Hollins, S. and Sireling, L. (1989) *The Last Taboo. A Video on Death and Mental Handicap*. Video, available from St George's Hospital Medical School, London.

Honey, J. (1989) *Does Accent Matter? The Pygmalion Factor*. Faber.

Hopkins, J. (1987) 'Failure of the holding relationship: some effects of physical rejection on the child's attachment and on his inner experience', *Journal of Child Psychotherapy* 13 (1): 5–17.

Hoxter, S. (1986) 'The significance of trauma in the ddfficulties encountered by physically disabled children', *Journal of Child Psych* 12 (1): 87–103.

James, Henry (1897) *What Maisie Knew*. Harmondsworth: Penguin, 1966.

Jelliffe, S. E. (1914) 'Technique of psychoanalysis', *Psychoanalytic Review* 1: 63–75.

Jones, D. P. H. (1987) 'Reliable and fictitious accounts of sexual abuse to children', *Journal of Interpersonal Violence* 2 (1).

Jones, E. (1959) *Free Associations: Memories of a Psychoanalyst.* Hogarth.

Judd, D. (1989) *Give Sorrow Words: Working with a Dying Child.* Free Association Books.

Jung, C. G. (1963) *Memories, Dream, Reflections*. Fontana.

Kafka, Franz (1916) 'Metamorphosis', in Kafka, *Metamorphosis and Other Stories*, trans. E. and W. Muir. Harmondsworth: Penguin, 1971.

Kennedy, J. (1963) 'Message from the president of the United States relative to mental illness and mental retardation', 88th Congress, 1st session, Document No. 58.

Khomeini, Ayatollah (1979) *The Little Green Book: Sayings of the Ayatollah Khomeini*. New York: Bantam Books.

Kilgour, A. J. (1936) 'Colonel Gheel', *American Journal of Psychiatry* 92: 959.

Klein, Melanie (1924) 'An obsessional neurosis in a six-year-old girl', in Klein (1975b), pp. 35–57.

—— (1930) 'The importance of symbol formation in the development of the ego', in Klein (1975a), pp. 219–33.

—— (1931) 'A contribution to the theory of intellectual inhibition', in Klein (1975a), pp. 236–48.

—— (1932) 'The sexual activities of children', in Klein (1975b), pp. 111–23.

—— (1935) 'A contribution to the psychogenesis of manic-depressive states', *Int. J. Psycho-Anal.* 16: 145–74.

—— (1946) 'Notes on some schizoid mechanisms', in Klein (1975c), pp. 1–25.

—— (1948) 'A contribution to the theory of anxiety and guilt', *Int. J. Psycho-Anal.* 29(3): 114–23.

—— (1952a) 'Some theoretical conclusions regarding the emotional life of the infant', in Klein (1975c), pp. 61–94.

—— (1952b) Postscript to 'Weaning' (1936), in Klein (1975a), pp.290–306.

—— (1975a) *Love, Guilt and Reparation and Other Works 1921–45. The Writings of Melanie Klein*, vol. 1. Hogarth/Institute of Psycho-Analysis.

—— (1975b) *The Psychoanalysis of Children. The Writings of Melanie Klein*, vol. 2. Hogarth/Institute of Psycho-Analysis.

—— (1975c) *Envy and Gratitude and Other Works. The Writings of Melanie Klein*, vol. 3. Hogarth / Institute of Psycho-Analysis.

Klein, S. (1985) 'The self in childhood: a Kleinian point of view', *Journal of Child Psychotherapy* 11 (2): 31–49.

Kops, B. (1963) *The World is a Wedding*. Vallentine Mitchell.

Kristeva, J. (1981) *Language the Unknown: An Initiation into Linguistics*, trans. A. M. Menke. Harvester, 1989.

Kundera, M. (1980) *The Book of Laughter and Forgetting*, trans. M. H. Heim. Harmondsworth: Penguin.

Lee, Wai-Yung (1986) *Sexuality Education Program for MTAMR Group Homes: A Developmental Project*. Toronto: MTAMR and Surrey Place Centre.

—— (1988) *Human Sexuality. A Staff Training Manual for Individuals with Special Needs*. Toronto: Surrey Place Centre.

Lewis, E. and Bourne, S. (1989) 'Perinatal death', *Baillière's Clinical Obstetrics and Gynaecology* 3 (4) Dec.: 935–53.

Lewis, M. and MacLean, W. (1982) 'Issues in treating emotional disorders', in Matson and Barrett (1982).

Lopez, Thomas (1974) 'Psychotherapeutic assistance to a blind boy with limited intelligence', *Psychoanal. Study Child* 29: 277–300.

Loveland, K. (1987) 'Behaviour of young children with Down's syndrome before the mirror; finding things reflected', *Child Development* 58: 928–36.

Lynch, M. and Roberts, J. (1982) 'Ill health and physical handicap', in M. Lynch and J. Roberts, eds, *Consequences of Child Abuse*. New York: Academic Press.

McCormack, B. (1989) Talk given to Tavistock Clinic Mental Handicap Workshop,

—— (1991a) 'Thinking, discourse and the denial of history: psychodynamic aspects of mental handicap', *Irish Journal of Psychological Medicine* 8: 59–64.

—— (1991b) 'Sexual abuse and learning disabilities', *British Medical Journal*, 28 July, vol. 303, pp.143–4.

McDonald, I. (1988) *From Seniority to Meritocracy*. Mental Handicap Services Unit, BIOSS, Brunel University.

—— (1990) 'Special villages and community care: the way forward', in S. S. Segal, ed. *The Place of Special Villages and Residential Communities*. Oxford: AB Academic Publishers.

McGee, J. (1989) *Being with Others: Towards a Psychology of Inter-dependence*. Omaha: Creighton University Department of Psychiatry.

McGee, J., Menolascino, F. *et al.* (1987) *Gentle Teaching: A Non-Aversive Approach for Helping Persons with Mental Retardation*. New York: Human Science Press.

Mahler, M. (1942) 'Pseudo-imbecility – the magic cap of invisibility', *Psychoanal. Q.* 11: 149.

Mahler, M., Bergman, A. and Pine, F. (1975) *The Psychological Birth of the Human Infant*. New York: Basic.

Main, Mary and Solomon, J. (1986) 'Discovery of an insecure–disorganized/disoriented attachment pattern', in T. B. Brazelton and M. Yogman, eds, *Affective Development in Infancy*. New Jersey: Norwood.

Main, Mary and Weston, D. R. (1981) 'The quality of the toddler's relationship to mother and to father', *Child Development* 52: 932–40.

Main, M. and Stadtman, J. (1981) 'Infant response to rejection of physical contact by the mother: aggression, avoidance and conflict', *Journal of Child Psychiatry* 20: 292–307.

Mannoni, M. (1965) 'A challenge to mental retardation', in Mannoni (1967), pp. 203–25.

—— (1967) *The Child, his Illness and the Others*, trans.. Penguin, 1973.

—— (1973) *The Retarded Child and the Mother*. Tavistock.

Markova, I., Stirling, J., Phillips, C. and Forbes, C. D. (1984) 'The use of tools by children with haemophilia', *Journal of Child Psychology and Psychiatry* 25 (2).

Mason, M. (1985) *Women's Health and Disability*. Women's Health Information Centre.

Matson. J and Barrett, R. (1982) *Psychopathology in the Mentally Retarded*. New York: Grune & Stratton.

Mattinson, J. (1975) *Marriage and Mental Handicap*. IMS. Tavistock Institute of Human Relations.

Miller, A. (1985) *Thou Shalt Not Be Aware: Society's Betrayal of the Child*. Pluto Press.

Moorcock, Michael (1988) *Mother London*. Secker & Warburg.

More, Sir Thomas (1557) In P. Johnson, ed. *The Oxford Book of Political Anecdotes*. Oxford University Press, 1986.

Morgan, S. R. (1987) *Abuse and Neglect of Handicapped Children*. Boston: Little Brown.

Mundy, L. (1957) 'Therapy with physically and mentally handicapped children in a mental deficiency hospital', *British Journal of Clinical Psychology* 13: 3–9.

Neham, S. (1951) 'Psychotherapy in relation to mental deficiency', *American Journal of Mental Deficiency* 55: 557–72.

Nietzsche, F. (1886) *Beyond Good and Evil*, trans. R. J. Hollingdale. Penguin, 1988.

Oberndorf, C. P. (1937) 'The feeling of stupidity'. Paper given to the Section of Neurology and Psychiatry, New York Academy of Medicine, 4 May.

Office of Census and Population Surveys (1988) HMSO.

—— (1989) *Disabled Children: Services, Transport and Education*. Report 6. HMSO.

Ogle, W. (1963) 'Psychotherapeutic treatment in mental deficiency – report of a case', Paper 3 in 'Symposium on psychotherapy in mental retardation', *Canadian Psychiatric Association Journal* 8(5): 307–15.

Office of Health Economics (1973) *Mental Handicap*. OHE Pamphlet 47. White Crescent Press.

Oliver, C., Murphy, G. H. and Corbett, J. A. (1987) 'Self-injurious behaviour in people with a mental handicap', *Journal of Mental Deficiency Research* 31: 147–62.

Oliver, J. (1988) 'Successive generations of child maltreatment', *British Journal of Psychiatry* 153: 543–53.

Onions, C. T. ed. (1966) *Sweet's Anglo-Saxon Reader*, 10th edn. Oxford: Clarendon Press.

—— (1980) *The Shorter Oxford English Dictionary on Historical Principles*. Oxford: Oxford University Press.

Orwell, G. (1946) 'Politics and the English language', in *The Orwell Reader: Fictions, Essays and Reportage*. New York: Harcourt Brace Jovanovich, 1956.

O'Shaughnessy, E. (1964) 'The absent object', *Journal of Child Psychotherapy* 1 (2): 134–43.

Oswin, M. (1971) *The Empty Hours*. Penguin, 1973.

Papousek, H. (1967) 'Experimental studies of appetitional behaviour in human newborns and infants', in H. W. Stevens *et al.*, eds, *Early Behavior*. New York: Wiley.

Penrose, L. (1963) *The Biology of Mental Defect*. Sidgwick and Jackson.

Phillips, I. (1966) 'Children, mental retardation and emotional disorder', in *Prevention and Treatment of Mental Retardation*. New York: Basic.

Pincus, L. (1981) *The Challenge of a Long Life*. Faber.

Pollard, A. (1982) 'Symposium overview: the black mentally retarded offender', in A. Harvey and T. Carr, eds, *The Black Mentally Retarded Offender*. New York: United Church of Christ Commission for Racial Justice.

Prouty, G. F. (1976) 'Pre-therapy: a method of treating pre-expressive psychotic and retarded patients', *Psychotherapy: Theory, Research and Practice* 13: 290–4.

—— (1990) 'Pre-therapy: a theoretical evolution in the person-centred experiential psychotherapy of schizophrenia and retardation', in G. Lietaer, J. Rombauts and R. van Balen, eds, *Client-centred and Experiential Psychotherapy in the 90s*. Leuven: Leuven University Press.

Rador Report (1908) *Report of the Royal Commission on the Care and Control of the Feeble-minded*. HMSO.

Rank, B. (1949) 'Adaptation of the psychoanalytic technique for the treatment of young children with atypical development', *American Journal of Orthopsychiatry* 19: 130.

Reid, A. (1982) *The Psychiatry of Mental Handicap*. Oxford: Blackwell.

Ricks, D. (1990) 'Mental handicap', in H. Wolff *et al.*, eds, *UCH Textbook of Psychiatry*. Duckworth.

Rieser, R. and Mason, M. (1990) *Disability Equality In the Classroom: A Human Rights Issue*. Inner London Education Authority.

Rix, B. (1990) 'The history of mental handicap and the development of Mencap'. 14th Annual Stanley Segal Lecture, University of Nottingham.

Robertson, J. (1952) *A Two Year Old Goes to Hospital*. Film produced by Tavistock Child Development Research Unit.

Robertson, J. and Bowlby, J. (1952) 'Responses of young children to separation from their mothers', *Courrier* 2: 131–42.

Robinson, H. B. and H. (1976) *The Mentally Retarded Child*. New York: McGraw-Hill.

Rogers, C. (1942) *Counselling and Psychotherapy*. Boston: Houghton Mifflin.

—— (1957) 'The necessary and sufficient conditions of therapeutic personality change', *Journal of Consulting Psychology* 21 (2): 95–103.

Rosenfeld, H. A. (1972) 'A critical appreciation of James Strachey's paper on the nature of the therapeutic action of psychoanalysis', *Int. J. Psycho-Anal.* 53: 455–61.

—— (1987) *Impasse and Interpretation*. The New Library of Psychoanalysis. Tavistock.

Rothstein, J. H. (1961) *Mental Retardation: Readings and Resources*. New York: Holt, Reinhart and Winston.

Rushdie, S. (1984) *Shame*. Pan.

Russell, P. (1990) *The Children Act 1989: Challenges and Opportunities for Children with Disabilities and Special Needs*. Voluntary Council for Handicapped Children.

Rutter, M., Shaffer. D. and Shepherd, M. (1975) *A Multi-axial Classification of Child Psychiatric Disorders*. Geneva: WHO.

Rutter, M., Tizard, J. and Whitmore, K. (1970) *Education, Health and Behaviour*. Longman.

Rutter, M., Tizard, J., Yule, W., Graham. P. and Whitmore, K. (1976) 'Research report: Isle of Wight Studies, 1964–74', *Psychological Medicine* 6: 313–32.

Ryan, J. (1987) *The Politics of Mental Handicap*. Free Association Books.

Sacks, O. (1976) *Awakenings*. Pelican.

—— (1985) *The Man Who Mistook His Wife for a Hat*. Duckworth.

Sandler, A. M. (1985) 'On interpretation and holding', *Journal of Child Psychotherapy* 11 (1): 3–17.

Saranson, S. S. (1952) 'Individual psychotherapy with mentally defective individuals', *American Journal of Mental Deficiency* 56: 803.

Sarwer-Foner, G. J. (1963) 'The intensive psychoanalytic psychotherapy of a brain-damaged pseudo mental defective fraternal twin', *Canadian Psychiatric Association Journal* 8 (5): 296–307.

Scott, Clifford. W. (1963) 'The Psychotherapy of the Mental Defective', *Canadian Psychiatric Association Journal* 8 (5): 293–5.

Scott, P. D. (1977) 'Assessing dangerousness in criminals', *British Journal of Psychiatry* 131: 127–42.

Seabrook, J. (1989) 'Reflections on a too short summer', *The Guardian* 18 January.

Segal, H. (1957) 'Notes on symbol formation', *The Work of Hanna Segal*. New York: Jason Aronson.

—— (1973) *Introduction to the Work of Melanie Klein*. International Psycho-Analytical Library. Hogarth/Institute of Psycho-Analysis.

Segal, S. S. (1967) *No Child is Ineducable*. Pergamon.

—— (1971) *From Care to Education*. Heinemann.

—— (1984) *Society and Mental Handicap: Are We Ineducable?* Costello.

Seguin, E. (1846) *Traitement moral, hygiène et éducation des idiots, et des autres enfants arriérés*. Baillière Tyndall.

Sgroi, S. M. (1982) *Handbook of Clinical Intervention in CSA*. Lexington, Mass.: Lexington Books.

Shaffer, D. (1977) 'Brain injury', in M. Rutter and L. Hersov, eds, *Child Psychiatry: Modern Approaches*. Oxford: Blackwell.

Shengold, L. (1979) 'Child abuse and deprivation: soul murder', *J. Amer. Psychoanal. Assn.* 27: 533–99.

Sinason, M. (1989) 'How can you keep your hair on?' Talk, Institute of Psycho-Analysis, London, 13 May.

—— (1990) 'What has psychosis got against psychotherapy?' Talk, St George's Hospital Medical School, London, 12 March.

Sinason, V. (1975) 'The History of Psychiatry', *New Psychiatry* 2.

—— (1985) 'Face values: a preliminary look at one aspect of adolescent subculture', *Free Associations* 2: 75–94.

—— (1986) 'Secondary mental handicap and its relationship to trauma', *Psychoanalytic Psychotherapy* 2 (2): 131–54.

—— (1987) *Inkstains and Stilettos*. Liverpool: Headland Press.

—— (1988a) 'Dolls and bears: from symbolic equation to symbol. The use of different play material for sexually abused children', *Brit. J. of Psychotherapy* 4 (4): 350–63.

—— (1988b) 'Smiling, swallowing, sickening and stupefying. The effect of abuse on the child', *Psychoanalytic Psychotherapy* 3 (2): 97–111.

—— (1988c) 'Richard III, Hephaestus and Echo: sexuality and mental/multiple handicap', *Journal of Child Psychotherapy* 14 (2): 93–105.

—— (1988d) 'Headbanger', *British Journal of Psychotherapy* 5 (2): 251.

—— (1989a) 'Sexual abuse' in H. Wolff *et al.*, eds, *UCH Textbook of Psychiatry*. Duckworth.

—— (1989b) 'Barry: a case study', in A. Brechin and T. Walmsley, eds, *Making Connections*. Open University.

—— (1989c) 'The psycholinguistics of discrimination', in B. Richards, ed., *Crises of the Self: Further Essays on Psychoanalysis and Politics*. Free Association Books.

—— (1989d) 'Psychoanalytical psychotherapy and its application', *Journal of Social Work Practice* 4 (1): 1–12.

—— (1989e) 'Uncovering and responding to sexual abuse in psychotherapeutic settings', in Brown and Craft (1989), pp. 39–49.

—— (1991) 'Interpretations that feel horrible to make and a theoretical unicorn', *Journal of Child Psychotherapy* 17 (1): 11- 23.

Solzhenitsyn, A. (1963) *One Day in the Life of Ivan Denisovich*. Pall Mall.

Sovner, R. and Hurley, A. (1983) 'Do the mentally retarded suffer from affective illness?', *Archives of General Psychiatry* 40: 61–7.

Sperlinger, A. *Making a Move*. National Foundation for Educational Research.: Nelson.

Spitz, R. A. (1946) 'Anaclitic depression', *Psychoanal. Study Child* 2: 313–41

—— (1950) 'Anxiety in infancy: a study of its manifestations in the first year of life', *Int. J. Psycho-Anal.* 31: 138–43.

—— (1951) 'Purposive grasping', *Journal of the Personality* 1: 141–8.

—— (1953) In R. Emde, ed. *Dialogues from Infancy*. New York: International Universities Press, 1983.

—— (1959) *A Genetic Field Theory of Ego Formation: Its Implications for Pathology*. New York: International Universities Press.

Sprince, J. and Usiskin, J. (1987) 'On running a group for women with learning difficulties'. Talk, Tavistock Clinic, .

Stanton, M. (1991) *Sándor Ferenczi: Reconsidering Active Intervention*. Free Association Books.

Stern, D. N. (1985) *The Interpersonal World of the Infant: A View from Psychoanalysis and Developmental Psychology*. New York: Basic.

Sternlicht, M. and Deutsch, M. (1972) *Personality and Social Behaviour in the Mentally Retarded*. Lexington, Mass.: Lexington Books.

Stokes, J. (1987) 'Insights from psychotherapy'. Paper presented at International Symposium on Mental Handicap, Royal Society of Medicine, 25 February.

Sturge-Moore, L. and Cameron, J. (1990) *Ordinary Everyday Families*. Mencap London Division: Under Fives Project.

Suskind, P. (1987) *Perfume, The Story of a Murderer*. Penguin.

Symington, N. (1981) 'The psychotherapy of a subnormal patient', *Brit. J. Med. Psychol.* 54: 187–99.

Szasz, T. (1962) *The Myth of Mental Illness*. Granada, 1972.

—— (1973) *The Second Sin*. Routledge & Kegan Paul.

Thomas, Dylan (1952) *Collected Poems 1934–52*. Dent, 1964.

Thorne, F. C. (1948) 'Counselling and psychotherapy with mental defectives', *American Journal of Mental Deficiency* 52: 263–71.

Tiffany, F. (1891) *Life of Dorothea Lynde Dix*. Boston: publisher?]

Tredgold, D. (1952) *Mental Retardation*. 12th edn, ed. Michael Craft. Baillière Tindall, 1979.

Tustin, Frances (1972) *Autism and Childhood*. Hogarth.

—— (1981) *Autistic States in Children*. Routledge.

—— (1986) *Autistic Barriers in Neurotic Patients*. Karnac.

Tyne, A. (1979) 'Who's consulted?' Enquiry Paper No. 8. Community Mental Handicap.

Vizard, E. (1988) 'Child sexual abuse: the child's experience', *Brit. J. of Psychotherapy* 5 (1): 77–91.

—— (1989) 'A child psychiatrist's perspective', in Brown and Craft (1989).

Vizard, E. and Tranter, M. (1988) 'Recognition and assessment of child sexual abuse', in A. Bentovim, A. Elton, J. Hildebrand, M. Tranter and E. Vizard, eds. *Child Sexual Abuse within the Family: Assessment and Treatment*. Bristol: John Wright.

Vygotsky, L. (1983) 'School instruction and mental development', in M. Donaldson *et al.*, eds, *Early Development and Education*. Oxford: Blackwell.

Weil, J. L. (1989) *Instinctual Stimulation of Children*. Framingham, MA: International Universities Press.

Willis, J. (1976) *Clinical Psychiatry*. Oxford: Blackwell.

Winnicott, D. W. (1949) 'Birth memories, birth trauma and anxiety', in Winnicott, *Through Paediatrics to Psychoanalysis*. Hogarth, pp.174–94.

—— (1952) 'Anxiety associated with insecurity', in Winnicott, *Collected Papers*, Tavistock, 1958, pp.97–101.

—— (1962) 'Ego integration in child development', in Winnicott, *The Maturational Processes and the Facilitating Environment*. Hogarth, pp.56–64.

Wolfensberger, W. (1987) *The New Genocide of Handicapped and Afflicted People*. Syracuse: Syracuse University Division of Special Education and Rehabilitation.

Woolf, V. (1938) *To the Lighthouse*. Everyman.

Woolridge, M. (1986) 'The anatomy of infant sucking', *Midwifery* 2: 164–71.

World Health Organization (1980) *International Classification of Impediments, Handicaps and Disabilities*, prepared by P. H. N. Wood. Geneva: WHO.

Wright, H. L. (1968) 'A clinical study of children who refuse to talk in school', *Journal of the American Academy of Child Psychiatry* 7: 603–17.

Yirmiya, N., Kasari, K. *et al.* (1989) 'Facial expressions of affect in autistic, mentally retarded and normal children', *Journal of Child Psychology and Psychiatry* 30 (5).

Zilboorg, G. and Henry, G. (1941) *A History of Medical Psychology*. New York: Norton.

LIST OF RELEVANT ORGANIZATIONS

Action for Research into Multiple Sclerosis (ARMS), Central Middlesex Hospital, Acton Lane, London NW10 7NS, UK; tel: 081-961 4911.

AIDS Awareness Sex Education (a project for people with learning difficulties), Room 61, Lime House, Harperbury Hospital, Harper Lane, Radlett, Herts WD7 9HQ, UK.

American Association of University Affiliated Programs for the Developmentally Disabled, 1100 17th Street NW, Washington, DC 20036, USA.

Amici Dance Theatre Company, 68 Barons Court Road, London W14 9DU, UK.

Anna Freud Centre, 21 Maresfield Gardens, London NW3 5SH, UK; tel: 071-794 2313.

Artshare, Southwest Bradninch Place, Gandy Street, Exeter EX4 3LS, UK.

Association for All Speech Impaired Children (AFASIC), 347 Central Markets, Smithfield, London EC1A 9NH, UK; tel: 071-236 6487.

Association for Child Psychology and Psychiatry (ACPP), 70 Borough High Street, London SE1 1XF, UK; tel: 071-403 7458.

Association for Dance/Movement Therapy, 99 South Hill Park, London NW3 2SP, UK.

Association for Psychoanalytic Psychotherapy in the NHS (APP), Mental Handicap Section, c/o Linda Kaufman, Tavistock Clinic, 120 Belsize Lane, London NW3 5BA, UK; tel: 071-435 7111.

Association of Child Psychotherapists (ACP), Burgh House, New End Square, London NW3 ILT, UK; tel: 071-794 8881

British Association of Art Therapists, 13c Northwood Road, London N6 5TL, UK.

British Association of Psychotherapy (BAP), 121 Hendon Lane, London N3 3PR, UK; tel: 081-346 1747.

British Council of Organizations for Disabled People (BCODP), St Mary's Church, Greenlaw Street, London SE16 5AR, UK; tel: 071-316 4184, 0773-40246.

British Institute of Mental Handicap, Wolverhampton Road, Kidderminster DY10 3PP, UK; tel: 0562-850251.

British Psycho-Analytical Society, 63 New Cavendish Street, London W1M 7RP, UK; tel: 071-580 4952.

Camphill Village Trust Ltd, Delrow House, Aldenham, Watford, Herts, UK.

Center for Developmental Medicine and Genetics, Albert Einstein Medical Center, York and Tabor Roads, Philadelphia, PA 19141, USA.

Centre for Studies on Integration in Education, The Spastics Society, 16 Fitzroy Square, London W1P 5HQ, UK; tel: 071-387 9571.

Child Development and Rehabilitation Center, Oregon Health Sciences University, PO Box 574, Portland, OR 97207, USA.

Childline, 2nd Floor, Royal Mail Building, Studd Street, London N1 0QW, UK; tel: 071-239 1000, fax: 071-239 1001.

Children's Legal Centre, 20 Compton Terrace, London N1 2UN, UK; tel: 071-359 9392.

CMH, Campaigning for Valued Futures with People who have Learning Difficulties, 12a Maddox Street, London W1R 9PL, UK.

College of Speech Therapists, Harold Poster House, 6 Lechmere Road, London NW2 5BU, UK; tel: 081-459 8521.

Council of World Organizations Interested in the Handicapped (CWOIH), c/o Rehabilitation International, 432 Park Avenue South, New York, NY 10016, USA.

DEAL Communications (Dignity, Education and Language for people without speech), c/o Rosemary Crossley (Project Co-ordinator), 538 Dandenong Road, Caulfield, Victoria 3162, Australia; tel: (03) 509-6324.

Diagnostic and Research Clinic, c/o Dr Al Pfadt, NY State Institute for Basic Research in Developmental Disabilities, 1050 Forest Hill Road, Staten Island, New York, NY 10314, USA.

Lifelong Education for Autistic People (LEAP), 6 Florence Road, Ealing, London W5 3TX, UK; tel: 081-579 6281.

Fairfields Counselling Centre (psychotherapy for individuals with learning difficulties), 'Falconhurst', 20b Cliddesden Road, Basingstoke, UK; tel: 0256-466308.

Family Planning Association (offers sexual education resources for handicapped children and adults), 27–35 Mortimer Street, London WIN 7RJ, UK; tel: 071-631 0555.

Federation of Jewish Family Services, Training Unit, 221 Golders Green Road, London NW11 9DW, UK; tel: 081-458 3282.

Geneva Centre (for pervasive developmental disorder), 204 St George Street, Toronto, Canada.

Group for the Advancement of Psychodynamics and Psychotherapy in Social Work (GAPS), Top Flat, 3 Streatley Road, London NW6 7LJ, UK.

Habilitative Mental Healthcare Newsletter, c/o Drs Robert Sovner and Anne DesNoyers Hurley, PO Box 57, Bear Creek, NC 27207, USA.

Institute of Child Health, University of London, 30 Guilford Street, London WC1N 1EH, UK; tel: 071-242 9789.

Institute of Social and Applied Psychology (major research centre on handicap), University of Kent at Canterbury, Canterbury, Kent CT2 7LZ, UK; tel: 0227-764000.

Intensive Support Team for People with Challenging Behaviour, Woodfield House, Bewdley Road, Kidderminster, DY11 6RL, UK; tel: 0562-825564.

International Resource Centre for Special Education, c/o Professor S. S. Segal, Computer Centre for the Disabled, Polytechnic of Central London, 115 New Cavendish Street, London W1M 8JS, UK; tel: 081-445 7810.

JANUS Consultancy, Developing Human Resource Potential through Excellence in Training, c/o Alexis Waitman, 19 Camden Grove, Chislehurst, Kent BR7 5BH, UK; tel: 081-467 7992.

Keep Deaf Children Safe (KDCS), Child Abuse Project, c/o Margaret Kennedy, Nuffield Hearing and Speech Centre, 325 Gray's Inn Road, London WC1X 0DA, UK; tel: 071-833 5627.

KIDSCAPE, 82 Brook Street, London SIY 1YP, UK; tel: 071-493 9845.

London Disability Arts Forum, The Diorama, Peto Place, London NW1, UK; tel: 071-935 8999.

MENCAP, 123 Golden Lane, London EC1Y 0RT, UK; tel: 071-250 4250.

MIETS Unit, The Bethlem Hospital, Monks Orchard Road, Beckenham, Kent BR3 3BX, UK; tel: 081-777 6611, ext 4139.

Muki Baum Association for the Rehabilitation of Multi-Handicapped Inc., c/o Dr Neheema Baum (Executive Director), 111 Anthony Road, Downsview, Toronto, Canada M3K 1B7; tel: 416-633 3971.

National Association for Deaf/Blind and Rubella Handicapped, 311 Gray's Inn Road, London WC1X 8PT, UK; tel: 071-278 1005.

National Association for the Dually Diagnosed, c/o Robert J. Fletcher, 110 Prince Street, Kingston, NY 12401, USA; tel: (914) 331 4336.

National Children's Bureau, Voluntary Council for Handicapped Children, 8 Wakley Street, London EC1V 7QE, UK; tel: 071-254 6251.

National Council for Special Education, 1 Wood Street, Stratford-upon-Avon CV37 6JE, UK; tel: 0789-5332 / 0437-84419.

National Deaf Children's Society, National Office, 45 Hereford Road, London W2 5AH, UK; tel: 071-229 9272.

National Fragile X Foundation, PO Box 300233, Denver, CO 80203, USA; tel: 1-800-835 2246, ext 58.

National Society for the Prevention of Cruelty to Children (NSPCC), 67 Saffron Hill, London EC1N 8RS, UK; tel: 071-242 1626, fax: 071-831 9562.

NHS Training Authority, The White Hart, Cold Bath Road, Harrogate HG2 0NF, UK.

Norah Fry Research Centre, c/o Dr Oliver Russell, University of Bristol, 32 Tyndall's Park Road, Bristol BS8 1PY, UK; tel: 0272-238137.

Nordoff–Robbins Music Therapy Centre, 3 Leighton Place, London NW5 2QL, UK; tel: 071-267 6296.

NUT Working Party on Disability, c/o Richard Rieser (Vice-Chair), 23 Walford Road, London N16 8EF, UK.

Parent to Parent, Tayside Scottish Child and Family Alliance, 55 Albany Street, Edinburgh EH1 3QY, UK; tel: 031-557 2780.

People First, c/o The King's Fund Centre, 126 Albert Street, London NW1, UK; tel: 071-267 6111.

Personal and Sexual Help for Disabled (PASH), c/o Peter McDonald, Chelston Vale, Mallock Road, Torquay, UK.

Practical Arts and Theatre with the Handicapped (PATH), c/o Sophie Kingshill, 38a Duncan Terrace, London N1 8AL, UK; tel: 071-359 7866.

Psychiatry of Disability Department, St George's Hospital Medical School (major treatment and research centre offering help with sign languages, courses, and books), Jenner Wing, Cranmer Terrace, London SW17 0RE, UK; tel: 081-672 9944, ext 55502.

RESCARE (National Society for Mentally Handicapped People in Residential Care), 17 Ford's Lane, Bramhall, Stockport SK7 1BQ, UK.

Research, Evaluation and Development Unit, c/o Dr N. Bouras, Section of Mental Handicap, Division of Psychiatry, Guy's Hospital, London SE1 9RT, UK; tel: 071-407 7600.

Respond (sexual abuse project for people with learning difficulties), c/o Tamsin Cottis and Steve Morris, 49 Forest Road, London E11 1JT, UK; tel: 081-539 8566.

Royal National Institute for the Blind (RNIB), 224 Great Portland Street, London WIN 6AA, UK; tel: 071-388 1266.

Royal Society of Medicine Forum on Mental Retardation, 1 Wimpole Street, London WIM 8AE, UK; tel: 071-408 2119.

Section for Independence Through Education (SITE), c/o Tamsin Cottis and John Hersov, The City Lit, Stukeley Street, London WC2B 5LJ, UK; tel: 071-831 6908.

Sexual Abuse Child Consultancy Service (SACCS), Mytton Mill, Montford Bridge, Shrewsbury SY4 1HA, UK; tel: 0743-850015.

Shape London, 1 Thorpe Close, London W10 5XL, UK; tel: 081-960 9245.

Sheltons Inc. Services to Handicapped People, Belchertown, MA 01007, USA.

Society of Analytical Psychology, 1 Daleham Gardens, London NW3 5BY, UK; tel: 071-435 7696.

Spastics Society, 16 Fitzroy Square, London W1P 5HQ, UK; tel: 071-387 9571.

Specialised Psychotherapy and Consultation Service, 2 Surrey Place, Toronto, Canada, M55 2C2; tel: (416) 925 5141.

SPIDA (Sexual Problems in Disabled People Association), c/o Mrs S. Marples, 35 Bronte Close, Monle Bretton, Barnsley, UK; tel: 0226-297487.

SPOD (Association to Aid the Sexual and Personal Relationships of People with a Disability), 286 Camden Road, London N7, UK; tel: 071-607 8851.

Stepping Stones Counselling and Supervision Services, c/o Michael Gold and Jean Dook, 48 Willow Court, Woodcote Road, Wallington, Surrey SM6 0PF, UK; tel: 081-647 0065.

Strathcona Theatre Company, Strathcona Social Education Centre, Strathcona Road, Wembley, Middlesex, UK.

Tao (training, books and videos), c/o David and Althea Brandon, 36 Victoria Road, Ashton, Preston PR2 1DT, UK; tel: 0772-726 031.

Toy Libraries Association, 68 Churchway, London NW1, UK; tel: 071-387 9592.

United Cerebral Palsy Association, 66 East 34th Street, New York, NY 10016, USA.

VOICE (legal advice regarding abuse of adults), Bushy Cottage, Grassy Lane, Burnaston, Derby.

World Programme of Action for Disabled Persons, United Nations Information Centre, Ship House, 20 Buckingham Gate, London SW1E 6LB, UK; tel: 071-839 1790.

INDEX

Annie's coming out
1984 / Australia

Walter